In honor of
Codman & Shurtleff's 150th birthday,
we would like to thank all our customers,
employees, neighbors and friends in Massachusetts
and around the world, who have contributed to our
growth and success. Our Company continues its
dedication to high social, civic, and professional
responsibilities while meeting the challenges
of the future. We trust you will share our
deep sense of pride and confidence
as you read this
historical review.

Roy W. Black
President

FROM COLONY TO COMMONWEALTH

MASSACHUSETTS

PICTURE RESEARCH BY RUTH OWEN JONES

"PARTNERS IN PROGRESS" BY DAVID HORN AND PIPPIN ROSS

PRODUCED IN COOPERATION WITH THE BAY STATE HISTORICAL LEAGUE

WINDSOR PUBLICATIONS, INC.
NORTHRIDGE, CALIFORNIA

FROM COLONY TO COMMONWEALTH
MASSACHUSETTS

BY JUDITH FREEMAN CLARK

To my grandparents
Frederick L. Worby and
Mary Andrea (Riedel) Worby

As early as 1638, their families took part
in Massachusetts' growth from colony to commonwealth

Title page: *English artist Thomas Charles Farrer painted this view of Northampton from the State Hospital Hill looking south to the Holyoke Range in 1863, before Smith College was built on the closer river. The distant river is the Connecticut, showing the oxbow section. Jenny Lind, the "Swedish Nightingale," called Northampton "the paradise of America" when she sang there in the 1850s. Courtesy, Smith College Museum of Art*

Right: *Boston is seen from South Boston in the mid-1800s. The State House stands on Beacon Hill in the distance. From Bryant,* Picturesque America, *Vol. II, 1874*

Windsor Publications, Inc.—History Book Division
Vice President/Publisher: Hal Silverman
Editorial Director: Teri Davis Greenberg
Corporate Biography Director: Karen Story
Design Director: Alexander D'Anca

Staff for *Massachusetts: From Colony to Commonwealth*
Senior Editor: Jerry Mosher
Picture Editor: Laura Cordova
Proofreader: Susan J. Muhler
Assistant Director, Corporate Biographies: Phyllis Gray
Editor, Corporate Biographies: Brenda Berryhill
Production Editor, Corporate Biographies: Una FitzSimons
Sales Representatives, Corporate Biographies: Hannah Dresser, Jim Herbert,
   Steve Hung, Fred Sommer, Mary Whelan
Editorial Assistants: Kathy M. Brown, Nina Kanga, Susan Kanga, Pat Pittman
Layout Artist, Corporate Biographies: Barbara Moore
Designer and Layout Artist, Editorial: Ellen Ifrah

Library of Congress Cataloging-in-Publication Data
Clark, Judith Freeman.
   Massachusetts, colony to commonwealth: an illustrated history / by Judith Freeman Clark; photo research by Ruth Owen Jones; "Partners in progress" by David Horn and Pippin Ross. —1st ed.   p. cm.
   "Produced in cooperation with the Bay State Historical League."
   Bibliography: p. 314
   Includes index.
   ISBN 0-89781-216-6
   1. Massachusetts—History. 2. Massachusetts—Description and travel—Views. 3. Massachusetts—Industries. I. Bay State Historical League. II. Title.
F64.C58 1987
974.4—dc19
                                                                    87-21006
                                                                    CIP

The property for the Martha Mary Chapel in Sudbury was bought by Henry Ford in the early 1930s. The chapel is named for his grandmother and is one of several nonsectarian chapels that Ford built around the country. Many weddings, christenings, funerals, and bar mitzvahs have taken place beyond the white pillars, seen here in autumn. Photo by Justine Hill

CONTENTS

AUTHOR'S FOREWORD

Few assignments could have been more challenging than this one. To chronicle events and issues specific to Massachusetts history was a welcome, if somewhat daunting, task. A lifelong resident of the state with a family history that reaches back to colonial times, I felt it a privilege to describe the individuals, places, and experiences that make Massachusetts one of the more unique states in the Union.

Drawing on various sources, from newspapers and government documents to other historians' written and verbal interpretations, I soon learned that writing Massachusetts' biography was a mammoth job. Where to begin and where to conclude? What facts were most critical, which ones were most entertaining, which the most obscure? Many sources had favorites; my problem was to select the most representative. Sometimes I faced eliminating particular tales or descriptions of famous individuals, a necessary but dissatisfying exercise. On the other hand, preparing this book meant sampling different accounts of Massachusetts as well as learning how the state has been viewed by others at various points in time. This project also enabled me to draw on the resources of several friends and colleagues. It would be remiss not to acknowledge Dr. Robert J. Wilson III, whose expertise and guidance were crucial in the final stages of editing this manuscript. Dr. Wilson provided immeasurable assistance willingly and with grace and good humor; his scholarly perspective and his droll wit made completion of this book less tedious, and he deserves a very special thank you. Similarly, I must acknowledge Professor Hugh Bell, of the University of Massachusetts, in whose classes I first learned about the "city upon a hill." Thanks also to Dr. Lynn Cadwallader of the Massachusetts Council on the Arts and Humanities. Dr. Cadwallader made many suggestions throughout the course of my writing this book and she deserves my gratitude for all her support.

Massachusetts claims a proud heritage. It is the "land of the Pilgrim's pride . . ." as the song goes. But it is also made up of more than dead, dry facts. Many things that make the Bay State an interesting, exciting place to live in the late twentieth century have existed in some form for several centuries: fine cultural and educational institutions, a demanding political arena, natural resources that offer everything from hydropower to fishing industry to dairy farming. The early settlers recognized the potential in Massachusetts, and surely entertained many hopes for that potential, even as the ink dried on the Mayflower Compact.

No matter how compelling the subject, a single volume cannot possibly detail every fact about so dynamic a state peopled by so complex a group of citizens. But this book is meant to be an overview, a taste, a sampling. All that, and perhaps something more. It is meant to provoke further exploration, to encourage curiosity the same way that early settlers' interests were kindled by tales about the New World.

Enjoy these chapters, the accompanying photographs and illustrations. This book, a journey into America's past, will tell you about the heritage all Americans share. This book will tell you many things about Massachusetts, and may tell you something about yourself.

Judith Freeman Clark
Northampton, Massachusetts

THE PLYMOUTH AND MASSACHUSETTS BAY COLONIES

(1620-1700)

★   ★   ★   ★   ★   ★   ★   ★   ★

The Mayflower II, *a replica of the ship used for the Pilgrims' 66-day voyage of 1620, is docked at the Plymouth waterfront. This 106½-foot vessel actually crossed the Atlantic in 1957, soon after it was built. Photo by Justine Hill*

Some three and a half centuries ago, one of many immigrant groups reached our shores. This group—a small band of English men and women—came in search of religious freedom and a new life which they could fashion according to their particular needs. To most people today, Plymouth Rock represents the foundation of that new life. That rough gray stone half-buried in the sandy Plymouth shore has become a symbol for all Americans—a visible reminder of our nation's humble, earnest beginnings.

The symbolic significance of Plymouth Rock notwithstanding, the first landfall of that hardy group was not on the coast by Plymouth but at Provincetown on the tip of Cape Cod. Subsequent generations have marked this first landing spot by raising, amid tide-swept dunes assailed by harsh winds, a stone tower that stands in mute testimony to the Pilgrims' sojourn. Swept north from their Virginia destination by

stormy weather, the Pilgrims weighed anchor in Provincetown Harbor in November 1620. After five weeks spent exploring the coast, their ship finally anchored in Plymouth, and the Pilgrims established a settlement there.

The Pilgrims came to the New World seeking respite from religious persecution. However, their journey had begun not in 1620 but in 1607, when they left England for the Netherlands where they hoped to be able to worship God in peace. It soon became clear, however, that the toleration and comfort they sought was not to be found either in Amsterdam, where they first settled, or Leiden, where they moved next. Although the Pilgrims could worship together in the Netherlands, life there was difficult, jobs were not plentiful, and as a group they feared for the future of their religion. Furthermore, their children were acquiring foreign ways and manners. Economic hardship and fears that their

On the day before they decided to settle at Plymouth, some of the Pilgrims explored Clark's Island and held a Sunday service there. This illustration from an 1869 book depicts John Carver (1575-1621), who had already been elected governor aboard ship, reading the Scriptures. From Mudge, Views from Plymouth Rock, *1869*

children would forget their homeland and their religious teachings made the Pilgrims decide to leave the Netherlands. However, their departure took time to arrange. The freedom the Pilgrims sought was impossible to obtain in England, but since King James I sought to rid his land of dissenters, the Pilgrims had been able to obtain a charter for land on the James River in Virginia. This charter was granted to the Pilgrims through the London Company, a joint-stock company controlled by London merchants. After more than a decade of deliberation, planning, and much disappointment, the Pilgrims finally left Leiden in 1620 and proceeded to Southampton where they set sail for America aboard the *Mayflower.*

Led both by a need for freedoms not easily found in Europe and by a desire

to be self-governing, the Pilgrims envisioned their future in a community in which harmony and cooperation abounded and which was, above all, led by God's gracious will. They were not anxious to invest their government with all-encompassing powers. Instead, they sought a separation of the secular and the sacred. The Pilgrims had too often experienced the oppression resulting from the combined power of church and state in their native England. They felt the church should be independent of state control, and this desire for religious autonomy resulted in a church separate from secular government but with spiritual power over its members. The Pilgrims were known as *Separatists,* a religious group broken away from the Church of England, although it did retain some of the basic teachings of England's

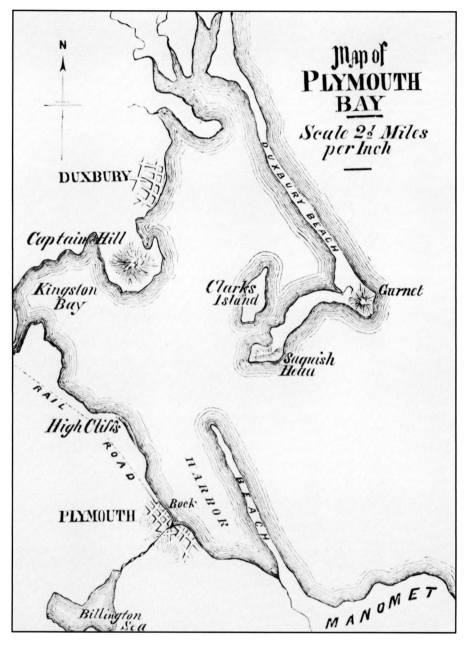

Map of
PLYMOUTH BAY
Scale 2½ Miles per Inch

This 1869 map of the Plymouth area (including a recently added railroad line) explains why the Pilgrims chose to finally disembark from the Mayflower *in December 1620. The geographically protected settlement site, combined with a mild winter, meant that some of the Pilgrims could survive despite being ill prepared for a New England winter. Bartholomew Gosnold was probably the first European to explore what is now the Massachusetts coast at Martha's Vineyard, Nantucket, and the Dartmouth area in 1603. From Mudge,* Views from Plymouth Rock, *1869*

state church. The unique combination of enterprise and piety that characterized their search for freedom spurred them to hard work and a determination to live according to God's laws. These ideas put their indelible stamp on the future both of Massachusetts and of the United States.

The relief the Pilgrims felt upon ending their long journey to the New World is not difficult to imagine. According to William Bradford's *A History of Plimoth Plantation,* after weeks of a confining voyage fraught with every imaginable discomfort and doubt, the Pilgrims "fell upon their knees and blessed the God of Heaven, who had brought them over the vast and furious ocean and delivered them from all the evils and mysteries thereof, again to set their feet on the firm and stable earth, their proper element."

FREEDOM DEFINED
On December 21, 1620, when the Pilgrims anchored at Plymouth, their search for a suitable site on which to build permanent shelter was over. They numbered 101 souls, including an infant, Peregrine White, born on board the

Many of the earliest shelters at Plymouth Colony were mud-daubed cottages with English-style thatched roofs similar to this reproduction at Plimoth Plantation. Photo by Justine Hill

Mayflower while it was anchored in Cape Cod Bay. He was the first child of English parentage born in New England. The Pilgrims stayed on board the ship while waiting for a break in the weather. Some of this time was spent discussing the form of government they were going to have. Since they had landed far north of Virginia and out of London Company jurisdiction, their charter was of no legal value. The Pilgrims therefore drew up a new charter known as the Mayflower Compact, which was signed by 41 freemen aboard the ship. The compact pledged allegiance to the English king but established a form of government by the will of the majority. Among the stipulations contained in the compact, one noted that, "We whose names are underwritten do by these Presents, solemnly and mutually in the presence of God and one another covenant and combine ourselves together into a civil Body Politick . . . and by Virtue hereof do enact . . . such just and equal laws . . . as shall be thought most meet and convenient for the general Good of the Colony." The agreement was similar to the church covenant that also guided them. It provided for full and equal participation of all signers in issues and concerns of the colony, including the annual election of a governor. The compact remained the basis of government in Plymouth for 10 years, and all later governments in the colony developed out of the compact.

Their government taken care of, the Pilgrims waited nearly a month before going ashore. Cramped and short of food, some became ill and all were without proper sanitation facilities or warm clothing. When spring finally arrived, they ventured onto land. By now, their faith and patience had been sorely tested—almost half of them had died. Yet despite disease, starvation, or exposure, none of them chose to return with the *Mayflower* to England. Among the surviving men were John Alden, William Bradford, William Brewster, Thomas Prence, Myles Standish, and

Variegated Indian corn was photographed in the fall at a roadside stand in Deerfield. Native to the Americas, corn was brought to Europe by Christopher Columbus, where it became popular as a vegetable dish and as a grain for bread. Corn bread, Indian pudding, succotash, corn meal mush, and other humble dishes were staples of Europeans in colonial Massachusetts. Photo by Paul A. Sherry

Edward Winslow (1595-1655) was elected governor of Plymouth Colony three different times. Winslow was well educated and well off—he brought two servants with him on the Mayflower. *Often in charge of "public relations" for the colony, he dealt with American Indians like Massasoit and was an agent sent to England. This portrait, painted by an unknown artist in 1651 in England, is the only actual portrait of a* Mayflower Pilgrim. *From Bartlett,* The Pilgrim Fathers, *1854*

William Bradford (circa 1589-1657) was elected governor of Plymouth Colony in 1621 upon John Carver's death. He held that office and used great authority nearly every year (except for a few years when he declined to serve) until his death in 1657. This is an 1888 artist's conception of what the Bradford house might have looked like in 1621. Today's Plymouth museum village has some reproduction houses with thatched roofs, but they are much more sharply pitched and altogether different. From a circa 1910 postcard

Edward Winslow, all of whom left an outstanding legacy of service to the new colony. William Bradford was governor of Plymouth Colony, serving several separate terms of office from 1621 to 1656, succeeding John Carver, who had been elected while the Pilgrims were still aboard the *Mayflower.* Carver had signed the famous compact but he died in the spring of 1621, so it was Bradford who served the colony with dedication for many decades. Dealing both with people and a harsh, primitive environment demanded foresight, patience, and skill, all qualities that Bradford possessed. It was his abilities that undoubtedly made the critical difference between Pilgrim

success and failure. Too, Bradford's *A History of Plimoth Plantation* has long been admired as a fascinating social history and valuable contribution to written accounts of English colonial life in America.

The sickness and privation that marked the Pilgrims' first winter in Massachusetts was mitigated somewhat by friendly support from Wampanoag Indians. Without their help, Plymouth Colony may not have survived to become a permanent settlement. The Wampanoag chief, Massasoit, who first approached the Pilgrims, remained steadfastly faithful to them for more than 40 years. Massasoit initiated the first agreement—the Seven Point Peace treaty—that aided both sides in settling

disputes for decades. The degree of peace and tranquility the two populations enjoyed was relatively constant until about 1660 when a growing white population encroached more and more on Indian lands.

The story of the first Thanksgiving has been told and retold and its origins now lie hidden in myth and folklore. But we do know that during October 1621, after a small harvest of corn, the Pilgrims celebrated their first Thanksgiving Day. Some 90 Indians joined the Pilgrims, who felt grateful to be alive and offered thanks to God at a meal that included four wild turkeys.

FREEDOM ESTABLISHED
Pilgrim men and women all made

NATIVE AMERICANS IN MASSACHUSETTS

Few people today give much thought to the human inhabitants of Massachusetts in the centuries preceding European colonization of North America. Thoughts of aboriginal Americans generally evoke images of either Pilgrim encounters with "noble savages" or somewhat later clashes between western settlers and the Indian tribes of the Great Plains. Seldom does the casual reader find an accurate, in-depth view of the North American continent and its inhabitants prior to its settlement by European colonists.

This lack reflects the dearth of extant written history from the pre-Columbian era. Although some artifacts and tools from that period have survived, the native Americans did not leave overabundant records of their existence before the arrival of the French, Spanish, and British. What does remain has been pieced together by anthropologists, archaeologists, and historians who have attempted to determine exactly who these early peoples were. But such piecemeal deductions can only partially satisfy our curiosity about pre-colonial culture in America.

Historical accounts of early Massachusetts colonization seem to relegate native Americans to a historical position of only auxiliary importance. The natives of Massachusetts who met and traded peacefully with the English—or made war on small bands of settlers who tried to carve a lifestyle out of an often forbidding land—have usually been overlooked in regional histories. Native Americans enter history only when they gave land to white settlers, or when they converted to Christianity at the urging of English clergymen.

However, native American culture flourished in the Northeast for thousands of years before European settlers took control of the land. Some 12,000 years ago, in the region we know today as Massachusetts, people were hunting, gathering, and eking out a simple life amid the woodlands and heavier forests

and along the coasts and marshes. These Indians had reached the Northeast from the south and the west. Until 10,500 B.C., the area had been covered for many millenia by a thick glacial ice cap. This ice cap retreated slowly, leaving in its frozen wake a growing profusion of flora and fauna which eventually encouraged human habitation. The Paleoindian culture of the region is known today principally through its stone implements, used in hunting and attendant tasks. Largely due to scrapers, points, and other items made of flint, chalcedony, and jasper, archaeologists have identified an Indian site in the northeastern region of Massachusetts by the New Hampshire border. Excavations at this site, called Bull Brook, indicate its inhabitants lived there for more than one season of hunting, fishing, and gathering. They hunted a variety of animals, including white-tailed deer, black bear, and elk, along with many smaller mammals and birds. They also fished in freshwater ponds, gathered shellfish, and collected roots and berries from plants growing wild in the region.

Later Indians practiced agriculture, growing corn and beans primarily. They eventually taught the white settlers to cultivate these crops. Still, the Indians

Camouflaged paleo-Indians are depicted hunting barren ground for caribou that lived as far south as Massachusetts about 10,000 years ago as the last glacier receded. Drawing by Marie Litterer. Courtesy, Pratt Museum, Amherst College

relied somewhat on hunting, particularly during the long New England winters. Shellfish added an important component to their economy, serving as tools, ornaments, and food. Most of these native Americans were Eastern Algonquins whose extended family groups lived in portable structures made from animal skins and wooden poles.

Calculating the number of Indians living in Massachusetts during the pre-colonial period can only be done by estimation. Some archaeologists have identified apparent fluctuations in demography around the first millenium A.D., although there are no reliable clues as to why the population declined nor to why it subsequently increased. Some suggest that disease may have been a factor in demographic change, but this is pure speculation. Other experts cite

environmental change as a likely explanation for population shifts. However it happened, before the European colonists arrived Massachusetts' native population had decreased somewhat from its former peak. By some accounts (meant only as a general guide rather than a definite index of tribal population) there were about 45 people per square kilometer in early seventeenth-century Massachusetts and the surrounding region.

As time passed, Indians formed more or less specific tribal groups. By A.D. 1600, they were identifiable as what we now term the Eastern Algonquin tribes in Massachusetts. By 1630, the major tribes had subdivided into fairly specific territories. These tribes were: the Pocumtucks, the Nipmucks, the Massachusetts, and the Pokanokets (or Wampanoags). While these tribes all belonged to the larger Eastern Algonquin nation, each had developed customs and language deviations setting them apart from others. Their territories, although identifiable, apparently shifted and blended, and by the late seventeenth century were less and less distinguishable.

War, both intertribal and with white settlers, combined with assimilation to the European culture and disease to change the native American way of life in Massachusetts. Change had formerly been internal or brought on by the environ-

This drawing of life in a Massachusetts Woodland Indian camp shows the people at everyday tasks in summer. Much of what we suppose to be their way of life is based on Europeans' early contact and reports to their sponsors or friends back home, but also from archaeological findings. Drawing by Marie Litterer. Courtesy, Pratt Museum, Amherst College

ment. Once Europeans settled in Massachusetts, external change was imposed on Indians through voluntary or enforced alteration of cultural patterns. The noble savage of myth and folktale in Massachusetts' early history was transformed almost beyond recognition by the late 1600s—and the "city upon a hill" envisioned by Governor Bradford was one in which there were no native American neighborhoods. The tribal lifestyles disappeared quickly through virtual genocide and assimilation of native American culture. By the time the U.S. Constitution was signed in 1789, aboriginal lifestyle in Massachusetts had become as much a part of the past as the era of the Founding Fathers seems to us today.

contributions of inestimable worth to the building of that first colony at Plymouth. By June 1621, title for land in Plymouth had been assigned in 100-acre parcels to each person. Fifteen hundred acres was set aside also as common land for the use of all settlers there.

As more ships arrived from England during the decade of settlement following 1620, the region's population grew. New colonists swelled the ranks of those who had arrived earlier, prompting the establishment of new communities. Most people hoped for a parcel of land on which to build a house, keep some animals, and raise enough food for their family's needs. Settlements grew, founded by *Mayflower* Pilgrims and their direct descendants, as well as by subsequent travelers arriving on ships similar to the *Mayflower*. Duxbury, a few miles to the north of Plymouth, was settled in 1631 and granted its own charter five years later. It was the second town in Plymouth Colony and relied primarily on farming in its early years. Later, Duxbury would see fishing, trading, and shipbuilding become part of the town's growth and development. The Congregational Church in Duxbury was organized by William Brewster, a signer of the Mayflower Compact. A church elder, he was an important leader in the colony, and the town of Brewster on Cape Cod, settled in 1656, was named in his memory.

Another well-known Pilgrim settler was Myles Standish. The first military leader of the colony, he successfully maintained cordial relations with neighboring Indians. In 1649, Standish purchased a large tract of land from Chief Ousamequin, which subsequently became part of what today is Bridgewater, Brockton, and surrounding towns. Standish was also instrumental in the founding of Duxbury along with William Brewster and John Alden.

The story of Myles Standish's courtship of Priscilla Mullens, with John Alden as go-between, was published in 1858 by Henry Wadsworth Longfellow in the poem, "The Courtship of Miles Standish." The story has no historical basis, but it remains a charming legend. In it, Alden plays the part of the romantic messenger for the couple, and the most often quoted line is Priscilla's parrying comment, "Why don't you speak for yourself, John?" Standish's intentions backfired, for, in reality, Priscilla Mullens married John Alden and the couple led a happy, fruitful married life. They are interred in Duxbury's Old Burying Ground, where Captain Myles Standish is also buried. The Jonathan Alden House in that same town, built by the couple's son, was their last home.

The number of towns in Plymouth Colony grew in response to the settlers' desires for larger farms and more spacious surroundings. Scituate was incorporated in 1636, followed by Barnstable in 1638 and Taunton in 1639. Marshfield was founded in 1640 and Eastham in 1644. The latter was a hoped-for relocation site for the original Plymouth Colony, but the proposed resettlement was discarded by the majority of settlers, who felt Plymouth should remain the central town of the colony. Rehoboth was founded in 1645, Bridgewater in 1656, Swansea in 1668, and Middleborough in 1669, to name a few other Pilgrim communities of those early years. The Indian chief Massasoit relinquished tribal jurisdiction over what is now West Bridgewater in 1645, according to legend, in exchange for a handful of "knives, hatchets, skins, hoes, coates [sic], and cotton."

Yet another settlement—one quickly earning a reputation for loose morality and questionable activities—was Mount Wollaston. It was founded in 1625 by Thomas Morton and was known also as Merry Mount. The town became a gathering place for traders and Indians who trafficked in firearms, furs, and spirits. William Bradford, then governor of Plymouth Colony, sent Myles Standish to arrest Morton on a variety of charges, among them encouraging celebration of

pagan festivals. Although he was banished to England in 1628, Morton returned to Plymouth Colony, only to be sent away once again in 1630. Mount Wollaston is located in the north part of Quincy, an industrial city south of Boston.

THE PURITANS SEEK FREEDOM
The Pilgrims, though generally thought of as the first, were not the only settlers of Massachusetts during the seventeenth century. In 1628, the nucleus of a Puritan colony was established at Naumkeag, in what is now Salem. Under the leadership of John Endecott, it displaced Salem's few English inhabitants (led by Roger

Top: *This is an 1869 artist's idea of what the Pilgrims' first meetinghouse probably looked like. It is known from a drawing that by 1683 they had built a larger, two-story structure of a much more sophisticated design with a belfry, clapboard cladding, and shingle roof, and a five-over-four window configuration similar to houses of the period. From Mudge,* Views from Plymouth Rock, *1869*

Above: *The John Alden House, built in 1653 in Duxbury (the second Pilgrim town, after Plymouth), is a timber-braced frame house that illustrates the early use of shingles for siding. From a circa 1910 postcard*

COLONIAL HOUSING AND APPAREL

Political and economic considerations aside, a people describes itself in general terms by means of various everyday practices and effects common to their social structure and culture. Among these are housing and apparel, inventions, and innovations. The early European colonists of Massachusetts accrued a record of such practices and effects throughout their first century that tell us a great deal about their individual and collective aspirations.

The tangible realities of life prior to the War for Independence are enumerated in all manner of private and legal documents—account books, diaries, wills, and marriage contracts. Some, such as William Bradford and John Winthrop, told of community happenings and described personal joys and sorrows. Others, such as firebrand patriot James Otis and his equally patriotic and articulate sister Mercy Otis Warren, left speeches, essays, letters, and pamphlets to illustrate points of honor and law. These records are invaluable, for they tell us about Massachusetts in its early years. But there are forms of records other than written ones, and they, too, define colonial life in eloquent, if unspoken, ways.

Although no pictorial record exists to chronicle the Pilgrims' landing at Plymouth, we know that when they came ashore they were weary, cold, and anxious to establish a means of shelter—however temporary—as soon as possible. The Pilgrims realized that New England's climate necessitated tight, weatherproof structures, and with warmth in mind they erected simple wattle-and-daub cottages. Humble homes perhaps, but welcome after a three-month ocean voyage. They were buildings which were thus to be replaced quickly with something more permanent. By 1623, according to one visitor to Plymouth Colony, there were about "twenty houses, four or five of which are very fair and pleasant." He noted that the homes were built with "clapboards, with gardens also enclosed behind and at the sides with clapboards." In just a few years at least some of the Pilgrims were thus able to satisfy their wish for more permanent dwellings.

Still, the houses were neither large nor elegant. They usually had only one-and-a-half stories, a thatched roof, and one or two tiny windows. After 1635, shingle and board roofing generally replaced thatch because of the threat of fire. Windows were thought of as luxuries and until 1640 were usually made from oiled paper or fabric rather than glass.

Edward Winslow, one of the original proprietors of Plymouth Colony, wrote to England with advice to a group of would-be emigrants to "bring paper and linseed oil for your windows." This meant that the Pilgrim houses were dark inside, and with often no more than one room at ground level, they lacked privacy as well. A fireplace on one wall dominated the room and provided the only source of heat as well as the cooking area.

Above, accessible by ladder or steep stair built close to the chimney, was a room often described as a "chamber"—the Pilgrims' term for bedroom. Some houses built with a larger floor plan had two rooms downstairs and a divided chamber upstairs, with a central fireplace, but these larger homes generally date from a slightly later and more prosperous period.

Only after the Pilgrims had attended to the colony's most basic needs did houses gain additional rooms. A lean-to was the most common addition. It sometimes served as a kitchen, but was just as frequently used for storage or sleeping. Some homes as early as 1640 also had cellars, which were either built under a portion of the main house or as part of the lean-to.

By twentieth-century standards, interiors of Pilgrim homes were sparsely furnished. However, inventories of the colonial period indicate that a wide range of prosperity existed in Plymouth. One man, Web Adley, was listed in 1652 as

A kitchen in a Massachusetts home circa 1700 would have probably looked like this, albeit more cluttered with food, ashes, and things like towels or potholders. Open-hearth cooking was the method of cooking until well after the Revolution. There was often a small oven in the wall of the brick fireplace. Courtesy, Connecticut Valley Historical Museum

having a total personal wealth of £3.7s., and another man, William Pontus, was assessed at just under £13. Yet another colonist, William Thomas of nearby Marshfield in Plymouth Colony, had land and possessions valued at £375. From the very beginning, economic diversity characterized life in Massachusetts.

The inventories list items such as chairs, beds, tables, and wooden cooking and eating implements, as well as pewter and—less frequently—silver cups, spoons, and beakers. Pilgrims possessed a few table knives, but forks were nonexistent since they were not yet in common use even in England. Many of these artifacts have been preserved and can be seen in museums and historic restorations such as Plimouth Plantation.

Another measure of wealth in Plymouth Colony (and in Massachusetts Bay Colony as well) was linens—bedsheets, napkins, petticoats, and handkerchiefs. All were woven and sewn by hand. The wealthier colonists had coverlets or bedspreads, blankets, and rugs as well as bed curtains. Feather pillows and feather beds were found in homes of the very richest people, but poorer folk slept on mattresses stuffed with scraps of wool and rags or hay and husks.

Pilgrim clothes were handmade of natural fibers—wool, linen, and leather. Cotton was rare in the seventeenth century and available only to the very rich. Some clothes were valuable enough to be left to ensuing generations, especially if they were heavy and very durable or very finely ornamented. This accounts for the careful listings in wills that show certain garments given as legacies to heirs, and it provides posterity with a very intimate peek at colonial life. In 1650, a woman's fine petticoat might be valued at £1.10s. The same amount of money would purchase a man's suit of clothes or be equal to the cost of a herd of goats or a large portion of wheat.

It is inaccurate to think of Pilgrims as dressing exclusively in somber colors, although it is true that they did not indulge in bright colors or elaborate clothes or ornamentation. Jewelry was

frowned upon; Pilgrim husbands and wives did not even wear wedding bands. The most common colors for daily wear in Plymouth Colony were hues of red or brown, but some blue, green, and yellow garments were also worn. The colors reflected the availability and range of homemade vegetable dyes rather than any desire to limit brightly hued clothing. Pilgrims did favor black for their best clothes, but this may have been because these were expected to last at least one generation and therefore needed to be conservative and serviceable.

Style of clothing varied little in Plymouth Colony. Most men wore a close-fitting jacket known as a doublet, knee-length breeches which were cut quite full, and a three-quarter length cloak. Sometimes a heavy sleeveless jacket known as a jerkin was worn in colder weather as a supplement to the doublet. Underneath was a linen shirt, stockings, and leather boots for everyday wear; shoes were used only for special

occasions. Men also wore a hat or a cap, but this was by no means required.

Women's clothing generally consisted of a three-piece dress with skirt, bodice, and sleeves. The latter were tied or laced to the armholes of the bodice. In colonial inventories sleeves sometimes were listed as bequeathed to a person separately from other portions of an outfit. There was usually a petticoat under the skirt and

often an underskirt under that. A chemise was worn under the bodice, and a loose smock was the basic undergarment. Leather shoes and woolen or linen stockings covered women's feet, although they often wore wooden clogs to protect their leather shoes from mud. A neck scarf and a cap completed the clothing for Pilgrim women. In fact, a woman's hair was bound tightly and covered completely

---

This dowry chest built in the 1770s is reminiscent of 1600s Pilgrim furniture. Made in the Northampton area for Sarah (Hooker) Strong (who married Caleb Strong, later governor of Massachusetts in 1777), the chest is one of the type called Hadley chests. From 1670 to 1730 this kind of hand-carved chest was especially popular up and down the Connecticut River. Courtesy, Northampton Historical Society

by a cap—it was considered immodest and wanton for women to be bareheaded, indoors or out.

The strict mores dictating style of apparel and the hardships of earlier colonial life gave way by the mid-1700s. Puritanism relaxed and Massachusetts became more cosmopolitan as its population grew, but these changes were slow to evolve.

Conant). In 1630, John Winthrop located the main Puritan settlement at Boston, which soon became the capital of the Massachusetts Bay Colony.

The Puritans, who settled the Massachusetts Bay Colony, differed from the Pilgrims (Separatists) in Plymouth Colony. Wanting only to *purify* the Church of England, the Puritans did not want to break away to form their own church. The Puritans' views, radical for their time, were not widely held and were as much concerned with governmental issues as with church issues. By 1630, 17 ships bearing more than 1,000 English Puritans had arrived on Massachusetts' shores and settled numerous towns, including Dorchester, Lynn, Roxbury, and Watertown.

Boston, founded on September 17, 1630, soon became the most prominent town in the Massachusetts Bay Colony. An important harbor community, its economic development flourished due to the constant influx of immigrants from England, many of whom stayed to contribute their talents to the growth of the city. Boston was designated the capital of the colony in 1632, and its settlement was guided principally by its third governor, John Winthrop, who in 1630 had led a migration of 900 Puritans from England. The Massachusetts Bay Colony was worthy of great admiration according to Winthrop, whose diary

entries anticipated that the Puritan settlement "shall be as a City upon a hill." Most Puritans worked tirelessly to promote their colony's success as envisioned by Winthrop and others like him. By 1642, there were nearly 10,000 people in the Massachusetts Bay Colony, some freemen and others who were servants or other non-property-owning individuals.

FREEDOM'S PARAMETERS

Initially, church membership was required of those sitting on the General Court. This being the case, decision-making rested firmly in the hands of the governor and a small body of clergy and church members. Later in the century, a 40-shilling freehold was substituted for the church membership requirement. This changed Winthrop's plan for a "holy commonwealth" and paved the way for a variety of other secular changes that soon transformed the entire colony.

During the first years of the colony, education was deemed of paramount importance. Boston Latin School, opened in 1635 as a school for boys, was the first free public school and the first secondary school in America. It was modeled, as were English private schools, along classical lines. Since the colony needed a college for training clergy, one was established in 1636 with a grant from the General Court. In 1638 it was named for

John Harvard, its first benefactor, who died that year, leaving an extensive library and half of his fortune to the school. The importance of education to the Puritans is evidenced by a 1647 Massachusetts General Court ruling that communities with more than 50 families must provide a teacher for their children. Towns with 100 families or more were required to establish a grammar school so that children might be educated. Books were also important to the colonists. Four years after Harvard College was founded in Cambridge, the first printing press was set up in the same town. Owned by Stephen Daye, it published the *Bay Psalm Book,* the first book in English printed in America.

Other General Court decisions affecting colonial life were less popular than setting up schools. By the 1650s, many people were unhappy with laws that extended voting privileges to church members only. These laws were related as well to church elders' worries that fewer adults were eligible for church membership. A decline in personal religious conversions—necessary for acceptance into membership—contributed to shrinking church membership. Everyone had to attend worship services each week, but this attendance did not automatically ensure church membership. Those seeking such membership had to publicly confess their sins. Each year, smaller numbers confessed and asked for acceptance into the communion of the church so as to receive community voting rights. The dwindling number of "visible saints," as this group of members was called, threatened church and community stability. By the middle of the century a solution to this legal and religious problem was deemed a critical necessity by the Puritans.

The *Half-Way Covenant,* adopted in 1662, permitted admission to church membership for those Puritans who had

This was Harvard as it appeared in 1721, 85 years after it was founded. On the left is Harvard Hall, built in 1672. Stoughton Hall, built in 1698, stands in the center, and Massachusetts Hall, built in 1720, is on the right. From New England Magazine, *October 1901*

By 1652 the Massachusetts Great and General Court authorized minting of the Pine Tree Shilling, the first coinage for use in the American colonies to be struck there. The motivation for this defiance of British authority was counterfeit coins that were plaguing the colony. In Boston's illegal mint the colonists minted their own coins: silver shillings, sixpence, and threepence. The obverse side had the pine tree surrounded by the word "Masathusets," while on verso was the year and the denomination. Courtesy, Berkshire Atheneum

not made a public profession of faith, but who led morally upright lives. As planned, the covenant strengthened the church and increased its membership—but only on a limited basis since a conversion experience, publicly confessed, remained an imperative qualification for full church membership.

This change in church doctrine was probably inevitable. Merchants in Boston and elsewhere were becoming increasingly prosperous and this prosperity extended to others as well. Manufactured goods flowed in from England, and the trappings of affluence were more available to the colonists. In 1651, the General Court passed laws regulating and limiting the wearing of fine clothes, which many Puritans considered an affront to God. This law indicates that the standard of living in Massachusetts Bay had improved somewhat since the 1630s.

FREEDOM AND COLONIAL INTOLERANCE

Children and grandchildren of the Puritans grew accustomed to material comforts greater than those enjoyed by the original colonists. Not surprisingly, attitudes about the fitness and legitimacy of amassing wealth shifted accordingly. This change placed a strain on Puritan spiritual life as the desire to "get ahead" overtook the need to be saved. Not all colonists were willing to confess their faith publicly, although most were anxious to remain part of the established church. By allowing for relaxed church membership rules, as with the *Half-Way Covenant,* Massachusetts Puritans acknowledged the colony's shifting social and economic fabric. At the same time, they hoped to maintain its moral stability and save the church from an untimely demise.

Although internal church structure accepted modification, Puritans (and Pilgrims as well) emphasized external adherence to church law. This was especially apparent in expressions of religious intolerance. Freedom of worship

was not allowed in the colony, and Quakers were among those who suffered the most from this intolerance. In the summer of 1656 when the first Quakers arrived in Massachusetts they were imprisoned and then forcibly ejected from the colony. By October, the General Court legislated a fine against anyone hiding a Quaker, and by 1658 the court had prohibited Quaker meetings. Two years later, however, the persecution abated after Charles II, a friend of Quaker leader William Penn, was restored to the English throne.

It was not only Quakers who suffered. In 1636, Anne Hutchinson, wife of one of Boston's leading citizens, was charged with heresy and banished from Boston. A woman of learning and great religious conviction, Hutchinson challenged the Puritan clergy and asserted her view that moral conduct and piety should not be the primary qualifications for "visible sainthood." Her preachings, labeled "Antinomianism" by the Puritans, were termed heretical since church teaching dictated the need for outward signs of God's grace as well as for an inward, direct experience of grace.

Threatened by meetings she held weekly in her Boston home, the clergy charged Hutchinson with blasphemy. An outspoken female in a male hierarchy, Hutchinson had little hope that many would speak in her defense, and she was tried by the General Court. After being sentenced, she went with her family to live in what is now Rhode Island. Several years later she moved to New York where she and some of her family died during an Indian attack in 1643. A descendant, Thomas Hutchinson, later became governor of Massachusetts.

Another dissenter, Roger Williams, was likewise banished from Salem, where he was known for his unconventional dealings with the Indians. His original tenure there as a minister had actually begun in Plymouth but was terminated after he challenged existing church teachings. At Salem, Williams was in violent opposition to almost every

established law and practice, both church and civil. A religious man, he nevertheless favored complete and absolute separation of church and secular government, even to the extent of repealing taxes in support of the church.

Williams criticized Puritan authorities' dealings with the Indians and advocated that settlers return Indian lands to their original owners. In 1635, he was tried by the General Court and banished. Williams fled to Rhode Island where he helped found Providence. He secured a royal charter in 1644, which established the Providence Plantations as a separate colony.

In both these cases, dissent represented such a threat to civil and church authority that it was dealt with in the most expedient, thorough, and extreme way. In Massachusetts Bay, the clergy and the General Court acted together to preserve the sanctity and integrity of the community. But it would not be long before even more serious issues threatened community stability.

Through banishment, fines, and even hanging (in the case of witchcraft and some other serious misdeeds), Puritan rulers kept a firm hold on the Massachusetts Bay Colony. Likewise, the Pilgrims exercised strong control over the Plymouth Colony. But laws, sermons, fines, and trials could not permanently forestall change in the social, political, and cultural spheres, change which pressed on all of the colonists during the latter part of the seventeenth century.

INDIANS CHALLENGE COLONIAL FREEDOM

It was not only religious life that changed during the seventeenth century in the Massachusetts Bay and Plymouth colonies. The settlers' relations with Indians changed, too. Like Roger Williams and Myles Standish, some colonists tried to maintain cordial relations with the Indians and a few, such as "Praying John" Eliot, tried to convert Indians to Christianity. Eliot translated the Bible into the Algonquin Indian language in an attempt to carry God's word to native Americans. He helped establish a community—a "praying" town—at Natick in 1651, and by 1674 there were around 1,100 Christian Indians in Plymouth Colony. Eliot's ambitions for his Indian proteges included a conventional education, and at least one Indian, Caleb Cheeshahteamuck, graduated from Harvard College in 1665.

Despite Eliot's best efforts, relations between whites and Indians deteriorated. Most settlers considered all Indians potential enemies, while non-Christian

John Eliot (1604-1690) was born in England and sailed to Boston on the ship Lyon *in 1631. He was pastor of a church in Roxbury, where he first came in contact with the native Americans. Eliot undertook to learn their language in order to convert them to Christianity, which he felt was their only salvation. He, like other Puritans, believed that the ability to read, especially to read the Bible, was a necessity. He translated the Bible into the Indians' language, and so published the first Bible in North America, paid for by friends in England. His attempt to make the Indians like English colonists failed during King Philip's War in 1675-1676. From Spencer and Lossing,* A Complete History of the United States of America, *Vol. I, 1878*

Indians rejected converts as colonial pawns. There was, in fact, some basis for colonists' fears. Settlers in Plymouth and Massachusetts Bay had expanded their hold on land in the region, and as colonists encroached on areas formerly inhabited exclusively by Indians, the latter responded violently. After 1662, when Massasoit's son Metacom (known to whites as King Philip) became Wampanoag chief, relations between the two groups deteriorated steadily.

King Philip, unhappy with the white settlers' overbearing attitude, was convinced that Indians were doomed if they did not resist further expansion into their tribal lands. To complicate matters even more, Philip was unwilling to make treaties with colonial governors. He preferred to deal directly with the King of England as befitted his own status as tribal leader. Philip ultimately planned war against the colonists with whom he could not agree, a conflict which broke out suddenly. It occurred after three Indians were hanged by the settlers for their role in a Massachusetts Bay Colony murder in 1675.

Incensed by this act of white justice, the Indians, under King Philip's leadership, attacked Swansea in June 1675 and killed all of its inhabitants. Other towns fell to the onslaught—Brookfield was destroyed in August. In Maine, which was then a part of Massachusetts, Indians rose up against the whites, and in neighboring Rhode Island, settlers were attacked by Narragansett Indians sworn to support King Philip in his attempt to rid New England of colonists. Deerfield, in western Massachusetts, was destroyed in the fall of 1675; no whites returned to the town for almost a decade. In February 1676, King Philip's warriors destroyed Lancaster, killing all the males and taking women and children into captivity.

By the time King Philip was killed in a small battle in Rhode Island in August 1676, one out of every 16 white settlers in New England (most of them in Massachusetts) had died at the hands of Indians. Angry white survivors treated their conquered foes harshly and all of Myles Standish's diplomacy was rendered futile. As a result of King Philip's War whites forcibly emptied praying towns of their Indian residents. They were relocated, often to remote spots without sufficient hunting or fishing resources, and many of them died as a result. The Indian population in New England was irreversibly affected by King Philip's War and its aftermath: the Wampanoag tribe, for example, suffered almost total extinction.

THREATS TO ECONOMIC FREEDOM

It was not only hostility between Indians and whites that threatened colonial existence. Both Plymouth and Massachusetts Bay colonies faced increasing internal and external discord as the seventeenth century drew to a close. Despite efforts of civic and church leaders, change was inevitable. Sometimes it was effected peacefully, as with internal shifts to a wealthier lifestyle. This type of change was absorbed gradually, but externally, strife meant ultimate confrontation—both among colonists themselves and between the colonists and English authorities.

Clashes over trade spelled tremendous upheaval for the colonies. In 1676, England declared Massachusetts in noncompliance with the Navigation Acts. These regulations, passed in 1660, required colonists to trade exclusively with England. Eight years later, in 1684, Parliament revoked the Massachusetts Bay Colony Charter for violations of trade restrictions.

In 1686, following the ascension of James II to the English throne, the Massachusetts Bay and Plymouth colonies became part of the Dominion of New England along with New York and New Jersey. The dominion represented perhaps the biggest shift in political structure the colonists had yet known.

Chief among the differences apparent after dissolution of the Massachusetts Bay and Plymouth colony charters was that the Dominion of New England was a civil commonwealth. Simply stated, this meant an individual could vote without being a church member. Not surprisingly, this law had a far-reaching effect on church power in Massachusetts and contributed to a growing mood of religious tolerance in the colony.

Sir Edmund Andros became the first royal governor of the dominion in 1686. By then, colonists had learned to enjoy their relative autonomy, and Massachusetts residents did not welcome the

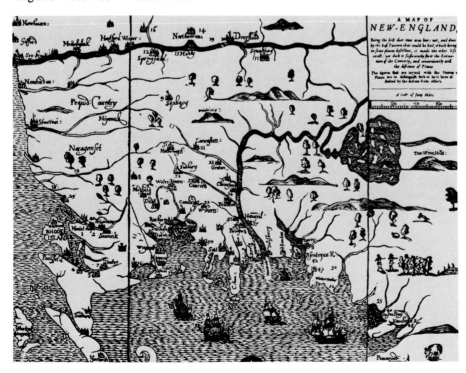

This early map by John Foster, first published in 1677 in the book Indian Wars in New England, *shows where the English had established themselves by the time of King Philip's War. Most of the towns were on the coast or along the Connecticut River. The map also tries to document which towns were attacked by Indians during the war. Ten to 15 percent of the English men, as well as numerous women and children, were killed. There were atrocities on both sides. For example, in Brookfield, colonists' heads were said to have been kicked around like soccer balls. And, after the war, Metacom's (King Philip's) head was displayed on a pike in Boston while his family was sold into slavery in the West Indies. From Waters,* Ipswich in the Massachusetts Bay Colony, *1905*

Left: *Built in 1681, the Hingham Meeting House is the only church from the 1600s remaining in New England, and it is still in use. It is known as the Old Ship Church because it was supposedly built upside-down in shipbuilding fashion by the seagoing settlers of coastal Hingham. The entryways were probably added later. Early meetinghouses were very simple in design; what is now considered the quintessential New England church, the white, end-gabled, Greek Revival edifice, was not built until the early 1800s. From Winsor,* Narrative and Critical History of America, *Vol. III, 1884*

Facing Page: *"The Landing of the Commissioners at Boston" illustrates the time when, after the end of Puritan Oliver Cromwell's rule and the crowning of Charles II, royal commissioners were sent to Massachusetts. The new king sent his commissioners in 1664 to correct whatever abuses they could find. The colonists were told to stop coining their own money and to say "God Save the King" after the reading of royal proclamations. From Stark,* The Loyalists of Massachusetts and the Other Side of the Revolution, *1910*

newly-appointed governor, who had a reputation as a military man. Quickly becoming unpopular, his efforts at ruling seemed both arbitrary and harsh. Angry citizens heard of the overthrow of James II in England and therefore deposed Andros in 1689 at Boston's Rowe's Wharf. Andros returned to England where the Glorious Revolution had restored William of Orange, and his wife Mary, to the throne, uniting England and Scotland as Great Britain.

Some colonists hoped the Glorious Revolution would reestablish an independent Massachusetts Bay Colony, but this did not occur. Two years after attempts to obtain a revived Massachusetts Bay charter failed, in 1691, the crown colony of Massachusetts was established, uniting the former colonies of Plymouth and Massachusetts Bay. The new royal governor of the colony was Sir William Phips, a Maine native, who arrived in Boston in 1692 just in time to play a role in one of Massachusetts' most infamous episodes.

THE UNEXPECTED FRUIT OF FREEDOM AND CHANGE

Puritan social order was disintegrating.

Plymouth's Pilgrims had been incorporated into Massachusetts, now a single political entity. Religious tolerance, while not flourishing, was permitted to the degree that Anglican church services were now held in Boston, that original bastion of Puritan dogma. But soon, the tragedy of the witchcraft trials at Salem in 1692 came to symbolize the intense disarray into which Puritan lifestyles had fallen.

In March 1692, a 73-year-old Salem woman—Rebecca Nurse—was accused of witchcraft. In July, along with four others, she was hanged as a witch. Just two months before Nurse was put on trial, a young girl named Betty Parris, daughter of local minister Samuel Parris, was afflicted with a strange, convulsive sickness: she writhed in pain and screamed that devils were tormenting her. Ultimately, her illness was blamed on witchcraft.

A curiously prevalent charge leveled against offenders in seventeenth-century Massachusetts, witchcraft was blamed in 1688 for the illness of several girls in Boston. Later, a woman was executed after being charged with witchcraft in connection with the girls' symptoms. In

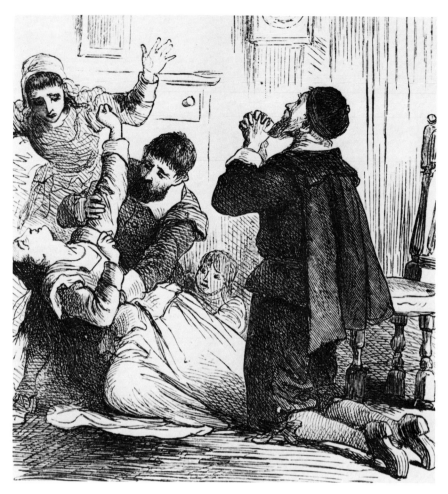

This 1880s depiction of the witchcraft hysteria shows the men with Lincolnesque beards which Salem men of 1690 did not have. However, the picture does illustrate the belief that prayers and fasting would deliver the afflicted one from the power of the witch. From Lossing, Our Country: A Household History of the United States, 1888

Salem Village a few years later, a West Indian slave named Tituba, who lived in the Reverend Samuel Parris' household, was implicated in the case involving Betty Parris, her cousin Ann Putnam, and several others. Tituba, under intense pressure from her interrogators, confessed to being a witch. She described in fantastic and imaginative terms the procedures she and the Devil supposedly used to hurt their victims. "The Devil came to me and bid me serve him," she said at one interrogation. Parris and his supporters were delighted to blame the young girls' strange and disturbing troubles on something as reprehensible as witchcraft. They proceeded to prosecute with a vengeance and Salem soon rocked with controversy as scores were accused and 20 were actually executed.

On the surface, witchcraft in seventeenth-century Massachusetts seems to have been frighteningly capricious—its victims and perpetrators were everywhere. But a closer look reveals that those labeled witches often held little power in the community. Tituba, a servant in the Parris home, was a black woman with no education. Others accused of being witches had reputations as jades, or disreputable women, and

were in frequent quarrels with neighbors. In Salem, feuds between relative newcomers to the community and older, established families seem to have been a contributing factor in the witchcraft hysteria there. Also, many witchcraft victims were young. Betty Parris was only nine years old and her co-accusers were within a few years of that age. Nearly everyone identified as a witch in the early stages of the craze was virtually powerless even before the scare became widespread, and this may provide a clue to their defenseless positions.

The hysteria of young witchcraft victims—many of whom hallucinated, had convulsions, and suffered odd speech and behavior—was terrifying to a society based on order and obedience. One observer told of the girls at Salem "getting into Holes, and creeping under Chairs and Stools, and . . . uttering foolish, ridiculous Speeches, which neither they themselves nor any others could make sense of."

The Reverend Parris and other ministers and magistrates who examined the victims were baffled. Chief Justice William Stoughton, lieutenant governor of Massachusetts, presided over the Salem witchcraft trials. He questioned victims closely, was convinced that their testimony rang true, and was determined to convict as many witches as necessary to put an end to society's torment.

As weeks passed, more and more accusations were made against people in and around Salem. Eventually, a few grew skeptical, even critical, of the shrieking, wailing victims who sat at the trials. But those who questioned the validity of witchcraft charges often found themselves accused. By September 1692, the hysteria resulted in the jailing of more than 100 people, both men and women, in Boston alone. The Massachusetts General Court restored a law making witchcraft punishable by death, thus paving the way for executions. Eight people were hanged in Salem on September 22, 1692, and throughout Essex County numerous strange episodes involving animal, as well as human, behavior seemed to confirm the alleged witchcraft.

No matter how respectable one was, it appeared nobody was safe from the victims' rantings. John Alden, son of John and Priscilla Alden, was asked to present testimony before a Salem court. Ultimately, he was arrested and jailed for 15 months on witchcraft charges, but he escaped to New York and stayed there until the terrors subsided. Alden was not alone in his peril. Ministers' wives were accused, as were friends of the royal governor, Sir William Phips. Even Phips' wife, the Lady Mary Phips, was accused of being a witch.

Cotton Mather, a well-known minister from Boston, was not convinced that hysterical testimony from young girls was sufficient to condemn a person to death. His father, Increase Mather of Cambridge, agreed, noting in an October 1692 sermon that "It were better that 10 suspected witches should escape, than that one innocent person should be condemned." Many agreed with the Mathers' opinions and in early 1693, Governor Phips ruled that nobody could be convicted of witchcraft solely on the basis of spectral evidence, that is, testimony of afflicted persons saying they had witnessed apparitions doing terrible things.

Of 52 cases tried in the courts during this latter period, only three resulted in convictions—and those only because the accused actually confessed to being witches. The governor reprieved those found guilty and saved them from hanging—much to the dismay and expressed displeasure of Lieutenant Governor Stoughton, who had spent so much time prosecuting witchcraft cases in Salem. In May 1693, John Alden was cleared of charges lodged against him and all others jailed on witchcraft charges in Massachusetts were set free. No more witches were hanged from the so-called Witches Hill gallows in Salem. Governor Phips' actions were based on his concern that the witchcraft episode, if allowed to

Cotton Mather (1663-1728) entered Harvard at age 11 and went on to became a teacher and a minister. In 1685 he wrote about cases of witchcraft that he had heard of, so he was hardly an impartial investigator of the Salem problems. This 1727 mezzotint, the first in America, was done by Peter Pelham, later the stepfather of John Singleton Copley. Courtesy, Mead Art Museum, Amherst College. Bequest of James Turner, class of 1908

continue, would have a detrimental effect on all of Massachusetts. He wrote to the Earl of Nottingham in February 1693 that he feared "the black cloud that threatened this Province with destruction."

In Salem Village, the Reverend Parris was the subject of an April 1695 meeting that resulted in a mutual agreement concerning his departure. By July 1696, he had left Salem Village and the ministry to become a teacher in a neighboring town. Afterward, Salem tried to erase the events that held the community in the grip of fear and horror for 12 months. Despite these efforts, however, Salem's name has been tied by historic record and public memory to witchcraft trials and to the deaths of those unfortunates ensnared in the web of fantastic accusations.

In the wake of these unsettling circumstances, most people in Salem and elsewhere set aside dissenting opinions concerning religious practices and social and economic change. The colonists were as eager as Governor Phips to erase the unwholesome blot of witchcraft from Massachusetts and they worked diligently to promote prosperity and progress in the eighteenth century. What colonists could not foresee, however, was a change in British colonial policy that heralded a new era for Massachusetts and all of North America.

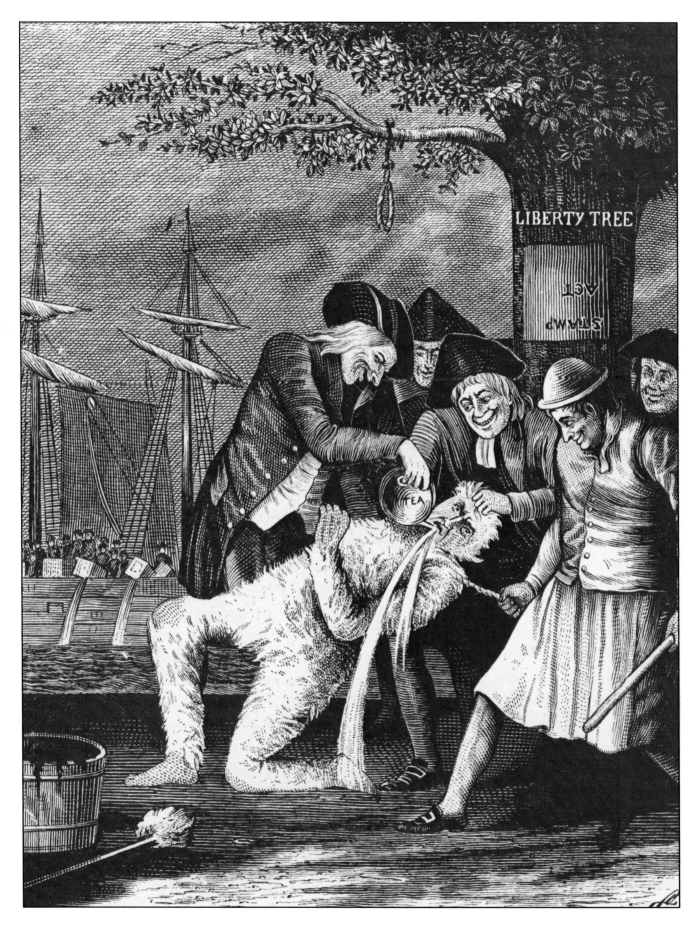

TRADE, TAXATION, AND THE WAR FOR INDEPENDENCE (1700-1780)

★ ★ ★ ★ ★ ★ ★ ★ ★

This cartoon published in London in 1774 attempted to illustrate how completely the rabble in the colonies disregarded government authority. To the artist, the colonists were an unruly mob of nasty people with no respect for proper authority. Patriot leader John Adams' statement made years later gives some truth to the London opinion. Adams said, "The poor people themselves, who by secret manoeuvres, are excited to insurrection, are seldom aware of the purposes for which they are set in motion or of the consequences which may happen to themselves; and once heated and in full career, they can neither manage themselves nor be managed by others." From Stark, The Loyalists of Massachusetts and the Other Side of the Revolution, *1910*

Compared to conditions suffered by colonists arriving in Massachusetts in the 1600s, eighteenth-century colonial life encompassed a considerable increase in material comforts and a wider latitude of individual freedom. In addition, political autonomy had developed to an extent satisfactory to most colonists. Although Britain established a board of trade in 1696 to regulate and deal with aspects of colonial administration, Massachusetts residents retained many decision-making powers, including legislative control, the right to levy taxes, and the right to approve governor's council appointees. For although named to his post by the king, the colonial governor consulted only with advisors acceptable to the colonists.

Some historians have referred to Britain's inability to regulate or effectively control affairs during this period as a time of "salutary neglect." Various results of this apathy would appear before the

end of the eighteenth century.

A GROWING SEPARATION

During the late 1600s and early 1700s, a lapse in well-established censorship policies fostered the growth of numerous publishing ventures in Massachusetts. However, they were closely monitored by conservative magistrates threatened by a press that challenged their authority. On April 24, 1704, the first regular newspaper appeared in Boston. The *Boston News-Letter*, published by John Campbell, postmaster, carried the phrase "published by authority," indicating nominal approval by the governor's council. In time, postmasters throughout Massachusetts came to expect that publishing duties and rights would accompany their other responsibilities. By 1723, little censorship was exercised by either royal authorities or church officials. Unlike the previous 90 years, clergy now found it difficult to dictate what could be published in Massachusetts. Control was limited to threats of libel suits by civil authorities. However, not until well after the War for Independence was the press in Massachusetts truly free in the sense that it is today.

Though prohibited in theory, smuggling was another activity carried out on a large scale. When British Parliament passed the Navigation Acts in 1660, there was little hope of their enforcement in the colonies due to the number of ships and ports requiring surveillance. Therefore, until the War for Independence, a great proportion of shipping originating from Massachusetts was illegal. Up and down the coast, merchant ships from Cape Ann to New Bedford maintained healthy trade relationships with countries other than Britain. Sugar, molasses, naval stores, furs, grain, and other items found their way into holds of ships plying Atlantic and Caribbean waters. The lucrative business resulting from these unlawful dealings launched the fortunes of more than one Massachusetts family.

To better describe the magnitude of this illegal shipping trade, one historian estimates that by 1748 there were 491 colonial ships sailing annually out of Boston Harbor and another 131 ships sailing out of Salem, the most important colonial port north of Boston.

Of course, some of this activity remained lawful. Fishing represented a major industry only a few years after the founding of the Plymouth and Massachusetts Bay colonies. The fleets that sailed from Nantucket, Martha's Vineyard, and other smaller ports were instrumental in establishing the financial stability of Massachusetts' fisheries. Abundant supplies of fish in Atlantic waters, which are warmed by the Gulf Stream, provided an economic windfall to the colonists. Massachusetts later recognized this boon symbolically: at the end of the 1700s, a Massachusetts House of Representatives resolution declared the new legislative body would "hang up the representation of a Codfish in the room where the House sits."

Not by caprice did the cod become a sign of the state's enterprise. According to

By 1765 Peter Folger II of Nantucket could afford to build this fine house on Centre Street. The receipt that dates it reads, "From Jethro Hussey, housewright, to Peter Folger II for 28 pounds, 10 shillings on account of building his house." The Folger family was on Nantucket in the 1600s and consisted primarily of merchants and inventors. Peter Folger II was a cousin of Benjamin Franklin. Photo by John H. Martin

THE BOSTON POST ROAD

Transforming a raw, untamed country into a thriving and dynamic society had taken more than a century. The first 100 years or so in which the colonists carved out a new existence in North America are noteworthy for the innovation, thrift, passion, and determination with which the settlers approached the challenges of their new life. By the time of the War for Independence, Massachusetts colonists had earned a reputation for hardheaded individualism, a taste for economic gain, a concern for religious freedom, and above all an overwhelming interest in making things better.

One way in which they attempted to improve their condition was by upgrading what we might now call their communications system. In the seventeenth and eighteenth centuries, that system was limited to travel on foot or horseback, or by carriage, coach, or boat. Although roads were generally primitive, the need for good ones was recognized early. In order to improve communications between the various colonies, a post road was opened in Massachusetts as early as 1673; it was used to transport mail between New England and New York.

On January 22, 1673, the first mail carrier left New York on his way to the capital of the Massachusetts Bay Colony. That initial dispatch arrived in Boston around February 1. Springfield, Brookfield, Worcester, and Cambridge were among the communities served by this postal carrier along a route known variously as the King's Highway, the Great Road, and later, the Boston Post Road.

Both Governor John Winthrop of Connecticut (son of the Massachusetts governor) and the royal governor of New York, Francis Lovelace, shared an enthusiasm for a regular post between their two colonies. They were encouraged in this endeavor by King Charles II, who supported a better communications system among all the colonies.

Initially, the 200-mile journey began on the first Monday of every month. After several years of interrupted service—due to Indian attacks on such postal station towns as Brookfield, and also due to the Dutch takeover of New York—the Boston Post Road finally saw regular mail service. By 1691, service was regularized and a royal patent was given to the individual in charge of colonial post offices. By 1751, two deputy postmasters—one of them Benjamin Franklin—were named by the crown.

Among the records of post road travel that exist today, the journal of Boston businesswoman Sarah Kemble Knight is vivid and insightful in its observations. In 1704, she traveled unchaperoned on horseback from her home near Dedham to New York, guided by a post rider. Knight acknowledged that her trip, both long and hazardous, was an "unheard of thing for an unaccompanied woman to do." The task of guide and traveler's aid was part of the mail carriers' job despite the requirement that post riders average 30 to 50 miles per day in summer months.

The post road journey being a lengthy one, it was not long before taverns and public houses were commonplace along the route. Establishments such as the Golden Ball Tavern in Weston and the Bunch of Grapes on Boston's King Street flourished in the years prior to the War for Independence. The Green Dragon, also in Boston, became legendary for its role as the place where the Sons of Liberty met before the Boston Tea Party.

In his diary, John Adams describes a Shrewsbury tavern, Major Farrar's, which he visited in 1774. He records that there he "sat down at a good fire in the barroom to dry out my great-coat and saddle-bags." While most taverns provided common rooms in which food and drink were served, few afforded their guests any real comfort—or privacy. Many public houses offered only the most rudimentary and sketchy sleeping arrangements, often with up to eight beds in a room and four people per bed. In her diary, Sarah Kemble Knight refers with no little disgust to having to share her already uncomfortable sleeping accommodations with several strange men.

As time passed, post road improvements accrued. Milestones were erected, in part as a way of determining postal rates. Early in its history, the charge to send a piece of mail along the post road was about three pence for a distance of up to 100 miles. During the War for Independence, these milestones were invaluable aids to intelligence efforts, since they allowed the patriots to report accurately on the movements of enemy troops.

The Boston Post Road saw the gradual demise of postal riders after the advent of stagecoach and wagon travel. Although this change occurred somewhat later than is generally imagined, by the late 1780s stage and wagon travel had been introduced and soon flourished. On October 20, 1783, along the post road from Boston to Hartford, a stagecoach was available to paying travelers for the first time. It made the journey in four days, stopping in Northboro, Brookfield, and Somers, Connecticut. This means of conveyance quickly grew popular, and in 1785 stagecoach owners Levi Pease and Reuben Sykes were granted the first contract to carry U.S. mail.

★   ★   ★   ★   ★   ★   ★   ★

Codfish caught in season could be dried into fish "flakes" on racks in the sun, as depicted here in Provincetown. The fish were usually caught, cleaned, and salted at sea, and rinsed and resalted ashore. The flakes were either covered or brought in at night or in rainy weather. From a circa 1907 postcard

In the 1890s Clifton Johnson photographed this scene which could have taken place at least a century earlier. Gloucester fish cleaners are preparing fish for salting away in barrels in the days before refrigeration. Such barrels were shipped from Gloucester to places all over the world. Courtesy, The Clifton Johnson Collection, The Jones Library, Inc., Amherst

Jonathan Edwards (1703-1758), a Northampton Congregational minister, led a controversial return to more strict Calvinist principles in the late 1730s. He felt sinners must recognize their own depraved natures and have an emotional awakening in order to obtain salvation. In a famous 1741 sermon he reminded his followers of God's power: "The God that holds you over the pit of hell, much as one holds a spider, or some loathsome insect over the fire, abhors you, and is dreadfully provoked." Edwards died from a smallpox inoculation shortly after accepting the presidency of Princeton. Engraved by S.S. Jocelyn and S.B. Munson from a circa 1750 oil painting. Courtesy, Forbes Library

Francis Higginson's observations of Massachusetts waters in 1630, "the Abundance of Sea-Fish are almost beyond believing and sure would I scarce have believed it except I had seen it with mine own eyes." Peter Faneuil, a prominent Boston merchant who gave Faneuil Hall to the city, built his fortune by shipping codfish to foreign markets. By the early 1770s, Chatham, on Cape Cod, boasted 27 cod-fishing ships. George Cabot, another prominent Bostonian, was a ship's captain by the age of 18 and was later the first American to send a ship to St. Petersburg, Russia, in 1784.

Although critical to coastal communities, the Massachusetts economy as a whole did not rely exclusively on fishing. By the mid-1770s a triangle of trade flourished in the Atlantic, both with the British West Indies *and* the French West Indies. Its growth encouraged the emergence of a new merchant class in Massachusetts and created growing tension between colonists and British authority once the Navigation Acts deemed this trade triangle largely illegal.

The triangle was based on specific commodities: whale oil (principally originating from ports at Dartmouth— later known as the town of New Bedford—and Nantucket); naval stores; furs (at least until the late 1760s); and rum. These were shipped to Africa (rum was the principal currency traded there) where they were exchanged for gold—and slaves. Slaves were shipped to the West Indies and exchanged for molasses, which was then transported to Massachusetts distilleries and used in rum production. Medford was but one community known for its manufacture of this lucrative molasses by-product.

While few records exist of many Massachusetts-based slave ships, we know that in 1700 several such vessels operated out of Plymouth and Boston. By and large, however, slave traders were British-based ships and profits from slavery accruing in Massachusetts were only indirectly linked to that tragic and peculiar institution on which the southern colonies became so dependent.

Another century would pass before Massachusetts became heavily embroiled in the public controversy surrounding slavery. But in the early 1700s, awareness of this and other ethical issues provoked concern over moral decline and roused the question of religious degeneration.

The religious revival that began in Northampton in 1734 is another example of how colonial thought and culture changed in spite of itself. Like the growth of the free press and the triangular trade, both this revival and the Great Awakening (which began in Boston in 1740) were phenomena that both shaped and were shaped by their participants. The first of many religious revival movements to spread through New England, the Great Awakening signaled a change in colonists' views of themselves and their communities.

An eloquent preacher, Jonathan Edwards (1703-1758), grandson of the respected Massachusetts clergyman Solomon Stoddard (1643-1729), kindled a religious revival along the Connecticut River Valley. The fervor spread like wildfire from Northampton, where both men had parishes, along the valley north to Northfield and south to Suffield. Entire communities were transformed, and the conversion experience represented to the colonists a common bond among hundreds in Massachusetts as well as many who lived outside the colony. Missionary zeal and millenial hopes went hand in hand. Revivalists became evangelists as well, and in 1751 Edwards himself went to preach in Stockbridge, an outpost in western Massachusetts. There, another minister, David Brainerd, had worked earlier to bring Christianity to the Indians.

The Great Awakening, which burned out by 1744, was a unique, specific religious phenomenon infusing new life into a Puritanism that was creaking with age. Although the Puritans had guided Massachusetts for more than a century, their influence was by now diluted. Revivals helped rejuvenate the colony's spiritual and intellectual climate, intensifying religious influence and resulting in funding for new schools and colleges as well as the revamping of established educational institutions. These schools would train a new generation of clergy, many of whom were to become involved in missionary work throughout the world.

More importantly than its specific religious impact, however, the Great Awakening encouraged people to look optimistically at life in America. Colonists had imagined themselves dwelling in a redeemed land, and the religious revivals resulting from the awakening promoted the idea that the "city upon a hill" was still viable. It was in part due to this renewed sense of religious authority that the political and moral issues of ensuing decades affected the colonists so deeply. To a large degree, the Great Awakening of the

1730s and 1740s strengthened the colonists' resolve so that continued encounters with British authority were treated as unjust and tyrannical acts against a godly people.

ESTABLISHING AN IDENTITY

A growing economy, a more dynamic political structure, and a more complex social environment all contributed enormously to changes in Massachusetts between the mid-seventeenth and mid-eighteenth centuries. But another factor affected the colonists even more directly: war between France and Britain.

This war was made up of several separate conflicts, beginning with King William's War (1689-1697), the North American extension of the War of the League of Augsburg in Europe. Frontier towns in New England were raided by

Benjamin Franklin (1706-1790) was born on Milk Street in Boston, the 10th son in his family. He went to school in Boston for a few years but was educated at home and by himself for the most part. At age 12 he was apprenticed to his half-brother, a Boston printer who began the New England Courant. *After a dispute with the half-brother, Franklin, at age 17 already an expert printer, left for Philadelphia. He of course became more than a printer: his future occupations included author, inventor, statesman, foreign diplomat, and scientist. Drawn by C.N. Cochin, engraved by A.H. Ritchie, 1777. From Duyckinck and Duyckinck,* Cyclopedia of American Literature, *1866*

Indians attacked the stockaded frontier village of Deerfield in 1704, killing some and taking the rest captive—only a few escaped. This scene depicts Rev. John Williams and his family trudging north to Canada with their captors. Mrs. Williams was slain not far along the trail, as she was weak from recent childbirth. Two of the Williams children were also killed. Some of the captives (including a Williams daughter) chose not to be ransomed and stayed on with the Indians. From Lossing, Our Country, A Household History, *Vol. I, 1888*

the French, who subsequently lost Port Royal, Nova Scotia, to the retaliating British. In 1697 the Treaty of Ryswick declared original settlers to be the rightful owners of these areas. King William's War was followed by Queen Anne's War (1701-1713), known in Europe as the War of the Spanish Succession. Queen Anne's War was followed by King George's War, or the War of the Austrian Succession (1740-1748), which was followed by the French and Indian War (1756-1763). The last and by far the most important of this series of conflicts, the French and Indian War left

a lasting impression on Massachusetts' development. This war fostered the Indians' hatred of the French in Canada and the British in New York and New England. Both the French and the British claimed to have some Indian allies, however, despite the Indians' general antagonism toward white colonists. Opposing forces from Great Britain and France continuously used Indians against colonial settlers to further English and Gallic political goals.

In 1704, during Queen Anne's War, a party of French, along with hostile Indians from Montreal, descended on the

Massachusetts town of Deerfield. It had been laid waste by an Indian massacre in 1675 and was once again attacked and 53 people were killed. Another 111 were taken captive by the French and the Indians and marched through bitter winter snows as far as Canada. Lancaster, which lay further east, suffered similarly. In 1708, Haverhill, near the New Hampshire border, was attacked, and about 40 people in that community lost their lives.

Although some towns suffered from Indian attacks more than others, some made alliances with Indians and thus were spared any violence. The Iroquois Confederation, known as the *Five Nations,* became closely allied with the British in America. These natives sold furs to colonists and fought alongside the

British during the French and Indian War. Opposing tribes allied with the French included the Delaware Indians.

When the French and Indian War erupted, many British settlers' lives were constantly threatened by Indian raids. Combined with the previous decades' conflicts, this promoted the colonists' willingness to fight back. British control of North America was finally secured with the Treaty of Paris in 1763, after British forces defeated the French in the Battle of Quebec. Among the leaders on the British side was General Jeffrey Amherst. The town of Amherst in western Massachusetts was named after this able soldier, who helped take Crown Point and Fort Ticonderoga in 1759. Fighting under the command of Amherst and numerous other officers, including George Washing-

Faneuil Hall, a gift to Boston from merchant Peter Faneuil, was to be used for public meetings and as a marketplace. Because of a speech by James Otis in 1763 dedicating Faneuil Hall to the cause of freedom for which he later fought, the structure became known as "The Cradle of Liberty" and in it were *hung portraits and memorabilia from the Revolution. In 1742 when it was built, Faneuil Hall served a new international trading center just blossoming near the waterfront, a shipping port of growing importance. From Barber,* History and Antiquities of Every Town in Massachusetts, *1839*

Boston lawyer James Otis (1725-1783) was the intellectual leader of Massachusetts' opposition to the English colonial tax measures after his 1761 court battle against the "writs of assistance," or general search warrants, which Crown officials used to search for smuggled goods. From Grafton, The American Revolution: A Picture Sourcebook, *Dover, 1975*

Right: *In 1762 a rumor spread around Boston and New England that the crown had appointed an Anglican bishop to sit in Boston, still a Congregational stronghold. Then in 1767 the spectre raised itself again when an Episcopal preacher was said to have written a letter to England requesting a bishop. The colonists were furious at the idea, and this cartoon shows the strong feelings aroused. There had been an Anglican church—King's Chapel—in Boston since 1754, and royal appointees were usually Episcopalian, but the thought of a bishop really rankled the anti-hierarchy Congregationalists. From Stark,* The Loyalists of Massachusetts and the Other Side of the Revolution, *1910*

Facing page, top: *On August 14, 1765, the Loyal Nine (a Boston social club of printers, distillers, and other artisans) and North and South End mobs rose up against the Stamp Act and the future stamp agent, Andrew Oliver. The mob hung Oliver in effigy, tore down a new building they assumed would be the stamp office, and built a bonfire with the wood near Oliver's home, where they smashed his windows. In this view sympathetic to Loyalists, the angry crowd is shown throwing stones and threatening the officials who came to disperse them. Andrew Oliver promised not to become the stamp agent. From Stark,* The Loyalists of Massachusetts and the Other Side of the Revolution, *1910*

ton, more than 6,000 Massachusetts troops lost their lives during these war years.

A separate set of events during this period marked a significant shift in British colonial policy. As victory over France became certain, British authorities began enforcing stiffer colonial adherence to crown policy. In 1761, Parliament had passed the Writs of Assistance authorizing general searches of homes and warehouses. The law seemed acceptable so long as war raged, but following the Treaty of Paris in 1763, colonists expected arbitrary searches to cease. James Otis, a noted Boston lawyer, carried their arguments against such searches and their demands for termination of the Writs of Assistance to the courts. Otis called on Britain to acknowledge the colonists' rights, but Parliament, deaf to his pleas, ignored these as well as subsequent demands for a hands-off colonial policy. By doing so, Britain unwittingly set the stage for colonial rebellion.

In 1764, James Otis published a pam-

Left: *Royal Governor Francis Bernard (1712-1799) was well liked by the people of Massachusetts when he was first appointed in 1760. By 1769 when he fled Boston back to England, he was despised as a person and as a symbol of British rule. While in office he acquired large tracts of land: all of Mount Desert Island in the Maine district, parts of seven townships in Vermont, one-third of a large town in the new Berkshire County, and a large estate on Jamaica Pond in Roxbury. He lived in Boston at the Province House, worshiped in the royal curtained box at Anglican King's Chapel, and had apartments at the fort on Castle Island in the harbor. This portrait was painted circa 1775 by John Singleton Copley. From Stark,* The Loyalists of Massachusetts and the Other Side of the Revolution, *1910*

phlet titled *The Rights of the British Colonies Asserted and Proved,* in which he avowed that Parliament could not legally tax colonial property. It was one of the early arguments in the most significant dispute yet between Britain and its colonies. Taxation without representation was the issue that would ultimately provoke the end of British rule in Massachusetts, as well as in the 12 other colonies.

Subsequent legal limitations placed on colonists were detailed in 1765 with passage of the Stamp Act, which required a stamp on all newspapers, pamphlets, legal documents, and other papers issued in the colonies. And the tightening of the 1764 Sugar Act, first passed in 1733, lowered a sixpence-per-gallon duty on imported molasses to three pence-per-gallon but threatened serious enforcement. It also meant that the British were less interested in regulating trade and more intent on raising revenues in the simplest way possible. The enforcement of duties on sugar affected the price of rum as well and further angered the colonists.

GROWTH OF DISSENT

Massachusetts had grown in population size and density since the 1680s. In 1643, the counties of Suffolk, Middlesex, and Essex had been established. Hampden County had been established in 1662, followed by Barnstable, Bristol, and Plymouth counties in 1685, and Dukes and Nantucket counties in 1695. The latter was named after the Indian word *nantican,* meaning "far-away land." Worcester County was established by the General Court in 1731. In 1760, Massachusetts' estimated population was 202,600, and in 1761, Berkshire County was established with Pittsfield as its county seat. It became more and more apparent that if challenged by Britain, Massachusetts would have both the moral inclination and the human resources and governmental structure to stand up to that challenge.

In June 1765, shortly after Parliament passed the Stamp Act, the Massachusetts Assembly proposed that an intercolonial

Stamp Act Congress should meet. Here, representatives from the colonies could discuss ways of legally protesting the new law. Britain expected to collect about £60,000 annually from these colonial stamp duties, but Parliament had failed to consider the colonists' willingness to pay the tax. Instead of generating colonial revenue, the Stamp Act provoked unanticipated resistance.

The Stamp Act Congress met in New York City in October 1765. It immediately adopted the Declaration of Rights and Grievances, which declared that freeborn Englishmen could not be taxed without their consent. It further stated that since colonists were not represented in Parliament, any tax imposed on them without their consent was unconstitutional. It was a repetition of the point James Otis had made the year before, in 1764, when protesting against the Writs of Assistance.

Meanwhile, rioting mobs in Boston were sympathetic to the Stamp Act Congress' aims. These mobs looted and burned both homes and offices of British stamp officials. Lieutenant Governor Thomas Hutchinson's Boston mansion was vandalized as a protest against his harsh, unyielding, and autocratic views. Stamp Master Andrew Oliver's house was attacked and his office destroyed. By November, when the Stamp Act was actually to take effect, British officials were left without any alternative but to ignore the act's regulations. Massachusetts colonists had made their point.

Methods other than rioting also were effective in expressing colonial dissatisfaction with British authority. By virtue of Massachusetts law, the colonial assembly approved individuals whose names were submitted as candidates for the royal governor's council. In 1766, the assembly refused to approve names submitted by Governor Francis Bernard, and although the royal governor became furious, his anger only strengthened the opposition. A group of men calling themselves the Sons of Liberty—James Otis, John Adams, Samuel Adams, Paul

Facing page: *The Province House, built in 1716 nearly opposite the head of Milk Street in Boston, was home to the royal governors. It was an imposing three-story brick mansion, set back and well-landscaped, with a stone walk and massive stone steps. On the lofty cupola turned a copper Indian weathervane—now at the Massachusetts Historical Society— made by Shem Drowne. Before the Revolution the royal governor fled the country; the Province House was soon seized by the colonists. After the Revolution it became the property of the state until 1811, when this sketch was made. In 1864 it burned, but traces of its brick walls were still in evidence in 1910 and may still be there. From Stark,* The Loyalists of Massachusetts and the Other Side of the Revolution, *1910*

This view of the Boston Massacre, March 5, 1770, portrays the British Redcoats being set upon by a rowdy bunch. The British almost look apologetic and chagrined at having to keep order in front of the Town House, now called the Old State House. Painting by Alonzo Chappel. From Spencer and Lossing, A Complete History of the United States, *Vol. I, 1878*

Revere, Benjamin Edes, and others—publicly asked for resistance against the governor. The Sons of Liberty held meetings, published statements in newspapers, and encouraged all the colonists not to cooperate with crown officials. Governor Bernard saw only too well what might happen and how impotent he was politically. In a 1765 letter to the Lords of Trade in London, Bernard had complained that he was "only a nominal governor," and that he was a "prisoner . . . wholly in the Power of the People."

Governor Bernard was able to sense what Parliament, at such a distance, was unable or unwilling to admit. Encouraged by the Sons of Liberty, Boston merchants signed nonimportation agreements—indeed, merchants throughout Massachusetts signed such contracts boycotting British goods. Both in Boston and in smaller cities and towns, people

refused to buy anything shipped from England. Those who did not comply with this new edition of colonial resistance were publicly denounced and derided by other colonists. The nonimportation boycott caused a trade loss resulting in the repeal of the Stamp Act by Parliament in 1766. This repeal occurred after British merchants complained that their businesses were in jeopardy.

Passed in 1765, the Quartering Act generated even more alarm and resistance in Massachusetts than had previous restrictive British regulations. Suddenly, residents faced the probability of increased numbers of British troops in Boston—troops toward whom Massachusetts colonists felt more and more hostile. The end of the French and Indian conflict led colonists to expect a respite from the presence of British regulars, but the British authorities decided otherwise.

In this version of the Boston Massacre by Paul Revere after a painting by Henry Pelham, the British are portrayed as the aggressors; the "poor colonials" were not really fighting at all and look quite innocent. The little dog in front was to remind the viewer that dogs licked up the blood when the fight was over and five colonials were dead. From Winsor, The Memorial History of Boston, 1630-1880, *Vol. III, 1883*

On October 1, 1768, two regiments of British redcoats—about 600 men— landed in Boston and disembarked at Long Wharf. The presence of these regiments (the 14th and the 29th) was in royal response to Massachusetts' call for intercolonial protest against the Townshend Acts. These acts had been passed the year before, shortly after repeal of the Stamp Act. Now, Massachusetts colonists hoped to provoke a nonimportation agreement similar to that launched after passage of the Stamp Act. In October 1767, Samuel Adams and his cohorts designated items taxed by the Townshend Acts to be boycotted if the acts were not repealed. The tax included such items as glass, lead, paper, and tea—materials and products in great demand in the colonies. Adams knew he would have little difficulty promoting a boycott. He also sensed that Massachusetts might be able to encourage other colonies to act against Britain and was soon gratified when Massachusetts took steps to ensure such group action. The Massachusetts General Court sent a circular letter to other colonial legislatures urging protest against the Townshend Acts. When word of this letter reached Lord Hillsborough, the British royal secretary of the colonies, he responded by sending two military regiments to Boston.

Ultimately, peaceful boycott of the Townshend duties led to the repeal of most of them by the British Parliament in March 1770. All taxes except those on tea were lifted. But news of that repeal reached Massachusetts too late to prevent a major clash between British troops and Boston residents. The encounter had been brewing for two years, since the troops had landed in Boston Harbor. Hostility ran high against British authority and sentries posted throughout the city were a too-visible reminder of that hated authority.

On March 5, 1770, fighting broke out in Boston's King Street, near the Custom House. Muskets fired—despite a British officer's orders against shooting into the crowd. Soon five men lay dead or dying, victims of the so-called Boston Massacre. The lieutenant governor was petitioned by a committee of colonists who demanded that the British troops be withdrawn from the city. The committee's message was direct:

That it is the unanimous opinion of this meeting that the inhabitants and soldiery can no longer live together in safety; that nothing can rationally be expected to restore the peace of the town & prevent further blood & carnage, but the immediate removal of the Troops; and that we therefore most fervently pray his Honor that his power and influence may be exerted for their instant removal.

Ultimately, nine British soldiers were arrested and put on trial for murder. Seven were acquitted of the charges and two were found guilty of manslaughter. These two were punished and discharged from the army. The two regiments were finally removed to Castle William, a fort

located in Boston Harbor.

Fanned to white heat during the two years leading up to the rioting, tempers cooled as time passed and repeal of the Townshend duties was publicized. By now, Massachusetts had a population of about 235,000, and few were eager to continue extremist opposition to Britain. Even Samuel Adams—the feisty, fire-eating Son of Liberty—recognized by 1771 that violent sentiment could not be maintained indefinitely: ". . . when at a lucky Season the publick are awakened to a Sense of Danger [and] a manly resentment is enkindled, it is difficult, for so many separate Communities as there are in all the colonies, to agree on one consistent plan of Opposition."

By this time, the current royal governor of Massachusetts, Thomas Hutchinson, relaxed a bit. For although British troops remained, the colonists seemed relatively calm. In fact, some of the more radical patriots such as Samuel Adams expressed open dismay at what they feared was deepening apathy. The solution, according to these patriots, was to form a Committee of Correspondence. This committee helped promote the idea that there remained many complaints to be lodged against Britain. Other colonies followed suit and formed their own organized protests. A short distance away, in Narragansett Bay, colonists in Rhode Island burned a British customs ship—the *Gaspee*—in 1772. Responsibility was claimed by the Committee of Correspondence there. The following year a far more colorful incident took place in Boston Harbor. The provocation was once more an act of Parliament designed to interfere with colonial trade.

Britain passed a Tea Act in 1773, granting the British East India Company monopoly on tea sales in the colonies. Suddenly, colonial merchants were no longer involved as middlemen in the lucrative tea trade. And since tea was a most popular eighteenth-century beverage, colonial merchants' losses were

Castle William on Castle Island in Boston Harbor was the strongest fort in New England and contained apartments for the royal governors. Governor Francis Bernard often avoided pre-Revolutionary War problems by having a 12-oared barge always ready to take him to Castle Island. When the unpopular governor and his son fled Boston in August 1769, they went to Castle William and then to England. The delighted Bostonians celebrated with fireworks. From Winsor, The Memorial History of Boston, 1630-1880, *Vol. III, 1883*

considerable. But more important, interference in their trade arrangements once again worried colonists. How long would it be before the British crown became involved in other aspects of colonial commerce?

As in the past, Boston's response was swift and effective. When the British ship *Dartmouth,* with a hold full of tea, arrived in Boston Harbor in December 1773, its captain waited to see if the tea would be unloaded. He needn't have wondered. It was taken—at night—by a band of "Indians" who dumped the entire shipment into the water. Of course, the group was not made up of real native Americans, but disguised Sons of Liberty. Their action prompted retaliation by Britain, and the resulting Coercive Acts placed severe restrictions on Massachusetts government and closed the port of Boston to all commerce. It would remain closed until the East India Company was paid for the tea.

By 1774, Britain's General Thomas Gage, commander in chief in North America, had been appointed governor of Massachusetts. Town meetings, ordinarily in session as frequently as necessary, were limited to annual gatherings. Provisions of the Coercive Acts were combined with terms of the Quebec Act and were labeled the "Intolerable Acts" by the colonists. Finally, Massachusetts and all other colonies had a mutual complaint. Colonial resistance to British tyranny was unified once and for all.

The Massachusetts royal charter had been annulled by the British in May 1774. By the time General Gage took over as governor, Massachusetts had set up an extra-legal Provincial Congress with John Hancock as head of the newly formed Committee of Safety. This group was empowered primarily with responsibility to train and to call out the militia if necessary.

War seemed inevitable. In February 1775, the second Provincial Congress of Massachusetts met, and later that month British troops arrived in Salem where military provisions had been stored. The redcoats were unsuccessful in their mission to seize those munitions and the colonists congratulated themselves—at the same time preparing for the inevitable future confrontation.

In addition to looking out for its own interests, Massachusetts rallied other colonies to action. In September 1774, Massachusetts sent delegates to the First Continental Congress held in Philadelphia, as did the other 12 colonies: Connecticut, Delaware, Georgia, Maryland, New Hampshire, New Jersey, New York, North Carolina, Pennsylvania, Rhode Island, South Carolina, and Virginia. Massachusetts' delegates were Thomas Cushing, Samuel Adams, Robert Treat Paine, James Bowdoin, and John Adams. The congress adopted the Suffolk Resolves, which demanded direct resistance to the Intolerable Acts and which were initially passed by Suffolk County delegates to Massachusetts' Provincial Congress. These delegates had first met in Dedham, then in Milton, to register a protest against the Coercive Acts. John Adams' *Declaration of Rights and Resolves* was also adopted enthusiastically by the First Continental Congress. This document articulated colonists' grievances against Britain but presented no new claims or disputes against the crown. Another boycott was established in which all colonies agreed not to import, export, or consume British goods.

Despite concerted action by all 13 colonies, British authorities—including King George III—believed Massachusetts to be the only colony showing signs of serious unrest. On the other hand, General Gage understood that Massachusetts was not alone in its resistance. In his position as royal governor and as a military commander of some experience, Gage recognized certain inevitabilities. Allied as one force, the colonies represented a formidable threat to Parliamentary authority. Gage knew militia were gathering and he also knew he had insufficient troops to suppress a colonial rebellion should one materialize.

Facing page: *The Liberty Tree, at the corner of Washington and Essex streets, was a giant and aged elm from which were hung likenesses of loathed Tories like the stamp collector. Patriots met under the Liberty Tree to plan the Revolution. The tree was thought to have been a seedling before Boston was settled by the Puritans in 1630 and was protected by a picket fence. That did not prevent the angry British from chopping it into 15 cords of firewood before they evacuated Boston. From* The London Illustrated News, *January 9, 1858*

On December 16, 1773, at Griffin's Wharf in Boston, a band of patriots, thinly disguised as Indians, boarded three British tea ships and threw overboard 342 chests of tea in protest against the British attempt that year to grant the East India Company a monopoly on tea sales in the colonies. From Grafton, The American Revolution: A Picture Sourcebook, *Dover, 1975*

DEFENDING LIBERTY

In April 1775, about 3,500 additional British troops were sent to North America at Gage's request, although this force was less than he had asked for. King George III instructed Gage to take whatever action he felt necessary. Since Gage knew Massachusetts patriots had munitions stored at Concord, he decided to march there and seize the weapons.

On April 19, 1775, 700 of Gage's troops set out for Concord. The "shot heard 'round the world" was fired when colonial militia fought with British troops that day, first at Lexington and then at Concord. The British first met the colonists at Lexington Green, a few miles short of their destination in Concord. No one is certain which side fired first, although many historians trust the accuracy of accounts holding the British responsible. Colonial Captain John Parker is alleged to have warned his minutemen against taking the initial action—"Stand your ground. Don't fire unless fired upon, but if they mean to have a war let it begin here."

Led by Major John Pitcairn, British regulars massed near the church on Lexington Green early on the morning of April 19. Pitcairn's shouted orders to the patriots—"Disperse! You damned rebels, disperse!"—preceded the melee, which lasted only a short time but left several Americans dead. The British troops continued to Concord where 450

colonial militia, under Major John Buttrick's command, waited near North Bridge. When the redcoats approached the colonists, the two groups exchanged fire. The patriots were anxious to protect Concord citizens from British troops, and large detachments of colonials from surrounding towns finally succeeded in pushing the redcoats back.

On their return trek to Boston headquarters, the British were harassed mercilessly. More than 4,000 colonial militia, alerted the night before, fired on retreating British troops along the entire 20-mile route. Paul Revere, William Dawes, and Dr. Samuel Prescott, riding the night before to warn colonists of British troop movements, had done their

job well. The British suffered 73 dead and more than 100 wounded during the retreat.

General Gage was denounced and the Provincial Congress proclaimed its need to raise 13,000 troops to defend the colony. By the end of May, 22 Massachusetts regiments had arrived in the Boston area, as well as another group of militia from colonies outside of Massachusetts. General Artemas Ward was named commander-in-chief, to be replaced later by the Continental Congress with General George Washington.

After the rout at Lexington and Concord, British troops stationed themselves in Boston, where colonial militia kept them sequestered during the building of fortifications around the city. At Breed's Hill and Bunker Hill, in Charlestown, about 2,000 colonial troops under the command of William Prescott prepared for battle, and on June 17, 1775, the redcoats attacked.

The first volleys were fired around 3 P.M. Although the colonials made earnest efforts, they ran short of ammunition and soon were forced to retreat. One British officer described the defeated colonists as fighting like devils. The redcoats—though winning a strategic victory at Breed's Hill—sustained major losses totaling upwards of 1,500 men. The colonial militia, on the other hand, suffered only about 100 dead and 300 wounded or captured. Among those who died on the American side were Dr. Joseph Warren, along with Colonel Thomas Gardner and Lieutenant Colonel Parker. Warren's death is immortalized in John Trumbull's painting, "The Battle of Bunker Hill," now hanging in the Yale University Art Gallery at New Haven, Connecticut.

General George Washington of Virginia, named head of the American Continental Army on June 16, 1775, assumed command of the army in Cambridge in July. Artemas Ward was named a major general and second in command to Washington. Three Massachusetts men—John Thomas, William Heath, and Seth Pomeroy—were

Above: *This is a 1901 look at the North Bridge in Concord, an 1875 replica of the 1775 rustic bridge. In 1909 a cement bridge safe for the new automobiles was built, but today, a wooden replica again marks the historic place. In the distance is the Concord Minute Man statue by Daniel Chester French, commissioned by the town in 1875 for America's centennial celebration. From* New England Magazine, *Vol. XXV, September 1901*

Right: *In this engraving from a painting by Alonzo Chappel, the British troops retreat down Concord's main road while being harassed from both sides by groups of militia. British losses for the day totaled 73 killed and 174 wounded; the colonials suffered 49 men killed and 41 wounded. From Grafton,* The American Revolution: A Picture Sourcebook, *Dover, 1975*

appointed brigadier generals in the American forces.

Thousands of American troops were already quartered in Cambridge, laying siege to Boston across the river. This siege lasted nearly 12 months before General Gage and his British troops finally were forced to leave the city in March of the following year, an exodus now celebrated in Boston as Evacuation Day. The inhabitants of Boston suffered greatly during this siege and the entire colony was relieved when the British departed. Their retreat was prompted in part by Henry Knox's ingenious strategy of aiming cannons at the British fortifications in Boston. Knox had gone to Fort Ticonderoga in New York in the middle of the winter to retrieve 55 pieces of captured artillery. It was due specifically to use of these cannons, shooting from the fortifications of Dorchester Heights, that colonists did not have to fight British troops on Massachusetts soil for the duration of the war. After March 1776 and the British evacuation of Boston, General Washington took the Continental Army to its war theater in New York.

Although there was almost no combat in Massachusetts, the War for Independence nevertheless had a great impact on the colony. Ship owners especially took advantage of wartime exigencies and many became rich from privateering. In practice, this meant raiding British ships—and Boston, as well as Salem and other smaller ports, was a center of operation for privateering until late in the war. By then, a British coastal blockade managed to put an end to this profitable illegal pastime. Captain Joseph Peabody of Salem was one of hundreds who made a fortune from privateering operations. Since Massachusetts no longer considered itself part of Britain, its ports were now technically open to foreign trading ships. It looked as if Great Britain's days of regulating trade in Massachusetts were over.

DECLARING INDEPENDENCE
By June 1776, John Adams of Braintree (now Quincy) and several others meeting in Virginia at the Second Continental Congress helped draft an independence resolution. In July, the Declaration of Independence was submitted to the congress for approval. Boston's John Hancock, president of the congress, was first in signing the document written to help Americans identify as a unified group rather than as residents of colonies with separate grievances against the crown.

That Massachusetts had a grievance was unmistakable. John Adams, in his diary for March 1776, reasoned that resentment ". . . is a Passion, implanted by Nature for the Preservation of the Individual. Injury is the Object which excites it . . . ought, for his own Seccurity and Honur, and for the public good to punish those who injure him, unless they repent . . . It is the same with Communities. They ought to resent and punish."

PROMINENT INDIVIDUALS
John Adams' name is remembered because of his contributions to the Declaration of Independence, his close friendship with its main author, Thomas Jefferson, and his term as second president of the United States. But there are many others from Massachusetts whose courage and conviction before, during, and after the Revolution have kept them prominent in Americans' memories. Few names evoke such a vigorous image as Paul Revere.

Immortalized by the poet Longfellow nearly a century later, Revere was a man of great talent and inventiveness. An accomplished craftsman, he was well known for his abilities as a silversmith and a master engraver. Many of his silver spoons, cups, salvers, salt cellars, and other items can now be seen on display in the Museum of Fine Arts in Boston. Revere's portrait, painted by John Singleton Copley—a prominent Bostonian whose Loyalist sentiments caused him to flee Massachusetts for England in 1774—hangs as part of the same museum's collection of early American paintings. The portrait shows Revere

This engraving from a painting by M.A. Wageman shows the British boarding ships to evacuate Boston on March 17, 1776. Cannon barrels are being dumped off a wharf to prevent capture. Accompanied by Loyalist colonials, most of the British fled to Halifax, Nova Scotia. Today, Evacuation Day is a state holiday which just happens to coincide with St. Patrick's Day. From Grafton, The American Revolution: A Picture Sourcebook, *Dover, 1975*

holding a teapot and gazing intently, but benignly, out of the canvas. It is easy to imagine him flinging himself onto the back of a horse, preparing to send the alarm throughout Massachusetts that "the redcoats are coming." Revere embodies the quintessence of Massachusetts patriotism—self-confidence, independence, and a desire only to live in peace without interference from external authority.

Another Massachusetts native with a reputation for independence is Deborah Sampson. Hers is among the more interesting stories of the period and concerns her role as a soldier in the Continental Army. Born in Plympton, near Plymouth, on December 17, 1760, Sampson enlisted in the army at age 22 by disguising herself as a man. Under the name Robert Shurtleff, she fought in the 4th Massachusetts Regiment. Wounded in a battle near Tarrytown, New York, Sampson was hospitalized and her deception was discovered. She was discharged from the army in 1783. Since she had actually been enlisted, Sampson-alias-Shurtleff was eligible for, and received, a military pension, the first woman in the nation to do so. In the years following her army adventures she married, had several children, and sometimes lectured publicly about her many experiences. Sampson died at the age of 66 in 1827.

Another unusual woman associated with early Massachusetts history is Phillis Wheatley. Born in Africa, she was sold in 1761 to a prosperous Boston family, who educated her and treated her as a

The Town House, built in Boston in 1711, is an early example of brick architecture. Built as a government center for Boston and the Province of Massachusetts, it housed courtrooms and a merchants' exchange. The Boston Massacre took place in front of the structure in 1770 when British troops were housed inside. The lion and unicorn, British symbols, were removed during the Revolution, and the Declaration of Independence was read to the people from the balcony. After the Revolution the building was used as a state house, a city hall, and a post office. Known today as the Old State House, it is the headquarters of the Bostonian Society with its library and museum, and the British lion and unicorn again stand on the stepped gables. From A Souvenir of Massachusetts Legislators, *1904*

Paul Revere (1735-1818) set himself up as a gold- and silversmith in Boston in 1758, but he also did copper-plate engraving. Among his prints were a view of the Boston Massacre and the design for Massachusetts' first paper currency. After his ride as special messenger for the Committee of Safety in 1775, he became a major and lieutenant colonel of a regiment of artillery. He returned to metalsmithing after the war and built a bell and cannon foundry. In 1801 he established a large, and possibly the first, copper-rolling works, at Canton. Oil portrait by John Singleton Copley, circa 1768-1770. Courtesy, Museum of Fine Arts, Boston. Gift of Joseph W., William B., and Edward H.R. Revere.

Phillis Wheatley (circa 1753-1784) was born in Africa, kidnapped, and sold at a slave auction in Boston to a family named Wheatley. Phillis learned English with remarkable speed, and, although she never attended a formal school, she also learned Greek. She became a sensation in Boston in the 1760s because of her excellent poetry. In failing health, Phillis Wheatley was taken to England in 1773 by the Wheatley son, where she charmed the nobility. Her first bound volume of poems was published in London in 1773 with a copper plate engraving of her from which this engraving was made. From Duyckinck and Duyckinck, Cyclopedia of American Literature, *Vol. I, Part 2, 1866*

John Hancock (1737-1793) was a Boston merchant who inherited a fortune at age 27 and then went into politics. He was the first to sign the Declaration of Independence, and then became a militia commander during the war that followed. Hancock was elected governor of Massachusetts, serving from 1780 to 1785 and from 1787 until his death. From Winsor, The Memorial History of Boston, 1630-1880, *Vol. IV, 1883*

family member. She developed a talent for writing and became the first black woman poet in America. Her verse having been widely published beginning in 1770, she traveled to Britain in 1773 with a member of the Wheatley family where she was a guest of the Countess of Huntingdon. She received her freedom and married a free black man in 1778 but suffered severe reverses of fortune and, despite her skills, was barely able to support her family. In 1784, she died in complete poverty. Only in subsequent years was interest rekindled in this remarkable woman's poetry, and today she is recognized for the iron will and incredible talent she displayed throughout her life.

John Hancock's name is instantly recognized by most Americans and has become a byword for signatures since his own was the first to appear on the Declaration of Independence. Although known today principally as a statesman,

Hancock was first a Boston merchant. Later Hancock, as president of the Provincial Congress in Massachusetts, issued calls for naval recruits in the year following the revolution's outbreak. He had hoped to be named commander-in-chief of the Continental Army, but that honor went to the more experienced George Washington. After Hancock was elected governor of Massachusetts, stories circulated concerning his lack of courtesy toward Washington. When the president visited Massachusetts after his election, it was said that an imperious and pompous Hancock still held a grudge against the first chief executive for the role he played in the War for Independence.

Samuel Adams (cousin of John Adams, America's second president) was one of the most outspoken of the Sons of Liberty. He took great pleasure in exciting the emotions of his fellow colonists, and some of the more moderate-minded considered his impassioned speeches and intemperate demands a liability. A driving force behind the nonimportation agreements and known as the "Great Agitator," Adams acted as a catalyst for interactions between Britain and the colonies. Without his determination, many attempts at obtaining justice would have achieved less prominence. Adams, a signer of the Declaration of Independence, was lieutenant governor under John Hancock in 1789 and was himself elected governor of Massachusetts in 1794.

No less a patriot than Samuel Adams, Mercy Otis Warren was known in pre-revolutionary times for writing political satire. Born in 1728, she authored both poems and plays. After she married James Warren in 1754, their home became a gathering place for patriots like the Adamses. Warren's outspoken writing was published in the *Massachusetts Spy* beginning in 1772, and her attacks on British authority continued for several years. Her brother James, a member of the Sons of Liberty, also attacked the British and supported colonial demands for repeal of several

acts of Parliament. Although the family lost its political prestige and power by the 1780s owing to its conservatism, Warren continued to write about political issues. Her major work was a three-volume history of the American revolution, published in 1805. Warren died in 1814 at her home in Plymouth.

These individuals and the efforts to which they devoted their lives are representative of thousands of Massachusetts residents who contributed to the colony's growth. Even those in remote areas—or those like Mercy Otis Warren and Phillis Wheatley who were subject to the gender and race discrimination of the era—left a rich legacy.

American patriot Mercy Otis Warren (1728-1814) was the sister of James Otis and the wife of James Warren. After writing poems, plays, and political satire for many years, Warren began in 1772 to attack the British in writings published in the Massachusetts Spy. *Her major work was a three-volume history of the American Revolution, published in 1805. From Ellet,* The Women of the Revolution, *Vol. I, 1818. Courtesy, The Jones Library, Inc., Amherst*

ECONOMIC AND POLITICAL FERMENT (1780-1814)

★   ★   ★   ★   ★   ★   ★   ★   ★

On August 19, 1812, the U.S.S. Constitution, *now preserved at Charlestown Navy Yard, vanquished the English frigate* Guerriere *in a 25-minute battle off Cape Race that wrecked the* Guerriere *but did so little damage to the* Constitution *that it was then called "Old Ironsides." The British lost 79 men, the Americans 14. When the* Constitution *sailed into Boston with its prisoners it received a grand welcome. It had made a new reputation for the young navy, challenging and bettering the proud British who had ruled the seas since the Spanish Armada. Engraved by James D. Smillie from a drawing by Alonzo Chappel. From Spencer and Lossing,* The Complete History of the United States, *Vol. III, 1878*

The economic chaos that ensued in the United States after the War for Independence had far-reaching effects on the formation of a federal government. In Massachusetts, virtually every resident experienced the postwar upheaval. While the revolution had freed North American colonies from a tyrannical British rule, it had also eliminated the commercial ties providing support for colonial prosperity.

New state governments, including Massachusetts', failed to meet their citizens' needs during this time of fiscal uncertainty and political change. Despite passage of a state constitution in 1780, in the Bay State there was little evidence that elected officials had either the will or the ability to govern wisely. And the crises resulting from poor decision-making had a profound effect on both state and national policy formation in the later years of the eighteenth century.

The new national government was defined by the Articles of Confederation, adopted by the Second Continental Congress in 1777 and ratified by the states in 1781. The articles deferred much authority to the individual state governments, as stated most clearly in Article 2:

Each state retains its sovereignty, freedom and independence, and every power, jurisdiction, and right, which is not by this confederation expressly delegated the United States . . .

Due to this power, the confederation could only suggest ways in which states could act collectively. Moreover, some very real fiscal problems resulted from the states' unwillingness to pay Congress monies needed for maintaining a federal government. In particular, refusal to fund back pay for soldiers in the Continental Army wreaked havoc at the local level. In all of the states in the confederation, soldiers returned home to farms and villages and wanted the money owed to them.

In addition to economic difficulties, the fledgling government wrestled with diplomatic problems. European powers viewed the new nation suspiciously and treated its representatives perfunctorily. But most of all, the confederation's fiscal limitations meant its diplomats and ministers had little hope of implementing policies that required budget decisions at home.

The new confederation seemed virtually gridlocked, its own definition of powers rendering it powerless. It lacked authority to collect taxes from the states, claimed no regulatory jurisdiction over commerce, as yet had no judicial or executive branches of government, and since representatives were elected annually, maintained little real continuity in government. Above all, the delay in back pay for former Continental Army soldiers symbolized completely the confederation's real impotence. Without fiscal independence, the confederation seemed doomed.

Economic paralysis and the inevitable inflation was not limited to Massachusetts, however. Slowly but surely the nation's currency eroded and the dollar plunged steadily downward in value. By 1780, continental currency was devalued to a point so low that $4,000 in paper money equalled only one dollar in gold or silver. A contemporary observer estimated Massachusetts farmers paid one-third of their income in taxes between 1780 and 1786. State debt hovered around $14 million after the war and Massachusetts legislators, anxious to lower that debt quickly, imposed excessively high taxes to help offset the deficit. Unfortunately, this burden was placed on the shoulders of those least able to pay—farmers and small landowners.

Bank foreclosures on homes and farms in Massachusetts between 1780 and 1786 ultimately led to revolt. Those who could not pay the nearly $1.9 million in taxes and whose property was doomed to be repossessed resorted to the only means left to them: armed rebellion.

GROWTH OF GOVERNMENT

In Massachusetts, the uprising in 1786-1787 that came to be known as Shays' Rebellion was relatively small and quite brief, but was by no means insignificant. In fact, it was symbolic of the nation's need for a stronger central government and of people's desires for more competent, responsive government officials. It also proved the truth of an observation made later by Thomas Jefferson. Commenting on Shays' actions and those of his followers, Jefferson said, "a little rebellion now and then is a good thing, and as necessary in the political world as storms in the physical . . . It is a medicine necessary for the sound health of government."

Jefferson's retrospective comment expressed an interesting philosophy, and since his words referred to a small, ultimately unsuccessful uprising, they could be read later without any real anxiety. But to Shays' supporters and to all those—including Jefferson—concerned about the nation's future, circumstances surrounding the need for armed revolt were grave, indeed.

Central and western regions of Massachusetts saw stirrings of really serious trouble in February 1782. The Pittsfield General Court was barred from sitting when angry residents barricaded courthouse doors after learning of pending property foreclosures which spelled certain disaster for area farmers. This violent action was followed by similar incidents in other communities, among them Northampton. In April that same year another group attacked the court as it attempted to assemble there. And in 1783, a Springfield mob tried to forestall the sitting of the Hampshire County Court.

All of these unlawful gestures were aimed at preventing further foreclosures, fines, debt imprisonments, and property confiscations. However, it was not only the farmers who were desperate for relief from increasingly burdensome taxes as well as from general currency devaluation. Some of the most outspoken critics

THE MASSACHUSETTS CONSTITUTIONAL CONVENTION

The framing of the Massachusetts State Constitution had direct and lasting influence on the later creation, in 1787, and subsequent ratification, in 1789, of the federal constitution. Until 1780, Massachusetts—like Connecticut and Rhode Island—continued to be governed by colonial charters, which had been confirmed by state legislative action. By 1779, the Massachusetts General Court recognized that discontented citizens who were clamoring for a new governmental framework must be presented with options for a new state constitution.

On February 19, 1779, the General Court offered Massachusetts towns an opportunity to say whether they would like to form a new government and whether they would send representatives to a convention established for its formation. With the votes strongly in favor of such a new government—6,612 in favor and 2,639 opposed—the delegates met at a state constitutional convention in Cambridge on September 1, 1779.

Among those 293 delegates were John Adams, Samuel Adams, James Bowdoin, George Cabot, John Lowell, and Robert Treat Paine. John Adams' draft of the state constitution was accepted after some revisions. On March 2, 1780, delegates voted in favor of submitting the final draft to the people of Massachusetts for ratification.

Ratification was effected via local assemblies—town meetings—during which the proposed constitution was reviewed and discussed. It was an eminently democratic procedure and the document was subject to a vote by all those eligible to cast ballots. This in itself underscored a new voting practice. In Massachusetts, an important change had occurred in voting law. Prior to this time, only those men who met certain requirements regarding ownership of

property were allowed voting privileges. By 1780 however, all free adult men, regardless of income level or property holdings, could vote. It would not be until the twentieth century that women were given voting rights in the state.

On June 7, 1780, after 14 weeks of local discussion, the state constitutional convention met again in Cambridge. On June 16, convention delegates announced the outcome of the popular deliberations: the people of Massachusetts had ratified their state constitution. October 25, 1780, was set as the date for the first elections under this new government to take place.

John Adams wrote from France, where he was traveling, that the Massachusetts state constitution was a "phenomenon in the political world that is new and singular." And in truth, it was the blueprint, in both form and procedures, for the U.S. Constitution created in 1787. As it had in the past, Massachusetts led the way for creative, responsive government that kept the needs and interests of its people in the forefront.

"Drafting the Constitution" is part of a large mural in the State House. Painted by Albert Herter and dedicated December 16, 1942, the scene depicts John Adams sitting at a table in his Braintree home, and Samuel Adams and James Bowdoin looking on. John Adams had by 1779 returned from his diplomatic mission to France and was appointed to the committee to draft a constitution for Massachusetts. He had already published an article in 1776, "Thoughts on Government," in which he outlined many of the ideas he later incorporated into the Massachusetts document. Courtesy, Massachusetts Archives

★   ★   ★   ★   ★   ★   ★   ★

of Massachusetts' financial policy were those who had served, many with distinction, in the army during the War for Independence. To these men, the deepening financial crisis across the nation called for vehement protest against unfair taxation and unresponsive government. Many of the rebels were incredulous at having to face these issues again after gaining independence from similar difficulties with Great Britain.

If elected officials in Massachusetts had been as wise as they were ambitious, some might have moved to assuage the fears of the populace. But instead of addressing the needs of the overtaxed and underfinanced, the House and Senate refused to reduce taxes. In 1784 in Worcester County, 2,000 cases for recovery of debts were on the books. A year later, records show that fully 94 of the 104 individuals jailed in Worcester County had been incarcerated for failing to pay debts they were unable to meet.

A Massachusetts newspaper reported in 1785 that "in almost all parts of the country, the people experience a scarcity of cash unknown in any former period. The jails [are] crowded with debtors, who find it impossible to raise money to pay their debts." By late 1787, people were allowed to pay taxes with beef, flax, iron, whale oil, and similar items. But legislation permitting such payments was the ultimate result of desperate public acts, chief among these the western Massachusetts uprising led by Pelham's Daniel Shays.

Many soldiers who fought in the War for Independence, and whose anger erupted into violence in 1787, were owed back wages for their military service. Grievances concerning military pay overlapped, and to some extent exceeded, those of overtaxation. Many former Continental Army soldiers were denied pensions to which they were entitled, and each—farmer, merchant, small landowner, and former soldier—sought redress by taking the law into his own hands.

ANARCHY THREATENS
Many historians feel Shays' Rebellion

might have occurred sooner had the national economy not received a much-needed boost between 1784 and 1785. In 1784, Congress ratified the final peace treaty with Great Britain and the next year farmers brought in a good harvest as well. But 12 months later inflation, delayed military back pay, and continuing debt provoked many citizens to meet in conventions all across Massachusetts. These gatherings were held during the summer of 1786, largely in Worcester, Hampshire, and Berkshire counties. Some attendees were conservative in their approach and wanted only to urge redistribution of the tax load and reduction of taxes in general. Many felt these actions were more appropriate than current government policies. Others—the more daring and radical of the convention delegates—demanded total abolition of the state senate. They even suggested drastic changes in the way the governor should rule.

In August 1786, a handful of those who had met in convention at Hatfield, in Hampshire County, forced the Court of Common Pleas and a General Sessions of the Peace to adjourn without making judgments for debt. Many similar disruptions of the state judicial process occurred throughout the late summer and autumn. Although they met with some opposition, rebellious crowds continued to garner more and more popular support. Anarchy seemed to be taking the upper hand and those who tried to prevent disruptions were thwarted at every turn. Men such as former general Artemas Ward, then a judge in Worcester County, David Cobb, chief court justice in Bristol County, Governor James Bowdoin, and others all hoped in vain to prevent impending disaster.

In all but a few cases, attempts to preserve the status quo were doomed to failure. In October 1786, Massachusetts Superior Court Justice David Sewall wrote of his apprehensions concerning unstable conditions in the state. Sewall readily blamed discontent on politicians whose words provoked local malcontents to action. Sewall's opinion of conventions meeting throughout Massachusetts left little doubt about his views and accurately predicted the events of the next few months as well:

The People must take care of themselves or they are undone. Stir up a County Convention and by Trumpeting lies from Town to Town get one collected and Consisting of Persons of small Abilities— of little or no property, embarrassed in their Circumstances—and of no great Integrity—and these Geniuses vainly conceiving they are competent to regulate the affairs of the State—make some hasty, incoherent Resolves, and these end in Sedition, Riot and Rebellion.

Some leaders of these uprisings were well known to Massachusetts residents before the War for Independence. Among them were Job Shattuck of Groton, Nathan Smith and his brother Sylvanus, Luke Day, and Daniel Shays of Pelham. At first, Shays was unwilling to take command of a serious revolt against the government and was quoted as saying in the fall of 1786, "I at their head! I am not." But others saw in Shays an impressive military record as well as a good reputation. He had held local public office after the end of the war and had proven that he was of temperate mind. Shays had become a farmer after leaving the army in 1780, but his economic position had deteriorated, as had that of many of his friends and neighbors in and around Pelham.

Onlookers in other states watched fearfully as uprising after uprising throughout Massachusetts predicted chaos, anarchy, and destruction for the new nation. A horrified John Adams wrote from London, inquiring about the "Seditious Meetings in Massachusetts" that eventually led to Shays' Rebellion. And General George Washington worried that the Massachusetts upheaval might spread. Washington was genuinely concerned that people might have some valid arguments against the state government. He asked for explanations: "What is the cause of all these commotions? Do they proceed from licentiousness . . . or real grievances which admit of redress?"

As a result of these inquiries and concern, in the fall of 1786 about 1,340 vol-

Daniel Shays from Pelham lived a very short distance from the meetinghouse on the right. Built in 1743, the meetinghouse is the oldest continuously used town meeting hall in the country. The church on the left was not built until 1839. From a circa 1912 postcard

69

On February 16, 1787, a state legislative act conditionally pardoned some of those who had participated in Shays' Rebellion. The next day Governor James Bowdoin issued this broadside proclamation, which was then posted throughout Massachusetts. Daniel Shays himself received a pardon in June 1788. Courtesy, The Jones Library, Inc., Amherst

Commonwealth of Maſſachuſetts.

By His EXCELLENCY

JamesBowdoin,Eſq.

GOVERNOUR OF THE COMMONWEALTH OF

MASSACHUSETTS.

A Proclamation.

WHEREAS by an Act paſſed the ſixteenth of February inſtant, entitled, " An Act deſcribing the diſqualifications, to which perſons ſhall be ſubjected, which have been, or may be guilty of Treaſon, or giving aid or ſupport to the preſent Rebellion, and to whom a pardon may be extended," the General Court have eſtabliſhed and made known the conditions and diſqualifications, upon which pardon and indemnity to certain offenders, deſcribed in the ſaid Act, ſhall be offered and given ; and have authorized and empowered the Governour, in the name of the General Court, to premiſe to ſuch offenders ſuch conditional pardon and indemnity :

I HAVE thought fit, by virtue of the authority veſted in me by the ſaid Act, to iſſue this Proclamation, hereby premiſing pardon and indemnity to all offenders within the deſcription aforeſaid, who are citizens of this State ; under ſuch reſtrictions, conditions and diſqualifications, as are mentioned in the ſaid Act : provided they comply with the terms and conditions thereof, on or before the twenty-firſt day of March next.

GIVEN at the Council Chamber in Boſton, this Seventeenth Day of February, in the Year of our LORD One Thouſand Seven Hundred and Eighty-Seven, and in the Eleventh Year of the Independence of the United States of AMERICA.

JAMES BOWDOIN.

By His Excellency's Command,
JOHN AVERY, jun. Secretary.

BOSTON : Printed by ADAMS & NOURSE, Printers to the GENERAL COURT.

unteer troops were called out. These troops were to be employed in Massachusetts, in case an armed uprising occurred there. In addition, Secretary of War Henry Knox arranged for more federal troops to be sent to Massachusetts since there was concern over safety of the federal arsenal at Springfield.

Major General Benjamin Lincoln was named head of state forces mustered to put down the rebellion. In November 1786, a group of angry citizens had tried to gain control of Middlesex County Courthouse, but Lincoln's militia maintained the upper hand. In the fighting there Job Shattuck was wounded, captured, and jailed for his efforts. But on December 5, a violent mob in Worcester closed the Court of Common Pleas. Help being nowhere in sight, the frantic sheriff realized he had no power to stop the angry people swarming up the courthouse steps.

At this point, Daniel Shays appeared with a group of 350 followers. Shays had hoped to avoid any fighting and told a friend he wanted to "have matters settled peaceably." Luckily for the crowds of people—both angry veterans and farmers as well as worried city officials—Shays counseled that a petition should be sent to the legislature. With armed confrontation averted, the rebels left Worcester unsatisfied but temporarily calmed.

In January 1787, the court of Hampshire County was scheduled to meet in Springfield, site of the federal arsenal. Springfield was a pivotal location for the rebels, who needed both additional weapons and another site at which to gather to show their defiance.

Shays, along with about 1,200 rebel troops, bivouacked at Wilbraham, several miles east of Springfield. At the arsenal, about 1,100 federal troops were under the command of General William Shepard. In addition to Shays' men, a group of about 400 rebels were posted at Chicopee and another 400, commanded by Luke Day, waited at West Springfield. Their plan was to join in an attack on January 25 and seize the arsenal.

Had Shays' attack been successful, our nation's history might have been different. But at the last minute, Day waited until January 26 to attack. Shays was sent a note informing him of the change, but the note was captured by Shepard's men and never reached Shays. The latter therefore attacked the Springfield arsenal as originally planned, in the belief that a force of nearly 1,000 men under Day's command would join him.

After two warning shots, Shepard's men fired a cannon directly into the midst of Shays' rebel forces. Three of Shays' men were killed and another lay wounded. Shays and the remaining rebels ran off. General Lincoln's federal troops pursued the main group under Shays' command while Shepard moved his troops north to prevent the rebels from regrouping there.

Shays attempted in vain to negotiate with General Lincoln for an unconditional pardon for himself and his men. Impossible to placate, the iron-willed Lincoln forced Shays to flee with his rebels further east, to Petersham. There Shays hoped to remain undisturbed, defended against the remote possibility that Lincoln would follow.

On February 3, however, Shays and his men suffered a surprise attack by Lincoln's troops. About 150 rebels were captured, but Shays and the rest escaped. By the beginning of March, Shays' forces had been broken. Lincoln routed most other groups of armed rebels across Massachusetts, although pockets of guerilla warfare continued in the Berkshires until the summer of 1787. The state government was free, ultimately, to take whatever punitive action necessary.

JUSTICE REESTABLISHED

The state legislature had been slow to act when people demanded relief from high taxes and exorbitant court costs, as well as full payment of back military wages. However, Bay State officials moved quickly in response to the threat posed by Shays' Rebellion. Two weeks after Shays' men were captured at Petersham, the legislature passed the Disqualifying Act, offering pardons to any rank and file soldiers or noncommissioned officers who

Federalist Caleb Strong (1745-1819) from Northampton was a state representative and county attorney when he was a delegate to the Massachusetts Constitutional Convention of 1779. He went on to become state senator and the Massachusetts representative to the U.S. Constitutional Convention of 1787. He was a senator from Massachusetts from 1789 to 1796, and was then elected governor from 1800 to 1807 and again from 1812 to 1816. Print by G. Stuart Pinx and J. B. Longacre. Courtesy, Forbes Library

had taken part in the uprising. While subject to certain restrictions in holding public office or voting, they would not otherwise be severely punished.

Leaders of the rebellion, and others from outside Massachusetts who had assisted in the attempted take-over of Springfield arsenal, were to be tried on charges of treason against the state. This decision caused an uproar. Many, even those who had actually opposed the rebel cause, were concerned that such measures would provoke further discord. It seemed to many elected officials that punishment of those responsible should be more temperate. Therefore, in 1787, the legislature reconsidered ways of dealing with the men not covered by the terms of the Disqualifying Act.

In April 1787, a new election spelled political defeat for many officials seeking severe penalties against participants in Shays' Rebellion. John Hancock was elected governor, succeeding James Bowdoin. But of 222 members of the House of Representatives, only 62 were reelected. Similarly, out of 24 senators, only 11 were returned to office. It was clear the public wanted a change of policy and this time peaceful, legal means were used to effect that change.

Many new officeholders were men who had openly supported, or actually taken part in, either the pre-uprising conventions or the rebellion itself. The new legislators repealed the Disqualifying Act and pardoned all participants—including Daniel Shays, who received his pardon in June 1788. He spent his remaining years in New York State and died there in 1825.

In the aftermath of Shays' Rebellion, the state legislature amended many laws dealing with taxes and payment of debt. It also fashioned a more responsive, flexible, yet strong, state government.

CONSTITUTIONAL CONVENTION

In May 1787, the Constitutional Convention met in Philadelphia to consider ways to formalize a federal government with credibility and utility. Among Massachusetts delegates whose presence at the Con-

Samuel Adams (1722-1803) of Boston became famous during the American Revolution as a spokesman for the Patriots. Having earlier earned a B.A. and an M.A. from Harvard, he was an articulate writer and speaker against the crown. In 1778 the town of East Hoosuck in the Berkshires was named Adams after this most effective revolutionary leader. The next year, with John Hancock as his running mate, Adams was elected lieutenant governor. When Hancock died in 1793 Adams became governor, serving until 1797, when he retired from public life. Oil portrait by John Singleton Copley, 50 x 40¼ in. Courtesy, Museum of Fine Arts, Boston. Deposited by the City of Boston

*Historic Deerfield's Wells-Thorn House (1717 &
1751) is painted a bright blue, thought to be an
authentic color as determined by paint chips. This
museum house is open to the public as an example
of life between 1720 and 1830 in a small
Massachusetts town. The 1717 section is in the
rear, a fortress-like, small-windowed structure. The
front section, added in 1751, has larger windows.
Except for the ornate pulvinated window caps it is
quite typical of the five-bay construction used in
eighteenth-century Massachusetts. Oil painting by
Wilbert B. Smith*

The Wilson Printing Office (circa 1816) is one of several museum buildings along "the street" at Historic Deerfield. Moved at least seven times around the village, and restored in the 1950s by Bill Gass, the shop has a reproduction printing press, a lathe, and an extensive collection of wood planes. The double chimney may be a feature added about 1850 when stoves became popular. Oil painting by Wilbert B. Smith

Above, left: *John Adams (1735-1826), the second U.S. president, was born in Braintree (now Quincy), the son of John and Susanna (Boyleston) Adams. He graduated from Harvard in 1755 and passed the bar in 1758. Considered by many to have been one of America's greatest political minds, Adams had a large part in drafting the Massachusetts Constitution, the outlines of which were used for the U.S. Constitution. Both documents have borne the test of time quite successfully. Pastel portrait by Benjamin Blyth. Courtesy, Massachusetts Historical Society*

Facing page, bottom: *Abigail (Smith) Adams (1744-1818) was the daughter of Weymouth minister the Reverend William Smith and his wife Elizabeth (Quincy). Abigail and John Adams had four children, one of whom also became president—John Quincy Adams. While her husband was abroad for years at a time, or in Philadelphia or New York or Washington, Abigail Adams ran the home farms and earned the money that kept the family solvent. She did accompany her husband for part of his years as ambassador to France, and then to England, and was with him during most of the years of his presidency. Her letters describing everyday life in Braintree during and after the Revolution are of great value for anyone studying the period. Pastel portrait by Benjamin Blyth. Courtesy, Massachusetts Historical Society*

One of the earliest known landscapes of Massachusetts, this autumnal scene was painted about 1832 as seen from Pelham looking west over Amherst and to the Berkshire Hills beyond. The artist, Orra White Hitchcock, was married to Edward Hitchcock, a geology professor and later president of Amherst College. In addition to illustrating his books and making enormous charts of his lectures, she reared a large family and executed the duties expected of the wife of a minister-professor-college president. Courtesy, The Jones Library, Inc., Amherst

Right: *When phrenology (the study of the contours of the human head) was first introduced in Boston in the early 1830s, some of the most influential scientific leaders embraced it as a wonderful tool for reforming society. They thought it would scientifically allow men and women to determine, by the shape of the head, what careers their children should pursue. One could, supposedly, determine who would grow up to be a criminal, and who would be over-strained by too much study. Education reformers like Horace Mann believed in phrenology at first. Phrenologists even promised to help people choose the perfect mate—a compatible head. It was sexist (men had larger heads) and racist (fair skinned people were preferable). By the 1860s phrenology was dismissed by most people as unscientific after all. However, some people still believe. From a home medical book published in 1901*

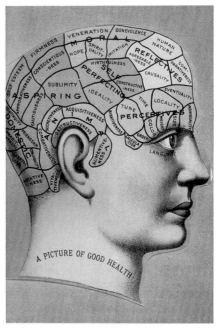

This mill complex in Lowell, now the Wannalancit Office and Technology Center on Northern Canal, was once a busy textile mill. Originally built in 1832 as the Suffolk Manufacturing Company when Lowell was a new experimental mill town, the buildings were rebuilt in 1862 and restored in 1983. Photo by Justine Hill

Sarah Elizabeth Ball, age 2, was painted circa 1838 by itinerant folk artist Erastus Salisbury Field. Miss Ball was the daughter of South Hadley minister Mason Ball and his wife, Orinda, who were also painted by the now-famous Erastus Field. Field, from Leverett, went to New York City in 1824 to study with Samuel F.B. Morse. In his career as a portrait painter, Field traveled primarily in central and western Massachusetts, as well as Connecticut. His paintings of folksy people and scenes now hang in prestigious museums and galleries all over the nation. Photo by David Stansbury. Courtesy, Mount Holyoke College Art Museum, South Hadley, Massachusetts

Trinity Row, in Wesleyan Grove on Martha's Vineyard, began in 1835 as a summertime Methodist camp meeting. The first year, there was a shed and nine large tents; by 1858 there were 320 tents and a few cottages. It is estimated that 12,000 people attended camp meetings there in 1857. By that time there were large boarding and lodging tents for guests, who slept on straw bedding. An 1866 New York Times article described the brightly painted cottages as the prettiest feature of Wesleyan Grove. Photo by John H. Martin

stitutional Convention guaranteed a pragmatic, all-encompassing document was Rufus King, later U.S. minister to Great Britain.

As with virtually all issues of the period, those surrounding the proposed federal Constitution provoked considerable debate. Among those who spoke out against the proposed Constitution was Mercy Otis Warren of Plymouth. A strong voice of dissent during the years preceding the War for Independence, she now attacked—from an anti-Federalist standpoint—various provisions of the pending Constitution.

In reference to a standing army, Warren cautioned that such military bodies had been "the nursery of vice and the bane of liberty from the Roman legions . . . to the planting of the British . . . in the capitals of America." Warren's caveat extended to the powers of the Supreme Court, the fallability of the electoral college system, congressional salaries, and the "dangerously blended" powers of the executive and legislative branches of government.

The anti-Federalist position, while not as strong as that which it opposed, claimed victory. For despite passage of a national Constitution binding all states into one government, the Bill of Rights, adopted December 15, 1791, addresses individual and state freedoms. These amendments to the Constitution exist in large part because of efforts like those made by Mercy Otis Warren. The first 10 amendments to the Constitution were passed in response to pressure from many Massachusetts delegates and others who feared a strong central government.

While Shays' Rebellion was small, it was an incident that prompted Constitutional Convention delegates to think carefully about federal response to future rebellions. Accordingly, Congress was empowered to call out state militia to "suppress insurrections." In this way, Daniel Shays and the others in Massachusetts who agitated for redress of their grievances helped effect lasting change in the way the nation's government was shaped and codified.

GROWTH UNDER "A MORE PERFECT UNION"

By 1788, despite dissenting opinions, the new constitution of the United States of America had been ratified by nine states. Massachusetts was the sixth state formally to support the constitution, voting "yes" on February 6, 1788. In the spring of 1789, George Washington was elected the nation's first president and Massachusetts native John Adams, who had received 34 electoral college votes, was named vice president. Adams would become the new nation's second president when Washington—besieged by ill health and advancing age—gave his farewell address

Eli Whitney (1765-1825) was born in Westboro, worked his way through Yale, and became a teacher in Georgia. By April 1793 he had built a machine, the cotton gin, that could take the seeds out of cotton. In 1798 Whitney obtained a government contract for manufacturing firearms and developed a manufacturing system utilizing interchangeable parts. He established a factory near New Haven which made him wealthy. From Cirker, Dictionary of American Portraits, *Dover, 1967*

Right: *Henry Knox (1750-1806) was a Boston bookseller married to a woman from an aristocratic Loyalist family when he joined the colonial army in 1775. He fought at Bunker Hill and proposed the gathering of cannons from Fort Ticonderoga in New York to drive the British out of Boston. Knox was given the task he proposed, and he brought the heavy cannons and stores across the state of Massachusetts on sleds in December and January of 1875-1876. The setting up of the cannons on Dorchester Heights forced the British to evacuate Boston. He became a good friend to General George Washington and fought well in the Battles of Trenton and Princeton. He was secretary of war from 1785 to 1795 and head of the navy department. He retired to a magnificent estate in Thomastin, Maine, which still exists. From Cirker,* Dictionary of American Portraits, *Dover, 1967*

Far right: *Samuel Osgood (1748-1813) was a merchant and civic leader who is remembered as captain of the Lexington Minute Men. He later served in the Continental Congress, was commissioner of the United States Treasury, and was postmaster general under President George Washington. From Cirker,* Dictionary of American Portraits, *Dover, 1967*

and announced his retirement in 1796.

With a federal government securely mapped out in the Constitution, states could begin to attend to local issues. In Massachusetts, the population had reached nearly 379,000 by 1790. During the next two decades the number of Massachusetts residents grew rapidly and by 1810, 472,000 people lived in the Bay State—an increase of nearly 25 percent during a 20-year period.

With population growth came establishment of new communities, some of which were originally part of much older towns in the Commonwealth. Many villages had grown since colonial times and portions of some had, by 1800, become incorporated as independent towns and cities. These include Amherst, which had previously been part of Hadley but was incorporated as a town in 1775; Dennis, on Cape Cod, incorporated in 1793 from part of Yarmouth; Easthampton, incorporated in 1809 from part of Northampton and Southampton; Lee, incorporated in 1777 from part of Great Barrington and Washington; Sterling, established in 1781 from part of Lancaster; and Somerset, incorporated in 1790 from a portion of Swansea.

There were various reasons for this growth, but among the most obvious was the state's rapidly expanding economy. Enterprise thrived in Massachusetts and by the turn of the century both industrial and agricultural expansion ensured that the Commonwealth would provide major

support for the new nation's fiscal stability. A major contribution to the rise in industry came from a Massachusetts native. Born in Westboro, Eli Whitney is best remembered for his invention of the cotton gin in 1793, which was to revolutionize the economies of both the North and the South. Whitney was also the genius behind a system of manufacturing interchangeable gun components. His system was later adapted to the manufacturing process as a whole and resulted in what we know today as the assembly line. As manufacturing concerns became an established and integral part of New England's landscape, Massachusetts natives were among the first to reap benefits accruing from these early factories and industrial enterprises.

Massachusetts made indisputable contributions to other efforts of the period—notable philanthropists, statesmen, artists, writers, educators, and reformers joined the ranks of inventors, clergy, sea captains, and entrepreneurs whose genius and determination transformed an entire continent. As it grew, the republic owed a continuing debt to men and women of Massachusetts whose legacies endure to this day.

From the start, qualified men from Massachusetts were named to high positions in the federal government. President Washington's choice for his cabinet of advisors included General Henry Knox as secretary of war and Samuel Osgood as postmaster general, both from Massachusetts. Knox had been instrumental in suppressing Shays' Rebellion and was well-respected by both the military and civilians. He was an ardent Federalist who supported a strong central government.

National events as well as state issues drew on the expertise of Massachusetts natives, and by the 1790s the state's economy had been affected positively by a variety of national experiences. Due to the fact that France and Great Britain were at war, the United States found it possible and profitable to enlarge its maritime economy. In Massachusetts, this spurred economic expansion and stability in a way that almost nothing else could have accomplished. The carrying trade—taking commercial cargoes from one port to another—became well established in Massachusetts during the 1790s. Unlike previous decades, Massachusetts enjoyed thriving finances during the waning years of the eighteenth century. Great fortunes were built up by ship owners and sea captains from Cape Ann, north of Boston, to New Bedford, along the southern coast of the state.

CHINA TRADE

Trade with the Orient had initially been established at Canton, China, the single Chinese port that permitted foreign trade. There, Yankee traders established mercantile bases in the 1790s, bases such as that of Shaw & Randall, or Perkins & Co. At first, Oriental trade involved just a single item: tea. Nearly 10 million pounds of tea were exported annually by American vessels from Canton by the end of the eighteenth century. Later this trade would expand to include silks, porcelain, and other products.

The youthful ages of Massachusetts men who shipped out to China is a matter of surprise today. One letter from a ship's clerk to its owner carries a postscript suggesting the writer's youth: "Sir, you'll please to let my mama know that I am well. Mr. Boit [the fifth mate, aged 17] also requests that you'll let his parents know he is in health." In 1792, the ship *Benjamin* left Salem under the command of Captain

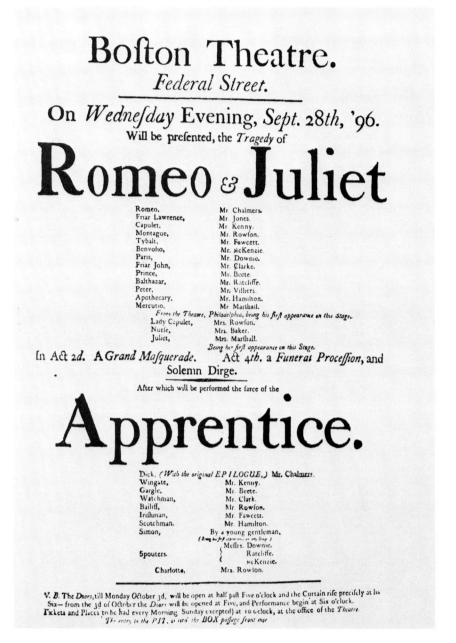

Nathaniel Silsbee, who was only 17. His first mate, Charles Derby, was 18, as was his clerk, Richard J. Cleveland. Due to the illness of the director of Perkins & Co. in Canton, the clerk of that firm, 16-year-old John Perkins Cushing, took over management of the company. After 30 years, Cushing became one of the most respected and successful of the China merchants. Another, 17-year-old Captain John Suter, left Boston for a life at sea in the year 1800.

Men who made their livelihood in the sea trade knew it was a hard life but that it held promise of great wealth. Salem merchants knew the East Indian trade was the

Puritan Boston had deliberately shunned stage plays; actors were considered to be immoral, and any play had to be performed privately until the late 1700s. An act of the Massachusetts legislature of 1750 was renewed in 1784 to discourage plays, and there were stiff fines for owners of buildings and actors if the audience numbered over 20. This broadside advertised one of the earliest of Boston's public plays, performed in a theater building in 1796. From Winsor, The Memorial History of Boston, 1630-1880, *Vol. IV, 1883*

The launching of the ship Fame in Salem Harbor, 1802, was painted in oils by George Ropes and here turned into an engraving for Harper's magazine in 1886. At its height in the early 1800s, Salem's port was a strong rival to Boston Harbor in the international trade. From Harper's New Monthly Magazine, Vol. LXXIII, September 1886

During the Federal period Massachusetts craftsmen executed some fine furniture. This semi-circular chest of drawers made by Thomas Seymour in 1808 was constructed of mahogany and satinwood in a highly patterned veneer and inlay technique with cast ornamental brass and paint. Courtesy, Museum of Fine Arts, Boston. From the M. and M. Karolik Collection of 18th Century American Arts

Ceres, the Roman goddess of agriculture and plenty, was popular as a ship's figurehead as well as for the name of ships. Newburyport alone had 17 ships named Ceres, *many with figureheads. This fine piece, made of pine with a graceful, spiral-draped classic gown, was found in a Boston shipyard and is thought to have been carved in the workshop of the Skillings family before 1815. Photo by E. Irving Blomtrann. Courtesy, Smith College Museum of Art*

key to prosperity and were willing to take the risks involved. That they did this so often and in such impressive numbers is a testimony to the unmistakable allure of Asian markets.

When the China trade opened fully, Massachusetts reaped undreamed-of benefits. Local sailing ships skippered by shrewd entrepreneurs were quick to establish commercial ties with other nations. In August 1784, the *Empress of China*, a 360-ton vessel, left for Canton with a cargo of export ginseng. This plant, valued as an aphrodisiac and prolonger of life by the Chinese, grew in North America as well as in the Orient. Enterprising Massachusetts businessmen such as Boston-born Samuel Shaw knew an investment in ginseng exports was a sure bet—and he reaped a tidy fortune through this trade.

In Salem, the merchantman *Grand Turk* sailed for China in 1795. One hundred years after its divisive witchcraft trials, Salem was thriving and prosperous.

When the *Grand Turk* returned from the East loaded with silks, porcelains, and tea, 34 captains of other ships left from Salem on similar voyages in search of equally fine—and saleable—cargoes. But they soon discovered that by trading in what are now known as the Hawaiian Islands, profits would exceed those accruing from trade with China alone. The Pacific trade routes were traveled extensively and regularly by Massachusetts ships throughout the last years of the eighteenth and the early years of the nineteenth century.

FRUITS OF STABILITY

In 1796, Salem's Chestnut Street had begun to reflect the prosperity and stability of its inhabitants. Most fine homes in this neighborhood were designed and con-

John Adams (1735-1826) was a lawyer, political science scholar, writer, wartime diplomat to England, vice president to George Washington, and then president. He was one of the authors of the Declaration of Independence and of the Massachusetts Constitution on which the U.S. Constitution was based. Ironically, both Adams and Thomas Jefferson died exactly 50 years after the 1776 Declaration of Independence, on the Fourth of July, 1826. From Spencer and Lossing, A Complete History of the United States, *Vol. I, 1878*

structed by Samuel McIntire, responsible for some of the most beautiful examples of Federal architecture in New England. Among those exemplary Salem houses are the Pierce-Nichols House (1792), the Cook-Oliver House (1804), Hamilton Hall (1805), and the Pickering-Shreve-Little House (1816). These homes are visible, lasting monuments to the lucrative shipping trade that blossomed at the turn of the century.

The wealth pouring into Newburyport resulted there, as it did in Salem, in lavish architecture, much of which was crafted by ships' carpenters. A visitor to Newburyport in 1800 noted that the homes there, "taken collectively, make a better appearance than those of any other town in New England ... upon the whole, few places, probably, in the world, furnish more means of a delightful residence than Newburyport."

International shipping and trade made Salem the main brokerage center for a number of exotic items, including pepper. The United States traded some 7.5 million pounds of this spice in 1805. Clever investors, many of whom were based in Salem, had wisely purchased the entire Sumatran pepper crop for resale that year. Earlier sales figures for this essential cooking ingredient and preservative indicate that in 1791 the United States had reexported only about 500 pounds of pepper.

Even without recourse to Oriental trade, some communities in Massachusetts established themselves via maritime exploits, principally in the form of shipbuilding, fishing, and whaling. By 1800, the region around the Merrimack River north of Boston grew richer as thousands of tons of sail, rope, iron, and fittings were manufactured for the many vessels launched there each year. Haverhill had several shipyards, as did Amesbury, Salisbury, and Newburyport. By 1806, the latter town had 60 ships involved in fisheries, which concentrated on the Labrador fishing banks. Others were active in the Caribbean trade, which resulted in a proliferation of distilleries for whiskey and rum in the region.

It is not surprising that Massachusetts grew economically stable thanks to contributions from its harbor cities. The state's coastline, totaling about 750 miles, offered opportunities at every inlet, from Cape Ann to Cape Cod to New Bedford, and to the islands of Nantucket and Martha's Vineyard.

POLITICS AND THE ECONOMY

The political climate that encouraged economic expansion in the late eighteenth and early nineteenth centuries was the combined result of a number of factors. In addition to changes in its local economy stemming from the United States' foreign relations, Massachusetts successfully weathered many political storms that blew across the new nation in the late 1700s. Civil conflict was not restricted to disgruntled ex-soldiers demanding back military wages. Federalists and Republicans came into direct confrontation both within the state's boundaries and in the nation's capital—the Federalist position supported most often by those with strong commercial interests. Farmers with large landholdings looked for stable markets for their agricultural surpluses and were inclined to support Federalist causes and a strong central government. And the split that inevitably widened into two distinct political parties catapulted John Adams to the presidency in 1796.

Adams served competently until 1800, helping guide the nation through a variety of touchy political situations. Among the more challenging was the XYZ Affair. In 1798, when France refused to receive the American minister, President Adams sent a negotiating team to establish friendlier relations. Using go-betweens, however, the French foreign minister demanded a bribe from the Americans. These go-betweens were identified only as X, Y, and Z, and when the American public learned of this charade of diplomacy, feelings ran high against France. Some Federalists, including Alexander Hamilton, demanded that President Adams declare war on France since the French navy recently had been attacking American

Boston Common, Beacon Street, and the State House are depicted about 1811. The Federal style brick homes included, on the left, the 1804 house of John Phillips. On the far right stands the 1804 Armory House. In 1858 the London Illustrated News *noted that "The great charm of the scenery of Boston is its 'Common' or Park—a piece of ground covering about forty acres, and open on one side to the Charles River." Watercolor by Andrew Ritchie from a sketch by J.R. Smith. From Winsor,* The Memorial History of Boston, 1630-1880, *Vol. IV, 1883*

merchant ships. Adams refused, although strong anti-French sentiment did continue.

During Adams' Federalist administration, passage of the Alien and Sedition acts in 1798 reflected continuing federal attempts both to limit foreign influence and to control growing Republican sentiment in the country.

The Alien Act extended the length of residency required of immigrants wanting to become citizens. These immigrant voters, reasoned the Federalists, posed a threat to the stable U.S. government which had been so painstakingly created. The act also gave the president power to expel enemy aliens in time of "declared war." The Sedition Act called for fines or imprisonment of individuals who opposed "any measures . . . of the government of the United States." This opposition included anti-government sentiment published in newspapers—effectively stifling those who spoke out against the Federalist administration. While some in Massachusetts and the nation applauded Adams' conservative

and repressive actions, others saw him as a betrayer of personal liberties.

These and other issues caused public consternation and promoted unrest and disruption. Adams seemed not to care, however. While he was president of the United States, he never worked at developing his popularity. In fact, there were those who absolutely detested him. But he was an able man and had many Massachusetts supporters. His cabinet included Samuel Dexter, U.S. secretary of war in 1800, who became secretary of the treasury under Jefferson in 1801 before Albert Gallatin replaced him later that year.

The power of the Republicans grew nationwide, however, and in 1800 Adams relinquished the presidency to an ardent Republican, Thomas Jefferson, his old compatriot. The 10-year Federalist monopoly was over, and after that the Republicans maintained the upper hand.

This shift in administrations spelled great changes for Massachusetts. The state's economy was directly affected by the change in presidential administration,

since much maritime activity on which the state so heavily depended during these years was touched by decisions of the new Republican president. Under Jefferson, a shipping embargo in 1807 precipitated yet another period of depressed prices. The Embargo Act of 1807 was a response to several years of harassment—often of Massachusetts ships and sailors—by the British fleet. The British harassment policy was a response to the United States' shipping of goods to France and its possessions at a time when war raged between the two European countries. Profits accruing to the U.S. from such trade were more than

the beleaguered British were willing to tolerate. In addition, the British navy was in need of sailors and impressment of American sailors was often the quickest, most effective solution to Britain's perennial shortage of manpower.

Under its maritime laws, the British navy felt it was unlawful to capture American ships carrying cargo to and from French possessions. But to Massachusetts sailors, the risk of being captured—or running the resultant embargo with its federally imposed fine—was worth the probable profits. It is estimated that the United States enjoyed a substantial increase in the

Beacon Hill was the highest of the three hills in Boston. The hill was gradually reduced, necessitating the moving of the Bulfinch column. The famous dome on the State House was not gold until much later in the 1800s. Drawn from an 1855 chromolithograph of an 1811-1812 sketch by J.R. Smith. From Winsor, The Memorial History of Boston, 1630-1880, *Vol. IV, 1883*

The Gerrymander was a salamander-shaped beast seen in an alignment of Essex County towns, rearranged by the Democratic legislature under Governor Elbridge Gerry in 1812. The new voting district created an unfair voting bloc and was returned to its former configuration in 1813 after this Gilbert Stuart cartoon was published in the Boston Gazette. *Elbridge Gerry went on to be vice president under James Madison. From Winsor,* The Memorial History of Boston, *Vol. III, 1881*

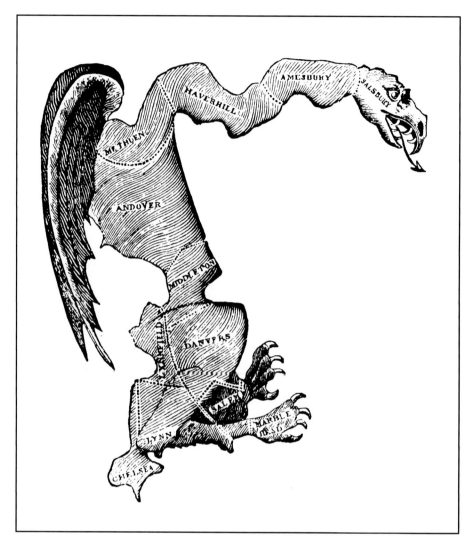

value of reexported products during this time. Trade figures for the period show that in 1803, the state brought in $13 million. By 1806, that number had increased to $60 million. And by 1807, the year the Embargo Act was signed into law by President Jefferson, the Massachusetts fleet was making $15 million in profits on freight charges alone. It is hardly surprising that the Embargo Act was extremely unpopular in the Bay State. One Massachusetts senator calculated that if, despite the blockade of its harbors, a single Massachusetts ship could get by the U.S. Navy, that ship would make a profit far outweighing any fines incurred by such illegal actions.

Despite frequent attempts to circumvent the Embargo Act, it spelled disaster for the nation's economy. In 1807, national exports totaled about $108 million. By the following year, exports had fallen to $22 million. Similarly, imports went from $138 million in 1807 to $57 million in 1808. For coastal communities in Massachusetts, there was little incentive to punish individuals who defied the embargo—since trade carried on by those ships was often the only thing that kept an area alive economically.

Massachusetts rallied to the defense of its maritime activities. In Gloucester, an angry mob destroyed a U.S. revenue cutter sent to guard the harbor and watch for smuggling operations. The situation echoed those of the pre-revolutionary era and some feared an outbreak of violence nationwide if the Embargo Act was not repealed. By the end of Jefferson's term of office this repeal occurred. The Embargo Act was replaced with the less sweeping Non-Intercourse Act, which only prohibbited trade with Great Britain and France. But it was also unpopular and difficult to enforce and did little to protect American ships and sailors from seizure by British navy vessels. President James Madison finally settled the situation by permitting trade with both European countries, and the Massachusetts economy boomed once more, albeit briefly. The War of 1812 loomed on the horizon, presenting another serious threat to maritime activity up and down the nation's coast.

WAR OF 1812

Although precipitated by a number of factors, the War of 1812 was caused chiefly by Britain's stubborn maritime policies. Westward expansion in the United States during the first decade of the nineteenth century promoted trade and contributed to a mounting sense of indignation against Great Britain. Expansion demanded increased trade opportunities with many nations. These were opportunities the British navy interfered with at every turn.

Tension between the two nations grew. Although some supported war and called it inevitable, many were worried that the United States lacked the naval strength to fight the British fleet. When war was finally declared on June 28, 1812, the U.S. Navy was greatly underfinanced and many Americans despaired of the country's ability to overcome British naval supremacy. But means by which the Americans could expand their limited naval capacity were quickly implemented. Privateering became an official part of the American war effort. Merchantmen such as the *America,* which called Salem home port, were thus responsible for capturing more than 1,200 British ships. The *America* claimed more than $1 million in seized British prizes. Privateers probably contributed more to the ultimate success of the United States in the War of 1812 than any other single factor.

By 1813, the British had blockaded New England ports and caused continuous panic among coastal communities. When the war neared its end in December 1814,

public sentiment against the conflict had reached an all-time high. Federalists, always anxious to go against the Jeffersonian Republicans, refused to support the war effort and would not agree to provide militia to fight in the federal forces. This dissent would not be silenced and New England merchants were among the most outspoken critics of the war. In early December, these critics met in the Hartford Convention, a body assembled to discuss ways in which individual states could protect themselves from federal demands.

The focal point at the Hartford Convention was the U.S. Constitution. Timothy Pickering of Salem was among those Federalist extremists who advocated solutions that included secession from the Union. Finally, in February 1815, before the group could do any substantial damage to federal unity, the Treaty of Ghent was announced in Boston, ending the War of 1812. The Massachusetts Federalists were reduced to ineffectual grumbling and criticism and merchants were relieved that they could now resume an honest foreign trade. And of course, cessation of the conflict meant resuming relations with Great Britain and France—and an increase in economic rewards for the entire nation.

Timothy Pickering (1745-1829) was an active patriot from Salem who wrote, among other pamphlets, "An Easy Plan of Discipline for the Militia," which was much used in the Revolution. He fought in the war himself, and later founded the United States Military Academy at West Point. He was U.S. secretary of state from 1795 to 1800, and U.S. senator in 1803. From Cirker, Dictionary of American Portraits, *Dover, 1967*

The Industrial Age and Currents of Reform

(1814-1861)

★   ★   ★   ★   ★   ★   ★   ★   ★

The first five decades of the nineteenth century brought to Massachusetts, as to other northern states, unprecedented opportunity for industrial growth. Employment figures for manufacturing in the United States increased from 75,000 in 1810 to 1,200,000 in 1850. The years from 1840 to 1850 saw an increase of more than 100 percent in all industrial output in the country. An extensive variety of products were made in Massachusetts, and very early in the century its factories were leaders in producing everything from boots, buttons, and iron, to hats, knives, rope, and wool and cotton textiles.

To support this growing industrial output, the state's factories needed more and more workers. This ever-present need for unskilled and semi-skilled labor gradually transformed Massachusetts' population. The state went from being a predominantly agricultural society of independent farmers to one increasingly dependent on manufacturing. Soon the native-born work force was insufficient, and particularly after 1850 immigrant labor became an integral part of the labor force. Once virtually nonexistent, women factory workers became a familiar sight by the 1830s in Massachusetts, particularly in the mill towns north of Boston—Lowell, Lawrence, and Haverhill. Children also were employed in the factories, but a gathering outcry against such practices brought about some legislative regulations and limitations of child labor in Massachusetts as early as 1842. Similar laws concerning women workers did not appear on the books until after the Civil War.

While those rooted in tradition mourned the passing of the agrarian age, others believed Massachusetts' future stability and prominence depended on a solid manufacturing base. Therefore, industrialists, philanthropists, and entrepreneurs encouraged and facilitated

By the 1820s whaling ships from Nantucket, New Bedford, and other Massachusetts ports were hunting whales around the world, sometimes being gone for years at a time. This engraving shows men harpooning sperm whales in 1833 near Hawaii where the whales came to calf in the winter. A "Nantucket sleighride" was the ride the men got when the harpooned whale furiously tried to get away. The print was inscribed by C.B. Hulsart, who had lost an arm while whaling and was on board the ship Enterprise *in this picture. Engraving by T. Birch, C.B. Hulsart, and J. Hill, 1838. Courtesy, Whaling Museum, Old Dartmouth Historical Society*

growth of factory towns and cities across the state—Bridgewater, Chicopee, Dalton, Fitchburg, and Plymouth. Immediately preceding the Civil War, most Massachusetts communities could point with pride to one or two thriving, small-to-medium industries that provided major economic support to the area.

GROWTH OF A NEW NATION

Rapid population expansion between 1790 and 1820 was an important factor in the success of manufacturing ventures. The population of the entire country grew during the years following the ratification of the U.S. Constitution. The nation's land area doubled, increasing from 888,811 square miles to 1,788,006 square miles in just 30 years. The number of inhabitants more than doubled, growing from 4 million in 1790 to 9.6 million in 1820. Only about 250,000 of these individuals were foreign immigrants, however. The majority were part of a national population explosion.

As the nineteenth century wore on, more and more towns were established. Massachusetts' population had been nearly 270,000 in 1780. Just 50 years later, in 1830, there were more than 610,000 residents in the Bay State. And while part of the population continued to support itself through agriculture, an increasing number turned to new industry and commerce like whaling and textile manufacture.

WHALING

Although dependent on whaling during the decades preceding the War for Independence, Nantucket fell on hard times immediately following the declaration of peace. During the war 150 whaling vessels had been lost, either through capture or wreck, and it seemed unlikely that Nantucket fisheries would recover. However, by 1789, there were 36 whaling ships involved in right whale and sperm whale hunting. In 1791, six Nantucket captains ventured into Pacific waters for the first time and began a business there that lasted throughout

much of the nineteenth century. Whale products commanded high prices, and European trade, as well as the domestic market, ensured that the names of Baker, Coffin, Hussey, and others would maintain their prominence on the island.

By 1810, Nantucket's population had doubled in comparison to pre-revolutionary times. England was the primary customer for sperm oil, but both France and Spain also purchased large quantities of whale oil. In 1839, the price of sperm

oil increased to more than one dollar a gallon for the first time since the War for Independence, and by 1855 sperm oil sold at $1.77 a gallon. Nantucket's prosperity continued through the 1840s, and by 1843 there were 9,000 residents on the island and a total of 88 whaling ships. In addition, Nantucket had 80 sailing vessels principally involved in the carrying trade up and down the Atlantic coast. By the time 30 more years had passed, however, Nantucket's golden days of whaling were over. The last whaling bark sailed from Nantucket Harbor in 1870.

Despite its eventual decline, Nantucket's contributions to the state economy during the first half of the nineteenth century were important. Next to shoe manufacturing and production of cotton textiles, whaling was the third most dependable contributor to Massachusetts revenues.

An average whaling voyage lasted

Bedford boasted 350 whaling vessels, more than any other whaling community in the world. Its population of 4,000 people in 1820 had increased to nearly 12,000 by 1840, when it was the fifth most active shipping port in the United States. The life and activity of this bustling whaling port inspired one of America's finest nineteenth century novelists, Herman Melville, to write a book which is among the greatest of all sea stories.

Much of what we know today of nineteenth-century Massachusetts sailors and whaling is due to Melville's inspired writing. He drew on personal experience of life at sea, for he had signed on to a whaling ship in 1839. Leaving from New York, he spent most of the next four years at sea. As Melville described so eloquently, American whalers sailed into every ocean and sea of the world. The Pacific, the Indian Ocean, and the Northern Atlantic all yielded their treasures of oil, whalebone, and other whale by-products. In 1851, Melville wrote in *Moby Dick* about Massachusetts whalers, observing that their vessels were "penetrating even through Bering's Strait, and into the remotest secret drawers and lockers of the world."

THE SHIPPING TRADE

Several impressive secondary industries were the direct result of successful maritime activity in Massachusetts. Among the most important was rope-making. In 1820, a total ship tonnage of about 21,000 shipped sugar, iron, and hemp between Boston, Havana, and Russia. The latter nation provided hemp from the Baltic region, which in New England was transformed into rope used for riggings on sailing ships. Even anchor cable, 120 fathoms in length, was made of hemp before the widespread manufacture of chain cable in later years.

Cordage was critical to the Bay State's economy, and one of its more important manufacturing firms was the Plymouth Cordage Company. Located in the community where the first permanent

between two and four years. In 1841, estimates set the average cost of outfitting a whaling ship for such a voyage at $20,100—half of which was the value of the vessel itself. One whaler, the ship *Lagoda,* made six voyages between 1841 and 1869, and returned an average profit of 98 percent for each trip.

But in spite of the island's success, Nantucket's early successes in whaling were overshadowed by that of the New Bedford whalers. New Bedford had the advantage of both a spacious, deep mainland harbor (in contrast to Nantucket Island's somewhat shallower waters) and access to railroads. The latter sped up distribution and sale of whaling products and helped create a solid niche in the region's economy. By 1847, New

Massachusetts settlement sprang up, it undoubtedly owed some of its success to that hardy group of Pilgrims who called the New World home. In 1824, when the Plymouth Cordage Company was established by Bourne Spooner, John Russell, and Caleb Loring, there was little at the factory site except for an ancient gristmill. A year later, in 1825, the owner of the brig *Massasoit* purchased 324 pounds of rope for $32.40. By 1837, the company had upped its capacity for production, but still made little more than 400 tons of hemp rope per year. Soon, however, manila rope was introduced and by the late 1860s was used on all American ships. Prior to the heyday of clipper ships Plymouth Cordage Company had employed fewer than 100 people, but by 1860 there were 140 on the payroll.

Advancing maritime technology—which cut down on the number of weeks in travel time—helped to expand the local, as well as the state, economy. As Lowell profited from its mills, so Plymouth benefited from the success of the ropemaking business, and everyone, from owners to stock boys, saw their fortunes increase. One young man who entered the company as an office boy at age 15 in 1859 earned three dollars a week. By 1867, he was an accountant earning $1,400 a year. His experience was repeated all over the state in a variety of industries, as by mid-century the national economy continued to expand.

CANALS FOR TRANSPORTATION

Manufactured goods demanded adequate means of transportation to various markets, but this was by no means unique to the nineteenth century. In Massachusetts, construction of the Post Road to New York had seemed a perfect solution to colonial transport problems in the late seventeenth and early eighteenth centuries. By 1808, the United States secretary of the treasury, Albert Gallatin, had devised a new plan to cope with the nation's transportation needs: a federally

funded system of turnpikes to connect the East Coast with the Mississippi River. Just two years before, Congress had given its approval to conduct surveys on which this National (or Cumberland) Road was to be based. Part of the overall plan described in Gallatin's extensive "Report on Roads and Canals" included a scheme to construct inland waterways as well as highways and turnpikes.

Supporters argued that federal funding for transportation was critical. John Quincy Adams, a native son of Mas-

John Quincy Adams (1767-1848) was the son of diplomat and Federalist president John Adams and Abigail (Smith) Adams. He had a long career as a diplomat, starting at age 14, and as a politician. He was a senator from Massachusetts, secretary of state under James Monroe, the sixth president of the United States (1825-1829), and after that was returned to Congress by his south shore constituents. From Spencer and Lossing, A Complete History of the United States, *1878*

sachusetts elected to the U.S. presidency in 1824, also agreed with this idea. A system of canals and highways could link different areas of the nation and contribute to general prosperity. However, Adams' strengths did not rest in powers of persuasion or cordial relations with political enemies, so he found it difficult to gain necessary congressional backing to support projects like a transportation system. Some of the era's most influential senators and congressmen, however, agreed with Adams' ideas about federal monies for communications links. In the northeast, by 1821, only $1.3 million had been spent on canal-building by public and private agencies. That figure rose quickly in just two decades, and by 1841 $8.8 million had been spent on transportation projects. In Massachusetts, canal building, although not backed heavily by state or federal funds, became a favored project in several areas. But no Bay State canal ever reached the degree of national promi-

nence claimed by the Erie Canal, built between 1817 and 1825. Wages paid to laborers working on the Erie Canal after its completion give an idea of its importance to the region's economy. In 1828, the common laborer there earned 71 cents a day. By 1861 that daily wage had risen to one dollar.

Several artificial waterways served important economic functions in limited areas of Massachusetts during the first half of the nineteenth century. The Middlesex Canal owed a great deal to improved granite-cutting techniques that helped speed up large building projects. These techniques also ensured greater precision when constructing canal locks, previously made of wood. The Middlesex Canal itself boasted 16 locks, stretching from Chelmsford to Boston. Completed in 1808, the canal provided easy transport from the Merrimack to the Charles River and was utilized extensively by various textile and shoe mills in the region north of Boston.

Charlestown, on the north rim of Boston Harbor, was drawn by John Warner Barber in the late 1830s from Copps Hill burying ground in Boston. An unfinished Bunker Hill monument on Breed's Hill is in the center, while the Charlestown Navy Yard, established in 1798, is on the right. Charlestown and the Charles River were named for King Charles I of England who was in power when the town was incorporated in 1635. From Barber, History and Antiquities of Every Town in Massachusetts, *1839*

The Middlesex Canal was built entirely without federal money. While the Massachusetts state government was not generous with support for canal building, it did provide a small grant of land for construction of connecting waterways north of the Merrimack River. For the most part, however, Bay State canal projects were privately funded affairs.

The very first of those canals in the Lowell area was the Pawtucket Canal, built in 1796 to circumnavigate Pawtucket Falls on the Merrimack River. This canal was designed to provide a viable route for rafts carrying timber and other wood products to shipping facilities at Newburyport on the coast. When Nathan Appleton, a major partner in the Merrimack Manufacturing Company,

Gridley Bryant built a horse-drawn railway in 1825 from Quincy's quarries to the Neponset River. Including branches, the railway was only four miles long, with stone ties and wooden rails at first; later, it even had stone rails. The railway made the granite age of architecture possible in Boston, encouraging the Greek Revival style. Although an early steam locomotive was already in use in England, and soon in America, the Granite Railway flourished for 40 years. The most difficult task for horse and driver was to hold the load of granite as it made the 84-foot drop from the quarry in just 315 feet of distance. From Winsor, The Memorial History of Boston, 1630-1880, *Vol. IV, 1883*

viewed the Pawtucket Canal—a rudimentary arrangement with wooden locks—he was impressed with the site's possibilities: "We . . . scanned the capabilities of the place, and the remark was made that some of us might live to see the place contain twenty thousand inhabitants." Appleton's prediction was well-founded, and the manufacturing concerns located in Lowell ultimately made private investors wealthy.

Despite the fact that it was enlarged and modernized in 1822, the Pawtucket Canal was soon supplanted by the Middlesex and other canals as the preferred transport route for raw materials and finished goods. In addition, the area's complex canal system included the Merrimack, the Lowell, the Western, Eastern, Hamilton, Lawrence, and Northern canals—all part of a system known as the Lowell Canals.

The eastern part of the state was not alone in canal-building. An inland waterway connecting Northampton, in western Massachusetts, with New Haven,

on the Connecticut coast, was begun in 1825. The Farmington Canal, completed in 1835, turned into a financial disaster. One historian referred to it as the nation's "longest and feeblest" canal, since it was 78 miles long but produced virtually no income. Although the Farmington Canal was intended to aid economic development of the Connecticut River Valley by bringing goods to the port of New Haven, it could not sustain the necessary traffic. Despite support from private sources and from Connecticut banks, a lack of public money, coupled with the area's terrain, made the Farmington Canal an impossible dream.

Nor could the Blackstone Canal, built in the 1820s to connect Worcester with Providence, Rhode Island, compete with less-costly railroads that soon provided area factories with an efficient, dependable means of transport for raw materials and finished goods. The Blackstone Canal—with 45 miles completed by 1828—received some support from the Rhode Island state bank, but it only remained in operation for two decades. Like the Middlesex and the Farmington canals, the Blackstone's brief existence was a testimony to the ingenuity of Massachusetts entrepreneurs and builders and to the precarious economic climate in which they operated. None of these inland waterways could be sustained as viable business ventures, and all ultimately failed in the face of burgeoning railroad development.

Another transportation project initially receiving at least some public support within Massachusetts' boundaries was a canal to reach westward to the Hudson River. In 1825, an engineer named Loammi Baldwin, Jr., completed a report on a canal to pass through the state's western region. In addition, its promoters asserted that it could tunnel under Hoosac Mountain, near Adams in the northwestern corner of Massachusetts. Although this project seemed preposterous at first, initial interest in this canal would later shift to a railroad connection through the same region. Unfortunately, this idea, too, proved costly, over-ambitious, and under-capitalized.

YANKEE INGENUITY AND ECONOMIC EXPANSION

Massachusetts' population and economy

grew in the early nineteenth century as a result of many entrepreneurial impulses. The Quincy granite works also contributed greatly to the permanence of the state's expansion.

During building of the Middlesex Canal, workers discovered that by drilling holes in the granite and splitting it along a line made by these holes, they could produce evenly hewn granite blocks. Very soon, granite became the preferred building material for many structures throughout the nation. In 1818, the city of Savannah, Georgia, ordered $25,000 worth of granite blocks for a church. Massachusetts architect Samuel Willard, who designed and superintended construction of the Bunker Hill monument commemorating an early battle in the War for Independence, chose Quincy granite as the preferred material for the monument. Willard also invented a wide range of machinery for quarrying and moving large blocks of the grey stone, devices instrumental in expanding the market for granite to a considerable degree. Willard noted that, due to construction of the Bunker Hill monument and the attendant publicity, "A business has grown . . . since the work commenced, and in a space of a few miles, amounting . . . to $3,000,000 which would not otherwise have been done at these quarries, and of which the work on the obelisk is but about one-thirtieth part."

By mid-century, granite was being used everywhere as a primary building material. Schools, churches, town halls, and courthouses were constructed of this hard stone. Among the more famous buildings constructed predominantly of Massachusetts granite during the period were the Astor House in New York and the Tremont and Customs houses in Boston. Mount Auburn Cemetery in Cambridge grew in prominence because of Jacob Bigelow's interest in the use of granite for driveways, portals, and stone markers. By the end of the 1800s, more than 60 million granite paving blocks were produced each year in New

England—the majority of them from Bay State quarries.

Interest in the further development of industry and manufacturing, coupled with a desire to use various New England resources, resulted in more comfortable lifestyles and the establishment of numerous personal fortunes. This expansion was paralleled by support for banking ventures. In 1791 the Bank of the United States had been established amid much controversy, and federal banks soon set the stage for state-chartered banks. In the last nine years of the eighteenth century, 29 state banks were set up in the northeast from New York City to Nantucket.

In Massachusetts, acceptance of state-chartered corporations meant that more manufacturing companies would spring up, as capital for investment was easier to obtain. In 1809 the Massachusetts legislature passed a law establishing rules for incorporation since there were so many individual requests to do so. As a result, by 1837 incorporation legislation appeared on the books in many states. In addition to the growth in corporate legislation, the business community received support between 1819 and 1824 from the U.S. Supreme Court under Chief Justice John Marshall. During this time, Supreme Court decisions on bankruptcy and taxes paved

Entrepreneur Frederic Tudor (1783-1864) was called the "Ice King" because he made his fortune by shipping Boston-area pond ice to tropical ports all over the world. In 1856 he sent 146,000 tons of cut ice in 363 cargoes to 53 places, including China. His business was an important factor in international trading and employed many people. It was said that he had ingeniously turned ice, a Yankee liability, into an asset. Courtesy, Graduate School of Business, Harvard University. From Cirker, Dictionary of American Portraits, *Dover, 1967*

the way for the pro-business legal climate so necessary to new companies during the first half of the nineteenth century.

A good example of the ingenuity common to Massachusetts politicians, entrepreneurs, inventors, and businessmen is represented by the successes of Daniel Webster, Frederic Tudor, Nathaniel Wyeth, and Francis Cabot Lowell. Although not a Massachusetts native, Webster later represented the state in the U.S. Senate and was an eloquent spokesman for pro-Union sentiment during antebellum years.

Bostonian Frederic Tudor began an ice business in 1806. At first derided for his unusual idea, he worked for 15 years to make the company successful, providing ice for chilling beverages in tropical climates and for storage of perishables. Tudor was one of many thousands of Americans during these years whose business interests helped promote a culinary fashion that remains today, since his early efforts bolstered the popularity of ice cream as a dessert. After months of exhaustive experimentation, Tudor designed an efficient ice house with a unique construction that cut down loss through melting to less than 8 percent a season in the tropical regions of the Caribbean. In 1824 Tudor teamed with Cambridge-born Nathaniel Wyeth, and the latter soon invented a way to harvest ice from New England ponds. By 1825 the two had reduced the expense of cutting ice to 10 cents a ton. Although they soon after dissolved their business

partnership, Tudor and Wyeth continued independently to reap large profits in the ice business.

Wyeth was successful in developing an ice cutter which he later used to free a Cunard ship frozen into Boston Harbor one winter. He also went on a westward expedition to Oregon and established Fort Hall on the California and Oregon trail. By the early 1830s, Tudor was shipping ice to locales like India and Persia, and would later ship to more than 50 destinations worldwide. Like some latter-day alchemists, the Yankee genius of Frederic Tudor and Nathaniel Wyeth turned ice—in monotonous abundance during long Massachusetts winters—into gold.

Massachusetts native Francis Cabot

Lowell was responsible for an even more significant transformation, having to do with the growth of factory communities. Lowell, sometimes called the "Father of American Cotton Manufacture," was determined not to duplicate the cramped, poverty-stricken living conditions of English factory centers.

In 1813, Lowell founded the Boston Manufacturing Company in the town of Waltham, just west of Boston, the first American factory to produce cotton textiles in one building. Soon, Lowell and his partners—other shrewd investors such as Nathan Appleton—were planning an enormous company town to the north in the small village of Chelmsford. The Merrimack and Concord rivers were among the natural resources available to

Lowell in the late 1820s is depicted by John Warner Barber from the Dracut, or north, side of the Merrimack River, with the Concord River entering the Merrimack on the left. Natural waterways were soon augmented by canals in Lowell, which was the fastest growing community in New England at this time, increasing from 2,500 residents in 1826 to 33,000 in 1850. Barber noted that there were 10 houses of public worship in Lowell, one of them Catholic, showing that a good number of Irish immigrants were already there by 1839. From Barber, History and Antiquities of Every Town in Massachusetts, *1839*

Designed by State House architect Charles Bulfinch, Massachusetts General Hospital was built in 1818 and opened in 1821. It was constructed of Chelmsford granite and was considered a model of architecture in its day. Ether was first demonstrated as a general anesthetic here in 1846. From Gillon, Early Illustrations and Views of American Architecture, *Dover, 1971*

fuel Lowell's Merrimack Manufacturing Company, and locks and canals built there helped establish the region's virtually unlimited potential. Although Francis Cabot Lowell died in 1817, his ideas were implemented by his partners, who built an enormous complex of textile mills, company-owned housing, stores, churches, and other facilities.

On March 1, 1826, the community of Lowell was incorporated and at that point had a population of about 2,500. Due to the rapid success of the Merrimack Manufacturing Company, however, the population quickly increased. Ten years later, Lowell had 18,000 inhabitants, and by 1856, 12,000 looms there produced cotton and wool textiles. Some 36 million pounds of cotton and 5 million pounds of wool were woven into more than 100 million

yards of cloth at Lowell during these years. The city's success was phenomenal and proved the utopian hypothesis of Francis Cabot Lowell and his partners. At least until the economic recession and increasing labor activity of the 1840s, Lowell appeared to have avoided the harsh excesses frustrating industrial centers in Great Britain. Massachusetts residents could point with justifiable pride to Lowell, the second largest city in the state, as the biggest and most productive cotton textile center in the nation.

Added to the factories themselves was the innovation of waterpower. The successful use of canals in Lowell foreshadowed the later success of railroads in transporting goods and materials from source to marketplace. As one historian noted,

Left: *Reformer Lucy Stone (1818-1893) was born in West Brookfield and graduated from Oberlin College. She lectured widely about slavery and women's lack of legal rights. In 1850 she headed the first national women's rights conference, which was held in Worcester. In 1855, when this picture was taken, she married Dr. Henry Blackwell, but shocked all by keeping her maiden name. Stone and Black-well noted that in 1855 the husband was in total legal custody of the wife and her material goods and earnings. She could not make a will, inherit property, sue or be sued, and if her husband died first, the wife inherited a much smaller interest in the husband's property than he would of hers had she died first. In short, the wife was treated legally as if she were a child, lunatic, or mentally retarded person. From Mary Thacher Higginson,* Thomas Wentworth Higginson: The Story of His Life, *1914*

Above: *Susan B. Anthony (1820-1906), antislavery and women's rights worker, was born in Adams, but by the age of six her family had moved to New York State where she resided for most of her life when not on the lecture circuit. She is shown here, in a black dress with lace on the front, at the 1897 summer reunion of her Anthony, Reed, Richardson, and Lapham relatives at her Grandfather Anthony's farm in Adams. She always considered herself a proud New Englander as she stumped back and forth across the country for more than 50 years in the cause of women's rights. From Harper,* The Life and Work of Susan B. Anthony, *1898*

The Lowell Canal System was one of the most impressive engineering achievements of nineteenth century America . . . the power canals which carried water to each major mill complex in the city were the product of engineering expertise and years of difficult labor. Water power was the source of Lowell's prosperity and Lowell was the pacesetter for a young industrial nation.

Not all was ideal, however. Lowell may have been a pacesetting city, but it ultimately proved profitable only for mill owners. Wages paid to those working in Lowell's mills seem low by today's standards and were, in fact, only barely adequate at the time. The average male worker earned between $4.50 and $12 for a 72-hour work week and women were paid between $2.25 and $4 a week for the same work. The industrial complex at Lowell was a model of manufacturing innovation and later the area would be a major attraction for waves of immigrants to the United States. But in the beginning, the mills were filled with native workers and none of the laborers—native-born or immigrant—found the streets paved with gold.

In the 1820s and 1830s, the specter of inflation and debt threatened towns and cities across the nation. One of the several fiscal questions of the day concerned a protective tariff on manufactured items and raw materials. New Englanders—and Massachusetts residents in particular—opposed the Tariff of Abominations, as it was called. In 1828, just as John Quincy Adams was leaving the U.S. presidency, the tariff passed into law despite attempts by New England politicians to amend it. As the presidential administration changed and Andrew Jackson assumed office, Massachusetts followed the national trend toward reform.

The era known for "Jacksonian Democracy" instilled in Americans a spirit of improvement and a desire to make life better. Accompanying this were many innovations in industrial development that marked the period. In fact, reform and technological advancement seemed to go hand in hand, each creating situations that could be aided, to some degree, by the other's attention.

Some of the more significant changes during this period were in areas of social and educational reform. Throughout the United States in the early nineteenth century, a number of different reform movements motivated people to attempt improvement in public education, care of the insane, women's rights, working conditions (especially for children), and care and education of the deaf and blind.

I HEREBY PROMISE, with God's help, for my own sake and the sake of others, that I will neither make, buy, sell nor use as a beverage, any Intoxicating Liquors.

Name,

Date, 18   Residence,

Witness,

Many prominent figures in these areas were natives of Massachusetts.

CURRENTS OF REFORM

Some reformers in the first half of the nineteenth century forever changed the way Americans perceived and treated workers, women, the handicapped, and the nation's youth. A few of these reformers traveled worldwide to deliver their messages. Margaret Fuller, a prominent transcendentalist and writer and one of the ablest critics in America, worked for social reform. Samuel Gridley Howe organized the Perkins Institute for the Blind in Boston in 1832, later becoming an influential abolitionist. In 1831, journalist and reformer William Lloyd Garrison, another abolitionist, moved to Boston and established the famous antislavery journal, *The Liberator*. In 1833, he founded the American Anti-Slavery Society. In 1834, Elizabeth Peabody and Bronson Alcott established a school based on new methods of teaching and handling children. Susan B. Anthony and Lucy Stone, two of the best-known early feminist theorists, were both born in Massachusetts, as was Mary Mason Lyon, founder of Mount Holyoke College—an educational institution that was among the first of its kind for women.

One of the most tireless reformers was Dorothea Dix. She almost single-handedly brought to public attention the plight of the insane. A former teacher, in 1841 she was involved in volunteer work at the House of Correction near Boston. She soon persuaded important state legislators and others active in reform to help her launch a crusade to change conditions in Massachusetts prisons. Men like Charles Sumner, Samuel Gridley Howe, Horace Mann, and many more joined Dix in her campaign to change the evaluation and treatment of the insane in public institutions.

Dix's work took her to virtually every jail and prison in the state, where she recorded the conditions and needs of inmates. What she saw in those

institutions led her to protest the "present state of Insane Persons confined within this Commonwealth in cages, closets, cellars, stalls, pens! Chained, naked, beaten with rods, and lashed into obedience!" By 1845, she had prepared detailed documentation of her findings. Almost immediately after reading Dix's report, the state legislature passed a law enhancing facilities of the Worcester insane asylum, legislation which became a model for that passed in other states.

Horace Mann's interest in education led him to establish the system on which all public schooling in the United States is now based. Mann, a lawyer and state legislator, helped found Massachusetts' first state board of education, serving as its first secretary and as a member of the board for 11 years between 1837 and 1848. According to Mann, "Education . . . is the great equalizer of the conditions of men—the balance-wheel of the social machinery . . . it does better than to disarm the poor of their hostility towards the rich; it prevents being poor." Because of Mann's energetic promotion of free public education, his standards for public schools were gradually adopted nationwide.

Religion also enjoyed a renewed enthusiasm among numerous Massachusetts residents in the 1800s. Some of the evangelical fervor associated with the

Horace Mann (1796-1858) was a lawyer, state representative, state senator, congressman to Washington, founder of the first American lunatic asylum, antislavery worker, and temperance and women's rights advocate, but he is usually remembered for his 11-year stint as secretary to the newly formed Massachusetts Board of Education, beginning in 1837. He worked against great opposition to make Massachusetts a model of modern educational reform. Mann improved the individual schools, lengthened the school terms which were often as short as eight weeks per year, began teacher training schools at a time when teachers were often college students on vacation or high school graduates at best, and tried to ensure a free public education to many more children than were then being educated. He declined the governorship in 1852 and went to Ohio to be president of Antioch College, where he died in 1859. From Mann, Life of Horace Mann *by his Wife, 1865*

Right: *Fidelia Fiske (1816-1864), from Shelburne Falls, was educated at Mount Holyoke Female Seminary with the class of 1842. She was caught up in the religious fervor of the time and dedicated her life to teaching and missionary work. A Congregationlist, she was the first unmarried woman ever to go abroad as a missionary. In 1843 she began a girls' school in Persia, living with the students, learning their language, and teaching them their lessons. For 16 years, despite cholera and typhoid epidemics, opposition from factions in Persia, and vast cultural differences, she worked to better the lives of young women who were sometimes taken from her for wealthy men's harems. After returning to Massachusetts, she taught at Mount Holyoke and lectured about her mission. Courtesy, Mount Holyoke College Library/Archives*

Facing page: *Ralph Waldo Emerson (1803-1882), poet and philosopher, was a Harvard graduate who left the Unitarian ministry to make his living as a writer and lecturer in the 1830s when that profession was new and unusual. He lived 50 of his years in Concord. This gifted speaker and thinker protested the materialism he saw changing his world with the advent of the industrial revolution. "Things are in the saddle,/ And ride mankind," he said. He felt people should find their true selves in nature: "Adopt the pace of nature; her secret is patience." From* New England Magazine, *Vol. XV, 1895*

Great Awakening in the past century simmered in New England and elsewhere until the 1820s and 1830s, when it once more burst into prominence. The Second Great Awakening, as it is sometimes called, drew on the efforts of many from Massachusetts, including William Miller and John Murray. The religiosity and ardor of this period spilled over into and directly influenced other reform move-ments, particularly women's rights, temperance, and abolition.

TRANSCENDENTALISM

Transcendentalists who flourished during the first half of the nineteenth century undoubtedly received the most lasting fame and had the most critical influence on American literature and philosophy at that time. Transcendentalists believed that

God is inherent in man and nature and that individual intuition is the highest source of knowledge. Their belief led to an emphasis on individualism, self-reliance, and rejection of traditional authority. Their acknowledged leader was Ralph Waldo Emerson of Concord, but the movement attracted many other writers and thinkers including Nathaniel Hawthorne, Henry David Thoreau, Margaret Fuller, Bronson Alcott, and George Ripley. In 1841, the latter founded Brook Farm in West Roxbury, a few miles from Boston. Based on cooperative living, the community expected each member to take part in manual labor in order to make the group self-sufficient. Brook Farm was established to further the philosophy these men and women espoused and provide a congenial setting for their intellectual efforts.

Many of Emerson's contemporaries were skeptical of his ideas and thought little of the transcendentalists. Emerson himself never lived at Brook Farm, confining his affiliation there to occasional visits. Other visitors included Dr. Oliver Wendell Holmes, Margaret Fuller, and the Reverend William Ellery Channing, who made frequent pilgrimages to Brook Farm during its short life (the experiment survived only until 1847). All of these visitors came to study and absorb the transcendental view of the world.

George Ripley's interest in establishing a community in which he and others could ponder life's mysteries is evident in his words to Emerson in this letter of 1840, the year before the founding of Brook Farm: "I wish to see a society of educated friends, working, thinking, and living together, with no strife, except that of each to contribute the most to the benefit of all." The almost evangelical tone of his message is similar to many of those written by Ripley's colleagues as well. Indeed, the entire period was one

Dr. Oliver Wendell Holmes (1809-1894) became famous for patriotric poems such as "Old Ironsides," which helped to save the old U.S.S. Constitution *from being demolished. His real vocation, however, was medicine, which he taught at Dartmouth and Harvard. His summers were spent in the Berkshires at Pittsfield, where he wrote novels and poems as well as hymns. Here, Holmes at age 80 sits in his study on Beacon Street in Boston. From* New England Magazine, *October 1889*

of intellectual, moral, as well as industrial, evangelism—much of it having its inception in Massachusetts.

Unlike some attempts at communal living, Ripley's bore fruit for a few years. When he and 15 others moved to Brook Farm, Hawthorne was on a committee for direction of agriculture, and he later affectionately satirized the entire experiment in *The Blithedale Romance.* For about four years the members of this utopian venture enjoyed a combination of industry, agriculture, education, and philosophy. In 1844, however, outside influences caused major revisions in the articles of association drawn up by the original members. The change spelled a swift and complete downfall of Brook Farm as a transcendentalist haven, and by 1847 the property was up for sale. Nevertheless, Brook Farm tested the practicality of Ripley's ideas and provided fertile ground for literary expression. It had been, according to Orestes Brownson, another trascendentalist, "half a charming adventure, half a solemn experiment."

LITERARY ACCOMPLISHMENTS

Certain other developments characterized the intellectual reform sweeping the state and the nation during these years. Nearly two centuries had passed since the *Bay Psalm Book* was published in Cambridge, and now Boston became noted for its diverse publishing establishments. The *North American Review,* founded in 1815 by William Tudor—brother of Frederic Tudor of ice-trade fame—became the foremost magazine of its type in the nation. Tudor, the first editor, encouraged the publication's high standards, and as a result the *North American Review* was the preferred forum for most, if not all, important writers and poets of the period—many of whom were from Massachusetts.

The *North American Review* was joined in the early decades of the nineteenth century by Ticknor &

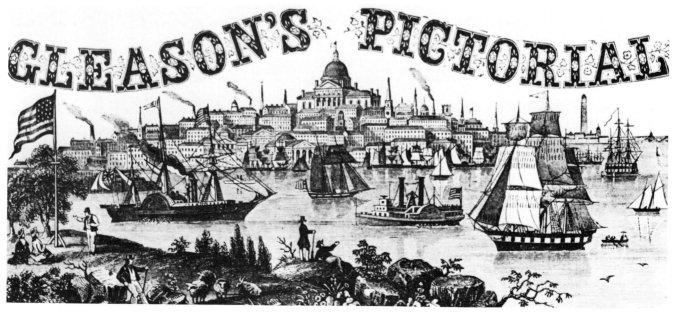

EMILY DICKINSON

Numerous critics have termed her the finest female poet in the English language, although fewer than a dozen of her nearly 2,000 poems were published during her lifetime. Emily Dickinson, born in Amherst on December 10, 1830, was to become a reclusive spinster who never ventured outside her family's home during the final decades of her life. Yet she also became known for her ability to write clearly and incisively in a direct, unaffected manner. Her poetry has a precision and grace that successors have imitated but never replicated.

Both of Emily's parents were of staunch New England stock. Her father, Edward, was a lawyer educated at Yale and a man well-respected for his pious, reverent attitude and his ability to get things done. Her mother, Emily Norcross, was from Monson, and was, in Emily's words, an invalid who was not available to her children. "I never had a mother," Emily once wrote in a letter to a friend.

Her life was shaped by her father's desires and opinions. Emily spent several years at Amherst Academy, graduating in 1847, and then attended Mount Holyoke Female Seminary for a year. After that time, she eschewed formal schooling and withdrew further and further from those whose religious inclinations led them on a path of vehement profession of faith. Emily described herself as "one of the lingering *bad ones*" with regard to formal Christianity. In this, she completely sidestepped her father's wishes.

So it was with poetry. Emily Dickinson read Emerson's *Essays* with her sister-in-law Susan, who had married Emily's brother Austin in 1856. It was during this formative period that Emily began thinking in terms of a life-long dedication to exploring themes of love and death. In choosing such a path, she

Emily Dickinson of Amherst is now considered one of America's best female poets and arguably one of the most talented poets of either sex in the world. Reclusive and odd in her adult life—she wore white all the time—Dickinson wrote compactly, concisely, and brilliantly. Her 1,775 poems and hundreds of letters continue to attract admirers, and they have been translated into several languages to satisfy the demand. Wood engraving by Barry Moser, Pennyroyal Press

Emily Dickinson was born in this house on Main Street in Amherst. She wrote most of her poems and letters here, and she died here. The east side is seen in winter, with a cupola just visible behind the chimney from which Emily could survey the Pelham and Berkshire hills, the Holyoke Range, and the sunrise and sunset. Thousands of visitors from all over the world visit the house each year, attesting to the universality of her appeal. Photo by John H. Martin

seemed instinctively to draw only select friends about her.

She was a humble, quiet person, whose self-portrait was penned in a letter: "I had no portrait, now, but am small, like the Wren, and my Hair is bold, like the Chesnut Bur—and my eyes, like the Sherry in the Glass, that the Guest leaves—."

By the 1850s, Emily was writing

poetry on a regular basis, although she kept it to herself for the most part. She did have several close male friends, and although attempts have been made to link Emily with one or the other of them, no real evidence of romantic entanglements survives. Benjamin F. Nelson, a law student in her father's office, was one such friend. Another was Henry Vaughan Emmons, also a student. Each of these

men encouraged Emily to write and to search her soul for the basis of the poems she produced during this period.

In 1854, Emily accompanied her family to Washington, D.C. for a year, as her father had been elected to Congress. The journey was to be one of her last trips—soon after returning to Amherst, Emily withdrew from society and remained steadfastly at home, going only to Boston several times during the 1860s for medical treatment.

By the 1860s, Emily Dickinson was turning out dozens, even hundreds, of poems. In 1862, she completed 366 poems; in 1863, another 141. In 1864, she wrote a total of 174 poems—but in all of this time she had never attempted publication. However, in 1862, an appeal from the editor of the *Atlantic* inspired her to write to Thomas Wentworth Higginson, a critic who became a staunch supporter of Dickinson's.

By the late 1860s, Emily Dickinson was a living legend in her own community of Amherst, although the townspeople never saw her and certainly most had no idea that she was the author of hundreds of poems. Emily refused social calls, staying on the second floor of her home, dressing constantly in white, and writing voluminously to many correspondents. Her parents died within a few years of each other, and Emily's strength grew strained to the breaking point as she helped nurse her mother through her last illness. Her own health was precarious, and she grew more and more frail as each year passed. She grew gravely ill in the autumn of 1885, and died quietly on May 15, 1886, at the age of 55. Buried next to her parents in a small Congregational cemetery in Amherst, Emily Dickinson had inscribed on her tombstone but two words, taken from one of her poems: "Called back."

★   ★   ★

Company (1833) and Little, Brown (1837), both Boston-based publishing houses of excellent reputation. The power behind these efforts came partly from a nucleus of expertise in Massachusetts that included historians George Bancroft of Worcester, Francis Parkman of Boston, Jared Sparks, numerous Adamses, as well as the transcendentalists Ralph Waldo Emerson, Bronson Alcott, and Henry David Thoreau. In addition, the novelist Nathaniel Hawthorne and poets Henry Wadsworth Longfellow, Emily Dickinson, and Walt Whitman contributed to the flowering of American literature in the early- to mid-nineteenth century. Massachusetts was a spawning ground for creative endeavors at that time, and the works of these individuals proved the success and endurance of that innovative zeal.

There was no one location where this literary flowering seemed to be centered. Yet, Bronson Alcott and his daughter Louisa May Alcott, whose stories for young people have delighted generations of readers, lived in Concord, as did many other writers, including Emerson, Thoreau, and, for a brief time, Hawthorne. Herman Melville, born in New York City, lived for a time at a house named "Arrowhead" in the Berkshires and wrote his classic tale *Moby Dick* there. In another generation or two, many writers and poets would flock to western Massachusetts, where the quiet hills and rural scenery provoked vivid, sensitive imagery. Emily Dickinson—a native of Amherst—was content to spend her entire life in her family home in that western Massachusetts town. A virtual recluse, Dickinson, born in 1830, saw only a few of her poems published in her lifetime. Her work was discovered after her death in 1886, and she has been recognized subsequently as one of America's greatest poets.

Unlike Dickinson, who lived a life bounded by Yankee convention, Edgar Allen Poe embodied daring and unrest in his writings as well as in his daily living. He wrote macabre tales and produced fascinating, convoluted verse dealing with sorrow, mystery, and horror. A native of

Massachusetts pottery industries in Whately and Dedham saw great success in the nineteenth century. On the left is a stoneware crock marked "S.D. Kellogg/Whately," and on the right stands pottery from Dedham, which often decorated its crackle-finished gray stoneware with a procession of handpainted rabbits or other animals. Stoneware was inexpensive compared to fine china in the nineteenth century, but commands high prices today. Photo by Randy Chase. From the Barbara K. Jones Collection

Lowell, Massachusetts, Poe was raised in Virginia and Europe. Although blessed with one of the most brilliant and original minds in America, he found it impossible to maintain a steady literary output and in 1849 died penniless, an addict of drugs and alcohol.

INVENTION AND LABOR UNREST
Much manufacturing in Massachusetts during the first half of the nineteenth century was carried out by factory workers whose days were more than twice as long as their contemporaries' would be in the late twentieth century. Wages were inadequate—at most, a laborer earned $12 a week. Many were in constant danger of falling into debt, and during the 1820s, records show that more than 3,000 people were jailed annually in Massachusetts for unpaid debts. In Lynn, a shoe factory worker might earn only five dollars a week for 72 hours of labor. A family of five needed a minimum of $10.37 per week just

to subsist. Women augmented family incomes, but were paid even less than men doing the same tasks.

On the other hand, owners of factories and mills earned increasing returns on their initial capital investment. In the 1850s, dividends at the Lawrence Company mills averaged 10.26 percent annually. Despite the broad gulf between worker and factory owner and despite nationwide inflation during the 1840s, there was little successful union activity across a wide swath of the factory population. Not until the 1870s did legislation effectively regulate the length of a worker's day.

Particularly after 1830, a demand for workers grew steadily all over Massachusetts until the Civil War. Much growth was due to the sheer increase in the number and variety of manufacturing concerns in the state. Textile mills more than any other factories typify nineteenth-century manufacturing in Massachusetts. Although work there was hard, with long hours and low

Although they worked extremely long, tedious hours in the mills, many Lowell women preferred their new life, away from seven-days-a-week farm work, in which they could now earn money of their own. The Lowell Offering, *the first magazine written exclusively by women, was a product of this short era, full of the promise of factory work accompanied by healthy conditions and a highly literate, cultural social life. Evening schools, lyceum lectures, self-improvement circles, and lending libraries also flourished in Lowell at this time. From* New England Magazine, *Vol. I, 1889*

An appointed commission presented a report on public health to the Massachusetts legislature on April 25, 1850, with this among the illustrations. It is Burgess Alley near Broad Street in Boston, the site of hundreds of cholera cases in 1849. Here recent Irish immigrants existed amid filth and squalor in overcrowded tenements and converted warehouses with inadequate sewerage. The commission made recommendations to the state on more stringent building inspections and zoning laws. From Report of a General Plan for the Promotion of Public and Personal Health, *1850*

wages, life for factory workers in the first decades of the century had positive aspects.

Among the written legacies of early textile mill life is Lucy Larcom's accounts describing Lowell during the 1830s. A poet who later wrote *New England Girlhood,* Larcom carefully detailed her experiences. While her tenure in the mills was brief, she provides a glimpse of the past that remains enlightening even today.

Larcom was typical of many hundreds of young women who left their families' rural homes to earn wages for a few years before marrying and settling back into an agricultural routine. In 1816, more than 50 percent of cotton mill workers in the United States were female. By the time Lucy Larcom found a position at Lowell, acceptability of such employment was largely dependent on the sheltering influence of the mill-owned boardinghouse. "Factory girls" like Larcom recalled advantages of the Lowell system that placed them in contact with other young women of their age and background:

The girls who toiled together at Lowell were clearing away a few weeds from the overgrown track of independent labor for other women. They practically said, by numbering themselves among factory girls, that in our country no real odium could be attached to any honest toil that any self-respecting woman might undertake.

Larcom's idealized view of her years in the Lowell mills was accurate. It is nevertheless true, however, that a female labor force had distinct advantages for mill owners. One of the original investors in the Merrimack Manufacturing Company knew that cotton textile production was a good investment risk because of low labor costs. According to Nathan Appleton, "the material is cheaper and the wages of labor, considering the larger proportion of female labor, scarcely anything higher."

Despite paternalistic corporate ideologies suffusing the mills and boardinghouses where women like Larcom lived, it was a lifestyle in which most women took pride. One testimony to its high ideals can be found in the *Lowell Offering,* a literary publication first appearing in 1840. Written entirely by Lowell mill workers, the magazine—consisting of several dozen pages devoted to poetry, essays, and letters—became famous throughout the world. To a certain degree it counterbalanced criticisms about low pay and long working hours. The impetus for publication of the *Lowell Offering* came from the Reverend Abel Thomas, and women such as Lucy Larcom, Harriet H. Robinson, and Harriet Farley contributed pieces over a five-year period. By the mid-1840s, demands for shorter working hours and better conditions negated the publication's message of "good news" for mill workers. The *Lowell Offering* was short-lived, but attempted to prove that factory work need

Above: *Worcester is shown here, looking north on Main Street, as it appeared in 1839 when John Warner Barber sketched it for his book. Established as a town in 1722, Worcester is the county seat of the county of the same name. During the reform era Worcester was the home of early organizations of abolitionists and women's suffrage workers, as well as the Free Soil Party. The city is known today for its varied industries, its colleges (especially Holy Cross, Clark University, and Worcester Polytechnic) and for the American Antiquarian Society and the Worcester Art Museum. From Barber,* History and Antiquities of Every Town in Massachusetts, *1839*

Above: *Isaiah Thomas, an impoverished child who grew up to be a patriot and the publisher of the* Massachusetts Spy, *the most successful newspaper of the Revolutionary era, founded the American Antiquarian Society in 1812. He began the library with his own 8,000 volumes, and he chose Worcester because that is where he had moved his printing presses in April 1775 to be out of reach of British guns.*

Today the society, the third oldest in the country and the first with national rather than regional scope, owns the world's largest collection of printed material from the first 250 years of United States history. These printed materials include three million books, pamphlets, broadsides, manuscripts, prints, maps, and a comprehensive collection of early American newspapers. From History of Worcester County, Massachusetts, *Vol. I, 1879*

Top: *John Warner Barber sketched this northwestern view of Millbury, six miles south of Worcester, in the late 1830s when Millbury was a small village with two centers and fewer than 100 houses. The boat is maneuvering the Blackstone Canal, which opened in October 1828. By 1837, Barber noted, Millbury had numerous mills, including six woolen mills employing 148 men and 128 women. From Barber,* History and Antiquities of Every Town in Massachusetts, *1839*

Above: *Berkshire County's town of North Adams, as sketched by John Warner Barber for his 1839 book on Massachusetts towns, shows a mill village just beginning on the Hoosic River. Agriculture is still very much in evidence in the background. Many mills employed farm girls at first, and in winter, the farmers as well. Settled in the late 1700s by Connecticut and Rhode Island families, North Adams became an early textile mill village. Susan B. Anthony's father started an early mill here and moved on to Battenville, New York, to start another. From Barber,* History and Antiquities of Every Town in Massachusetts, *1839*

not be dull or harsh. It helped attract young women workers by offering training and a chance for intellectual stimulation among their comtemporaries.

In spite of the availability of willing factory workers in the first half of the nineteenth century, there were rumblings of labor unrest. In 1809, dissatisfied printers in Boston formed a union, and in 1825 the Columbian Charitable Society of Shipwrights and Calkers was established. The latter resulted from an unsuccessful shipbuilders' strike in Medford six years earlier. In 1825, 600 Boston-area carpenters attempted to obtain contracts for a 10-hour day, but their organizing efforts were too weak to have any positive results in the state.

Social reformers interested in promoting cooperatives as a way of bypassing the evils of labor-management issues found fertile ground in Massachusetts. By 1831, Boston workers had gathered to discuss the formation of a cooperative group to be known as the Association of Farmers, Mechanics and Other Working Men. The following year, leather workers who were part of the vast shoe manufacturing industry in Lynn met to form a cooperative. These efforts were doomed, however, as the outbreak of the Civil War caused an abrupt change in the national economy.

As the 1840s drew to a close, the working population in Lowell and elsewhere gradually changed. Immigrants flocked to the United States and economic depression threatened. The mill girls slowly disappeared from Lowell, replaced by immigrant labor. The neat, well-run boardinghouses gave way to crowded tenements, and Lowell's shining promise grew tarnished.

The growth of cities—both in size and in number—was directly related to the success of Massachusetts' industrial ventures. Boston claimed a population of about 36,000 by 1815, and on February 23, 1822, it was incorporated as a city. Urban life seemed to go hand and hand with wealth and ambition, which, always evident in Boston as well as in other Massachusetts cities, flourished and cre-

ated a distinctive social upper class.

The influx of Irish, Scottish, and German immigrants, part of the first of three great waves of immigration to the United States, contributed to a more distinctly stratified social fabric. The divisions, particularly with regard to the Irish, were especially evident in Boston and surrounding towns. Newburyport, to the north, saw a gradual but definite shift in population as that community became a favorite destination for Irish immigrants seeking escape from famine at home via work in the United States.

To the west of Boston, Worcester, established as a town in 1722, was incorporated as a city in 1848. Its industry included an active publishing business, which had been located there since before the War for Independence. Isaiah Thomas was publisher of the *Massachusetts Spy,* an influential newspaper during the years 1770 to 1776. He established a printing shop in Worcester after smuggling his printing press out of Boston in 1775 to escape British censorship. Thomas, who lived from 1749 to 1831, used the motto "Open to all Parties, but Influenced by None," for the *Spy.* It underscored the independence and single-minded Repub-

licanism that flourished in the Bay State throughout the Federal period. This Republicanism carried a strong belief in the importance of a stable state government and of noninterference by federal bureaucracy.

In addition to his reputation as a printer, Isaiah Thomas was also a noted historian and founder of the American Antiquarian Society. The society, set up in 1812 at Worcester, is famous for its collection of historical documents; it claims to have in its archives two-thirds of all materials printed in the United States up to the year 1820.

INDUSTRIAL EXPANSION
Worcester, with its mills and thriving mid-state economy, was typical of the many Massachusetts communities that, through industrialization, gradually grew in economic strength during the early nineteenth century. Shoes, paper, textiles, and cutlery were among the products made in these factories, of which many were small but remarkably efficient.

In Holyoke, to the west of Worcester, construction of a dam at South Hadley Falls in 1828 provided waterpower for many manufacturing concerns located

Charcoal for industrial uses and restaurants such as Durgin Park in Boston was manufactured at rural charcoal kilns like these two in Pelham on the road to Prescott. Ironically, the business was burned, reportedly by drunken employees who let the charcoal get too hot. Today the site is near the shore of the Quabbin Reservoir on the road to Prescott, a town that no longer exists. From a circa 1910 postcard

Gleason's Pictorial *featured this Gloucester schooner in an 1854 story when Gloucester was already famous for fish. The writer noted that there were more than 200 such schooners in Gloucester, each with a crew of 10. They caught mackerel and cod primarily, laying up in port in the winter when Gloucester was most lively. The mackerel was sorted, salted, and packed in barrels and kegs. Cod, haddock, and pollack were prepared for drying. The story also declared that there were no very poor people in Gloucester, nor any very rich. From* Gleason's Pictorial, *1854*

along the Connecticut River. Similarly, Lee, in the western region of the state, boasted three paper mills by 1821, all of which were powered by water. One of the most famous of the many Massachusetts paper mills is located in Dalton in the Berkshires. Crane Paper Mills was established there in 1801 and is still producing high-quality paper for a variety of markets. Leominster, just north of Worcester, was a farming community that had, by the mid-1800s, about two dozen comb factories in operation. One of the first manufacturers of these combs, made from horn, was Obadiah Hills. Combs were worn as ladies' hair ornaments in the nineteenth century, and Hills, recognizing their commercial potential, set up a thriving business based on production of this finery.

East of Worcester, the town of Hudson was the home of a shoe manufacturing plant founded in 1816 under the direction of Daniel Stratton. By 1835 shoe production was that town's chief industry. Then Francis Brigham

brought automation to the manufacture of shoes there, based on waterpower from the nearby Assabet River. Soon, other factories, including tanneries, textile mills, and box makers, were all part of the local industrial scene.

Other towns, such as Blackstone near the Rhode Island border, added to Massachusetts' industrial output via production of textile goods. Blackstone entrepreneurs built the first cotton mill there in 1809 and set up a wool mill in 1814. Bridgewater, in the same region of the state, was the location of a mill established in 1817 to construct cotton gins. It was this technology that ultimately transformed the processing of cotton in the United States and was, most historians agree, a major factor in furthering economic patterns that eventually led to the Civil War. Bridgewater was no stranger to profits connected with war efforts, however, since during the eighteenth century it had been a major iron producing center. Factories in Bridgewater had manufactured the majority of cannons used by colonials during the War for Independence.

Sterling, north of Worcester, saw the beginning of a scythe business in 1828, after Silas Lamson patented a procedure for making these sharp-bladed grass cutters. This agriculturally-oriented business indicates that, although industry was well-established in Massachusetts, the nation as a whole retained its agrarian economic base.

By 1806, a paper mill had been set up in Chicopee, and in 1822 Edmund Dwight established a cotton mill in this western Massachusetts community bordering Holyoke. In Chicopee in 1829, the Ames Company was founded by two brothers, Nathan Peabody and James Ames, who made table cutlery as well as swords and knives.

CLIPPER SHIPS AND THE GOLD RUSH

Much of the expansion of manufacturing and economy in Massachusetts was a result of improved transportation. About the time that Lowell mills were turning out miles and miles of textiles, and canals in Massachusetts were providing efficient transportation to Boston, another innovation had occurred. The clipper ship, larger and faster than whalers or other sailing vessels, began to dominate the maritime scene.

The China trade continued to prosper during the mid-1800s. With repeal of the Navigation Acts in 1848, Great Britain opened its markets to New England goods. And in 1839, Samuel Hall of East Boston built the *Akbar,* a 650-ton ship that was unusually fast and carried a considerable cargo. Just nine years later, when news arrived of the gold discovery at Sutter's Mill in California, vessels like the *Akbar*—one of the many new clipper ships—carried fortune hunters around Cape Horn to San Francisco. During a one-year period, 25 percent of Nantucket's voting population left for California in search of gold. Eight hundred men left the port of New Bedford beginning in 1849, hoping to get

rich quickly and return to Massachusetts with a fortune.

Most of these 49ers returned to the Bay State, a few with more money than they had when they left. Some tried to exploit their fellow prospectors, and some, such as Dr. Samuel Merritt, tried to emulate past entrepreneurial success. Merritt copied Frederic Tudor and attempted to supply ice to the San Francisco area. His supply was to come from Puget Sound, off the coast of Washington State. Merritt found little ice at Puget Sound, however, but instead began supplying pilings for San Francisco wharves out of the vast Pacific Northwest timber reserves. Soon, Merritt was importing oranges from the Society Islands to the California coast, and his fortune was established. A multimillionaire, and one of the fortunate Massachusetts sons who stayed in California, Merritt founded the city of Oakland. When he retired he was known for having the largest yacht on the Pacific coast.

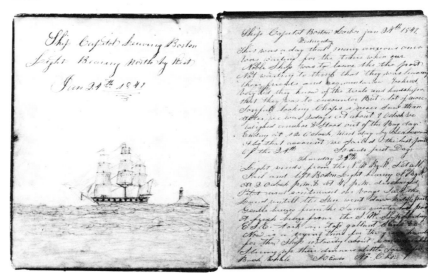

Merritt was not alone—gold-rush economy translated into incredible markups on ordinary items. A barrel of flour shipped from Massachusetts mills fetched $4 in 1849. Potatoes sold then for $16 a bushel; eggs went for $10 a dozen. All of this meant that Bay State ship owners grew rich quickly. Medford's *Argonaut,* built by John E. Lodge, was paid for even before it weighed anchor,

Not only was the merchant fleet growing before the Civil War, but the U.S. naval fleet was multiplying as well. Shown here in a London magazine illustration is the Charlestown Navy Yard as it looked in 1853. The drawing by Baker Smith-Andrew depicts the new 74-gun Vermont *of the Japan expedition. In the foreground stand natural elbow-like pieces of trees that were used in interiors of ships and called "ship's knees." From the* London Illustrated News, *January 22, 1853*

thanks to freight charges that were higher than ever in the history of shipping.

But the boom was short-lived—by 1851, goods sent to California by clipper sat rotting on San Francisco's streets. As with many other ventures of the period, it was only the quick-thinking, fast-moving individual whose success had any enduring quality.

The clippers carrying Massachusetts fortune-seekers and various cargoes around the Horn were packets that freighted cargo at rates of up to $60 per ton. Considering their size—the *Gamecock* of Boston was 190 feet long and was registered at 1,392 tons—these clippers made excellent time. The *Northern Light,* built in 1851, made the round trip from Boston to San Francisco in seven months. Donald McKay, a Boston shipbuilder, pioneered the 1,500-ton class of clipper in 1850 with the *Stag-Hound.* Soon after he built the famous *Flying Cloud,* the fastest vessel of its type ever in the United States. The *Stag-Hound* held the world record for sailing from Boston to the equator,

having made the trip in 13 days. It also held the second-best record from San Francisco to Honolulu—8 days, 20 hours. The *Stag-Hound*'s owner, McKay, was a master shipbuilder whose vessels made more under-100-day voyages around Cape Horn than did those of any other shipbuilder of the time.

During the clipper ship era, various commercial ventures were built up on this new mode of transportation—cod-fishing and whaling reached their peak in the antebellum years. Federal expenditures for rivers and harbors also increased from $26,000 in 1824 to $704,000 by 1833. Coffee, as well as tea, was traded and shipped by clipper, although this means of transport declined somewhat as steamships traveled between Europe and South America. Exports of ice from Boston increased 100 percent between 1847 and 1856, and rum producers enjoyed a thriving trade, as did Massachusetts manufacturers of shoes and boots. The port of Boston hummed with trade, and shipments of almost anything could be found there, from Australian wool to California wheat to

On July 4, 1854, Messrs. Sanderson and Lanergan entertained enormous crowds on Boston Common with fireworks made in their East Cambridge laboratories. Shown here is their grand finale, a "National Tableau." The whole display was arched and illuminated by flights of rockets, shells, mines, and stars. From Gleason's Pictorial, *July 8, 1854*

SHOW BUSINESS AND MEDICINE SHOWS

The decades preceding the Civil War were not marked exclusively by debate and dissent over slavery. Americans of the period readily took part in a variety of cultural pursuits and they readily flocked to any new educational or entertainment innovation. One such novelty was Jenny Lind, the "Swedish Nightingale," whose debut in New York City was sponsored by P.T. Barnum. In 1850, Lind traveled to a number of American cities, and when she appeared in Washington, D.C., Daniel Webster, the famous senator and orator from Massachusetts, acknowledged her with a dignified bow from his front-row seat. In Boston, one eager concert-goer paid $625 for a ticket to Lind's appearance there, the highest price anyone had offered for any of her concerts. The poet Longfellow also attended that Boston recital, and in his words, "her presence . . . takes her audience captive before she opens her lips. She sings like the morning star; clear, liquid, heavenly sounds." Miss Lind was married in Boston, in February 1852, only months before her retirement from the American stage. She spent her honeymoon in Northampton, naming Paradise Pond at what is now the Smith College campus.

As at other times in the nation's history, fads of various kinds swept the country, proving P.T. Barnum's maxim, "There's a sucker born every minute." In some cases, consumers were persuaded to purchase medicines that were not in the least effective, but which were sold with a great deal of gusto and enthusiasm by their clever promoters. Massachusetts had its share of patent-medicine producers who sold nostrums not on the basis of medical endorsement but on sheer brazen chicanery. These cure-alls were advertised as the answer to colds, muscle sprains, kidney disease, tuberculosis, toothache,

"female complaints," and hair loss. Furthermore, these miracle cures could supposedly be depended upon after one or two doses. James C. Ayer, a clever Massachusetts entrepreneur, was one of the most successful of these patent-medicine men. His "Ayer's Cathartic Pills" and "Ayer's Cherry Pectoral" were both produced in Lowell throughout the 1800s. The town of Ayer, to the west of Lowell, was named for this beneficent gentleman whose philanthropy was based on the exploitation of thousands of trusting customers.

Patent medicine humbugs were not regarded with much respect by members of the legitimate medical community. In Massachusetts, most citizens had looked for quality medical care to the Massachusetts General Hospital in Boston since the early nineteenth century. Founded partly as a charitable organization,

The Ayer Company had remedies for almost any ailment, as shown in this April 28, 1885, Boston Globe advertisement. Endorsements by local people puffed the product line for sarsaparilla.

Massachusetts General was the site of the first surgical procedure involving anesthesia (ether), on October 16, 1846. This hospital, along with others and institutions such as Harvard Medical School, founded in 1782, helped put Massachusetts in the forefront of medical research and assured patients—who came to the Bay State from all over the world for treatment—that they received the best care possible.

★　　　★　　　★　　　★　　　★　　　★　　　★

goatskins and ostrich feathers from South Africa.

SHADOWS OF WAR

Not until September 1857 was there a lull in business. By then, Boston was overrun with East India Company goods shipped out from markets in Calcutta. Because of the sepoy mutiny in India, British merchants were anxious to leave, and the overabundance of their merchandise in the U.S. caused a drop in prices for about two years. This precipitated a concurrent decline in shipping, which led to a shipping trade depression. Slowly, however, the merchant fleet went back into operation. By 1860, Boston Harbor was thriving once more, and in one year 13 American ships were launched there, including four iron-screw steamers more than 200 feet long.

The latter—yet another maritime innovation—were the *Massachusetts,* the *South Carolina,* the *Merrimack,* and the *Mississippi.* They had been built in South Boston by Samuel H. Pook

and were designed by Harrison Loring. It seemed that the merchant fleet, particularly the one sailing from Massachusetts, would see a record-breaking amount of tonnage launched there during the following decade.

This might have occurred but for storms brewing on the political horizon. From April 12, 1861, when Fort Sumter was fired upon, signaling the start of the Civil War, the next four years saw Massachusetts ship owners busier than ever. Their energies were aimed, not at commercial profit, but as historian Samuel Eliot Morison noted, at "preserving the Union." The Civil War brought to the Massachusetts maritime industry the challenges and problems of blockades, as well as the ultimate threat that if the South won the war, there would be a drastic change in the northern economy. Along with the rest of the Union, Massachusetts set its sights on victory and did everything in its power to ensure a southern defeat and an end to the Confederacy.

This British sketch of Tremont and Park streets in Boston in 1858 was accompanied by a report on the best way to travel from New York to Boston. One should travel by steamboat the 200 miles to Fall River, and then by rail the 54 miles to Boston, although the reporter found American rail travel disagreeable. "Such easy luxury as that of a first-class carriage in England or France is not to be had for love or money. The servant and the mistress, the navvie, the pedlar, the farmer, . . . governor of the state, and even the Irish bogtrotter, who before he left Ireland would have as soon as thought of taking the chair from the Viceroy . . . as of traveling in a first class carriage, but who in this country handles more money in a day than he saw in the old country in a month . . . mingle together in one long car." From the London Illustrated News, *January 9, 1858*

125

THE CIVIL WAR AND THE GILDED AGE (1861-1890)

★　★　★　★　★　★　★　★　★

The American Civil War was not a single-issue conflict between two geographic regions about slavery. It was, rather, a bundle of disputes that ranged from states' rights to protective tariffs, from land policy to slavery. Affecting virtually every U.S. citizen, no matter how far removed from the actual fighting, the Civil War began at Fort Sumter, South Carolina, on April 12, 1861.

Residents of Massachusetts may have been spared the trauma of Civil War battles within their state's boundaries, but its citizens were by no means immune to the upheaval and tragedy of war. In fact, Massachusetts soldiers were the very first to die in Civil War-related fighting, even before large-scale battles began.

An understanding of the full effects of the horror and waste this civil conflict engendered best proceeds after considering the factors that led the country to war. From the very beginning, the United States grappled with the slavery issue. Delegates to the Constitutional Convention in Philadelphia in the 1780s argued about whether slaves should be counted as citizens. Resolution of this issue would determine a state's share of federal taxes. As could be expected, different opinions concerning inclusion of slaves in this head count came from northern and southern convention delegates. As early as the late 1600s, vastly different economies in North and South had emerged, and these differences caused constitution delegates in the 1780s to clash. Chief among their disputes, slavery presented a major stumbling block. The North wanted slaves counted as citizens for tax purposes, but the South wanted slaves excluded from the tally. Inconsistently, the South demanded slaves to be counted when state representation in the House was to be determined—even though slaves could not vote. Finally, the "three-fifths

Born in Newburyport, William Lloyd Garrison (1805-1879) started the radical abolitionist paper, The Liberator, *in Boston in 1831. By calling for immediate emancipation of all slaves Garrison made enemies in the South, where a price was offered for his capture, and, reportedly, a higher price if he was brought in dead. But he was also despised by a large group in Boston who, in 1835, dragged him through the streets with a rope around his neck. From Winsor,* The Memorial History of Boston, *Vol. III, 1881*

compromise" was reached, which stated that three-fifths of "other Persons," that is, slaves, be counted for both purposes: taxes and representation. As far as the slavery controversy was concerned, the convention ended with agreement that importation of slaves should not be forbidden before 1808. This was the first in a number of compromises hammered out between North and South during several decades before the Civil War.

Slavery was not the only issue of dispute between North and South. Trade was also a difficulty, particularly since southern states disliked export taxes. These taxes, they argued, would affect southern states most extensively since their goods (largely cotton) were for foreign export. The North was concerned only marginally with this issue since much of the manufacture in the northern states was for the domestic market and thus would not be affected as severely by export taxes.

By the beginning of the nineteenth century, southern life and culture had evolved as distinctly different from that in the North. The South was primarily agricultural, the North increasingly dependent on factories and mills. Cotton was an important crop—both to the South which grew it and the North which processed it. This had become even more true since the 1793 invention of the cotton gin, which allowed for faster processing of raw cotton fiber. Northern mills depended on cotton for textile manufacture, and both regions enjoyed increasing prosperity due to the success of cotton production and export. Both sides had an interest in keeping conflict to a minimum, but both sides

were destined to fail in their attempts to preserve peace. The agricultural way of life that made cheap cotton cultivation possible was predicated on slavery. And the abolitionists of the North were determined to put an end to the enslavement of other humans.

THE PECULIAR INSTITUTION

Southern cotton production resulted both in overwhelming economic reliance on the crop and on ever greater reliance on slaves for its cultivation and harvest. In 1800, there were about 90,000 slaves in the United States. By 1860, the eve of the Civil War, there were at least four million slaves at work on plantations all across the South. Because of slaves' efforts, cotton production increased steadily. The "peculiar institution," as one historian has called it, gave the South its unmistakable and inimitable culture, and gave the North justification for its charges of the moral degradation of slave labor. Questions surrounding the institution of slavery and the culture it supported helped build the foundation on which the Civil War was ultimately based. Abo-

lition of slavery became a rallying point for opponents of the entire southern way of life.

Abolitionists in Massachusetts were numerous, and none was more famous or more effective than William Lloyd Garrison. He was founder, in 1833, of the American Anti-Slavery Society, and his magazine, *The Liberator*, became reformers' main vehicle for popularizing the antislavery cause nationwide. Abolitionists such as Garrison were vehement in their opposition to slavery and adamant in their attempts to outlaw slavery both in theory and in practice.

"I am in earnest. I will not equivocate—I will not excuse—I will not retreat a single inch—and I WILL BE HEARD!" Garrison left little doubt about his position or his sincerity. His emphatic, forceful prose motivated thousands to stand behind the abolitionist cause, and as the nineteenth century wore on, his views carried more and more weight in states across the North.

By the second decade of the nineteenth century it was clear that the political and economic unity of the North

The Liberator was founded by William Lloyd Garrison because he had found, on a speaking tour of New England, " . . . prejudice more stubborn, apathy more frozen, than among the slave owners themselves." He wanted immediate emancipation: "On this subject, I do not wish to think or speak or write, with moderation . . . [would you] tell the mother to gradually extricate her babe from the fire into which it has fallen?" The masthead of the paper shows a slave auction in view of the nation's capitol, an embarrassment to many in a land where all men were, supposedly, created equal. Garrison published his incendiary paper until after the Civil War when his cause was finally won; a bronze statue was later erected in Boston in his memory. From New England Magazine, December 1890

129

Samuel Bowles (1826-1878) was the capable editor of the Springfield Republican, *which he developed from a weekly into a world-class daily in the mid-1800s. A provincial paper, it was national and even international in scope and was read widely outside of its geographic area. Bowles was a Republican when the new party was born in 1856; the paper had been the* Republican *since 1824. He denounced slavery and its spread to the West, and editorialized against the hanging of John Brown. After the Civil War he continued his reformatory zeal in attacking political and financial corruption characteristic of the new era. From Everts,* History of the Connecticut Valley in Massachusetts, Vol. II, 1879

was greatly dependent on industrial production that often involved southern cotton. Furthermore, southern cotton was the crop that determined the relative economic success of the United States in the world market. As several historians have noted, northern industrial cities such as Lowell depended on continuing shipments of raw cotton from the South. Cotton was very much "king," even in the North. In many northern mill communities abolitionist activity was therefore unpopular, as it represented a threat to the economy. An abolitionist newspaper, *The Middlesex Standard,* was edited in Lowell from 1844 to 1845 by John Greenleaf Whittier, but was unable to sustain itself for more than a few

months. The pro-South/pro-cotton bias of many mill owners and most workers prevented the abolitionists from becoming powerful in this area before 1860. In other Massachusetts cities, however, there was criticism of the connection between "the lords of the loom and the lords of the lash," as mill and slave owners were described. A related article in the *Springfield Republican* noted that "prosperity . . . has frequently stood in the way of very necessary reforms."

The South had virtually none of the factories characterizing cities such as Lowell, Lawrence, and Waltham. The entire southern identity was predicated economically and culturally on its dependence on cotton cultivation and slavery. Unlike the North, which had a diverse economy based on agriculture *and* industrial production, the South was totally dependent on one crop.

The two regions—along with the ever-increasing western portion of the country—were affected simultaneously (but often in opposite ways) by various issues. Free trade versus protective tariffs divided them, with New England almost always favoring some protective tariff. National banking likewise affected the North and South differently, as did land policy. But no issue was more divisive, more persistent in its ability to cause conflict among elected officials and private citizens alike, than slavery.

Importation of slaves to the U.S. ceased in 1808. Although slave smuggling continued after 1808, it was seen only as part of the larger issue of slavery. Smuggling was not, in itself, an overriding concern of most abolitionists. In fact, between 1840 and 1860, the U.S. Navy captured only 50 ships attempting to smuggle this pitiable human cargo. Most abolitionist efforts focused on complete eradication of slavery from the nation. In 1819, there were 22 states in the Union evenly divided between those permitting slave ownership and those that were "free." Free and slave states continued to join the Union in balanced

Sojourner Truth (1790?-1883), an escaped Michigan slave, came to Massachusetts between 1842 and 1846 and lived for a time in a utopian community with abolitionist sentiments in the Florence section of Northampton. In such a community everyone was expected to help with the work, and Truth took it upon herself to do the laundry, as depicted in this 1867 drawing by Charles C. Burleigh. She became famous in the years before the Civil War for her moving antislavery lectures and efforts to free her fellow blacks. Photo by Ecclestein. Courtesy, Northampton Historical Society

numbers, and it looked as if slavery would continue as a way of life, at least in the southern states, for decades to come.

The year 1820 proved critical to future disputes over slavery. That year, the nation's growing rift was clearly illuminated. Many observers publicly stated that, unless the North and the South could find ways of eliminating their grievances, future conflict of a more serious and debilitating nature was inevitable.

Missouri was admitted to the Union in 1820 as a slave state along with Maine. The latter was previously a part of Massachusetts and was admitted as a free state. This enabled maintenance of the balance of free and slave states, and the Missouri Compromise, as the events of these state admissions were known, underscored the importance of a bal-

MASSACHUSETTS, MAINE, AND THE MISSOURI COMPROMISE

Beginning in 1691, Massachusetts officially held the land bordering on Canada which we know today as the state of Maine. At the time Massachusetts was admitted to the Union as the nation's sixth state, Maine continued to be part of the Commonwealth—albeit a distant, non-contiguous portion of it. A few decades later, events conspired to provoke a political separation of the two areas which had long been separated by geography.

The Missouri Compromise in 1820 was Congress' solution to an ongoing pro-slavery/antislavery debate. The debate was not new and the decisions made in 1820 were not to last past 1854. But the decision made by Congress, creating both a new slave state (Missouri) and a free state (Maine), changed Massachusetts forever. Because of the compromise, Massachusetts lost valuable ports and some 31,000 square miles of timber and farmland. Maine, the 23rd state, was created in response to the admission of Missouri as a slave state, so in a sense Massachusetts sacrificed valuable territory on behalf of a greater national need: to maintain a balance in the Senate between free and slave state factions.

Sectional issues, slavery among them, were clearly defined during the early decades of the nineteenth century. This heated but not-yet-open confrontation would burst into the inferno of civil war by the 1860s. The division of Massachusetts and creation of Maine as a separate state meant that 12 free states would counterbalance 12 slave states. Maine was literally born out of the abolitionists' desire to save the Union from slavery, although pressure for Maine statehood had existed since the 1780s. But skeptics knew that the sacrifice of this northern part of Massachusetts would not delay the inevitable.

John Quincy Adams, sixth president of the United States (1825-1829) was one of those who recognized the gravity of the

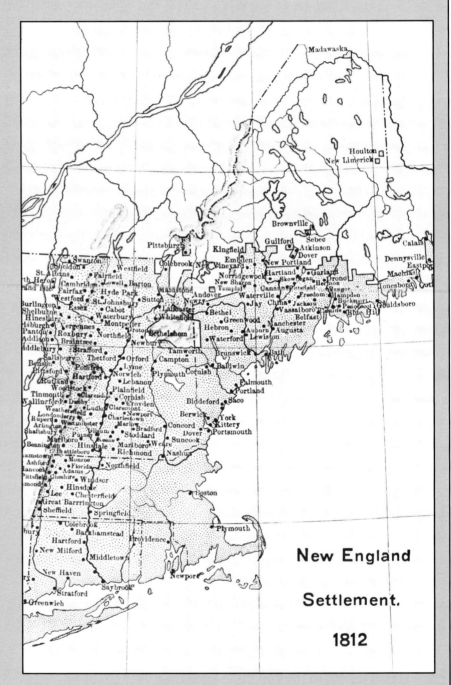

New England

Settlement.

1812

problem. He knew that merely to divide states into slaveholding and non-slaveholding areas was only a temporary solution, not a final answer. Adams looked with rue at the Missouri Compromise in 1820 and commented that the decision represented a "title page to a great, tragic volume."

By 1820 Maine's population was large enough to justify statehood status. Incidentally, Bowdoin (founded in 1794) and Colby (1813) were colleges in Maine chartered by the Massachusetts government. From Mathews, The Expansion of New England, *1909*

anced U.S. Senate. If Missouri had entered singly as a new slave state, there would have been greater slave-state representation in Congress. This was unacceptable to northern senators and congressmen alike, anxious that the will of the South not predominate in matters of national importance.

The more far-reaching effects of the Missouri Compromise "forever prohibited" slavery north of 36° 30', the western extension of Missouri's southern boundary. The compromise passed the U.S. House of Representatives by a vote of 90 to 87—with all slave states voting negatively as a bloc. The almost equal division of national political sentiment was clear—and Thomas Jefferson, himself a slave owner, was quick to point out that "we have the wolf by the ears, and we can neither safely hold him, nor safely let him go."

There was solace in the fact that Congress remained able to settle serious disagreements with comparative dignity and success. But those who hoped other issues would be handled similarly were disappointed. Even the Missouri Compromise ultimately was repealed in 1854 with passage of the Kansas-Nebraska Act, which itself was declared unconstitutional by the Supreme Court in 1857 in the Dred Scott case.

EXPANSION AND COMPROMISE

The 1840s saw major geographic expansion of the country. In 1848, the United States won the Mexican War and received, through the Treaty of Guadalupe Hidalgo, Texas, New Mexico, Arizona, and Upper California. Now, all of the Pacific coast from south of San Diego to the 49th parallel was part of the United States. Although the newly-acquired region was 3,000 miles from Massachusetts, it would have lasting impact on New England's future, as well as on that of the rest of the country.

Acquisition of new land again raised the slavery issue, bringing it to the forefront of national political debate. President Taylor, anxious to avoid a long,

acrimonious argument in Congress over disposition of slave territory, suggested that California be admitted immediately—as a state, rather than as a territory. As a state, it would be free to decide whether to permit slavery within its borders. The California state constitution was drawn up and ratified quickly. The constitution of the new state excluded slavery, and the South, fearing such a precedent might leave slave states in an ever-dwindling minority, protested in Congress.

The result of this protest was the Compromise of 1850, one more uneasy and somewhat tenuous agreement between North and South. Senators Henry Clay and Daniel Webster were among the chief proponents of the new compromise, which allowed California its free-state status in return for organization of remaining Pacific territory (as well as that in the Southwest) without mention of slavery. More importantly, a new, more rigorous federal Fugitive Slave Law was enacted as part of the Compromise of 1850, and it contained a special provision that the law be strictly enforced in the North. Finally, slave trade was to be abolished in the District of Columbia as of January 1, 1851. That these measures all passed was indicative of the nation's ability to expand while continuing to maintain a peaceful balance in the face of the most extreme political diversity.

THE IRREPRESSIBLE CONFLICT

Speaking to the Senate on March 7, 1850, Daniel Webster of Massachusetts tried to forestall the outbreak of war by appealing to reason on the part of the South *and* the North. With characteristic eloquence, Webster stated his case. His defense of the Fugitive Slave Law angered northerners, but Webster staunchly advocated a policy that would avoid extremism. His opening words in the famous Seventh of March speech give an idea of how desperately Webster sought to avoid war: "I wish to speak today not as a Massachusetts man, not

Right: *Charles Sumner (1816-1874) was a young Boston lawyer when he became caught up in the antislavery movement of the 1830s. He wrote against slavery in the South—it had been unlawful in Massachusetts since the Revolution—and became especially vocal after 1850 and the passage of the Fugitive Slave Law, which meant that northerners must return escaped slaves. He was elected to the U.S. Senate, where his fiery speeches irritated southern leaders. In retaliation for one speech, the cousin of the slandered southerner in question beat Sumner with a cane until he lay senseless on the Senate floor. His seat was left vacant and his attack became the focus of outrage from the North, while southern leaders upheld the attack as deserved. From Stearns,* Cambridge Sketches, *1905*

as a northern man, but as an American. I speak today for the preservation of the Union. Hear me for my cause."

Webster's opponents were not moved. Senator John C. Calhoun, old and ill, spoke only as a South Carolinian: "I cannot agree that this Union cannot be dissolved. Am I to understand that no degree of oppression, no outrage, no broken faith, can produce the destruction of this Union? The Union *can* be broken."

As the decade unfolded, increasing numbers of incidents involved pro-slavery and antislavery groups. Economic issues attending slavery could not be overlooked, and as the nation entered the 1860s, many counseled against future compromise. Some predicted accurately that the gathering clouds of dissent meant only one thing: the storms of war.

Senator Charles Sumner of Massachusetts stated his feelings in a letter to a friend in 1857. A staunch advocate of abolition, Sumner said the practice of slavery "degrades our country and prevents its example from being all-conquering." As the 1860s wore on, Sumner became an ultra-radical Republican known for his support of total freedom and full civil rights for all black Americans. He also became an arch foe of southerners who demanded states' rights.

Shortly after the attack on Fort Sumter, South Carolina, the Massachusetts militia was activated and led to Washington, D.C. On its way to the nation's capital the Sixth Massachusetts Regiment commanded by General Benjamin Franklin Butler passed through Baltimore, where it was set upon by angry, pro-Confederate rioters. The mob attacked the Bay State troops on April 19, 1861, killing four soldiers and causing the deaths of nine civilians. These casualties occurred 86 years to the day after the War for Independence had begun with the battles of Lexington and Concord in 1775. Although General Butler was not directly involved at Baltimore, having arrived in Washington, D.C., he became associated historically with this engagement that preceded the more devastating encounters between North and South later in the war.

The Sixth Massachusetts Regiment was quartered in the Senate chamber when it reached Washington. President Lincoln personally welcomed this first fighting unit as it set up its temporary headquarters in the Senate. It was joined in strategic defense of the city by the Fourth Massachusetts Regiment, based at Fort Monroe, Virginia.

Within a few weeks of the Baltimore event military victims of the clash were buried in their native soil in Massachusetts. The soldiers—the first Civil War fatalities, for the bombardment of Fort Sumter had killed no one—were Sumner H. Needham of Lawrence, Luther C. Ladd and Addison O. Whitney of Lowell, and Charles A. Taylor, whose residence was unknown.

General Butler, of Lowell, was one of a handful of Massachusetts natives whose connection with the military granted a prominence he might otherwise not have enjoyed. Butler's activities during the Civil War were both notorious and notable. A lawyer, he had twice run unsuccessfully for governor before the war, but later was elected to that office in 1882. Butler was a Republican congressman during the postwar years, and he ran for president of the United States in 1884 on the Anti-Monopoly and Greenback tickets. He was perhaps best known for his behavior during the occupation of New Orleans.

In May 1862, just after becoming military governor of that Louisiana city, General Butler issued a document to its citizens, a decree known as General Order Number 28, or the "Woman Order." In it, Butler made clear his uncompromising position toward the conquered city and its proud residents. The text of Order Number 28 reads in part, "As the officers and soldiers of the United States have been subjected to repeated insults from the women (calling themselves ladies) of New Orleans . . . when any female shall . . . show contempt for the United States, she shall be regarded as a woman of the town plying her avocation."

It was due in part to this ill-mannered and unnecessary directive that President Lincoln removed Butler from command in December 1862. Butler's disregard for convention and lack of tact in dealing with the inhabitants of New Orleans was long remembered as another example of Yankee bad manners. In Butler's defense, it is true that none of his military successes are recalled when Order Number 28 is cited as an example of his incompetence as a military leader.

Another famous Massachusetts native

Below: *On December 11, 1862, Massachusetts and Michigan volunteer troops cross the Rappahannock River toward Stafford Heights, Virginia, in an effort to drive off Confederate sharpshooters who are aiming at the soldiers assembling prefabricated bridge sections. The result of this battle was 300 Union men killed, and possibly more than that number of Confederate dead, as the North took possession of the riverfront, finishing the bridge for future assaults. From Mottelay and Campbell-Copeland,* Frank Leslie's Illustrations: The Soldier in Our Civil War, *Vol. II, 1900*

Clara Barton (1821-1912), the founder of the American Red Cross, was born on a farm in Oxford, Massachusetts. She became a teacher, then worked in the Patent Office in Washington. After the Battle of Bull Run she saw the suffering of the wounded and ran an ad in the Worcester Spy *asking for supplies to help them; so much came that she began a dispensing agency. Barton was not primarily a hospital nurse, but worked heroically at several battle scenes, providing medical supplies. In 1869 she went to Europe for a rest, but worked there with the International Red Cross. When she came home she began the American Red Cross. Courtesy, National Headquarters, American Red Cross, Washington, D.C.*

made a major contribution toward the Union war effort: Brigadier General Joseph Hooker. A native of Hadley, Hooker graduated from West Point and was named brigadier general of volunteer troops in the Washington, D.C. region between August and October 1861.

A tall, blue-eyed man described by a contemporary as "the handsomest soldier I ever laid eyes on," Hooker was named the fourth head of the Army of the Potomac in 1862. He held this post for six months but resigned from his command a few days before the battle of Gettysburg and was replaced by George Meade.

As the war dragged on, President Lincoln put out a call for additional militia from all states. Among those who answered that call was the 54th "Colored" Regiment from Massachusetts, under the command of Colonel Robert Gould Shaw, a white officer. The poet Henry Wadsworth Longfellow, observing this regiment of black soldiers drilling in the streets of Boston, commented that it was an "imposing sight, with something wild and strange about it, like a dream." Shaw and his regiment were memorialized by a Saint-Gaudens sculpture now on the Boston Common. The 54th Regiment was one of many black regiments fighting for the Union during the Civil War. An intense desire to rid the nation of slavery was a common bond among all Union soldiers, black and white, and there was a total of 53,000 black enlistees from free states

The Civil War experience probably had one positive result in the improved efficiency of local fire companies. Here the Pontoonsuc Engine Company shows off in Pittsfield in December 1867. Courtesy, The Berkshire Atheneum

such as Massachusetts.

While the Civil War fighting raged out of state, much war-related activity occurred in Massachusetts. Massachusetts was joined early in its efforts to preserve the Union by 17 other nonslave states—Maine, New Hampshire, Vermont, Rhode Island, Connecticut, New York, New Jersey, Pennsylvania, Ohio, Indiana, Illinois, Wisconsin, Iowa, Minnesota, Kansas, Oregon, and California. The western part of Virginia had opposed that state's secession from the Union, and with its almost total absence of slavery the region had separated from the state. West Virginia was admitted to the Union as a state in 1863. Four border slave states—Kentucky, Delaware, Missouri, and Maryland—also remained loyal to the Union.

Massachusetts, the site of the initial battles of the War for Independence almost a century before, was saved from the destruction and ravages of the Civil War experienced by the southern states.

However, Bay State soldiers enlisted and died in large numbers to save the Union. Massachusetts suffered 13,942 casualties during the war out of a total state enlistment of 122,781 white troops, 3,966 black troops, and 19,983 sailors.

Battles in which Massachusetts regiments participated ranged from Antietam to Fredericksburg, Cold Harbor to Malvern Hill, and Gettysburg to Appomattox Courthouse.

Throughout the hard, lonely months of fighting and waiting for battles to begin, Yankee soldiers comforted themselves with stories of home and songs of sweethearts, bravery, and patriotic pride. Among these songs was the *Battle Hymn of the Republic,* written by Massachusetts native Julia Ward Howe. She composed the words in the early weeks of war while her husband, Dr. Samuel Gridley Howe, was inspecting Bay State troops in the nation's capital. It was a haunting hymn that soon came to represent all the Union army stood for.

WAR MANUFACTURE AND WAR PROFIT

During the war, manufacture of firearms was centered chiefly in New England, which supplied regiments such as the Sixth Massachusetts, the 54th, and others. Smith & Wesson of Springfield was, next to Colt Firearms in Connecticut, the foremost manufacturer of revolvers. Most of these saw little use during actual battle, however, as their range was too limited. Only after the Civil War did Smith & Wesson develop revolvers in a caliber high enough to be useful in large-scale combat. But Smith & Wesson undoubtedly benefited from the lessons learned during the many battles fought. That weapons manufacture, founded by Horace Smith and Daniel B. Wesson in 1853, along with the Springfield Armory (maker of the "Springfield" rifle), made this western Massachusetts city prominent in arms manufacture right through to the twentieth century. In Chicopee, north of Springfield, Savage Arms began producing major armaments for the United States military in 1864. However unpleasant their business, it is clear that

arms manufacturers of Massachusetts and surrounding areas gained a great deal from the suffering of the country as a whole.

Massachusetts was not new to innovation, either in arms manufacture or in other entrepreneurial areas. For more than two centuries, the state had been home to a number of inventive geniuses, and despite interruptions of the Civil War the state's cities and towns continued to be spawning grounds for new ideas in manufacture, agriculture, science, and education.

The town of Sterling, north of Worcester in central Massachusetts, was home to tailor Ebenezer Butterick, inventor of the first standardized paper patterns for shirts, suits, dresses, etc. Butterick's 1859 invention was a sweeping success that grew into the large company now known as Butterick Patterns. Sterling was also the home of two brothers, Silas and Lucian Stuart, who devised a way to mass-produce sewing machine needles. Nearby Spencer was home to Elias Howe, inventor of the home sewing machine, which was patented in 1846.

An anti-Catholic mob of hundreds burned the Charlestown convent of St. Ursula on the night of August 11, 1834. Fire companies responded to the alarm, but did very little to douse the flames. The ruins were left for many years, a stark reminder of the mob's violence. From Winsor, The Memorial History of Boston, 1630-1880, *Vol. III, 1881*

IMMIGRATION AND XENOPHOBIA

After the Civil War ended, Massachusetts—like other states across the war-weary nation—was affected by the inevitable chaos occurring with a shift to a peacetime economy. Returning soldiers needed work, and immigrant labor was gradually increasing in number. In Boston, the population grew at a steady pace following the Civil War. By 1880, there were 1,783,000 people in Massachusetts of whom 362,839 lived in the state capital. In 1890, Boston's population had grown to 448,477. The entire population of the United States stood at 50,155,783 in 1880—much of it clustered along the Atlantic seaboard in the Northeast.

The state population in the decades following the Civil War is of continuing interest to historians. Among the most obvious changes in Massachusetts' demography during these years was an increase in non-native-born citizens. Although immigrants were common prior to 1860, the state's population expanded tremendously after 1870 as French Canadians, Scandinavians, Eastern Europeans, and some Asians joined the thousands of Bay State factory and agricultural workers in cities like Boston, Springfield, Worcester, and Pittsfield.

For example, in 1875, 60,000 foreign-born Irish called Boston home, and by the end of the 1890s the Irish represented about 35 percent of the city's entire population. By the final decade of the nineteenth century, the influx of Irish had abated slightly, only to be replaced by a wave of Jews, Italians, Poles, and others from Eastern Europe.

The pattern was the same, whether it was Boston, New York, or Chicago. Immigrants worked hard, putting in long hours at factories or on farms. Women and children joined husbands, fathers, and brothers in sweatshop factories, pooling their wages into a meager total per family. All were determined that Massachusetts should live up to the promise it held out to them: freedom and a new way of life, a release from oppression, hunger, and fear.

Despite their high hopes, many immigrants found life was not easy in the United States. Before the Civil War, a nativist influence in the Massachusetts state government tolerated anti-foreign, anti-Catholic sentiments, provoking a considerable number of confrontations between native-born Americans and immigrants. Riots involving foreigners, who were usually Roman Catholic, and native-born Massachusetts residents, who were often Protestant, were all too frequent. In 1834, a Roman Catholic convent in Charlestown was burned to the ground. Such incidents and other manifestations of a growing nativist influence had, by the post-Civil War era, proved that native-born citizens feared losing their jobs and were outraged by religious practices contrasting so obviously with their own. But immigrants to Massachusetts were tenacious. They did not succumb to intimidation and threats of harm, as their desires for comfort, a steady living, and a safe life matched those of the native-born. Somehow, the two groups maintained an uneasy coexistence, and in many communities they learned to work side by side for the good life they all hoped for.

Newburyport, north of Boston, saw an influx of Irish Catholics during the middle to late decades of the 1800s, and Lawrence became heavily Roman Catholic during the same period. In 1881, an Irish Catholic became mayor of that city, the first non-Protestant elected to office there. Southbridge saw an influx of French-Canadian immigrant labor that soon transformed the community, a phenomenon as much the result of active recruiting on the part of manufacturers as it was a result of chance immigration.

This immigrant wave was the second of three such surges of foreigners who sought a new beginning in America. The first wave, between 1820 and 1860, brought mostly Germans and other Northern Europeans to Massachusetts. Most were Protestants, but already some groups of Roman Catholic immigrants had settled in the Bay State. The second immigrant wave arrived between 1860 and 1890 and comprised about 15 million people, as compared to 5 million in the earlier group. Boston was the nation's second-largest port of entry in 1880—58,000 immigrants arrived there in one year. Of the city's total population in 1880, 54 percent were Massachusetts-born, 32 percent were foreign-born, and

This cartoon in the Boston Sunday Globe in 1886 reveals the fear generated by "anarchist" immigrants from Hungary and Poland, as well as the fact that most of these immigrants were attracted to America by the availability of jobs—jobs that were provided because they would work for less than those already here. The caption reads: "Uncle Sam: 'Who are these fellows? Why are they coming here?' Mr. Contractor: 'I sent to Hungary and Poland for them. They come cheaper than the natives or the decent immigrants.' Uncle Sam: 'Yes, but they are bomb-throwers. Who's going to pay the police and military bills?' Mr. Contractor: 'That's your lookout. My duty is simply to buy my labor in the cheapest market.'" From the Boston Sunday Globe, May 16, 1886

The pride of Fitchburg was its magnificent railroad station, which handled Boston-to-Albany passengers and most of the east-west, west-east traffic in the 1870s and 1880s. From Jewett, History of Worcester County, *Vol. I, 1879*

the rest were born elsewhere in the United States.

This changed ratio of foreign-born to native-born meant that change in the social fabric of towns and cities was inevitable. Furthermore, relations between workers and employers were changing. Labor union activism was perceived as a direct result of immigrant labor. It represented foreign influence on a democratic, capitalist society. By the 1880s, when labor union activism in Massachusetts and elsewhere provoked demonstrations and riots, newspapers pounced on these incidents as proof that something terrible was happening. The effect of such reporting increased nativism and xenophobia and caused more suspicion and hatred among Massachusetts residents who were different from each other.

One facet of mutual distrust was the growing favor parochial schools held with Roman Catholic parents. Such schools, set apart from the public schools that native-born children attended, were seen by the native-born as threatening imminent takeover by Rome. In Boston, a minister with well-developed nativist leanings—the Reverend Justin Fulton—spoke to enthusiastic crowds of fearful residents who worried that the pope was going to usurp all parental (and governmental) power in the United States. It was a time of almost unrelieved suspicion and antagonism, inevitable to a certain degree, but these impulses existed alongside other, more constructive ones that helped build the Bay State into a stronger, more flexible and welcoming

No. 24 B.

1892.   Corrected to June 6.   1892.

Official Time-Table

OF THE

BOSTON & ALBANY

RAILROAD COMPANY.

Subject to Change and Corrections without Notice.

This Time-Table shows the times at which trains may
be expected to arrive at, and depart from, the several
stations; but their arrival or departure at the times stated
is not guaranteed, nor does the Company hold itself
responsible for any delay, or any consequences arising
therefrom.

* ——INCIVILITY.—— *

Passengers are respectfully requested to report to the
General Superintendent any instance of incivility on the
part of employés of this Company. While it is the aim
of the Company to redress just grievances, it is suggested
that courtesy is equally commendable, whether practised
by the railroad employé or the passenger.

H. T. GALLUP,   A. S. HANSON,
Gen'l Superintendent,   *Gen'l Pass'r Agent,*
SPRINGFIELD.   BOSTON.

B. A. SUPPLY CO., BOSTON.

*Railroad tickets from the 1890s were
often specific about behavior aboard
the trains. Incivility was not to be
tolerated. Courtesy, The Walter C.
and Sarah H. Jones Collection*

environment for all citizens, immigrant or
native-born.

RAILROADS AND LABOR MOVEMENTS

Railroads were one development that
helped provide a leavening agent. After
1860, more and more rail activity
occurred throughout the United States.
Before the Civil War, only a limited
amount of railroad lines were available,
about 65 percent of them in the
Northeast. Massachusetts had committed
nearly $7.2 million to railroad promotion
by the time of the Civil War. But despite
its promise, railroads had only limited
usefulness, as the existing mass of
track—some 35,000 miles total
throughout the nation—was made up of
small, local lines using different track

gauges. Soon after the Civil War, 10,000
miles of new track was hammered into
place—most of it in standard gauge. This
resulted in an enormous railroad network
connecting all areas of the country. This
development continued, and by the
1890s, tracks in the United States
represented one-third of the entire
railroad mileage in the world.

A postwar burst of industrial activity
was concurrent with general railroad
expansion but lasted little more than a
decade. In 1873, a series of economic
depressions affected virtually every part
of the nation, hitting especially hard in
Massachusetts factories, prompting
wholesale layoffs and a drop in textile
workers' wages for those lucky enough to

THE HOOSAC TUNNEL

Amid the bustle of early nineteenth-century American life, a constant clamor for new technologies produced revolutionary items like the cotton gin and the sewing machine. Eventually, these two inventions would help boost the textile output of Massachusetts, placing the state in the forefront of northern industrial economies. Other inventions were designed to further various interests in the Bay State and elsewhere. Some were successful, like the revolver, the steel plow, and the process of vulcanizing rubber. Others have long been forgotten. Among innovations that helped transform America was dynamite, the product of years of research by Swedish scientist Alfred Nobel. Dynamite led directly to a project of some importance in western Massachusetts: the Hoosac Tunnel.

This engineering marvel of the 1800s, located near North Adams, was the brainchild of Alvah Crocker. A prosperous Fitchburg industrialist, Crocker hoped to tap into the lucrative shipping trade of the Erie Canal. But in order for Crocker's mills in Fitchburg to access the Erie Canal, it was necessary to devise a quick, relatively inexpensive means of transport across western Massachusetts. There the craggy, uneven terrain made overland transportation costly and time-consuming and construction of a canal impossible.

Crocker's solution was a tunnel. Construction of this tunnel was begun in 1851 and its ultimate purpose would be to speed up rail shipment of goods and materials to and from Fitchburg.

Hoosac Mountain was the natural stone barrier through which Crocker's engineers would drill. Crocker's expectation was that this tunnel would take three years to build. But after 10 years,

using steam drills and black powder, workers had only gone about one-third of the way through the mountain rock.

Nobel's invention—dynamite—was a major contributor toward hastening the project. And Alvah Crocker's willingness to invest in new technologies brought compressed air drills and remote control detonators to the site. The Hoosac Tunnel was thus integral to the development of industrial America. Without this Massachusetts mill owner's desire to increase his productivity, many of the skills and procedures developed during the building of the Hoosac Tunnel may have been longer in coming.

Crocker's desire to complete the tunnel within three years was unrealistic at best. The Hoosac Tunnel was 24 years in the making and was a project that claimed the lives of 195 miners between 1851 and 1875. The opening at the eastern end of the tunnel carries the inscription "1875," and bears only a mute testimony to those nearly 200 workers who spent many hard, fruitless hours tunneling through the solid facade of Hoosac Mountain. And along with Crocker's need to complete the project within a handful of years was his expectation that the tunnel would result in increased profits for his Fitchburg mills. Ultimately, Crocker was proven wrong about this as well. Over the 24 years that it took to build, the Hoosac Tunnel cost $14 million and was never able to develop Crocker's mills into the most important economic factor in Massachusetts.

The entrance to the 25,031-foot tunnel is still visible, tucked away in the overgrowth on the side of Hoosac Mountain. Nowhere to be seen are the two million tons of rock, removed during

excavation. Neither is it possible to view easily the 20 million bricks used to line the inside arches of the tunnel for nearly five miles. But the now-obsolete tunnel remains a monument to the miners, engineers, and common laborers who devoted their working lives to its completion. The vitality of these men represented the economic vigor surging through the state and the nation throughout the nineteenth century. It was this vigor that paved the way for even greater industrial and technological innovations in the twentieth century.

In an article titled "Feats of Railway Engineering," Scribner's Magazine *in July 1888 ran this picture of a tunnel construction technique that was pioneered during the building of the Hoosac Tunnel. Wood framing was used to line the tunnel as it was bored out, while rock and debris were removed by shovel and cart.*

★　　★　　★　　★　　★　　★　　★

The Montague Paper Company in the village of Turner's Falls, Montague, was organized in 1871 by Colonel Alva Crocker of Fitchburg and Edwin Bulkley of New York, both of whom also owned the pulp company next door. Employing 250 people, they daily manufactured 10 tons of newsprint and book paper in 1879. From Everts, History of the Connecticut Valley in Massachusetts, *Vol. II, 1879*

hold their jobs. In the immediate postwar years, while industrial expansion continued, there was a gradual increase in labor activism. Ira Steward, a factory worker in Boston, organized the Grand Eight-Hour League of Massachusetts, hoping to promote legislation supporting shorter work days. The league became a model for other groups throughout the country also wanting to improve working conditions for average laborers.

Another union group involved shoemakers—the Knights of St. Crispin, one of 32 national trade unions in existence by 1870. Many Massachusetts workers belonged to this union, particularly in centers such as Lynn, the top shoe-manufacturing city in the country. The union gave both identity and a degree of political power to its members. In 1887, the Massachusetts Federation of Labor was formed, part of the national organization known as the American Federation of Labor, or A.F. of L. The latter replaced the defunct Knights of Labor, the first nationwide labor union of its type in the United States.

Much of this labor activity was a facet of general attempts to change society during what was known as the Gilded Age. For radical labor activists, this change helped workers. Other activists bent on different kinds of reform saw change as a means of upgrading the quality of living for others. Schools, museums, new church buildings, religious evangelism, new types of books and learned essays on all subjects, as well as actions taken by self-styled social welfare workers, characterized the three or four reform decades leading to the turn of the century.

EXCELLENCE IN EDUCATION

In Northfield, near the Vermont border and close by the Connecticut River,

A prominent Massachusetts woman of the nineteenth century was Maria Mitchell (1818-1889) from Nantucket and later from Lynn. A capable astronomer who had won fame early when she discovered a comet, she became Vassar's first professor of astronomy in 1865. Miss Mitchell was a role model for her students and other women, who saw her achievements as an example of what a woman could accomplish as a scholar. From Kendall, Maria Mitchell, Life, Letters, and Journals, *1896*

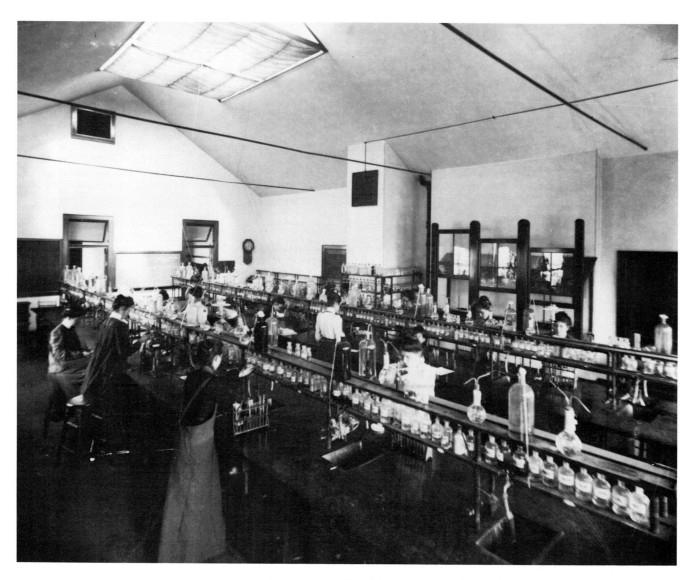

Above: *Young women at Mount Holyoke College in South Hadley are shown here about 1900 conducting experiments amid Florence flasks and test tubes in Shattuck Hall, the physics and chemistry building that has since been demolished. Courtesy, Mount Holyoke College Library/ Archives*

Left: *H.H. Richardson's Trinity Church faces the Boston Public Library across a refurbished Copley Square in Boston. Richardson had the rough granite edifice, with its cavernous arches and asymmetrical lines, built on 4,500 wooden piles in the soggy Back Bay of 1872. Architects of public buildings across Massachusetts and the nation copied Richardson's Gothic style. Today the interesting lines are reflected wonderfully in the mirroring sides of the towering John Hancock Building next door. Photo by John H. Martin*

Facing page, bottom: *Under the 1862 Morrill Land Grant Act, states were given land in the West to be sold in order to finance the establishment of agricultural colleges such as Massachusetts Agricultural College, seen here in 1871. Another proviso required the young men (there were no women at Mass Aggie until 1899) to have military training. The name was changed to Massachusetts State College in 1931, and to the University of Massachusetts in 1947. Today there is a two-year Stockbridge School of Agriculture and four-year majors in agriculture-related fields, but the departments are small and overshadowed by the arts and sciences, and by engineering, computer, and business schools. In this 1871 view, the year the first class graduated, South College is on the left, North College is in the center, and the Old Chemistry Building is on the right. Courtesy, Special Collections and Archives, Library, University of Massachusetts at Amherst*

evangelist Dwight L. Moody's interest in religious education led him to found the Northfield Seminary in 1879. Moody, a Northfield native, had moved to Boston shortly before his 20th birthday. In 1856, after experiencing a religious conversion, he moved to Chicago where he began his evangelical work with orphaned children and with the poor. Moody garnered support from rich and influential people like Cyrus McCormick and George Armour. Moody was president of the YMCA in Chicago and a few years later preached in England, campaigning for converts and telling people that eternal life was theirs.

The Northfield Seminary, a school for young women, was mirrored in 1881 by a similar institution for young men, the Mount Hermon School, also in North-field. The schools merged in 1971 and are now known as the Northfield Mount Hermon School, a coeducational, college preparatory school of high quality and

fine reputation.

Other new educational institutions of the period include Smith College in Northampton, founded in 1875 through the generosity of Sophia Smith, a native of nearby Hatfield. Smith College was designed to promote the development of "the intelligent gentlewoman," and was well regarded as soon as it opened. Similarly, Wellesley College, founded in 1870, and Radcliffe College, founded in 1879, contributed to Massachusetts' prominence in post-secondary education of women. Mount Holyoke College had been founded in 1837 and was, like the others, part of a larger, national trend. Post-secondary education for women was new, and some institutions dedicated to this goal existed outside of New England. In Massachusetts, however, women of the late nineteenth century found a wide variety of educational opportunities.

In 1862, the United States Congress passed the Morrill Land Grant Act,

Daniel Webster (1782-1852) was born in New Hampshire, but became famous in the government of Massachusetts. A lawyer and popular orator, Webster championed states' rights, but as a U.S. senator from Massachusetts he changed his mind and delivered great pre-Civil War speeches about compromise between the North and South. He died in Marshfield at his home before the Civil War erupted. Painting attributed to Joseph Alexander Ames. Courtesy, Massachusetts Historical Society

Winslow Homer (1836-1910) was born in Boston, reared in Cambridge, and apprenticed for two years to a Boston lithographer. The Berry Pickers is a watercolor painted during the summer of 1873, which Homer spent on an island in Gloucester Harbor, away from his New York studio. Homer is famous for his marine paintings, but he often sought out gentle scenes reminiscent of old-fashioned rural life. Courtesy, Harold T. Pulsifer Memorial Collection, Colby College Art Museum, Waterville, Maine

In Boston Common at Twilight, *Frederick Childe Hassam captures a rather well-to-do woman and two girls admiring the birds on the Tremont Street side of the famous green. Behind them bustle the horse-drawn cars and private carriages of 1885 Boston. Courtesy, Museum of Fine Arts, Boston. Gift of Miss Maud E. Appleton*

Above: *The vista of the Connecticut River Valley from Mount Holyoke has attracted numerous artists and writers as well as sightseers. This view was painted in 1903 by David John Gue (1836-1917). Mount Holyoke rises 954 feet on the east side of the river, while Mount Tom rises on the west side. Dinosaur tracks can still be found in the shale on the river's edge nearby. Courtesy, Mount Holyoke College Art Museum, South Hadley, Massachusetts. Gift of Mr. John Dwight, 1903*

Left: *In 1905, before the era of the affordable automobile, this Trolley Wayfinder was essential to many New Englanders. Red areas indicate parks, red lines indicate electric railways, and blue lines indicate steam railways. The map cost 10 cents and folded conveniently for pocket use. With the advent of this system of inexpensive travel, many people could now move out of the cities and commute to work. Whole new suburban neighborhoods sprang up in the era of the trolley, and new recreation areas vied for the business of working people on Sundays. Photo by Paul Carew. Courtesy, The Jones Library, Inc., Amherst. Gift of Mildred H. Dickinson*

Facing page: *The flowering court at the Isabella Stewart Gardner Museum on the Fenway in Boston is part of a setting envisioned by Mrs. Gardner when she collected art pieces and built her great mansion. The galleries of her Venetian Palazzo, finished in 1902, hold Whistlers, Matisses, and Titians, as well as seventeenth-century tapestries, exquisite examples of needlepoint lace, ceramic tiles, and tooled leather wall coverings. She lived on the top floor from 1902 until her death in 1924. Today, the museum maintains the courtyard and galleries as she wished, and holds musical programs three times a week. Courtesy, The Isabella Stewart Gardner Museum*

The Wayside Inn Gristmill in Sudbury, built in 1929 by Henry Ford and J.D. Campbell, grinds corn and wheat into flour, as did an older mill near the same site. It operates from April 1 to November 30 each year and draws more visitors than the historic inn itself. Photo by Justine Hill

Boston's "New Old South" Church, completed in 1874, utilized the then-fashionable Northern Italian Gothic style with a campanile, decorated belfry, pyramidal spire, and low-pitched roof. From Gillon, Early Illustrations and Views of American Architecture, *Dover, 1971*

which provided each state with acreage for an agricultural college. Massachusetts located its institution in Amherst, later branching out into several other areas of the state. The $208,464 allotted for the Massachusetts Agricultural College, or "Mass Aggie," was funding that helped establish the state's later prominence in agricultural and scientific research and development. Smaller state-sponsored colleges would later flourish, all having grown from this original Civil War-era legislation.

ARCHITECTURE, ARTS, AND LITERATURE

Other manifestations of post-Civil War reform impulses could be seen in architecture, which lent itself to both creative expression and visible environmental change. Some architectural projects that now grace Massachusetts cities and towns are memorials to the ideas that grew so rampantly in the 1870s, 1880s, and 1890s.

Trinity Church, at Boston's Copley Square in the Back Bay, was designed and built by Henry Hobson Richardson. Its construction period extended from 1872 to 1878 and provided a livelihood for many workers throughout the first of several economic downturns. Richardson was one of the paramount figures in Massachusetts architecture, and edifices which were the result of his enthusiasm for Romanesque style include railroad

stations in Auburndale and Wellesley Hills, both built during the early 1880s. He also designed the Woburn and Quincy public libraries, built in 1877 and 1880, respectively.

The new Back Bay church erected by the Old South Church congregation was the project of architect Charles Cummings, a student of John Ruskin, who designed and built Harvard College's Gothic style Memorial Hall. A contemporary of Richardson, Cummings, and Ruskin, Charles Follen McKim, designed the Neoclassical revival-style Boston Public Library, which was completed in 1895. The library contains many other examples of the creative genius of this period, among them bronze bas-relief doors by sculptor Daniel Chester French and murals painted by John Singer Sargent. Throughout the state, numerous libraries, town halls, churches, and schools copied fashionable styles promoted by these leading architects of the Gilded Age.

Literature of the post-Civil War period changed along with the physical surroundings in which it was written. Nathaniel Hawthorne and Henry David Thoreau had been published for several decades when styles in popular reading matter began to change. William Dean Howells and Henry James wrote con-

The original Museum of Fine Arts in Boston, built on Huntington Avenue at Dartmouth Street in 1876 and 1890, was constructed by Sturgis and Brigham in an extravagant Ruskian Gothic style of terra cotta ornamentation on a vivid polychrome facade. Incidentally, the two towers shown here were never finished. The museum boasted a gallery of casts—reproductions of Greek, Roman, Egyptian, and Assyrian sculpture. It also had a school of drawing and painting, as well as a school of carving and modeling, to train people for careers in art. In 1912 the museum moved out to the Fenway, and the Copley Plaza Hotel took this site. From Gillon, Early Illustrations and Views of American Architecture, *Dover, 1971*

Winslow Homer (1836-1910) spent the summer of 1873 on an island off Gloucester where he painted this watercolor, "Boys Wading." This tranquil low tide harbor scene of blue water and sparkling light reveals another side of Homer, whose more famous paintings are often violent and wild ocean scenes. Courtesy, Colby College Art Museum

Edwin Romanzo Elmer's "A Lady of Baptist Corner, Ashfield, Massachusetts," painted in 1892, depicts the artist's wife, Mary Jane (Ware) Elmer, twisting silk thread into a buggy lash on a machine supplied by the Westfield Whip Company. Many area women made money at this unusual cottage industry. The artist, whose masterful use of light is particularly evident in this painting, was unknown until recently. Courtesy, Smith College Museum of Art, gift of E. Porter Dickinson

vincingly about Boston, although James (and his psychologist-brother, William James) was born in New York City and Howells was a midwesterner by birth. Poet John Greenleaf Whittier, of Haverhill, was well-loved for his writings, among them the poem "Snowbound," written in 1866, which countless schoolchildren have since been required to memorize and recite. Among great historians of the nineteenth century, Francis Parkman, of impeccable Boston Brahmin lineage, was perhaps the most famous. George Bancroft of Worcester became celebrated for his 10-volume *History of the United States,* published between 1834 and 1874.

Many painters and artists in various media lived and worked in the Bay State during the late 1800s. One of the best-loved was Winslow Homer, whose seascapes, many of them painted in Maine, represent the quintessential New England scene. James McNeill Whistler was another Massachusetts native, born in Lowell, who found it more reassuring to paint elsewhere. Whistler went to Paris to study painting when he was 20 and never returned to the United States, refusing even to admit any connection at all to his Bay State heritage. According to a biographer, Whistler would cheerfully and emphatically deny his Lowell birth.

An American accosted Whistler in the Carlton Restaurant, London: "You know, we were both born in Lowell, Massachusetts, and at very much the same time."

"Most interesting, no doubt, and as you please," Whistler replied, "But I shall be born when and where I want, and I do not choose to be born at Lowell."

Daniel Chester French, the sculptor who created the bronze doors for the Boston Public Library and the statue of Abraham Lincoln for the Lincoln Memorial in Washington, D.C., was not a native of Massachusetts, but he studied in Concord and Boston. He worked for a period with May Alcott, sister of the novelist Louisa May Alcott (and

daughter of transcendentalist Bronson Alcott). In 1875, French was acclaimed as a great talent with the unveiling of his monument, *The Minute Man*, at the Old North Bridge in Concord. He also worked with architect Charles Follen McKim to produce the statue *Alma Mater* for Columbia University.

French's summer retreat in the Berkshires was the site of his early studies for the Lincoln statue. Known as "Chesterwood," the home was purchased in 1896 and French said about it, "I spend six months of the year up there. That is heaven." He was among many wealthy and creative individuals for whom the Berkshires was a summer resort. The area's development was

Sculptor Daniel Chester French (1850-1931) lived as a young man in Amherst and Concord. He maintained a studio in New York City, but he spent summers at his estate/studio, Chesterwood, in Stockbridge. Some of French's most well-known sculptures are "John Harvard," the bronze doors at the Boston Public Library, the Concord "Minute Man," and "Abraham Lincoln" at the Lincoln Memorial in Washington, D.C. His Stockbridge estate, where he died, is now a National Trust property open to the public. From Cirker, Dictionary of American Portraits, *Dover, 1967*

greatly enhanced by the contributions of these sometime inhabitants, right through to the late twentieth century. Today, the entire French estate, including his studio, is part of the National Trust for Historic Preservation and is open to public view.

Patron of many Massachusetts painters, literary figures, musicians, and other celebrities, Isabella Stewart Gardner and her husband, financier John Gardner, assembled an outstanding collection of classical and contemporary paintings and art objects. She gave

famous parties and receptions and was known for her self-indulgent eccentricities. Upon her death in 1924, the reproduction villa built to hold her art collection was willed to the city of Boston as a public museum to be preserved without change. Isabella Stewart Gardner was a part of the last great flowering of art patronage that occurred prior to the turn of the century.

Other Massachusetts natives prominent in public life during the mid- and late nineteenth century include elected

Left: *Isabella Stewart Gardner (1840-1924) was 48 when John Singer Sargent painted her portrait. Mrs. Gardner is wearing three ropes of her famous pearls, each rope hung with a large ruby. Courtesy, Isabella Stewart Gardner Museum*

Far left: *In the middle to late 1800s scenic vistas became popular with artists, and the hilly, western part of the state, with its river valleys and craggy peaks, was painted frequently. Here the Connecticut River Valley is seen from Mount Tom, as reproduced in an 1874 book of scenic places. To be published in a book, the painting had to be transformed into print form. By the 1890s the technology for reproducing photographs into print was achieved, but putting color paintings onto the printed page was a long way off. From Bryant,* Pictorial America, *1874*

and appointed officials in various presidential administrations. Many of them came from distinguished lineages that had seen decades of stalwart service to state and nation. Others were new in the public arena but competent and dedicated nevertheless. Those named to the cabinet post of U.S. secretary of state were Daniel Webster (1841-1843 and 1850-1852), Edward Everett (1852-1853), and Richard Olney (1895-1897). George Boutwell (1869-1873) was U.S. secretary of the treasury and Caleb Cushing was U.S. attorney general (1853-1857), as was Ebenezer Hoar (1869-1870), General Charles Devens (1877-1881), and Richard Olney (1893-1895). These men made contributions to national development during years when both territorial and economic growth were at an unprecedented high. Much of this growth laid the foundation for future expansion and increased power in the twentieth century when the world was unwittingly preparing for the changes to be wrought by war, severe economic chaos, and a more complex diplomacy.

URBANIZATION AND LABOR UNREST (1890-1914)

★   ★   ★   ★   ★   ★   ★   ★   ★

This photo of a Boston three-decker was used in a state report on immigrants and their housing and the "problems" of Americanizing the newcomers. From Report of the Commission on Immigration on the Problem of Immigration in Massachusetts, *1914*

During the last half of the nineteenth century, political turmoil and disorganization marked election activities in the United States. In Massachusetts this upheaval both paralleled and reflected changes in Bay State social fabric. The Democrats were in the minority. There were no Democratic congressmen from Massachusetts until 1876, so strong was Republican sentiment in the state.

Among leading Republican party members were Henry Cabot Lodge of Boston and George Frisbie Hoar of Worcester, the latter a follower of the outspoken Massachusetts antislavery advocate, Senator Charles Sumner. Hoar was also an ardent abolitionist, and was best known for his role as chief author of the Sherman Antitrust Act of 1890. At a time when imperialism ruled the nation's foreign policy, Hoar was one of the few politicians who did not support the U.S. effort to conquer the Philippines during the Spanish-American War.

Although many in Massachusetts agreed with Hoar's anti-imperialist views, he and his supporters were in the minority.

Imperialism held sway in the United States in 1895 when Cuba, off the coast of Florida, was in rebellion. All over the United States newspapers carried stories of struggles between Cuban rebels and the island's Spanish government. The situation seemed in some ways to replicate the story of the colonists' bid for self-government and freedom from British rule 120 years earlier. In Massachusetts, the battles of Lexington and Concord in 1775 appeared to be historic blueprints for Cuban action in 1895. Those whose interests warranted it called for U.S. intervention and aid on behalf of Cuban rebels fighting what was termed an undesirable government. Senator Henry Cabot Lodge was one of those most eager for the United States to get involved in the Cuban rebellion.

After several unsuccessful bids for

Mary Baker Eddy (1821-1910) from New Hampshire founded the Christian Science Church in Boston in 1879. In 1892, when this photograph was taken, the First Church of Christ Scientist in its present form was begun in Boston. Mrs. Eddy had written the religion's textbook, Science and Health with a Key to the Scriptures, *in 1875, and one of her final achievements was the founding of the widely respected newspaper,* The Christian Science Monitor, *in 1908. Used by permission of the Christian Science Board of Directors*

public office, Lodge had been elected to Congress in 1886. He thereafter enjoyed a prominent position in the Republican party for almost 40 years. In 1893, he became a United States senator—with a decidedly pro-imperialist position concerning the brewing Spanish-American conflict. Lodge was also an ardent proponent of immigration restrictions, and his activities on behalf of native-born Americans—and against the nation's immigrant population—were enthusiastically supported by many like-minded conservatives. Perhaps most important of all, Lodge was a friend of Theodore Roosevelt. Lodge, an instructor at Harvard University when Roosevelt was an undergraduate, was to be the progressive president's staunchest Mas-

sachusetts supporter in the early years of the twentieth century.

In 1898, Lodge saw his hopes realized for military action against the Cuban government. On February 15, 1898, the U.S. battleship *Maine* was blown up in Havana Harbor. More than 250 U.S. naval personnel were killed in the attack, the origins of which were never definitely determined, although Spanish complicity was suspected. U.S. public opinion was aroused and pro-war sentiments grew. The *Maine* incident's effect on the nation was electrifying. The pro-war faction—with Henry Cabot Lodge at its head—demanded instant and thorough vindication of the terrible "act of dirty treachery," as the *Maine*'s destruction was called by Theodore Roosevelt, who at that time was assistant U.S. secretary of the navy. By April 1898, President William McKinley reluctantly persuaded Congress that armed force in Cuba was the best way to stave off future difficulties with Spain. The warmongers were thrilled. Most people in Massachusetts and elsewhere supported the president's action as the only possible response to the *Maine* incident.

For most Massachusetts citizens, the declaration of war meant little, but it did provoke excitement and flurries of preparatory activity as several units of the military looked forward to mobilization. "Remember the *Maine*" was the rallying cry heard all across the state and the nation, as soldiers assembled prior to departure for the Cuban war theater.

About 20,000 Bay State soldiers took active part in the Spanish-American War. The Sixth Massachusetts Regiment, an infantry unit, was called to duty once more. This regiment, remembered for its early role in the Civil War, asked for and received permission to travel through Baltimore on its way to Cuba, retracing its route of nearly four decades before. This time the Sixth was greeted warmly by residents of the city who cheered the gallant Bay State soldiers on their way south.

Although the Sixth Massachusetts did

not see action during its short tour of duty in Cuba and Puerto Rico, the Second Massachusetts Infantry was part of the legendary battle of San Juan Hill on July 1, 1898. The Ninth Massachusetts Infantry was also sent to Cuba, and during 18 days at the scene of battle there, it lost 177 men.

Hostilities in Cuba ended when an armistice was signed in August 1898. The war officially concluded with the signing of the Treaty of Paris on December 10, when Cuba was freed but placed under U.S. jurisdiction. Meanwhile, an outbreak of military activity in the Philippine Islands introduced another phase in the conflict with Spain. First, annexation by the United States prompted a Philippine revolt, and occupation of the islands by U.S. troops provoked a war lasting three years. President Theodore Roosevelt eventually proclaimed an end to the Philippine insurrection on July 4, 1902.

SOCIAL REFORM

The nation turned hopeful eyes on the future, and many leaders in the late nineteenth and early twentieth centuries were known as zealous reformers. They hoped to improve everything from urban slums and public education to race relations and labor conditions. Between 1880 and 1920, there was an air of optimism that seemed to promise big improvements in many areas. In Massachusetts, there was an early effort which reflected the nationwide settlement-house movement. At Boston's Andover House, just as at the more famous Hull House in Chicago, social workers dedicated their energies to upgrading the lives of neighborhood people. Many of these social workers

W.E.B. Du Bois (1869-1963) is at front left in this photograph of people active in the Niagara Movement in 1907 in Boston. Du Bois is considered by some to be the father of the black-power movement, which later tried to blend civil rights integration with the more militant black nationalism. Courtesy, Special Collections and Archives, Library, University of Massachusetts at Amherst

often were graduates of Massachusetts women's colleges such as Smith, Mount Holyoke, Wellesley, and Radcliffe, as well as of coeducational institutions. These women were highly motivated, well-educated, and eager to take an active role in the reform of American society.

These reformers hoped to salvage urban dwellers from poverty and ignorance, but the urban poor represented only a small percentage of Massachusetts' total population. For the most part, Bay State residents had until now lived in smaller cities and towns where opportunities for aiding the less fortunate were generally limited. Between 1880 and 1920, however, the population increase in Massachusetts began to take place in cities rather than in the rural areas.

Many of those living in Massachusetts in the late nineteenth century were factory workers whose jobs were continually threatened by a major decline in the textile and other manufacturing industries. Reformers were for the most part unable to alter economic conditions creating recessions and depressions. Nor were they able to amend the social conditions surrounding the very real racial segregation that existed in northern, as well as southern, states at this time.

American blacks enjoyed little in the way of social or political progress. Some black leaders tried to effect change, however. Among them was William Edward Burghardt Du Bois. Born in 1868 in Great Barrington in western Massachusetts, he received a Ph.D. from Harvard University and became a spokesperson for black citizens who desired equality, an integrated society, and fair treatment. Du Bois was a cofounder of the committee which later became the National Association for the Advancement of Colored People. Formation of the NAACP marked a break between Du Bois, an integrationist, and Booker T. Washington. Washington preached self-sufficiency and segregation, promoting establishment of a black community operating separately from the white world, a community which would nevertheless be maintained without a radical departure from middle-class norms.

Du Bois was for the most part disappointed in his efforts to promote sweeping reforms for blacks in America and elsewhere. He spent the last two years of his life in Africa and died in 1963 after years of hard work. Du Bois' papers are maintained in a special collection at the library of the University of Massachusetts, Amherst. A memorial park is located on the site of Du Bois' childhood home in Great Barrington in the Berkshires.

Blacks were not alone in their struggle for integration. Massachusetts was changing and immigration was chiefly responsible for the new, and some said stronger, social fabric. Although nativists such as Henry Cabot Lodge were loathe to admit it, immigrant labor and the cultural pluralism resulting from a mix of nationalities across the state produced a more vital, vigorous population.

By the middle of the nineteenth century, Roman Catholic immigrants made up fully one-fifth of the Massachusetts population, most of them of Irish descent. The election of an Irish Catholic mayor, John Breen, in Lawrence in 1881, was symbolic of the gradual transformation of public opinion toward immigrants. Boston saw another Irish-born Roman Catholic, Hugh O'Brien, elected mayor in 1884. By 1885, the formerly antagonistic relationship between native-born Yankees and foreign-borns, such as O'Brien and Breen, had changed. In Boston, Thomas Gargan, an Irish lawyer, was chosen that same year by the Democrats to give the traditional Independence Day oration. Following the acceptance of Gargan, native-born and Irish Catholic speakers alternated as Fourth of July speakers each year thereafter.

Another Irish immigrant and Fenian nationalist who had fought for Irish independence from England, John Boyle O'Reilly, became prominent in Boston as editor of the *Pilot*, a widely read Roman Catholic newspaper. O'Reilly found acceptance throughout the ranks of Massachusetts literati, and in 1889 some of his poetry was read at the rededication of Plymouth Rock.

Many women worked long days on their feet in paper mills like this one in Holyoke, circa 1900. The photographer labeled this image "In the Rag Room." The census of 1900 counted 2,805,346 people in the state, 329,033 of them women in "gainful occupations." Of these women, only about 12 percent were married. This count of working women did not include the thousands of women who worked on farms or in family-owned businesses, since they did not get paid wages. Photo by Clifton Johnson. Courtesy, The Clifton Johnson Collection, The Jones Library, Inc., Amherst

LABOR REFORM

Political upheaval went hand in hand with labor struggles, and both marked the late nineteenth and early twentieth centuries in Massachusetts. A critical factor in the state's industrial decline rested in the fact that textile mills were no longer lucrative, low-cost operations. During the heyday of the early industrial revolution wages were low, but labor costs continually increased after 1830.

During the depression of 1873, many factory workers left Massachusetts. Those who stayed looked for ways to obtain real bargaining power and guarantee job security. Their success in this search was only moderate. In 1893, about 15,000 mill workers in Lawrence were out of work, and all the mills in the city shut down. By 1909, prosperity had slowly regained a foothold, and the average weekly wage for most male workers hovered around nine dollars. For women, earnings were slightly lower, averaging eight dollars a week. By 1911, all workers in Lawrence were limited to a 54-hour work week as a result of new state legislation governing the number of hours that women and children could work. Some maintained that this protective legislation was needed, but others—including many of the workers themselves—demanded further changes. Their complaints fell on deaf ears, for there was little labor organizing occurring then. The enormous mill complexes— American Woolen Company's Wood Mill, the Arlington Mills, and the Pacific Mills—remained peaceful and seemingly placid industrial centers without overt labor dissent. But this did not last.

By the beginning of 1912, mill workers in Lawrence expressed their dissatisfaction over working conditions. The 54-hour work week had brought a decrease in wages that most families could ill afford to absorb, and laborers were finally speaking out.

On January 12, 1912, at the Wood textile mill, angry workers, many of them immigrants, burst into a frustrated rampage, destroying machinery, telling co-workers to quit, and defying police sent in to quell the disorder. On Monday, January 15, about 8,000 striking mill workers picketed the Wood mills and several other Lawrence factories, preventing other workers from going to their jobs. The International Workers of the World (IWW), whose members had organized the strike, called for help, both financial and otherwise, for striking workers and their families. By Wednesday of that week, 10,000 striking

New England Magazine *described the 1912 Lawrence strike as "a small Civil War." As many as 15,000 strikers took part; many are seen here, marching down the snowy streets of Lawrence. From* New England Magazine, *March 1912*

workers gathered to listen to the radical views of union agitators Big Bill Haywood, Elizabeth Gurley Flynn, and the Socialist poet Arturo Giovanitti. Two weeks later more strikers mobbed the streets, and headlines in the *New York Times* read "Real Labor War Now in Lawrence." One striker was killed and a police officer was stabbed. Giovanitti was arrested for inciting trouble, and the children of many striking textile workers were evacuated from the city in order to secure their safety.

Several weeks after the main outbreaks of violence, mill owners, anxious to get factories back into production, offered pay increases of nearly one dollar a week to most workers in hopes of encouraging their return. Almost all the textile workers agreed to the terms of the concessions offered, much to the owners' relief. They had worried what further disruptions in their production might do to the already tenuous economic balance.

The year 1912 was pivotal in terms of ultimate settlement of labor disputes, although the rift between immigrant workers and police took years to mend. The old division between native-borns and immigrants, including Italians, Irish, Poles, and Franco-Americans, was less apparent as union organization became mutually important to these ethnically diverse groups. Union membership in Massachusetts went from 4,000 to 17,000 in one year, giving workers the strength to make subsequent demands.

After the 1912 strike was over, immigrant workers began to leave Lawrence. In 1920, they represented only 42 percent of the population, while in 1910, they had made up nearly half. This shift took place without a corresponding increase in the general population of the city. By the eve of World War I, immigrants in Lawrence had begun to identify more closely with native-born Americans rather than with their own ethnic roots. Liberty bond drives yielded several million dollars from the foreign-born during World War I, and immigrants and their sons enlisted in the

An early streetcar line was run by the Holyoke Street Railway Company, whose South Hadley-to-Sunderland route was staffed in 1901 by John Haskins and Fred Garey. Some streetcars had passenger and driver's seats that turned around at the end of the line. The car was then driven "backwards" on the return trip, with the driver in the rear of the car. Courtesy, The Baxter Eastman Collection

Nantasket Beach was newly commercialized and popular in 1882 when Harper's Weekly *featured it on its cover with a caption that began "What Coney Island is to New York, Nantasket Beach is to Boston—the great popular summer resort for the masses, easy of access, crowded, noisy, bustling, and democratic, with some corners devoted to the* elite *. . . ." Nantasket could be quickly reached from Boston on the steamer or the Old Colony railroad, and most people could afford the fare. From* Harper's Weekly, *August 19, 1882*

NANTASKET BEACH—DRAWN BY J. A. S. MONKS

military, died for their new country, and were memorialized by their survivors, native-born and foreign together. It appeared by the second decade of the twentieth century that the previous friction and unrest between the two groups had largely abated.

TRANSPORTATION

The Boston Post Road in the seventeenth century had been the major artery in and out of several cities. Then, it traversed the Commonwealth on its way to New York State, but now, in the early twentieth century, there were other means of transportation. Eastern Massachusetts residents could select one of several as yet rudimentary but viable methods of getting from place to place. Most exciting was the advent of the automobile. Few had access to this new conveyance, but those who did were able to travel much farther and more frequently. Among the first manufacturers of this new mode of transportation were Charles and Frank Duryea, credited with building the first really successful gasoline automobile, in

Springfield in 1893. In 1896, they made the first auto sale in the United States, kicking off what was to become one of the nation's largest, most important industries. Eventually the brothers went their separate ways, and in 1900, Frank Duryea opened a factory named the Stevens-Duryea Company, located in Chicopee Falls.

Common to more residents of Massachuetts was a different, yet still fairly innovative, form of transportation: the streetcar. At first it was drawn by horses, but by 1900, streetcars in many urban areas had been electrified. In 1891, there were 245 miles of trolley track in Boston alone. All over the greater Boston area, from the North Shore to the South, and westward with ever-expanding regularity, the streetcar unified the region. In 1850, there had been a three-mile streetcar radius in Boston; by the turn of the century, that radius exceeded 10 miles.

One of the early streetcar promoters was Stephen Dudley Field, a resident of Stockbridge. His interest in electricity was

Lake Pleasant, a village of Montague, was a summer camp meeting pláce for spiritualists—those who believe that the dead communicate with the living. Tiny lots for tents around a common were soon used for cottages, and the cottages grew and grew on the same small lots. The July 8, 1888, edition of the Boston Globe *noted that beautiful summer places, "models of architectural design," were being built at Lake Pleasant. As the belief in spiritualism declined over the years, so did the beauty of the Lake Pleasant community. Another spiratualist mecca was located at Silver Lake in Plympton. From a circa 1908 postcard*

At the turn of the century a cleaner Charles River was popular with canoeists. This picture from a circa 1906 postcard may have been taken at the Forest Grove area in the Waltham section of the river.

provoked at an early age by an uncle, Cyrus W. Field, who was responsible for the laying of the first submarine telegraph cable between the United States and Europe. The younger Field worked with dynamos, experimenting with ways to employ them in streetcar operation. His work was critical to the evolution of the modern rapid transit system common to Boston today, and thanks to Field, the electric streetcar soon replaced the horse-drawn variety. According to one historian, the electric streetcar moved twice as fast as the horse-drawn vehicle and tripled the street-railway's passenger capacity.

Early in the 1900s, the inhabitants of southeastern Massachusetts marveled at an engineering feat which many had long sought. On July 29, 1914, engineers opened the Cape Cod Canal, started five years earlier in 1909. Symbolic of many technological advances that had their inception in the Commonwealth during the twentieth century, the project actually had been discussed seriously a century earlier. The canal was a shining example of the type of advance that benefited thousands while boosting the state's commercial abilities. The waterway connects Cape Cod Bay with Buzzards Bay south of the Cape. Discussion concerning building a canal had begun in

1697, but not until the early 1800s did widespread interest in the project grow. State and federal authorities brought up the topic for consideration several times, but canal construction did not get under way until the twentieth century.

There were various reasons for building this type of canal in this location. Among the most pressing were considerations of safety for both lives and property. Between 1875 and 1903, nearly 700 vessels were lost in the waters off the Cape, and 105 lives were lost in these shipwrecks as well.

In June 1899, the Boston, Cape Cod and New York Canal Company signed a construction contract. On June 22, 1909, the first shovel of earth was turned and work began in earnest. By the end of the year, 200 workers had been engaged and by 1912, 750 men were employed on the project in various capacities. They worked 10-hour days for between $1.50 and $2.00 an hour. When it was completed, the canal eliminated the need for ships from New York and points south of New England to navigate treacherous shallow waters off Provincetown in order to access Boston Harbor and points north. Completion of the canal meant Barnstable County was now technically an island. In 1935, the Bourne Bridge was constructed, con-

necting Cape Cod with the mainland. In later years, this bridge was supplemented by the Sagamore Bridge. Both received increasingly heavy usage as Cape Cod became a popular vacation spot following World War II.

TIME FOR LEISURE

Thanks to innovations such as the automobile and the streetcar, cities from Boston to Pittsfield extended their boundaries. From Boston, people could now travel to other locations to enjoy leisure activities. The entire North Shore area, from Beverly to Salisbury, changed into an important playground for both rich and poor in the late nineteenth century. By the early twentieth century, the South Shore had also become popular. Resorts such as Nantasket Beach, Revere Beach, and Lincoln Park, near New Bedford, all were populated heavily during summer months by pleasure-seeking people from all over eastern Massachusetts and beyond.

Another spot that grew in popularity as a summer resort was Martha's Vineyard. Originally, it was a Methodist meeting ground for religious revivals, but was discovered by "ordinary" vacationers and became an exclusive summer destination. Its only means of surface access is by ferryboat, as is that of Nantucket, the island to the east of Martha's Vineyard. Both had relied earlier on fishing and whaling as main sources of income, but by the twentieth century, this maritime economy was replaced forever by tourism.

The growing number of talented foreign-born and native-born residents of Massachusetts, combined with improved transportation networks and an increase in leisure time, meant that new institutions would continue to grow and acknowledge culturally-diverse factors. Wealthy, well-educated citizens of eastern Massachusetts rejoiced in 1881 in the formation of the Boston Symphony Orchestra. Henry Lee Higginson, a wealthy Boston Brahmin, donated money and put in considerable time and effort to establish the symphony, of which some musicians were trained at the New England Conservatory of Music, established in 1867. Others, however, came from the increasing ranks of artistically gifted immigrants. In 1900, construction of Symphony Hall, the future home of the Boston Symphony, was begun at a location off Huntington Avenue in the city's Back Bay.

Less sedate pastimes included baseball, which grew in popularity as the Boston

Dr. James Naismith of Springfield invented the game of basketball in this gymnasium in the school for Christian Workers in December 1891. He hung a peach basket on each end on the area below the overhead running track. Eighteen players took part in the first games played here. Courtesy, The Naismith Memorial Basketball Hall of Fame, Springfield

Baseball Club, active since 1871, became the delight of hundreds of avid fans. Similarly, boxing had aficionados who grew ecstatic when Boston-born John L. Sullivan became national boxing champion in 1882. Conversely, they despaired when he lost the title in 1892. A new sport, basketball, had been invented in Springfield in 1891 by James A. Naismith. He was an instructor at the YMCA College in Springfield (now Springfield College), and devised the game as a way of ensuring his student athletes would stay in good physical condition during the winter months.

Naismith's ingenious idea consisted of attaching overhead peach baskets to the walls on opposite sides of the gym and then having opposing teams try to throw soccerballs through the baskets. His game basically remains the same today as it was when invented nearly 100 years ago, although there have been important upgradings of equipment.

ART AND ARCHITECTURE

Statewide interest in culture resulted in the establishment of a number of important museums by 1900. The largest and most generously endowed was the Museum of Fine Arts in Boston. Founded in 1870 at Copley Square, it was moved in 1909 to its present site on Huntington Avenue in a building designed by Guy Lowell. The museum faced the Fenway, part of the "Emerald Necklace" designed by the famous urban planner and landscape architect, Frederick Law Olmsted. His idea of connecting important residential and commercial areas of Boston resulted in the lovely strip of parks that begins at Boston's Public Gardens and ends at the Fenway, near Isabella Stewart Gardner's former home.

Just as the period 1790 to 1830 produced architectural gems in residences throughout the state, in 1900 similarly grand architectural displays were in

In 1899 the new South Station was the largest railroad station in the world, according to an article in the New York Sun. This circa 1911 postcard shows the exterior; the interior was noted for its complicated turntables for the engines that stationed there.

vogue. Constructed in part as a result of the economic boom enjoyed by important industrialists (so aptly described in William Dean Howells' *The Rise of Silas Lapham*, these homes reflect the affluence of the age.

In Worcester, the Salisbury Building marked the beginning of that city's apartment-house boom. Three-decker homes were popular at this time also, springing up especially in middle-class or working-class neighborhoods where families did not have the income to sustain large, single-family dwellings but still had pretensions to middle-class lifestyles. Chicopee also sported many new homes in the 1890s and early 1900s, most of them ornately designed and decorated with gingerbread trim, many with mansard roofs. Again, much of this urban, and later suburban, growth was made possible by expanded transportation networks enabling people to live farther away from their workplaces. Boston's first skyscraper, the Ames Building, located near the Old Statehouse, also dates from this period.

A loose assemblage of Impressionists, the group of painters known as the Boston School, came to enjoy world renown. This is somewhat remarkable, considering that many of them drew on inner resources fueled by the beauty and tranquility of the same region—Massachusetts. The Boston School included Frank Benson, Joseph DeCamp, Childe Hassam, Philip Hale, his wife Lilian Westcott Hale, William Paxton, his wife Elizabeth Paxton, and Edmund Tarbell. Many had studied in Paris or other European cities, yet returned to paint scenes and individuals in Massachusetts, thereby immortalizing the region of their birth. The legacy these artists left is one that represents Massachusetts during one of its most interesting periods of growth and change.

By 1900, Massachusetts' population had grown to 2.5 million people, most of whom lived in urban centers. Vestiges of rural life remained throughout the state, however, particularly in smaller

communities to the west of Worcester. Like few other states, Massachusetts successfully clung to both the charm of an agrarian past and the challenge of brisk, industrial lifestyles. This pluralism was in part represented by the distinct divisions still remaining between native-born and immigrant. It was clear that in factory cities like Lawrence this division often meant trouble, for fear and uncertainty provoked by cultural differences erupted into violence. Underneath the facade of progress, both groups clung to the known. Labor agitators, political splinter groups, and most of all, the horror that World War I brought to the entire nation, were as much a part of Massachusetts' experience in the first two decades of the twentieth century as had been the patriotic fervor of the 1760s and 1770s in the Bay State.

America's premier landscape architect, Frederick Law Olmsted, is probably most famous for his design for Central Park in New York City, but he did commissions across the country. By 1881 he was living in Brookline, which was to become his home and office headquarters and is now a National Historic Site. In Massachusetts his work includes the Emerald Necklace park system in Boston and numerous other contracts. Olmsted's social and design principles are as appropriate today as in the 1800s, and his work is enjoying a revival of appreciation. A thorough inventory of his commissions is being made by the Massachusetts Association for Olmsted Parks, a pilot survey meant as a model for other states. From Cirker, Dictionary of American Portraits, *Dover, 1967*

WORLD WAR I AND THE ROARING TWENTIES (1914-1930)

★　★　★　★　★　★　★　★　★

The first decades of the twentieth century brought not only progressive reforms but the specter of world conflict as well. Some were comforted by the fact that the United States did not play an active military role in World War I until April 6, 1917, but there was, nevertheless, much military activity in the United States as soon as war broke out in Europe in 1914. Battle preparations began almost immediately after news of the European conflict reached our shores.

Across the nation, military preparedness camps abounded. Special units were set up for the first time so that women could enlist directly in the military service. People everywhere were exhorted to contribute to the war effort. In Massachusetts, newspapers carried feature articles such as "Self Helps for the New Soldier" and "What are You Planting," the latter referring to the "Victory gardens" popular in many communities. But their widespread appeal provoked fear among some agricultural officials who worried that neophyte gardeners would waste valuable seed, precipitating a shortage during a time when steady supplies of food for troops and civilian allies was most critical.

Home defense league drills became increasingly popular also. In Chicopee in 1917, a state home guard unit was organized by 84 men. That same year, women streetcar conductors were hired in Springfield and Boston for the first time. Their presence outraged conservatives who believed such employment was an affront to femininity. According to conventional standards, service on public conveyances was not fitting work for women.

Civilian life during early months of the war was affected in many different ways. Consumer prices rose immediately, but compared to prices in later decades, the costs people faced in 1917 were low.

One Massachusetts restaurant advertised a 50-cent-per-plate lunch. Hotel rooms were offered at 75 cents and up per night. Coal sold for $9.50 a ton, and ladies hats could be purchased on sale for $2.50.

The legislation that created a military draft in the U.S. was passed by Congress on May 18, 1917. This draft law assured the government that sufficient numbers of troops would be available for battle "over there." Although President Woodrow Wilson advocated conscription, it was not a popular move, and during debate about merits of a military draft prior to passage of the bill, even the House Military Affairs Committee opposed it. Representative Richard Olney of Massachusetts noted that the terminology "draft" and "conscription" were offensive to most Americans. He suggested instead the term "personal obligation to service."

No matter how it was labeled, military service remained, for most, a duty to be performed like any other. And in reality, despite congressional debate on the subject, there was less opposition to

President Wilson's call for conscripts than there had been in Abraham Lincoln's time, during the Civil War, or would be later under President Lyndon B. Johnson during the Vietnam conflict.

HOW MASSACHUSETTS HELPED

Camp Devens, in Ayer, Massachusetts, was a base for new army recruits. Approximately 100,000 soldiers encamped there, out of a total of 24 million American men in military service during the entire war. Of these troops about 200,000 were from the Bay State. Only about 83,000 were actual conscripts, however—the majority of Massachusetts soldiers were volunteers.

American soldiers were sent to France as early as June 1917. They were under the command of General John J. Pershing, who had served during the Spanish-American War. Pershing worked closely with allied Commander-in-Chief Marshal Ferdinand Foch, although U.S. troops were a distinct and separate unit for the duration. At no time were American soldiers integrated with foreign

Although the United States had not yet declared itself in World War I, it was wary of the threat from abroad as shown in this June 1914 New England Magazine *photograph from an unidentified beach on the New England coast.*

service units. For close to a year, trench warfare was the major action American doughboys experienced. In March 1918, Germany began an offensive known as the Second Battle of the Somme. From this point on, all the important battles of the war claimed many American lives. In subsequent years, the nation would commemorate those who had fallen at Belleau Wood, Ypres, Saint-Mihiel, the Meuse-Argonne Forest, and many other locations. Of those who died, some 5,200 were Massachusetts natives. These losses finally ended on November 11, 1918, when Germany surrendered and signed the Armistice.

During the months that the United States was actively engaged in war, there were no special provisions for formation of exclusive state military units. Nonetheless, most Massachusetts recruits served in the 26th Yankee Division under the command of Major General Clarence Edwards. According to reports,

the first shot fired by U.S. troops in France came from the 26th Yankee Division.

Another military outfit in which Bay State soldiers enlisted or were placed after conscription was the 82nd Division. A portion of this group consisted of the 401st Telegraph Battalion. This unit was promoted by the New England Telephone and Telegraph Company. Dr. Harvey Cushing, a prominent brain surgeon from Boston, oversaw operation of a 2,000-bed hospital which was part of the 82nd Division.

The war effort needed more than soldiers. It required armaments as well. In Massachusetts, the M1903 Springfield rifle was manufactured in the city of the same name. This standard item, produced at Springfield Armory (established in 1794), was among many pieces of equipment issued to all U.S. Army recruits. At Boston Navy Yard ships were both prepared and repaired, and con-

During World War I, male students at Massachusetts Agricultural College (now the University of Massachusetts) were required to take military training. Here, young men learn to lob grenades under the watchful eye of their leader. The college's horses were used to train some students for the cavalry. Courtesy, Special Collections and Archives, Library, University of Massachusetts at Amherst

struction of battleships occurred at Quincy's Fore River Shipyard. Many small but critical items were also provided by Bay State industries, among them, shoes, boots, uniforms, pistol belts, and incendiary cartridges. This intense effort was a boon to the economy while it lasted, but later caused major portions of Massachusetts industry to grind to a halt after the Armistice. Portions of the state's economy were then left in a precarious position, and many able workers were unemployed.

THE STATE ECONOMY AFFECTED

Changes in the nation's economy due to wartime were reflected in the increase in union membership rolls. In 1916, before the United States entered the war, there were about two million members in the American Federation of Labor (A. F. of L.), but by 1920 that figure had grown

to 3.26 million. War manufacture also provoked federal government involvement in economic production. Centralized bureaus such as the War Industries Board monitored coordination of war goods manufacture, and the National War Labor Board helped negotiate settlements between employers and workers. Most often, the board favored the union position. Federal control was clearly necessary during wartime, but after the Armistice was signed and soldiers returned to civilian life and work, government involvement in business and industry was no longer necessary.

During World War I, shoe and textile factories in Massachusetts had experienced a burst of activity. Production demands of wartime provided comfortably for workers during wartime and augured well for the future. In addition, war-related shipbuilding created many new jobs in the state. But the economic prosperity reigning in Massachusetts throughout the war diminished following the Armistice. Postwar recession spelled economic downturn in Massachusetts, and meant a decline in manufacturing production and employment statewide. Still, in 1919, the state's factories were producing $4 billion in products compared to only $109 million in farm income. There were about 700,000 industrial workers in Massachusetts by this time—almost six times the number of farm workers. By 1920, some factories were closing down since defense-related production was no longer required. Even so, that year Massachusetts produced 6.4 percent of all U.S. manufactured goods. However, it was increasingly common for big investors to move plants to other parts of the country, where better risks for capital investment were located. This combination of factors meant layoffs and factory shutdowns across Massachusetts. Added to the inevitable postwar decline, yet another issue caused difficulty throughout the state. An increase in labor union activity across Massachusetts meant greater demands for higher wages among those workers who had kept their jobs.

Some recalled the textile factory strikes of 1912 during the Boston police strike of 1919. During this incident Calvin Coolidge, a somewhat obscure Republican from Northampton, achieved national prominence and respect through his terse, direct approach to the strike. As Massachusetts' governor, Coolidge demanded that striking police officers return to their jobs, which they did after an interlude of only two days. The fortunate Coolidge was credited with efficient handling of a potentially dangerous situation. He went on to win the Republican nomination for vice president in 1920, largely on the strength of his performance during the strike.

A DECADE OF CONTROVERSY

Massachusetts residents looked to the future with ambivalence. Changes of every type in every area of life were inevitable. Some embraced these changes willingly; others attempted to forestall them through various legislative means. Some legislation of this period was propelled by attitudes and ideologies that were questionable at best. The 1920s were of pivotal importance for the United States. A more sophisticated

Calvin Coolidge (1872-1933) was born in Vermont, but graduated from Amherst College and became a lawyer in Northampton. After holding various civil offices there he became a Massachusetts representative in 1907. From 1910 to 1911 he was mayor of Northampton, then went back to Boston as a state senator. Coolidge was lieutenant governor from 1915 to 1919, then governor from 1919 to 1921 when he became vice president under Warren Harding. When Harding died in 1923 Coolidge became president, and he was reelected in 1924. The Coolidges retired to a modest home in Northampton, where he died in 1933. Here Coolidge and his wife, Grace, enter their car circa 1928 when they retired from the White House to Northampton. Courtesy, Northampton Historical Society

Right: *Imagine this Roaring 20s flapper with a broad red ribbon around her cloche hat, bright red lips, and a red collar. Then imagine her inviting you to meet her at the fair, as advertised on this 29-inch-diameter tire cover on the back of a Model A Ford sedan. The Three County Fair (Hampshire, Hampden, and Franklin counties) is the longest continuously running fair in the country. It was founded in 1818 by such men as Judge Joseph Lyman and Noah Webster. The early fairs, held after harvest season, offered premiums for the best bull, milk cow, oxen, sheep, cheese, knitted mittens, handwoven diaper fabric, and sheeting. Breeding stock and new seed varieties were bought and sold or swapped; important advances in agricultural techniques were shared. The first fairs also held oratory competitions featuring the more vocal of the civic leaders. Photo by Kathryn Stadler. Courtesy, The Collection of Walter C. and Sarah H. Jones, gift of Albert Omasta of Hatfield*

Facing page, top: *The appointed state commission on immigration in 1914 reported to the legislature that immigrant living conditions were unacceptable. This picture from the report showed a room, probably in Worcester, in which 10 Turkish people slept in day and night shifts. The commission declared such overcrowding bad for health and morals. They noted that only a small percentage of immigrants were women—94 percent of Turkish immigrants in 1911 to 1913 were male. The commission recommended that housing laws be enforced but it had no ideas on how to alleviate the Turkish men's general forlornness. Having no normal social relations, the men's lives were open to temptation and vice. From* Report of the Commission on Immigration on the Problem of Immigration in Massachusetts, *1914*

Facing page, bottom: *The 1914 Commission on Immigration report included this picture of immigrant men in a construction workers' shanty near Boston, where the extension of the steam and electric railroad was in progress. The report noted that 80 percent of the workers were foreign-born, mostly from Italy but also from Portugal, Poland, Greece, and Russia. The men were required to live in camps even if their homes were nearby. Sometimes they were billeted in old box cars or sheds of corrugated iron. Bags of straw served as mattresses, laid on platforms the length of the building. The report was critical of the fact that water was often hard to acquire, so that men with standards of cleanliness soon lost them. From* Report of the Commission on Immigration on the Problem of Immigration in Massachusetts, *1914*

culture, combined with new technologies and an upward trend in the nation's economic picture, now contrasted sharply with the Victorian-era mores and manners of the previous century. The population was growing rapidly: from 1900 to 1910, the number of people in the United States grew by 21 percent. Demographic shifts, from a mostly rural settlement pattern to one where more than 50 percent of U.S. homes were in cities or towns with more than 2,500 inhabitants, signaled both the end of a lifestyle and the beginning of a new age. In 1920, the U.S. census showed that 94.8 percent of Massachusetts residents lived in urban areas. Perhaps even more significant was the fact that in 1920, for the first time, people who worked in some type of industrial job outnumbered those in agricultural jobs by five to four.

Immigrants continued to swell the ranks of the state's population, and the implications of this continuing wave of

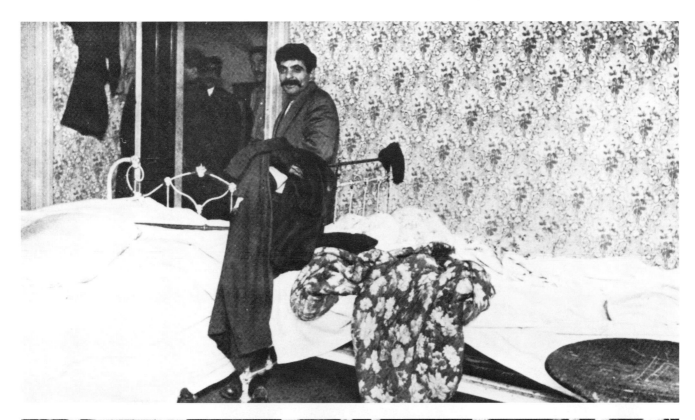

John Francis Fitzgerald, "Honey Fitz" (1863-1950), the son of Irish immigrant parents, was a newspaper publisher, insurance broker, banker, and a leading Boston Democrat in the most rowdy era of American politics. He began in the Common Council in 1892, was a state senator in 1893-1894, was a United States representative from 1895 to 1901 and again for six months in 1919, was mayor of Boston from 1906 to 1907 and from 1910 to 1914, and was an unsuccessful candidate for governor in 1922. Prominent as he was in politics, Fitzgerald is best known to today's voters as the father of Rose Fitzgerald Kennedy and grandfather and great-grandfather to the Kennedy candidates. From Boston Statistics Department, The Municipal Register for 1910, *1911*

foreign immigration worried many state and federal officials. Their concern was fueled by a nationwide nativistic impulse that emphasized the perceived virtues of the native-born and the disadvantages of welcoming more immigrants into the United States. This attitude resulted in federal immigration restriction laws in 1921 and 1924. Among the most vociferous supporters of this legislation was Massachusetts senator Henry Cabot Lodge.

In Massachusetts, changes in demography due to foreigners were quite apparent. The nation's heaviest concentrations of immigrants were in the cities of Boston and New York, and the greatest population density for the nation overall was found in the Northeast. In 1920, several Massachusetts cities—among them Springfield, Worcester, Lynn, and Lowell—had populations of well over 100,000 people; Boston had 750,000 residents; 81.6 percent of the state's citizens lived in communities of at least 10,000 people; and 66 percent lived in cities of 25,000 or more. The fact that Massachusetts was becoming more urban, as well as absorbing ever larger numbers of foreign-born, was of great concern to a vocal majority of politically-influential individuals.

The largely Roman Catholic population in and around Boston continued to be a cause of friction. By 1920, only 31.9 percent of the Commonwealth's citizens were "native white of native parentage," according to census reports. Nearly 67 percent were either immigrants or offspring of foreigners.

Immigrants threatened what was, for the native-born in Massachusetts, a comfortable economic status quo. Staid Yankees of the region—white, Anglo-Saxon Protestant descendants of those who had settled Massachusetts in the seventeenth century—probably agreed with immigrants on a few things, however. The 1920s posed a threat to a seemingly safer, more secure time. Antiradical sentiment ran high and

reached a peak with the Sacco-Vanzetti case, which brought Massachusetts' politics into national prominence. Two Italian immigrants, Nicola Sacco and Bartolomeo Vanzetti, had been charged with robbing a shoe factory and murdering two employees there. The climate of the times carried a distinct note of hysteria against suspected anarchists and communists, and the Italians had little hope of a fair trial. As many of their supporters feared, the men were found guilty and executed. Their case prompted a wave of liberal-radical outrage expressed in a variety of ways, among them, a poem titled "Justice Denied in Massachusetts" by Edna St. Vincent Millay (who made her home in the Berkshire Mountains, just over the Massachusetts border in New York).

Changes in public morals and manners in the 1920s alarmed all but the most avant-garde thinkers. Together,

Due to overcrowded schools, young Syrian immigrant women were obliged to meet in a Boston kindergarten room when they attended classes to learn English. The women were taught such words as "millinery," "piece," "sale," "special," "bargain," "department," "change," and "gentlemen," probably in anticipation of their likely employment as salesgirls. From Report of the Commission on Immigration on the Problem of Immigration in Massachusetts, *1914*

both immigrant and native-born decried the daring explicitness of new novels, and the unashamed boldness of popular silent films and the newer "talking" pictures. They shuddered at the shocking freedom of behavior exhibited by the younger generation. In the eyes of many, smoking, drinking, and sexual activity equaled moral degradation. The nation's future

as a pacesetter in medicine and in a range of industrial technologies.

Certain trends that showed up early in Massachusetts would later affect the entire country. Among these was a growing tendency toward prohibiting alcoholic beverage consumption. As early as April 30, 1908, the city of Worcester voted to become "dry." This move made

Women and some men worked actively to get women the vote in Massachusetts from the early 1850s; by 1895 they were still petitioning the state legislature. This 1895 cartoon shows the fears some men seemed to have concerning women voting. The Nineteenth Amendment to the Constitution finally gave women that privilege in 1919. From the Boston Sunday Globe, *January 13, 1895*

seemed imperiled, and as a defense there were attempts to resist and limit change by more powerful citizens (usually native-born, although their numbers included some Irish-Catholic politicians in the Boston area who had grown increasingly influential, as exemplified by Boston mayor "Honey" Fitzgerald's success). Some efforts were successful, such as restrictions on foreign immigration. Any change, demographic or otherwise, carried with it the suggestion of crisis, and Americans who recalled the more genteel manners of the nineteenth century were aghast at the contemporary decline they now witnessed.

SHIFTING POLITICAL WINDS

Like most of the nation, Massachusetts enjoyed a variety of industrial innovations and technological advances during the initial decades of the twentieth century. The Bay State was a leader in education, particularly of women, as well

Worcester, at the heart of the Commonwealth, the largest dry city in the United States. Smaller communities would follow suit, foreshadowing passage of the Volstead Act in 1919. This federal legislation mandated prohibition nationwide and ultimately provoked such illegal activities as bootlegging (importing alcoholic beverages from outside the United States) and operation of clandestine stills and speakeasies for the production and serving of alcohol.

Across America, people either applauded or decried ratification in 1920 of another constitutional change: the Nineteenth Amendment to the Constitution, guaranteeing suffrage to women. The first presidential election in which women were eligible to vote catapulted Massachusetts politician Calvin Coolidge to the U.S. presidency. He had risen from small-town lawyer to popular state governor to inoffensive vice president. From there, it seemed inevitable that

Coolidge would become president. In 1923, after President Warren G. Harding's untimely death, Coolidge stepped with characteristic diffidence into the White House. And in 1924, Coolidge's 2-to-1 popular vote margin in the race against Democratic challenger John Davis ensured his victory. The nation's 30th president, Coolidge was the first Massachusetts president to be elected since John Quincy Adams.

TECHNOLOGICAL ADVANCES

Numerous new gadgets, machines, and novel technologies became popular and widespread during the 1920s. The automobile grew ever more popular, amateur photography became increasingly common, the marvel of the helicopter expanded the possibilities of the aviation industry, and use of electrical power in American homes and factories grew. In 1900, the nation's electrical output was only about six million kilowatt-hours—one-twentieth of all the power used by factories in the United States. By 1927, two-thirds of industrial power in the nation was generated by electricity, and use was just under 120 million kilowatt-hours. A great many of these manufacturing facilities were located in New England, despite the pull-out by some large investors shortly after World War I. Power used in the area was generated by hydropower facilities situated along the region's powerful rivers.

Radio became more and more popular in the 1920s. At Medford, the first radio station in Massachusetts accessed the airwaves and began broadcasting in 1921. Six years later, in 1927, there were about 10 million radio sets in use throughout the nation. Despite public fascination with radio in the late 1920s, the popular topic of conversation in Massachusetts (and the nation) had little to do with airwaves—but a lot to

In 1916 women still could not vote, but these women celebrating Enfield's centennial dressed up like their mothers and grandmothers in parody of women's rights activists. From a 1916 postcard. Courtesy, Special Collections and Archives, Library, University of Massachusetts at Amherst

do with air.

Charles A. Lindbergh's 1927 nonstop transatlantic solo flight captured the imagination of millions of Americans, and the subsequent efforts of many less-publicized pilots caught the nation by storm. The idea that humans could actually fly had been tested and proven by the Wright brothers at Kitty Hawk, North Carolina, in 1903. After that, hundreds of people attempted to further the science of aviation by a variety of means. Among the most significant of these efforts were a series of experiments conducted in Worcester. The year before Lindbergh's famous flight, a virtually unknown researcher was bent on proving the viability of air and space exploration. Dr. Robert H. Goddard successfully fired a liquid-fueled rocket that achieved a height of 41 feet, and in so doing, ushered in the modern space era. Goddard was highly optimistic about the ramifications of his modest success. However, he was slightly inaccurate in a 1918 Smithsonian Institution report concerning future space exploration. In

his report, Goddard predicted the world would see human exploration of the moon's surface by the year 2000—a guess that was late by more than three decades.

Within 10 years of his original experiment, Goddard built and tested rockets that went 700 miles per hour, reached heights of 7,500 feet, and exceeded the speed of sound. However, not until the nation's defense needs expanded rapidly during World War II did Goddard's pioneering work with rocketry receive the credit—and the financial support—it deserved.

Statewide interest in science extended to areas of direct human benefit as well. Medicine, its study and practice, had been held in high regard in Massachusetts as far back as the seventeenth century. Boston in particular has a long tradition of excellence in medicine and has long been a center of the highest quality medical care and research. The history of formal support for medical practice in Massachusetts was highlighted in 1797 when Samuel Adams, one of the original

A supervisor poses circa 1903 in a 7½ x 13-foot steel pipe in Wayland during construction of the Weston Aqueduct. The new aqueduct had to go under railroads as well as roads and through a boulder clay ledge in its nearly mile-long route. At its peak, 125 men and 22 horses worked on the project. From Second Annual Report of the Metropolitan Water and Sewerage Board, *1903*

On May 19, 1938, the first mail plane to fly out of Pittsfield was captured on film by a photographer. The destination of the plane is unrecorded; perhaps it flew to Boston over the Old Post Road? Photo by Gravelle Pictorial News Service. Courtesy, The Berkshire Atheneum

Sons of Liberty, helped found the Massachusetts Medical Society. Well over a century later, in 1926, two Boston doctors, George R. Minot and William P. Murphy, developed a successful treatment of pernicious anemia. This condition had previously been fatal, but due to Minot and Murphy and their research, lives could now be saved. The pair, along with Dr. George H. Whipple, received the 1934 Nobel Prize for Medicine as a result of these findings.

In addition to these physicians, other doctors based in Boston during the 1920s and later deserve mention because of the comprehensive quality of their medical contributions. Neurosurgeon Harvey Williams Cushing was surgeon-in-chief at Peter Bent Brigham Hospital and professor of surgery at Harvard Medical School. He received a Pulitzer Prize in 1925 for a biography of the Canadian physician Sir William Osler. Cushing was also known for his work with the United States Army during World War I.

The well-known heart specialist, Paul Dudley White, began his career at Massachusetts General Hospital in Boston. Research in cardiovascular diseases led him to become attending physician during President Dwight D. Eisenhower's recovery from a heart attack in the 1950s. White, through his position as executive director of the National Advisory Council of the National Heart Institute, is credited with saving thousands of lives. Due to his efforts, the American public was educated about the causes and prevention of heart disease.

Individual physicians' contributions to research and medical treatment helped increase the quality of life for all Americans and made possible a longer life span. Some outstanding Boston-area medical institutions that grew up during the early twentieth century were critical to these individual contributions. Massachusetts General Hospital, which was founded in the early nineteenth century, was joined in the first few decades of the 1900s by Peter Bent Brigham Hospital, Beth Israel Hospital, the Floating Hospital, Children's and Infants Hospital, the Lahey Clinic, and Boston University Hospital. The reform efforts connected with these medical institutions represented positive forces at work in Massachusetts up through the 1920s.

MASSACHUSETTS IN THE MODERN ERA (1930-1985)

★　　★　　★　　★　　★　　★　　★　　★　　★

After the stock market crash in October 1929, the national economy plummeted. And as the difficulties continued into the new decade, there appeared to be little hope of a quick solution to the fiscal crisis. The idea of retrieving one's savings, deposited in local banks, was quickly thwarted as banks closed, not one by one but dozens at a time. Runs on local banks further weakened local economies, and it was clear that the entire United States was in severe difficulty. Headlines for that ominous first week of stock market chaos reflected the desire for calm. "Banking Officials Optimistic Over Future for Business and Not Alarmed By Break," shouted the *Boston Globe* for Tuesday, October 29, 1929, the day called "Black Tuesday." The following day, three-inch headlines proclaimed, "Big Banks Ask Only 25 Percent Margin," and "Stocks Rise After Big Losses in Wild Opening." One analyst said the stock market opening "was

dramatic, spectacular, ruinous." Capital investment dropped from $10 billion in 1929 to $1 billion in 1932. Some 110,000 businesses collapsed during the same period. A half year after the stock market crashed, three million Americans were out of work, and by 1933 more than 12 million individuals were unemployed. Figures in Massachusetts mirrored the national trend. In 1930, the first year after the stock market crash, 116,210 people in the Bay State were unemployed—75 percent of them males. This figure represented nearly 3 percent of the state's working population, of which another 1.1 percent were laid off without pay. The unemployment figures rose throughout the decade and by 1940 they had reached 206,000, or 11.2 percent of the total state work force. In addition, there were 103,400 people on relief work—another 5.6 percent of the total working population. In the early 1930s officials predicted increasingly dire

circumstances as more and more businesses failed, and few people could rely on regular work hours or the security of a weekly paycheck.

ECONOMIC DISASTER

Despite his intentions, President Herbert Hoover (elected in 1928 and an ally of private industry) was unable to reverse the terrible economic slide. It was a descent that plunged the entire country into chaos. The handful of programs established during Hoover's administration, such as the Reconstruction Finance Corporation (RFC), helped only a few people. The president, true to his conservative economic theories, claimed that only voluntary self-help programs could be applied to the nation's problems, despite the reality of a 25 percent unemployment rate from coast to coast. There was little Hoover could do since he staunchly insisted that relief was *not* the business of the federal government. He was adamant that the private sector must rely on itself for support and

solutions. However, this national crisis ultimately spelled failure for the Republican administration, and by 1932 most Americans looked hopefully toward the next election as an opportunity to stave off future catastrophe.

The Democrats won an easy majority of congressional races almost everywhere in 1932. Unlike its voting record in previous presidential races, Massachusetts did not follow the lead of Connecticut, New Hampshire, and Vermont. Instead, the Bay State joined the rest of the nation and was among all but five states casting their electoral votes for Franklin D. Roosevelt. Roosevelt won 23 million popular votes while Hoover garnered only 15.8 million of those votes. The nation wanted a change, and within a few years the results of this change were clear in Massachusetts.

THE QUABBIN RESERVOIR

Construction of Quabbin Reservoir in the central part of Massachusetts was a project representing many decades of planning. In fact, as early as the first quarter of the nineteenth century officials in the eastern part of the state looked to the Swift River Valley as a potential source of drinking water for Boston's growing population.

Despite the political wheeling and dealing so inevitable in a project of this magnitude, a study group finally was formed in 1919. Its express goal was to seek a solution to Boston's water-supply problems. In 1926, legislation known as the Ware River Act formally created the Metropolitan District Water Supply Commission (MDWSC). This agency would study and make plans for building a dam, flooding the Swift River, and creating a reservoir. The name of the reservoir would be *Quabbin,* an Algonquin name meaning "well-watered place." Native American tribes living in this area of the Swift River Valley had been ruled by a sachem known as Nini-Quaben. It seemed natural to derive the name of the reservoir from this once-powerful ruler's name.

Because reservoir construction coincided with the high unemployment of the 1930s, the state-funded plan became one of the biggest public works projects in the state, offering jobs to large numbers of Bay State workers. This project ultimately resulted in a 38.6-square-mile reservoir in the state's central region to the west of Worcester. In order to carry out the project, it was necessary to expropriate great parcels of land. The entire towns of Dana, Enfield, Greenwich, and Prescott were bought up, their inhabitants moved, and their boundaries flooded. Since these communities—along with many in the Swift River Valley—were sparsely populated, such upheaval was not as far-reaching as it might seem. More importantly, for the flagging economy of the 1930s, construction projects of the magnitude of Quabbin meant jobs, income, and security. The work involved in moving people out and demolishing buildings was considerable, but it was dwarfed by the construction task itself. As part of the

Top: *Many local men were hired to clear the land and burn brush on the ground that would be covered with the Quabbin Reservoir's water. This photograph, taken on February 27, 1939, shows the magnitude of the job as an Oshkosh tractor drags a tree to the fire. Courtesy, Massachusetts Archives*

Above: *To clear the Swift River Valley, many houses, inns, stores, and churches were burned. Others were taken apart board by board and erected elsewhere, while some were disassembled for the lumber, windows, or mantels alone. But some homes or parts of homes could be towed; here, the Thayer house is moved from Greenwich on March 21, 1939. Courtesy, Massachusetts Archives*

The Chandler Place, the best located large home in Enfield, was kept by the state as the Enfield office until the last possible moment. This photograph was taken September 1, 1939, looking north to the cleared valley that would soon become an 18-mile-long reservoir, with the hills in the distance becoming islands. Courtesy, Massachusetts Archives

Quabbin project, the Winsor Dam was built to hold back the many tons of water that would engulf the land and create the state's largest man-made reservoir.

Engineers had determined early which areas would be flooded by the reservoir. By March 27, 1938, the MDWSC had filed necessary paperwork with the state to take 117 square miles of land by eminent domain. People were paid for their property, although for most the state's remuneration in no way made up for the total loss that they experienced. Everyone who lived within the marked areas was instructed to evacuate by July 1, 1938.

The actual flooding was not to begin until 1939, so the region's inhabitants left slowly. But as poignant as their departure seemed, they were not leaving behind a land of promise. The economy of the region had been deteriorating for decades, and for most people, relocation suggested an opportunity to begin again, in prosperity.

The move could not be effected merely by relocating people, however. Special legislation was needed in order to disincorporate the four towns to be flooded. In addition, towns had to hold special meetings to finalize municipal affairs and dismantle their individual governmental structures. Special celebrations, as well, marked the demise of these tiny central Massachusetts communities. The most widely publicized was the Enfield Firemen's Ball, held on April 27, 1938. It was a social affair of memorable proportions, and several thousand people attended. Publicity surrounding the event was wide-ranging. For months, newspapers that had carried progress reports on reservoir construction now focused on this last, festive occasion. The *Springfield Union* described the ball in vivid terms: "Muffled sounds of sobbing were heard, hardened men were not ashamed to take out their handkerchiefs, and even children, attending the ball with their parents, broke into tears." It was a curious blend of celebration and funeral. From the perspective of the region's economy, the death of the four towns was inevitable—the Quabbin project merely hastened the process along—but for town residents, it was sorrowful.

In September 1938, the few buildings and municipal properties remaining in the four communities were auctioned off.

Late in the month, a hurricane swept through the empty towns—a final, vehement salute and farewell to the hundreds who had lived and struggled there for several centuries. After flooding started on August 14, 1939, the ghostly remains of abandoned towns remained visible for almost the entire seven years it took for Quabbin Reservoir to fill with water.

THE NEW DEAL

During the initial months of Franklin D. Roosevelt's administration, some important legislation was passed. Affecting all Americans, the set of bills was designed to provide comprehensive relief to farmers and to industry. Three major efforts of the early Roosevelt years—establishment of the National Recovery Administration (NRA), the Agricultural Adjustment Administration (AAA), and the Public Works Administration (PWA)—aimed at encouraging factory and agricultural production without dismantling the concept of private industry.

Many disagreed with the president's policies. Some feared what extensive government intervention would do to the economy, while others felt that too little was being done. Controversy reigned, and in Massachusetts, as in other states, skeptics criticized Roosevelt while supporters argued on behalf of his programs. It was some years into the New Deal before Roosevelt's legislation had a major effect on the Massachusetts economy. Eventually, however, Bay State citizens benefited in a variety of ways from the Works Progress Administration (WPA), the Civilian Conservation Corps (CCC), and the Federal Emergency Relief Act (FERA).

The annual report of the Metropolitan District Commission for 1937 detailed the success of the CCC camp at the Great Blue Hills Reservation near Boston. The camp operated at Blue Hills until September of that year, although there

The least controversial and most popular of all the New Deal federal legislation was the Civilian Conservation Corps. In 1933 Franklin D. Roosevelt requested money for a peacetime army to work against the destruction of national resources. In time 50 camps of men were at work in Massachusetts, planting trees, building dams, fire towers, and bridges, and clearing beaches and campsites. This photo was taken at the Mount Greylock CCC camp in the Berkshires, where unemployed males between 18 and 25 were given jobs. Clothing and equipment were mostly World War I surplus, and the camp was run like a military camp. Courtesy, Massachusetts Department of Environmental Management, Division of Forests and Parks

On January 23, 1938, one of the first snow-ski trains arrived from New York City at Pittsfield's South Street station, and the tourist ski industry in Massachusetts was launched. Photo by Gravelle Pictorial News Service. Courtesy, The Berkshire Atheneum

were other CCC camps at other locations in the state. The 1937 report noted that the Blue Hills camp, which helped preserve and upgrade recreational facilities at Blue Hills, was a leader of "First Corps Area camps in general excellence and was flying the honor pennant as the best camp in New England when it ceased its operations" that year. This federally-funded corps of young male workers constructed roads, built a stone observation tower, sprayed extensively to control gypsy moths, completed construction of cross-country ski trails, and planted 15,000 pine and spruce seedlings. The report indicates that 22,000 work hours were spent on CCC work at the Blue Hills reservation that year.

The WPA funded employees in a variety of projects across the state. Together with a basic grant of $50,000

from the legislature, the WPA brought about $550,000 into the Commonwealth for a total of 22 new projects in 1937 alone, in addition to some projects carried over from previous years. These projects included landscaping, construction of MDC buildings, and continued work on public golf courses, tennis courts, and baseball diamonds. Other similar projects involved development of major waterfront recreation areas such as Nahant Beach and parks such as the Middlesex Fells Reservation.

MDC reports indicate that in 1938, 36,602 work hours were expended by the CCC across the state, some of which included work done after the infamous hurricane of that year. This disaster required extensive clean-up as well as repairs to roads and highways. The hurricane struck on September 21, felling

trees, flooding roads, farms, and towns, stranding hundreds of residents in their homes. Some Massachusetts residents lost their lives. The *Boston Globe*'s headlines the next day read, "11 Deaths in Line Storm, Roads Out," and "State's All-Time Rainfall Record for September Broken, 12.49 Inches." Nearly $1 million in state funds were required for the clean-up.

WORLD WAR II

Despite the hardship and tragedy of the Depression years, the country was secure and at peace. Rumblings of war in Europe provoked debate in the U.S., but throughout the 1930s the nation was able to remain detached. Massachusetts, along with the rest of the nation, was shocked into action, however, by the news of Japan's attack on Pearl Harbor on December 7, 1941. With that single, devastating strike, occurring at 8 a.m. local time, Pearl Harbor's Battleship Row—where the nation's most valuable naval vessels were moored—was in flames. Nearly 2,300 service personnel died, as well as 68 civilians.

The following day, President Roosevelt asked Congress to declare war. Despite several years of isolationist activities and major reluctance to become involved in global conflict, Americans rallied around the president. Few had any real reservations now, since the country had little choice but to fight back. In fact, most isolationists agreed that "that date ended isolationism for any realist," according to Senator Arthur H. Vandenberg (R-Michigan).

Demands placed on American industry during the war were diverse and complex. Recruitment of workers, expansion of facilities, conversion of old plants, and construction of new industrial sites, as well as problems imposed by wage and price ceilings and rationing of resources, meant that the home front needed to exercise ingenuity, caution, and a sense of unity far greater than they had shared for several decades.

Various factories throughout Massa-

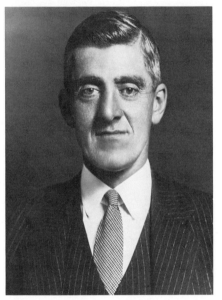

Above: *The Richardson Trail in West Townsend's CCC Camp was built in 1937 in what is now the Townsend State Forest in the north-central section of the state. One camp in the Berkshires cleared a ski trail to boost the state's tourist industry. Courtesy, Massachusetts Department of Environmental Management, Division of Forests and Parks*

Above: *Leverett Saltonstall, born in 1892 in Chestnut Hill, earned his law degree from Harvard in 1917. He served as an alderman in Newton from 1920 to 1922, as Middlesex County assistant district attorney from 1921 to 1922, and in the Massachusetts House of Representatives from 1922 to 1937. This photograph was taken when he was speaker of the House. A Republican, he was elected governor in 1938, defeating James Michael Curley. Saltonstall then served three terms as governor and in 1944 was elected to the U.S. Senate, where he served until his retirement in 1967. Courtesy, Massachusetts Archives*

Right: *On March 22, 1942, Bobby Ford, 7, Malcolm Keeler, 9, and Paul Mathews, 4, piled up salvage to contribute to the war effort from Tyler Street in Pittsfield. Rubber and metal were especially needed for reuse, and every bit helped. Photo by Gravelle Pictorial News Service. Courtesy, The Berkshire Atheneum*

Left: *During World War II, certain consumer items were earmarked for the war effort, or were not available because raw materials from foreign countries were not easily obtained. Ration coins and coupons were distributed by the War Price and Rationing Board and were needed when purchasing a car, gasoline (farmers were given more coupons for vehicles and fuel), and for scarce consumer goods like butter, sugar, and coffee. Photo by Brenda Lilly. Courtesy, The Walter C. and Sarah H. Jones Collection*

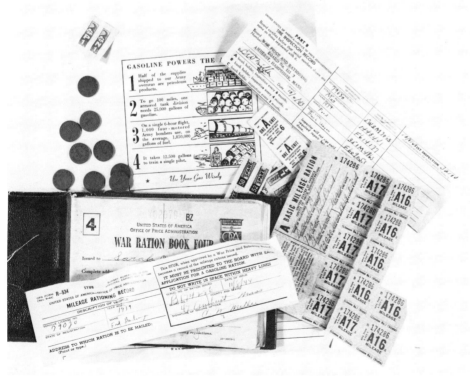

chusetts were converted to defense production. In Worcester, Harrington and Richardson produced Reising submachine guns for the marines. Like the Springfield Armory, they also manufactured M1 rifles. At Savage Arms in Chicopee, hundreds of workers produced Thompson submachine guns. Raytheon produced a range of electronic equipment, including radar for use by the Air Force. A number of shipyards such as Fore River and Lawley's turned out naval vessels. At the Boston Naval Shipyard, ships came in for repairs and new vessels were outfitted. Smaller arms were important as well as large battleships and tanks, and Smith & Wesson in Springfield manufactured revolvers for the United States military as well as for the allies in Britain.

Ammunition, aircraft, heavy weapons and tanks, and ships poured out of American factories just a few months after Pearl Harbor. By 1943, twice as much freight was shipped by rail as had been transported in 1940, and three times as many passengers traveled via railroad. The latter increase was due to the fact that few automobiles, and even fewer replacement parts for existing cars, were available. In particular, rubber rationing meant that tires on cars would have to last for the duration of the war.

In Massachusetts, researchers at medical facilities worked to come up with solutions to problems that plagued doctors and nurses close to the battlefield. On May 3, 1944, two chemists at Harvard University, Doctors Robert B. Woodward and William E. Doering, announced that they had successfully produced synthetic quinine to alleviate suffering from malaria, among the most

Above, left: Dorothy Luz of Pittsfield had been, for nine years, a supervisor at the Elmvale Worsted Company when World War II was declared. She joined the Red Cross Ambulance Corps motor unit, and when the WACs were organized, she was the first woman from Berkshire County to enlist. Photo by Gravelle Pictorial News Service. Courtesy, The Berkshire Atheneum

Above, right: Corporal John Collins of Pittsfield was a proud young marine on the Solomon Islands when he smiled for a photographer in 1942. He was killed in action later that year. Courtesy, The Berkshire Atheneum

205

troubling illnesses in the Pacific theater.

During the war, consumers found many common items unavailable, and they struggled with limited quantities of whatever *was* still produced for civilian consumption. Grocery shelves were stocked meagerly, if at all, with butter, sugar, and coffee. There was some attempt in 1943 to freeze prices on consumer goods, but this was not successful, as it was difficult to enforce a price freeze. New items entering the marketplace (such as margarine) did not fall within established price guidelines for standard items (butter).

Massachusetts provided a solid number of service personnel throughout the entire war—550,000 people either volunteered or were drafted into the military. Fort Devens in Ayer once again became an induction center, and at Otis Air Force Base on Cape Cod a military training center was established.

It was a challenge to decide how best to allocate human resources available during the war. In order to utilize talents most efficiently, the War Manpower Commission, set up in 1942, determined where workers were needed and how to divide their efforts among various industries and the military. This federal agency acted as a coordinator, not as a controller. This fact, plus the emergency nature of wartime, meant that few people reacted negatively to the commission, although there were some pockets of resistance to military service.

Most Americans contributed their time and efforts willingly. One of the most interesting phenomena on the home front was an increase in women workers, particularly in previously male-dominated jobs. Because of defense needs, women were hired to build planes, tanks, and battleships and to produce munitions—bullets, guns, and bombs. Throughout the nation, women expressed pleasure at the opportunity to earn substantial wages and to participate in a war effort that produced such tangible and gratifying results.

About 10,632,000 women were part

of the U.S. work force in 1930. Immediately after Pearl Harbor in 1941, defense plants began hiring women as replacements for military recruits who had left for the front. Actually, women had been entering the work force even earlier than that, for as it became clear to many that U.S. entry into the war was only a matter of time, factories began hiring more and more women. By 1940, there were 13,840,000 women employed outside the home. Four years later, at the height of the war, 18,449,000 women worked at a variety of factory and other industrial jobs. By the end of the war, that number had been reduced to 16,323,000, and the decline from the peak years continued as many women were laid off from war-related jobs or in order to open up jobs for returning GIs.

Above: *In the 1940s a chestnut tree blight struck Massachusetts full force. This man was obliged to cut down an enormous, but dead, chestnut tree on the Sumner lot in Leydon. The lumber from the tree might well have been used for postwar construction that answered the demands of the returned service people. Courtesy, The Walter C. and Sarah H. Jones Collection*

Facing page: *The battleship* Missouri *docked in Boston Harbor for a ceremony commemorating the surrender of Japan during the 1946 encampment of the Veterans of Foreign Wars. John F. Kennedy, soon to be a U.S. representative, was in charge of the local arrangements. Courtesy, John F. Kennedy Library*

Joseph P. Kennedy, Sr., was on the Post-War Rehabilitation Commission immediately after World War II to study the Commonwealth's economic position. This photograph is thought to have been taken at a black tie dinner meeting of that commission. To the left of Kennedy sits a young Massachusetts legislator named Thomas P. "Tip" O'Neill. Courtesy, The John F. Kennedy Library

Christian A. Herter (1895-1967), shown here about 1939 when he was speaker in the Massachusetts House of Representatives, was a 1915 Harvard graduate and had been an assistant to Herbert Hoover from 1915 to 1924, then editor of the Independent *from 1924 to 1928. He was elected to the Massachusetts House in 1938, where he served until 1943 when he was elected to the U.S. House of Representatives. A Republican, he was a congressman for Massachusetts until 1952 when he returned to Boston to become governor from 1953 to 1957. In 1959 he was appointed secretary of state under President Eisenhower. From 1961 to 1962 he was chairman of the U.S. Citizens Committee on NATO. Courtesy, Massachusetts Archives*

POSTWAR ADJUSTMENTS

Most people in the United States believed the war would end in allied victory. But there were concerns over what U.S. soldiers would do when they returned from the battlefields. Massachusetts attempted to forestall any serious assimilation difficulties by advance planning. In 1943, the state legislature established a Post-War Rehabilitation Commission to investigate and make recommendations concerning the state economy. As a result of its work, the commission published a report in 1945 detailing its findings and explaining where the economy's most pressing needs were. Particular attention was paid to agriculture—still an important part of the economy in this predominantly industrial state. Housing, urban redevelopment, and industrial development were also discussed by the commission. It was clear that Massachusetts would suffer if these economic factors were not addressed with consideration of the large numbers of returning soldiers and the shift to peacetime production.

Recommendations of the Post-War Commission said it was critical to provide for the employment, housing, and hospitalization needs of former military personnel. The reality for returning soldiers held both promise and challenge. Throughout the nation, housing was at a premium. GIs were anxious to take advantage of benefits offering them a college education in return for their military service. During the postwar years, colleges and universities in Massachusetts would see a marked increase in freshman enrollment based on the benefits of the GI Bill of Rights. In Amherst, the University of Massachusetts was just one of many

Provincetown, the northern extremity of the arm of Cape Cod, is just 55 miles by water from Boston. In 1620 the Mayflower *stopped at Provincetown's good harbor before sailing down the inner Cape to Plymouth. This photograph was taken near the Chrysler Art Museum looking back at the docks and the townscape in the late 1970s. Photo by John H. Martin*

Dawn breaks at Edgartown, Martha's Vineyard, as a lone fisherman tries his luck in the harbor between Edgartown and Chappaquiddick Island near the ferry run. Photo by Richard W. Wilkie

Above: *The Mount Holyoke College women's crew team works out in the foggy early morning hours on the Connecticut River near Brunelle's Marina in South Hadley. Photo by Michael Zide. Courtesy, Mount Holyoke College*

Facing page: *In this icy scene, a waterfall flows from Upper Pond at Mount Holyoke College in South Hadley. Ham Hall, a dormitory, stands in the distance. Photo by Clemens Kalischer. Courtesy, Mount Holyoke College*

Above: *In Rockport Harbor on Cape Ann this fisherman's shack is known as* Motif #1 *and is the town's most photographed and painted landmark. In fact, it is perhaps the favorite artists' subject on the entire East Coast. During the blizzard of 1978 the shack was destroyed, but through funds raised by town citizens it was soon restored. Photo by Justine Hill*

Facing page: *Richard W. Wilkie, a University of Massachusetts professor of geography, photographed these Whately farms during two different seasons. First owned by people of English descent, the farms feature predominantly mid-nineteenth-century buildings on extremely fertile river valley land next to the Connecticut River just south of Mount Sugarloaf. The dairy barns were often connected by sheds to the main house, enabling one to get to the barns in comfort during the winter. By the end of the 1900s many of the farms had been bought by Polish immigrants who began as hired help. Today one farm in the picture is owned by a Chinese-American who owns restaurants and sells his surplus vegetables in Boston.*

The John F. Kennedy Library and Museum commands an ocean view at Columbia Point in the Dorchester section of Boston. Designed by I.M. Pei and built with donated funds, the building was donated to the U.S. government and opened its doors in October 1979. As a presidential library it is now part of the National Archives and belongs to the people of the United States. Photo by Justine Hill

institutions across the nation with enrollments suddenly loaded with former military personnel now seeking an education.

DEFINING THE NEW ECONOMY

As the nation resumed peacetime production efforts, many regions were anxious to examine relations between labor and management. The crisis of the 1930s had made leaders of both groups wary, and New Deal legislation had changed the face of union organization with passage of major bills such as the National Labor Relations Act, also known as the Wagner Act.

In Massachusetts, Governor Robert F. Bradford appointed a special labor-management committee to study the effects of marketplace trends on the state's economy and to make suggestions about how best to handle the relationship between union leaders and industry spokespersons. Nine persons representing top industry and labor interests made up the committee. In their March 1947 report to the governor they stressed several points: the state was advised to make legislative provision for facilitating collective bargaining procedures, and was urged to "set up a new and stronger service of conciliation and arbitration." Amendments to "bring into balance" the State Labor Relations Act and ways in which to mediate labor-management disputes were also recommended.

In his response to the report, delivered to the state House of Representatives and the Senate, Governor Bradford encouraged adherence to the committee's recommendations. In his words, "This is the first time in industrial history that so comprehensive a subject has been so conscientiously studied . . . by representatives of every group affected. Moulded . . . into legislation, the Massachusetts plan can become a modern Magna Carta for labor and industry."

Elected and appointed officials in Massachusetts recognized, as did labor and management leaders, how the

immediate postwar years could bring recession and even another economic depression. At this time, many industries—particularly textile works—moved to warmer climates, predominantly in what is now termed the "Sunbelt." This exodus was the result of lower wages and greater tax benefits to industry in the South. The attempts of the Bay State labor-management committee indicate one way in which future planning was intended to stave off any further drain of industrial activity and help build the state into an economic giant in the Northeast. Several decades later, Massachusetts had proven that this

In the summer of 1966, before the student uprisings, a young Edward M. (Ted) Kennedy and Secretary of the Interior Morris Udall visited the University of Massachusetts. Kennedy is shown here with Nikaii Amarteifio, a foreign student from Accra, Ghana, who was about to enter Wesleyan and would go on to earn an M.B.A. from Harvard in 1973. Courtesy, The Walter C. and Sarah H. Jones Collection

JOHN FITZGERALD KENNEDY

Fueled by the ambition of several generations of Irish-American politicians, John F. Kennedy stepped into the arena of public life in 1946, winning the race for a Massachusetts congressional seat in the 11th district. The slot had opened up in 1945 when James Michael Curley made a successful bid for mayor of Boston. Kennedy, recently discharged from the U.S. Navy, ran a zest-filled campaign and won the election. He arrived in Washington, D.C., in 1947, joining the 90th Congress, and was subsequently reelected in 1948. Soon, he would run for (and win) the more influential post of U.S. senator—defeating Massachusetts' Republican Henry Cabot Lodge, Jr., in 1952.

In Washington, Jack Kennedy was among the most eligible bachelors of the decade. He had looks, charm, and money, and he soon met Jacqueline Bouvier, a reporter-photographer for the *Washington Times-Herald.* Gossip columnists followed the pair with a curiosity vindicated on September 12, 1953, when Senator John F. Kennedy and Jacqueline Bouvier were married in the "wedding of the year" in Newport, Rhode Island.

That both Jack and his wife were ambitious was unquestionable. That they were also polished, clever, and generally accustomed to having their own way was also true. And the nation, watching this enchanted couple rise from senator-and-wife to president-and-first lady, accepted these attributes as part of the Camelot-like dream that seemed to follow the Kennedys. Indeed, the 1960s began with an almost myth-like idealism.

Kennedy's administration promoted an expansive social policy. His stand on civil rights, buttressed by his brother Robert F. Kennedy's zeal as attorney general of the United States, promised to advance liberal causes. Kennedy's foreign policy experience was limited, yet he managed to convey a hard-line approach toward communism that served the country well during the 1962 Cuban Missile Crisis.

The president's words at his inauguration foreshadowed the strong approach he would take when confronting challenges and problems. His remarks in January 1961 reflected the idealism in all of Kennedy's choices and decisions during those early days in office: "We shall pay any price, bear any burden, meet any hardship, support any friend, oppose any foe, to assure the success and survival of liberty."

In choosing his brother as attorney general, JFK further emphasized the Kennedys' strong family traditions. Among other appointments and reappointments to the Kennedy administration were Robert McNamara as secretary of defense, J. Edgar Hoover as head of the Federal Bureau of Investigation, and Allen Dulles as director of the Central Intelligence Agency. Kennedy's decisions were representative of his desire to have policies executed quickly, with as little interference as possible.

JFK's "New Frontier" would present the young president with burdens and challenges. But for Massachusetts, at least, the continuing theme was one of pride and overwhelming support for this native son.

Kennedy's tenure was not without its rocky moments. And none of his mistakes were as obvious or as potentially disastrous as the failed Bay of Pigs invasion of Cuba in April 1961. This CIA-sponsored project was the brainchild of a Kennedy advisor, but reportedly did not have the president's out-and-out support. JFK refused to guarantee complete military air capability to back

On June 16, 1946, when John F. Kennedy won the 11th Congressional District primary, thus assuring him of victory and a seat in the U.S. House of Representatives in the fall election, there was a festive victory party. Helping him celebrate were his parents, Rose Fitzgerald Kennedy and Joseph P. Kennedy, Sr., and his maternal grandparents, Josephine (Hannon) Fitzgerald and John F. "Honey Fitz" Fitzgerald. Courtesy, The John F. Kennedy Library

The Kennedy family in 1931 at Hyannis Port did not yet include Teddy. From left to right are Bobby, Jack, Eunice, Jean, Joseph P. Sr., Rose, Pat, Kathleen, Joe Jr., and Rosemary. Courtesy, The John F. Kennedy Library

up the invasion, a limitation that proved fatal to the entire operation. Subsequently taking full blame, the president tried to redeem himself publicly for creating an atmosphere in which this type of failure could occur. He was later to lament that the episode damaged his reputation as well as the nation's. Further, it eliminated his plan to accomplish a major policy success within the first 100 days of his administration.

Still, the president remained popular. The October 1962 missile crisis involving the Soviet Union and Cuban-based missiles gave Kennedy a chance to deal firmly and resolutely with a foreign power. This restored faith in his abilities, although there were Republicans (and some Democrats) who remained critical of Kennedy.

As JFK advisor, Harvard historian Arthur M. Schlesinger, Jr., aptly commented that, following the Cuban Missile Crisis, Kennedy displayed a "combination of toughness and restraint, of will, nerve, and wisdom, so brilliantly controlled, so matchlessly calibrated, that dazzled the world. It displayed the ripening of American leadership unsurpassed in the responsible management of power."

U.S. foreign affairs were in an increasingly strong position after the crisis. In October 1963, Kennedy signed the Limited Test Ban Treaty. Ideally, this would prevent continued build-up of nuclear weapons, curtailing such activity by both the United States and the Soviet

Union. Domestic issues received attention as well, as JFK gave the go-ahead for the attorney general and the Congress to take action in a number of areas.

Kennedy supported programs aiding the disadvantaged. Throughout his term he saw numerous bills passed that would increase the minimum wage, fund urban development projects, propose social security benefit increases, and establish a medical program for the nation's elderly. Added to these was a stepped-up war against organized crime.

Kennedy's popularity was at its height in late 1963. He had support from family members, friends, and politicians. His wife and his two children—Caroline and John F. Kennedy, Jr.—were the darlings of the press. His policy-making was regarded as solid. It seemed that he faced a relatively simple reelection campaign.

The trip to Dallas, Texas, in November 1963 was critical to this reelection, however. Having won by a small margin in 1960, a margin relying heavily on Texas votes, Kennedy was determined to guarantee chances for a second term of office by paying respects now to Lone Star State voters.

It was critically important to garner Democratic support in Texas, and the popularity of the president and the first lady were exploited fully in this November visit, just as it had been during their successful European visit in 1962.

At 11:55 a.m. on November 22, the presidential limousine prepared to enter

Dallas. Jackie, wearing a pink suit and matching hat, sat beside JFK in the back seat. Texas governor John Connolly and his wife, Nellie, sat in front. It was the final appearance for John F. Kennedy—shot and killed by an assassin's bullets as the presidential entourage drove slowly past the Texas Book Repository in Dallas. By 1 p.m. Kennedy was pronounced dead at the Parkland Hospital. By 2:45 p.m. his body was on its way to Bethesda Naval Hospital aboard Air Force One, accompanied by his grieving widow and newly-sworn-in President Lyndon B. Johnson. LBJ was a Texas Democrat whose political support had helped elect Kennedy in 1960.

At the Washington, D.C., funeral on Monday, November 25, 1963, the eyes of the world focused on a somber ceremony. Communications satellites—a product of Kennedy's support for the nation's space program—gave global access to a scene that reminded some observers of FDR's burial train in the 1940s.

A riderless horse and flag-draped caisson emphasized the country's loss. Onlookers wept during the service at St. Matthew's Cathedral, the prayer of Boston's Richard Cardinal Cushing (long-time Kennedy family friend and advisor), and the playing of "Hail to the Chief." And most of all, a small boy's farewell salute to his assassinated father reminded the nation of its absolute loss.

This nuclear power plant at Rowe, called "Yankee," is one of two in Massachusetts. Seen shortly after it was built in 1960, it is now the oldest operating nuclear power plant in the United States. By 1987 Yankee had generated 28 billion kilowatt hours. Designed by Westinghouse as an Atoms for Peace project and built by Stone and Webster, Yankee has ". . . a documented record of safety, reliability, and inexpensive electricity," according to a company spokesman. Courtesy, Yankee Atomic Electric Company of the Massachusetts Electric Company

type of forecasting was the key to success.

THE COLD WAR

The postwar era signaled the start of another phase in America's obsessive fear of communism, codified in 1947 by the Truman Doctrine. This set of policies stipulated that the United States would help defend free countries of the world in their fight against communist takeover. In announcing this policy, President Harry Truman ushered in ongoing debate over how best to fight communism. Conflicting opinions held by various government officials resulted in argu-

ments over anti-communist strategies. Among those involved in the debates was John F. Kennedy. By the mid-1950s, the Massachusetts senator was known as one of the staunchest proponents of a strong national position opposing communism.

Kennedy, a native son of Massachusetts, would become one of the century's most popular presidents. Elected in 1960, his political career and personal style were in marked contrast to those of his predecessor, Dwight D. Eisenhower. Eisenhower had been elected president in 1952, riding the crest of a wave of popularity following his military career. This included a stint as

The Chantavong family of Greenfield, recent Laotian immigrants, came to the United States to begin a new life after the Marxist-Leninist Lao People's Revolutionary Party gained control in their native country in 1975. From left to right are Bounma (in back), Souk, Siene, and Philavanh Chantavong, and family friend, Khambone (the father and oldest daughter were away at the time). Photo by Samuel Pettengill. Courtesy, Special Collections and Archives, Library, University of Massachusetts at Amherst

head of the North Atlantic Treaty Organization (NATO). At the end of his two terms, Eisenhower gave endorsement to Vice President Richard M. Nixon. This former congressman from California was known chiefly for his aggressive tactics on the House Un-American Activities Committee.

President Kennedy was heir to decades of shrewd political know-how handed down to him by both his mother's and father's families. His maternal grandfather had been mayor of Boston, and his father, Joseph P. Kennedy, was U.S. ambassador to Great Britain from 1937 to 1940. John Fitzgerald Kennedy's road to the White House was not without obstacles, but his victory over Nixon assured good visibility and promised popular support for his first term in office. Particularly in the eastern part of Massachusetts, ecstatic response to Kennedy's election was repeated over and over in headlines and news stories.

A DECADE OF CHANGE

During the 1960s, the entire nation became intimately acquainted with the Kennedy family and thereby became more conscious of Massachusetts as a force in contemporary politics. Not only did JFK reach the presidency, but his two brothers, Robert F. Kennedy and Edward M. Kennedy, climbed into the political spotlight as well. By the 1980s, RFK's son Robert F. Kennedy, Jr., would be a successful contender for a congressional seat from Massachusetts.

The state political and cultural milieu changed during the 1960s. In 1964, Massachusetts' electorate extended the governor's term of office from two to four years. The year before, the state voted to ban public school prayer, an action viewed unfavorably by many Roman Catholics in Massachusetts. In 1966 Massachusetts Republican Edward W. Brooke was elected as the first black U.S. senator since Reconstruction, and the governor also signed into law that year a bill permitting distribution of birth control information. This law eliminated a ban of 87 years against such dissemination—making Massachusetts

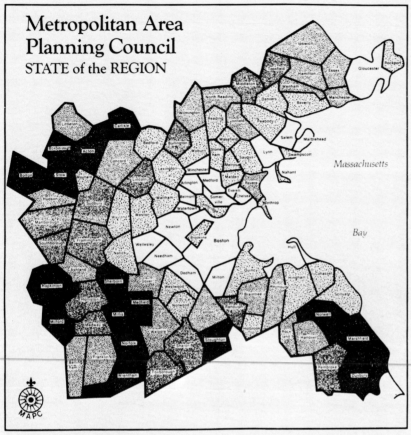

Metropolitan Area Planning Council
STATE of the REGION

Massachusetts

Bay

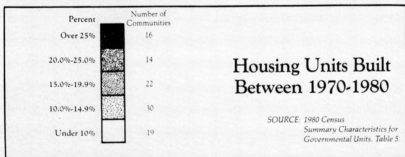

Percent	Number of Communities
Over 25%	16
20.0%-25.0%	14
15.0%-19.9%	22
10.0%-14.9%	30
Under 10%	19

Housing Units Built Between 1970-1980

SOURCE: *1980 Census Summary Characteristics for Governmental Units. Table 5.*

The Metropolitan Area Planning Council charted the growth of the Boston suburbs in the 1970s. The darkest areas, 16 communities, had more than 25 percent of their housing units built in that short decade. The white areas had the fewest additions to the housing supply. From Carnahan, State of the Region: A Statistical Portrait, *1975*

one of the few states in the nation where birth control information could be obtained easily and legally.

Kennedy was the first Massachusetts-born president since John Quincy Adams (Calvin Coolidge, although a resident of Massachusetts, had been born in Vermont). The positive atmosphere that surrounded Kennedy seemed to reflect a similar optimism that pervaded Massachusetts as a whole. Throughout the first two postwar decades, Massachusetts residents moved into new suburbs and many new industries were launched, particularly during the mid-1960s. In the 1950s, housing construction increased, as did the demand for new schools to accommodate the postwar baby boom that had hit the nation. In 1950, nearly 4,700,000 people lived in Massachusetts; by 1960, that figure had grown to almost 5,150,000. In 1970, the state population hit almost 5,700,000, and by 1980 there were 5,737,000 residents of the Bay State.

Thanks to the enthusiasm of the Kennedy administration, the U.S. space program created hundreds of jobs for Massachusetts citizens. Along Route 128—the state's "Technology Highway" that encircles Boston—companies turned out all sorts of products used to support NASA's space programs. Were it not for the vision of John F. Kennedy, Massachusetts might have lagged behind in the national economy. As it was, his intent that the United States would send a man to the moon before 1970 resulted in stable growth for the Bay State.

DEMOGRAPHIC CHANGE
Attempts to establish good state employment policies and an atmosphere of welcome for new business and industry bore fruit. By 1960, the Bay State was thriving; it was a good place to live and work. Across the nation, cities were growing and suburbs were springing up around them, but in Massachusetts a somewhat different set of demographics were at work. Between 1950 and 1960, there was about a 10 percent gain in the

state's population, compared to an 18.4 percent growth rate for the nation as a whole. Large numbers of people were not resettling in Massachusetts. While states such as Florida and California experienced major population expansions, Massachusetts was 34th among all the states in growth.

Like many areas of the country, Massachusetts saw its fastest population growth in the suburbs. While urban decentralization was a characteristic of the 1950s, suburbanites continued to commute to work in the cities through most of the 1960s. The move of resources away from urban centers into the suburbs and bordering regions became pronounced in the late 1960s and continued into the 1970s and 1980s.

By the 1970s, suburbs had largely replaced cities as the places to live *and* work, both in Massachusetts and across the nation. The Standard Metropolitan Statistical Area (SMSA), a measure devised to define the parameters of an urban area, in 1960 defined and described Massachusetts via the following approximate populations:

Boston:	697,000
Brockton:	73,000
Fall River:	10,000
Fitchburg-Leominster:	71,000
Lawrence-Haverhill:	117,000
Lowell:	92,000
New Bedford:	102,500
Pittsfield:	58,000
Springfield-Chicopee-Holyoke:	289,000
Worcester:	186,500

These figures contrast markedly with similar figures for some of the same cities in previous years, and they serve as a gauge against which future demographic shifts can be measured. The move away from cities and toward suburbs was both a reflection of and a precipitating factor in social, cultural, and economic shifts within Massachusetts during the 1970s and 1980s.

CHANGING ECONOMIC PATTERNS

In the 1970s, high-tech industry offered undreamed-of opportunity for thousands of Massachusetts workers. By the 1950s, more individuals were training for technical positions. For example, there were an estimated 13,000 engineers in Massachusetts in 1950, a figure that had grown to 26,000 by 1960. One decade later, 40,000 engineers lived and worked in the Bay State. A similar increase was seen in the percentage of technical and professional workers in the greater Boston area (the most populated part of the state). In 1960, about 12 percent of the population fell into this job category. By 1970, this group had increased to 20 percent.

Soon after the Route 128 region became home base for a variety of high-tech firms, Bay State companies were producing everything from electronics to software to computer microchips. The basis for much of this research and development in high technology had been established earlier by several Massachusetts residents. In the 1920s, Dr. Vannevar Bush, then a professor at the Massachusetts Institute of Technology (MIT), was responsible for building the differential analyzer, a forerunner of today's computational devices. The first electronic digital computers constructed and used on a large scale were designed in the 1940s by mathematicians at Harvard University.

Although Massachusetts' population leveled off during the 1970s and into the 1980s, the state's economic abilities were not hampered by lack of an adequate labor force. Overall, the state economy grew 25.7 percent between 1974 and 1984. In fact, Massachusetts' economy increased at a rate faster than that of the rest of the nation between 1980 and 1984. During that period, the state population grew by about one percent (62,000 people), up slightly from the 0.8 percent growth rate between 1970 and 1979. Massachusetts is a state where the majority of people currently enjoy a

Governor Michael Dukakis met some future voters at an undated and unidentified patriotic parade. Courtesy, Press Office, Office of the Governor

higher per capita income than in other parts of the country. This growth and stability is likely to continue, since residents are likely to remain in Massachusetts rather than move to other parts of the nation.

In many respects, Massachusetts is considered an ideal place to live, despite the high cost of living there during the past several decades. In the mid-1980s, it cost a family of four 15 percent more to live in Massachusetts than to live in a comparable location in Texas. State unemployment hovered around 11.2 percent during the nation's 1975 recession, a figure higher than the national average. By 1978, however, Massachusetts' jobless rate fell below the national average and by the 1980s unemployment rates in Massachusetts were the lowest in the entire United States. Part of this was due to the strong trend toward continued job growth, particularly in the high-tech and service sectors, in contrast to heavy industry, which continued to locate elsewhere during the 1960s, 1970s, and 1980s as energy costs rose. Low business taxes, combined with somewhat lower wages than some areas and the availability of skilled or educated workers, make Massachusetts more and more

attractive to new businesses. Since early in the postwar era, Massachusetts has steadily shifted from traditional mill-based industry, (i.e., paper manufacture, textiles, and shoes) to high-technology industry. This shift has resulted in an increase in white-collar jobs in the state.

There have been changes in regional population distribution within Massachusetts in recent decades. Boston showed a slight population increase in the 1980s, but in general Bay Staters moved to the suburbs, as well as to smaller cities and towns. The southeastern portion of the state saw the largest population gain—Plymouth County grew by 3 percent in the 1980s, the Cape and Islands by 10.6 percent. The latter increase reflects a growing elderly population in the state. Reflecting national trends, more and more of Massachusetts' citizens are elderly—the state's population was the seventh oldest in the nation in 1980.

LABOR IN THE 1980s

While it is true that the recession of 1974-1975 hit Massachusetts particularly hard, recovery seemed to come more quickly there. The gross state product dropped faster than the GNP in the

1970s, but between 1980 and 1982 Massachusetts' total output grew 3.2 percent compared to the national growth rate of only 0.7 percent. During the early 1980s, personal income in Massachusetts climbed 18 percent, while the national average hovered around 11.8 percent. This ranked Massachusetts third in the nation, behind Texas (with personal income growth at 18.7 percent) and Florida (22.5 percent). Most of the recovery and expansion is attributed to the high-tech industry—35.7 percent of manufacturing in Massachusetts is high-tech in nature. Financial and other service industries, real estate, and insurance also account for a large number of employed persons in the state. In 1985, Massachusetts women represented 54.5 percent of all workers compared to 43.3 percent in 1970.

An important factor influencing the lower wage and salary scales is the generally lower union membership in the Bay State. Of the entire non-farm work force, only 24.9 percent are unionized. Most northern industrial states, such as Michigan and New York, have much higher union membership, 37.4 percent and 38.7 percent, respectively. Massachusetts also suffers less time lost due to strikes and labor disputes. This union situation is undoubtedly considered a positive factor when business and industry locate a plant in Massachusetts. But for workers, lack of union activity means less take-home pay. Combined with the high cost of living, this means many people in Massachusetts are making few gains in the quality of their life. In Boston, data processors earn about 10 percent less than their counterparts in other areas of the country.

State Democratic party supporters attribute economic stability in Massachusetts to Governor Michael Dukakis. A native of Lowell and the son of Greek immigrants, Dukakis was a state representative between 1963 and 1971. He became a strong, effective leader and was elected governor in 1974. Defeated for

reelection by Republican Ed King (governor from 1978 to 1982), Dukakis was elected again in 1982 and reelected in 1986. The "Duke," as he is called, announced his candidacy for the Democratic presidential nomination in early 1987.

LEARNING IN THE COMMONWEALTH

Since the 1630s, when the first free public school was established in Boston and Harvard College was founded in Cambridge, Massachusetts has been in the forefront of education. From these great beginnings, a tradition of excellence in education prompted many to agree that Bay State institutions offer some of the finest educational opportunities in the world. These comprise a concentration of post-secondary schools including MIT, Harvard University, and several of the country's oldest women's colleges,

Robert Frost was born in San Francisco but grew up in Lawrence, Massachusetts, his father's hometown. Frost graduated as co-valedictorian from Lawrence High School and attended college at Dartmouth and Harvard but never earned a degree. In this circa 1952 photo, a still from a film made by the U.S. Information Service, Frost is interviewed at Amherst College, where he had been poet-in-residence several times since 1917. Frost was Simpson Lecturer at Amherst from 1949 until his death in 1963. Used by permission of the Robert Lee Frost Estate. Courtesy, The Jones Library, Inc., Amherst

COURT-ORDERED BUSING IN BOSTON

Massachusetts has never been immune to the problems inherent in absorbing ethnic and racial changes in its population. In particular, the Boston public schools have for years faced challenges posed by various immigrant groups. Early in the nineteenth century, older white Anglo-Saxon residents of the city felt threatened by large numbers of Roman Catholic Irish immigrants who moved into the Boston area. They brought their own customs with them, customs that often clashed with established traditions of long-time Boston residents. Among the bases for these confrontations was the education of children, which Irish Catholics often left to the Roman Catholic Church. This led to violent anti-Catholic riots, and in some cases to attacks on the nuns who taught in Catholic schools. In the early twentieth century, other foreigners—notably Italians and Poles—emigrated to Boston and subsequently provoked violent reaction. The famous Sacco-Vanzetti trial showed to what extent xenophobia could carry defenders of the status quo.

But among the most pervasive and disruptive problems facing Boston as a community in the latter years of the twentieth century was court-ordered busing of black children into predominantly white neighborhood schools. Most of this busing focused on South Boston schools, an area of some isolation from the rest of the city.

"Southie," as it has been known for generations, is a predominantly working-class, Irish Catholic area. Geographically it is part of Boston but is set off by the Southeast Expressway, by myriad railroad lines, and by its staunchly parochial identity.

Nonetheless, this strictly homogeneous group displayed some of the most severe reactions to school desegregation that had yet occurred anywhere in the United States.

It might seem that racially-provoked violence would be more common to areas where racial segregation had been first accepted and then later legally denied continuance. But in states where all-white or all-black restaurants, public transportation, and schools were no longer legally supported, school desegregation had been effected with relative ease (after initial attempts to block it). The positive results of the 1954 Supreme Court ruling in *Brown v. Board of Education* were clearly evident in southern school desegregation. Such positive changes were not easily wrought, however, in Boston in the 1970s.

Boston's Irish-Catholic mayor, Kevin White, had been elected in 1967. Less than a decade later he faced the almost insurmountable challenge of persuading a recalcitrant school committee to accept busing of black students to white schools. It was no simple task for him to persuade his ethnic peers to comply with a law that seemed to threaten their heritage.

White himself was skeptical about forcing the desegregation of Boston's schools, stating openly that "it's a lousy law." But by 1974, even schools in cities like Charlotte, North Carolina, and Jacksonville, Florida, where racial tensions had been extremely apparent, complied with federal laws concerning racially-integrated student populations. Boston residents, on the other hand, continued to reject desegregation outright. They rejoiced that the Boston School Committee refused to fall into line.

In June 1974, U.S. District Court Judge W. Arthur Garrity, Jr., ruled that the Boston School Committee must approve a citywide desegregation plan for all public schools by September 1975. The committee refused to cooperate. It filed a court appeal, but was defeated when Garrity's decision was upheld.

The public nature of school authorities' defiance gave Southie residents, their children, and others with anti-busing sentiments an excuse to take their anger and frustration into the schools and onto the streets.

Riots in and around the South Boston schools became commonplace throughout the early part of the 1974 academic year. Yet it soon became clear that violence would not solve the deadlock concerning desegregation. Arch-foes of desegregation, like School Committee member Louise Day Hicks, grew fearful as incident after incident erupted in the schools and in the streets. Yelling racial epithets, thousands of parents gathered when black students were bused into the previously all-white school district. In December 1974, an 18-year-old white youth was stabbed at South Boston High School and a black was charged with the crime. This provoked more violent demonstrations. And a few months before, a black Haitian immigrant had been the innocent target of a severe beating.

Southie residents traditionally relied on their church and on the police force (largely Irish-Catholic) for protection and guidance. But in this issue, the neighborhood priests failed to give their approval. After being denied help by federal marshals, Mayor White turned to city law officers to protect schoolchildren before, during, and after school. Mayor White even suggested closing South Boston High School as a way to prevent further violence. This was no idle threat, since federal support for all Boston public schools was at risk due to the city's non-compliance with desegregation laws.

Southie parents felt betrayed. They could no longer rely on their police force, and the Church failed to help, as not one priest would participate in anti-busing activities.

Gradually, the violence abated. After months of anguish, mothers from both South Boston and Roxbury (home for most black students) offered to form patrols in school buildings. They hoped their presence might reduce hostility and violence. Black and white high school students formed biracial committees to investigate causes of their mutual difficulties. And parents from both black and white areas of the city agreed to sit on a biracial peacemaking council.

In the face of threats to their children's welfare and serious disruption of the educational process, parents in Southie began to look beyond their initial distrust of change. School authorities gave in and complied with desegregation plans, keeping the schools open and operating in more or less orderly fashion.

Although this compliance was made grudgingly at first, by the early 1980s Boston schools were different. They had grown more responsive to the needs of all students. Anti-busing factions were, for the most part, absent from the school committee. A professional administrator had been hired to upgrade the educational system and make it accountable to parents and to the city. The corporate community provided support for education in the form of guaranteed hiring priorities for Boston high school graduates in entry-level positions. This gesture of confidence helped turn around the previously high dropout rate.

Racially-provoked incidents still occur in Boston, and the secondary schools still have racial issues to contend with. But the city's population shift during the 1970s and early 1980s resulted in a student body that was 67 percent minority (black, Hispanic, and Asian). This natural population shift probably served more than any other factor, including court-ordered busing, to desegregate the Boston public schools permanently and in a positive manner.

BALANCING THE PUBLIC SCHOOLS

Desegregation in Boston and Springfield

These schoolchildren were photographed for the cover of a 1975 state commission booklet on de facto *segregation and its remedy. From*

Massachusetts State Board of Education, Balancing the Public Schools: Desegregation in Boston and Springfield, *1975*

Radcliffe, Wellesley, Smith, and Mount Holyoke. College students represented 7 percent of the state's total population in 1984.

Three out of five college students in the state attend privately-funded institutions. But public spending on higher education in Massachusetts was below the national average until the mid-1980s, both in elementary and secondary education. From 1970 to 1983, spending on this segment of education grew only 23 percent in the state, compared to 32 percent nationally.

Statewide public school education was further affected, negatively, by legislation aimed at reducing property taxes. Proposition 2½, enacted in 1980, stopped the increase in per capita spending on public school students. Spending dropped by nearly $300 per student in 1981 and 1982 following this tax limit law. Many parents and educators had spoken out against the tax reduction bill, although these protests were doomed to failure in the face of demands for lower taxes. Concerns that Massachusetts students would suffer if fewer tax dollars were available for state schools were well-founded. In 1979, Massachusetts spent about 24 percent more per student than the national per capita average. By the time Proposition 2½ impacted local budgets, Massachusetts' per capita rate was only 3 percent above the national average. In fact, during the first year after Proposition 2½, Massachusetts dollar amounts spent on public-school students fell by 11 percent.

There was simply not as much money available to cities and towns after this tax limit law passed. Because of it, income from property taxes fell by 18 percent during that first year, affecting not only spending on students but also limiting money available to pay public school teachers. This contributed to the further erosion of an already low salary scale for educators in Massachusetts. Attempts to repeal Proposition 2½ have been unsuccessful. However, local groups in some communities have passed overrides of the tax limit law, thereby increasing some school districts' funding. Elsewhere, communities have seen athletic programs limited, certain academic projects and curricula eliminated, and repairs and upkeep to aging school facilities ignored.

A STATE OF CONTRASTS

Massachusetts is a state with strong ties to the Democratic party. Its state legislature remains predominantly Democratic in the mid-1980s, with little indication of a change, although some areas are strongly Republican in political makeup. The Commonwealth has a firm economic base—its reliance on high-tech industry has continued to bear fruit—and the trend toward approval for taxing foreign imports is likely to benefit the Bay State even more.

The state has been a leader in cultural and educational issues for centuries. It boasts three native sons as former presidents of the United States, with the possibility of another before the end of the twentieth century. Many state citizens have contributed to the country's industrial development, its scientific and medical advances, and its agricultural pursuits. The majority of Massachusetts towns are steeped in history and tradition of national significance, ranging from the landing of the *Mayflower* on Cape Cod to the culturally-rich Berkshires, where the Boston Symphony Orchestra makes its summer home at Tanglewood. Both residents and visitors delight in the leisure pursuits offered by the state's tourist industry. There is little missing from the Bay State. Colonists settled in Massachusetts during the seventeeth century, patriots from the state fought for a nation's liberty during the eighteenth century, and inventors and philosophers developed their ideas in the settled security of nineteenth-century Massachusetts. In the twentieth century, statesmen and politicians have strived, along with reformers and entrepreneurs, to make Massachusetts a shining example of democracy at work.

As a result of peace activism, especially among college students, and because of the Vietnam War, Massachusetts felt Far Eastern cultural and religious influence in the form of this Buddhist peace pagoda on a hilltop in rural Leverett. Built by monks and nuns and interested volunteers affiliated with the Nipponzan Myohoji, the pagoda opened in October 1985. The group plans to have a Japanese landscaped environment for the site, complete with reflecting pools and flowering plants. Photo by Evan D. Jones

PARTNERS IN PROGRESS

On April 18, 1775, when Paul Revere spotted two lanterns in the belfry arch of Boston's Old North Church, he galloped off to "spread the alarm through every Middlesex village and farm . . ." Massachusetts was predominantly agricultural then, but the economy would soon begin changing rapidly. Within the next 45 years the state's population grew from 270,000 to over a half-million; urbanization became inevitable.

The change from an agricultural society to an industrial economy was not confined to major cities, such as Boston and Worcester, but affected every town and hamlet in the Commonwealth. The population grew, but the amount of arable land remained the same. Revolutionary War veterans, well established on their farms, watched sons and grandsons move west to seek available land. Ingenius Yankees thus became one of the Commonwealth's first exports.

In farming villages industry began modestly, almost unnoticed. Sawmills, paper mills, and carding mills—taking advantage of abundantly available waterpower—sprang up to meet the needs of local farmers. Farm families began to supplement their incomes with cottage industries that gradually became full-time occupations. And before long, nonagricultural production exceeded the needs of local villagers and had to be transported to other towns where demand was greater. To reduce the cost of this transportation, the public supported construction of canals, turnpikes, and, after 1830, railroads.

Massachusetts capitalists were making elegant profits in global trade, and began investing in factories only after the Trade Embargo of 1807 shut down most of their markets. Income from industrial investment could not compete with fortunes made through commerce until a few far-sighted, courageous entrepreneurs decided to invest heavily in the textile industry. The first large-scale textile mill began operation in 1815 in Waltham and included dormitories for 200 mill workers.

By 1860 Massachusetts was an industry leader, not only in textiles, but also in shoe manufacturing. The era of self-sufficient farming began to decline.

The War Between the States stimulated Massachusetts industry, providing incentive for more mass production which soon required a larger pool of labor. This need was partly met by a massive wave of immigrants from Ireland, who came to Boston at the rate of 1,000 per month between 1846 and 1856.

By the beginning of World War I Massachusetts' factories were experiencing hard times. Demands of wartime again boosted production, but only until armistice day. The postwar recession of 1921 hit hard, complicated by developing labor unions demanding higher wages. After the stock market crash in 1929, total recovery did not arrive until World War II stimulated production in 1940.

The postwar years saw increased international competition for Massachusetts' share of the textile and shoe markets, but government investments in defense bases and projects during the Cold War helped sustain the state's economy. Electronic research carried on during the war eventually spawned a new scientific industry known as "high-tech," and service industries evolved to meet the needs of an increasing middle class.

The organizations whose stories are detailed on the following pages have chosen to support this important civic project. They illustrate the variety of ways in which individuals and their businesses have contributed to the growth and development of the Commonwealth. The civic involvement of Massachusetts' businesses, institutions of learning, and government, in cooperation with its citizens, has made the state an excellent place in which to live and work.

BAY STATE HISTORICAL LEAGUE

"For the purpose of stimulating interest in historical matters and to become better acquainted with local organizations and what they are doing in the way of historical work, I would ask your opinion as to the advisability of forming a society composed of representatives from all the local organizations within the limits of Middlesex and Essex counties."

John Ayer, president of the Somerville Historical Society, wrote that message in 1903 to the presidents of the historical societies of his neighboring towns. Thus was the Bay State Historical League born. It has "stimulated interest in historical matters" ever since. For his efforts, Ayer has been memorialized in the John Ayer Award, presented annually by the league to an individual who has made a major contribution in the field of local history.

The association was formed as part of a broad movement of concern for the past, stirred in large part by reaction to the large wave of immigrants that came to America at the turn of the century. The movement was conservative and protective of a long-ago time. The societies that multiplied so rapidly throughout the commonwealth focused on the colonial past and were generally the province of a closed society of white Anglo-Saxon Protestants.

The vehicles chosen by the original organizers of the league would remain virtually unchanged for the history of the organization. These included quarterly meetings hosted by a member society with tours of local historical sites as the feature attraction. In addition, occasional publications kept the organizations informed of each other's activities, and eminent scholars offered opinions on the purpose of local history.

Membership growth was constant and quickly outgrew the northeastern base. The league had a statewide constituency by its 15th anniversary. In September 1930 the first issue of the *Bulletin* appeared. It was a quarterly listing of the activities of the society's 85 members, and also included a report of the previous quarterly meeting and plans for the next one. The plain, six-page format would remain unchanged for the next 40 years.

The American Association for State and Local History was formed in the early 1940s, and the league's affiliation with that national body gave it access to assistance and technical information on a scale not previously available.

The Bay State Historical League underwent a dramatic revision in the 1970s. Membership grew rapidly. More than 300 organizational members were joined by new, individual members—a category added in 1971. The *Bulletin* was expanded to a slick, magazine-size professional publication. Quarterly meetings added lectures and workshops to the traditional tours. And leadership came more frequently from professional historians connected with the commonwealth's museums and educational institutions.

The historical "renaissance" of the 1970s was part of a nationwide interest in local history, a by-product as much of the Bicentennial as of the growing interest in historical preservation and new methods of studying local history.

The professionalization of the league continued with the addition of an executive secretary from 1975 until 1982, the evolution of the *Bulletin* to an informative journal, and the offering of a monthly calendar of events. Services were expanded to include technical workshops, seminars, speakers' lists, and consultants.

A grass-roots membership drive in 1980-1981 increased the Bay State Historical League's membership to nearly 1,000 organizations, libraries, and individuals.

ZAYRE CORP.

In 1956 the Max and Morris Feldberg family, owner of a chain of ladies' apparel stores, launched a new concept in retailing. They predicted that discounting would be the growth direction of the future and opened America's first neighborhood, self-service, general merchandise, discount department store.

Today Zayre Corp., a 70,000-employee company named for the Yiddish expression "zehr gut" (very good), has grown from its small, experimental origins into one of America's largest retail organizations, operating more than 1,200 stores in 42 states coast to coast. The Framingham, Massachusetts-based firm has been on the leading edge of retailing concepts for over 30 years.

Each Zayre Corp. business represents a distinctive marketing strategy. Zayre Stores, the largest division, operating in close to 30 states, boasts nearly 400 full-line discount department stores. T.J. Maxx, established in 1977, is the nation's second-largest off-price retailer with 250 stores selling discounted brand-name family apparel and giftware in 33 states. Hit or Miss, offering style-conscious career-oriented women first-quality apparel at low retail prices in more than 500 stores in 33 states, has expanded these fashion lines in a new mail-order catalog, "Chadwick's of Boston." BJ's Wholesale Club is a self-service, cash-and-carry warehouse selling general merchandise and food at wholesale prices. BJ's serves small businesses, professional offices, institutions, and other groups on a membership basis. The newest Zayre division, HomeClub, is a chain of membership cash-and-carry warehouse outlets selling brand-name, home-improvement products at discount prices.

The Zayre commitment to community service is manifested in contributions of more than five million dollars annually to numerous charitable organizations with emphasis on those that provide health and social services for the elderly, handicapped, minority groups, women, and children. Zayre has responded to the mounting

One of the largest discount and specialty retailers in the United States, Zayre Corp. represents five separate retail businesses: (clockwise, from top) Zayre Stores, T.J. Maxx, Hit or Miss, BJ's Wholesale Club, and HomeClub.

national concern about missing children and is one of Child Find's largest corporate sponsors, displaying photographs on in-store posters and community bulletin boards throughout the country. Zayre also prints pictures of missing children on several million items it sells each year. Customers can report lost children on a specially provided toll-free hotline.

The Zayre good-neighbor policy has resulted in significant growth for the company. Extensive expansion of retail space, technical support, and management continues to spur sales and earnings, and by the end of the decade Zayre Corp. expects to see volume surpass $10 billion.

PARKER BROTHERS

In 1883 an enterprising 16-year-old boy named George S. Parker took nearly all of his life savings and three weeks off from school to publish and market a game he invented called Banking. Little did he know that this small investment would lead to the founding of one of America's oldest and largest game manufacturers, Parker Brothers.

Over the past 104 years Parker Brothers has published more than 1,200 different games. Many have enjoyed continual popularity throughout the years, such as world-famous Monopoly®, Risk®, Clue®, and Sorry®. Today, as Parker Brothers enters its second century, the company continues growing with the times, shown by its 1982 introduction of video games and its 1983 entry into personal-computer software.

Although Parker Brothers is now a subsidiary of Kenner Parker Toys Inc., it was a family affair for more than 100 years. Until 1985 it was headed by Randolph P. Barton, grandson of founder George S. Parker.

Parker was born in 1867 in Salem, Massachusetts. He aspired to be a journalist, but was also a great games enthusiast and spent much of his leisure time playing games with friends. Forming an informal "club," they played parlor games of the era—Authors, Everlasting, Around the World, and Parchesi.

Card playing was discouraged in many New England homes because of its association with gambling; but making money was not forbidden, so George chose this theme for his first game, Banking. He invented it for his friends, and it soon became their favorite. After countless playing sessions to iron out wrinkles, clarify rules, and polish it up, George Parker submitted Banking to two Boston publishers. Both turned it down. One recommended that George publish it himself, which he did, and within a few months had sold nearly 500 copies. Besides earning back his $50 investment, he cleared a profit of almost $100.

After graduating from Medford High School, George Parker was a reporter for the *Commercial Bulletin* in Boston, but he never lost sight of his embryonic game business. At the urging of his brother Charles, he soon left journalism to form the George S. Parker Company in Salem. Two years later Charles became a partner, and the firm was renamed Parker Brothers.

George focused his efforts on developing new games and play-testing them. "There are many games on the market that, though bright and interesting in external appearance, are found dull and unentertaining when played," he wrote. To ensure that Parker Brothers games remained fun to play, George personally wrote the rules for every new game.

In 1888 Parker Brothers' catalog described 29 games, most invented by George Parker. The firm experienced a burst of growth during the Gay Nineties. It was a time when the public was eager for fun, while interest in culture

Front of Salem plant in early days.

and education was also growing. Popular Parker Brothers items included Game of American History, Story of the Bible, Baseball, and The Game of Travel. As the country approached its entry into the Spanish-American War, George Parker introduced The Military Game, Hold the Fort, War in Cuba, Siege of Havana, and other new games. Turn-of-the-century titles also reflected the times, including The Motor Carriage Game and Klondike, based on the Alaska gold rush.

Since bridge was banned by millions of conservative American families in the early 1900s, George Parker saw the need for a substitute card game that could not be associated with gambling. Pit®, introduced in 1904, had the excitement of regular playing cards, but individual cards depicted grains with point values, thus avoiding any gambling connections. Flinch® soon followed, for a time outselling every other card game on the market. Finally in 1906 Parker Brothers introduced Rook®, the most successful card game ever produced by the company. Within

Parker Brothers' corporate headquarters, Beverly, Massachusetts.

seven years it became the best-selling game in the country, and today more than 55 million decks have been sold.

Always looking for a new, enjoyable pastime, Parker Brothers applied the puzzle technique to pictures with a series of jigsaw puzzles named Pastime Picture Puzzles. These puzzles were considered works of art because expert woodcutters cut the pieces into recognizable shapes, such as snowflakes, lobsters, and stars. Demand was so overwhelming that in 1909 all other game production was stopped in the Salem plant. A special building was rented where 150 additional employees handled the flood of puzzle orders. High production costs forced Parker Brothers to discontinue the puzzles in 1957, but not before it had been enjoyed by millions, including the Russian emperor, Teddy Roosevelt, and the Queen of England.

Parker Brothers continued to grow throughout the Roaring Twenties, due partly to ownership of the license for mah-jongg, a game craze then sweeping the country. But the Depression took its toll on everything, including the game business. Just when the firm was "within an inch of disaster," recalled Parker's son-in-law, Robert Barton, Parker Brothers introduced its most popular game, Monopoly®. "It was a godsend," Barton added. During a time of financial hardship, "It let people fantasize that they could win in the real estate market."

Monopoly® was brought to Parker Brothers in 1933 by Charles Darrow of Germantown, Pennsylvania, but was turned down by company executives who claimed it had more than 50 fundamental playing errors. Undaunted, Darrow proceeded on his own, and when reports of the game's success began to reach Parker Brothers, the firm reconsidered and bought the rights in 1935.

Monopoly® was the biggest thing to ever hit Parker Brothers. Production rose to 20,000 sets a week, but orders poured in so quickly that they had to be stuffed in huge laundry baskets and stacked in the hallways. Today Monopoly® is produced in 29 countries and 19 languages including Chinese and Arabic.

In 1953 George Parker, the firm's founder and guiding spirit, died at the age of 86. A legend in his own time, he had lived long enough to see Parker Brothers become a major force in the home entertainment industry.

235

PRIME COMPUTER, INC.

By 1972 the minicomputer was a well-established product. A number of companies were marketing these small systems that took computing power out of cloistered environments of mainframes and put it in users' hands.

To stand out in this kind of competition, a start-up would have to do something dramatic. It needed a really *different* idea, one that excited not only the scientific, technical users of the day but that also appealed to business people, who worried about the cost and potential obsolescence of the systems.

Eight men founded Prime Computer, Inc., on such an idea. They took an operating system that had been created for a mainframe computer and converted it to power a much smaller system, a minicomputer. This new system would process information twice as fast as existing minicomputers. More important, it was the first small computer that let many users run a variety of tasks simultaneously.

To do this the founders of Prime developed the software, then built the hardware around it. This unique "software first" philosophy became the foundation of the firm's fully compatible product line. Software running on one system could run on any other. Therefore, when customers upgraded their computers, they could do so without costly, time-consuming software rewrites.

That first minicomputer, the 200®, enabled Prime to offer the features of a $10-million machine on one that cost roughly $100,000. It became a magnet for technically sophisticated users who wanted to run large applications, such as scientific analyses, on a minicomputer. It also launched a corporation that has grown into a *Fortune* 500 company and one of the world's largest superminicomputer vendors.

Between 1967 and 1972 there were some 50 computer start-ups in the United States. Prime is one of only two minicomputer companies from that era

Prime Park in Natick has been the world headquarters of Prime Computer since 1980.

succeeding today as an independent corporation.

From sales of $12,000 that first year, Prime vaulted to the $11-million mark in 1975 and to $153 million in 1979. As a result of this tremendous market acceptance, it was listed on the New York Stock Exchange in 1978—the youngest company ever listed up to that time.

One reason for this growth is Prime's international perspective. The company realized early that the international market was ripe for a product such as its minicomputer. As a result, less than one year after its founding, Prime opened its first office overseas. The office consisted of a single marketing representative working over an appliance store in West London.

That British sales office was the first of what has become 15 subsidiaries, plus numerous international distributors. Today approximately half of Prime's revenues comes from sales outside of the United States. Along with its international sales presence, Prime

has opened research and development facilities in England and Australia, as well as manufacturing operations in Ireland and Puerto Rico.

Another key to Prime's success has been its investments in research and development. The company has produced an impressive string of "firsts" in the computer industry. In addition to the 200®, Prime introduced such innovations as the first virtual memory minicomputer in 1973; the first 32-bit, virtual memory, large-scale supermini in 1976; the first token-based communications network and million-byte memory board in 1979; and the first large-scale superminicomputer to use emitter coupled logic (ECL), the 9950®, in 1984.

Prime currently reinvests more than 11 percent of its annual revenue into research and development. In addition to developing faster, more powerful superminicomputers, the company is exploring such highly specialized arenas as supercomputing and sophisticated graphics.

The use of Prime computers has mirrored the evolving acceptance of minicomputers. From the onset users in the scientific and engineering communities used Prime's systems in complex computational areas such as geophysical engineering, aerospace engineering, energy, and scientific research. This technically sophisticated audience remains one of the biggest users of Prime equipment.

In the late 1970s minicomputers started moving out of laboratories and into commercial offices. Among the first systems to make the transition were Prime systems, since they were easy to develop applications on and could communicate well with equipment from other vendors. Today Prime systems can be found from classrooms to government offices, from manufacturing sites to brokerage houses.

The third major market in which the firm competes is computer-aided design and computer-aided manufacturing (CAD/CAM). Only entering the fray in 1981, Prime's product offering and targeted marketing have helped it become one of the top 10

CAD/CAM vendors in only six years.

Fifteen years ago Prime Computer was eight men. According to company lore, they produced one system in 1972; it was swaddled in a blanket and delivered in a station wagon to the customer. Today Prime is a major player in the intensively competitive information processing industry. It is particularly known for its reliable products and its exceptional financial management. The company's heavy research and development funding has resulted in one of the newest, most advanced product lines in the industry.

The company employs more than 8,600 people worldwide, with a marketing presence that reaches more than 60 countries on six continents. More than one-third of Prime's employees are professionals working outside of the United States. The corporate headquarters is located at Prime Park in Natick, Massachusetts. Research, development, and engineering is conducted at nearby Framingham; in Bedford and Stevenage, United King-

The 200® was Prime Computer's first product.

dom; at Coolock, Ireland; and at Canberra, Australia. At each location, the firm uses its computers as part of a worldwide network to provide a laboratory for future development.

"Every company says it is committed to excellence. That is the business buzzword for the eighties," says Joe M. Henson, the firm's president since 1981. Prime Computer, Inc., demonstrates its commitment to excellence through its products and through its customer relationships.

Prime Computer's latest superminicomputer, the 6550® system, introduced the next level of power for its class by providing the performance of a mainframe at the price and size of a supermini.

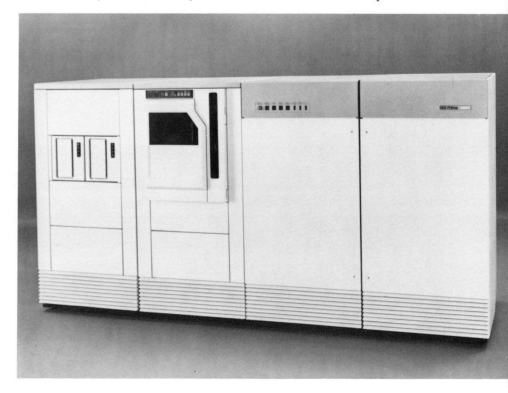

BOSTON'S BETH ISRAEL HOSPITAL

The major mission of Beth Israel Hospital is to deliver patient care of the highest quality, in both scientific and human terms. Although the strong humanist tradition that characterizes Beth Israel Hospital arises in part from its Jewish community origins, it has been nonsectarian from the beginning, offering patient-centered care to the sick and disabled of every race, creed, color, and nationality.

To support the humanistic aspect of patient care, the hospital's modern medical center houses 460 adult inpatient beds in medicine, surgery, obstetrics and gynecology, orthopedics, psychiatry, neurosurgery, neuromedicine, and medical and surgical intensive care units. More than 25,000 patients are served by these facilities each year. The hospital's 24-hour Berenson Emergency Unit is part of the Longwood Area Trauma Center, and responds to more than 35,000 patient visits annually.

But Beth Israel's commitment to patient-centered care is best expressed in its pioneering use of "primary nursing." Under this system each patient is assigned a registered nurse who is responsible for developing a 24-hour nursing care plan, looking after the patient while on duty, and monitoring the care while others are on duty. Unlike traditional team nursing, which is fragmented, primary nursing is personalized care, from admission to discharge. Beth Israel was the first institution in the United States to institute primary nursing on a hospitalwide basis.

In addition to providing an unusual level of individual patient care, Beth Israel Hospital has been on the leading edge of biomedical research for many years. The history-making cardiac pacemaker was first developed here, along with techniques for dissolving life-threatening blood clots following heart attacks. Medication to improve the function of impaired hearts has been clinically tested—and found successful. America's oldest clinical research facility, Harvard-Thorndike Laboratory, has been located at Beth Israel Hospital since 1973. Significant research is now under way in areas of nutrition and metabolism, endocrinology, hematology, oncology, cardiology, nephrology, obstetrics, surgery, and pulmonary disease.

In a city renowned for excellence in medical care, Beth Israel is a living tribute to the vision of its founders. Established in 1916 by the Boston Jewish community to meet the needs of a poor and growing immigrant population, it provided an environment where their special cultural, dietary, and language requirements could be met. These standards are still honored whenever necessary, although less than half of the hospital's patient population today is Jewish.

Patient-centered care, history-making research, and quality teaching continue to be the triad whose combined level of excellence details the success of Beth Israel Hospital. Carefully balancing thoughtful personal care with technical expertise, Beth Israel respects the "art" as well as the "science" of medicine—concerned not only with today's illness, but also with tomorrow's health.

Established hospitalwide over a decade ago at Boston's Beth Israel Hospital, primary nursing gives nurses the authority and responsibility to make patient care decisions at the bedside. Beth Israel's nurses helped establish the hospital's international reputation for warm and personal care of the highest quality.

Boston's Beth Israel Hospital, a teaching hospital of Harvard Medical School, is recognized for a particular sensitivity to the personal needs of patients. Beth Israel published a statement on the rights of patients in 1972 that has since served as a model for other hospitals and for state legislation.

G&H POULTRY & PROVISIONS, INC.

The story of G&H Poultry & Provisions, Inc., is also the story of George Matthews, a man who "does not know the word 'fail,'" according to one colleague. Matthews, who has been involved with the firm for more than 25 years, brings unique experience to his business. He's been a chicken plucker, retailer, chain store buyer, and today is a full-line distributor.

Matthews grew up on a farm in the Dutch country of Pennsylvania, and was first involved in processing chickens and selling them at local farmers' markets. Then he took a job at College Hill Poultry, a pioneer in the cut-up chicken business. Among other things he was a live chicken buyer, truck driver, and plant worker.

After serving in World War II he rejoined College Hill in the Washington, D.C., area, operating retail poultry concessions in Giant Foods stores. When Giant Foods took over its own poultry marketing, he joined the firm as a buyer in charge of retail operations.

Four years later Matthews moved to Grimes & Hauer in Fredericksburg, Pennsylvania, as retail sales manager. Grimes & Hauer had 95 retail poultry stores and concessions from Ohio to Pennsylvania to New England.

In 1960, in partnership with Lloyd Hauer, Matthews bought the firm's wholesale operation in Boston and changed the name to G&H. Eventually they sold the poultry stores, focusing on the distribution end of the business. Six years later, when Lloyd Hauer died, Matthews bought his share of the business and has run the operation ever since.

G&H Poultry & Provisions operates from the New Boston Food Mart, a 22-acre wholesale food distribution complex in the South Bay area of South Boston. In addition to his poultry business, which serves customers within a radius of 60 miles from Boston, Matthews also has a brokerage operation, primarily for turkeys, although he is willing to include anything in the poultry line.

Matthews was the first distributor ever to be named director of the National Broiler Council. He was named Man of the Year by the National Independent Poultry and Food Distributors Association in 1981, a year after being honored by *Poultry & Eggs Marketing* as Merchandising Man of the Year. Matthews has been praised for his work

George Matthews, president, who brought his expertise to G&H Poultry & Provisions, Inc., to make it a full-line distributorship.

with retailers that has increased the use of turkey and chicken in his marketing area, and for his successful support of the National Chicken Cooking Contest. He also actively supports his local church and various civic projects in the Boston area.

"We're fully committed to service and quality," says Matthews, which explains why G&H Poultry & Provisions, Inc., today has an annual sales volume of more than $60 million.

SYMMONS INDUSTRIES, INC.

If you have ever been shocked by suddenly chilled or unexpectedly hot water while taking a shower, you will appreciate what this Massachusetts-based company manufactures. Since 1939 Symmons Industries, Inc., in Braintree has produced pressure-balancing shower valves that prevent sudden changes in water temperature. After nearly a half-century so many homes, hotels, hospitals, and public buildings use the Symmons valve that the firm has become one of the leading shower system manufacturers in the country.

When Symmons was established in 1939 and began to study the problem of sudden temperature changes in the shower, it discovered that the basic problem was one of pressure. Shower water got suddenly hot when someone elsewhere in the building turned on a cold water faucet or flushed a toilet. Conversely, turning on a dishwasher or clothes washer might cause water in the shower to become cold.

Symmons perfected a valve—after considerable research and testing—that was essentially the same as the one produced today. It uses a hydraulic piston as the prime control unit. As soon as the valve is turned on, both hot and cold water exert pressure on opposite

A page from a 1947 catalog illustrating the original Symmons pressure-balancing valve.

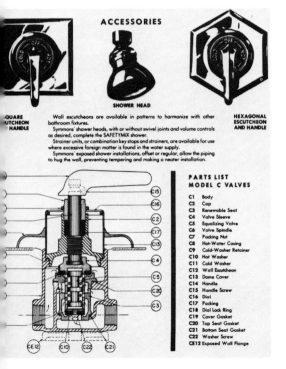

The present Symmons plant, housing the offices and manufacturing facilities in 100,000 square feet of floor space.

ends of the piston, holding it in a balanced position in the valve. If the hot water pressure drops, the piston reacts and reduces the cold inlet opening. The piston continually equalizes the pressures of hot and cold water, even when supply pressures change suddenly or drastically.

The main operating spindle can be set to mix any proportion of hot and cold water for any desired shower temperature. The operating chamber of the spindle will continuously be fed with hot and cold water under equal pressures and the set temperatures will be maintained.

The Symmons pressure-balancing valve has significant safety advantages over conventional two-handle or single-handle valves. Not only does it prevent sudden uncomfortable or dangerous temperature changes in shower water, but it also eliminates the serious accidents that can result when people—particularly the elderly—try to back away from scalding or freezing water.

In 1967 Symmons introduced a competitively priced pressure-balancing valve, much lower in cost than its original heavy-duty product. This new valve made it possible to market a product for all residential applications that had originally been equipped with conventional two-handle shower controls. Symmons attributes the introduction

of this product with being a major factor in its dynamic growth and market dominance in the pressure-balancing valve field.

Following the trend of industry needs, a product was introduced in 1975 that was specifically directed toward health care institutions—a pressure-balancing valve with a built-in thermometer. This product allows a nurse in a hospital or attendant in a nursing home to accurately set the proper water temperature for all bathing purposes.

The federal government now requires that all housing for the elderly that it helps to fund must have safety-type shower valves. Many states have amended their plumbing codes to demand the use of safety-type showers in "all shower applications" or in specific commercial, institutional, or public facilities.

Since its patent expired in 1960 Symmons is no longer the exclusive manufacturer of these valves, but is still a major producer, because many manufacturers now use Symmons valves in their shower fixtures.

When Paul C. Symmons invented the first pressure-balancing shower valve and started his company in 1939, he and a handful of employees located in the vacant Chickering Piano Building on Tremont Street in downtown Boston. "Paul made the original patterns himself, out of wood," recounts company president Albert G. Fehrm. "During the war years, when all manufacturers were supporting the defense effort, one of Paul's colleagues was a torpedo inspector for the Navy. Symmons Industries retooled to supply essential parts for torpedos, and received an award for the excellent quality of its work. In addition, we received some of the earliest postwar contracts from the government to make shower valves for military barracks and other federal housing."

The company left its Tremont Street home in 1956, moving to larger facilities in South Boston. Eleven years later it expanded to its present Braintree facility.

Today Symmons Industries is the largest manufacturer of pressure-balancing shower valves. "Our plant is not a pure assembly line," explains president Fehrm. "We are automated, using dedicated equipment that can do varied and complex tasks. This unique equipment has not put anyone out of work, however. Increased production and our elaborate quality-control procedures continue to boost our work

Shown in the Sales Training Laboratory are founder and current chairman Paul C. Symmons (center); his brother Thomas F. Symmons, retired executive vice-president (right); and current vice-president and general manager Kevin V. Symmons.

force annually." The firm attributes its high degree of quality control to complete in-plant production, right up to the final chrome plating.

While pressure-balancing products account for a significant portion of Symmons' business, the firm also produces a wide range of associated products such as thermostatic controllers, metering valves for both the shower and lavatory, and single-handle kitchen and lavatory fixtures. The most recent addition to its line of products is a stylish line of bath and lavatory fixtures in polished brass to answer the demand for the high-fashion decorator market.

Symmons Industries, Inc., firmly believes that its pressure-balancing valves are the finest that money can buy, in front of the bathroom wall and behind it, too. The firm cautions that if you use another brand, you might find yourself in a lot of hot water!

Some of the computer-controlled automatic machines producing Symmons products.

VICTOR COFFEE COMPANY

The Boston Tea Party is a favorite history lesson of schoolchildren—a colorful and dramatic protest against "taxation without representation." The political consequences of King George III's tea tax are known to all Americans, and where coffee was not similarly taxed, the beverage gained in popularity. Most of the green coffee was brought into the country through the Port of Boston, with the coffee merchants congregating on lower State Street.

In 1796 Shapleigh Coffee Company was founded and is still in Boston, operating today under the ownership of Victor Coffee Company, thus making it the oldest coffee house in the United States in continuous operation. Until the outbreak of World War I, the Victor logo—a Roman chariot in full charge—was the subject of a most original promotional campaign. An accurate replica of a racing chariot, drawn by four white horses and driven by a charioteer, was transported around New England in a specially constructed railroad freight car. The chariot would parade through the main street of the town, coming to rest outside the local store selling Victor Coffee.

Victor Coffee, a division of Stanley W. Ferguson, Inc., has been owned and operated since 1935 by the Ferguson family, there now being a third generation to continue the founder's policy of highest quality in manufacturing and service. In 1946 the company moved from State Street to its present location at 365 C Street. Today Victor sells exclusively to hotels, restaurants, vending, office coffee, and manual feeding operations. Manufacturing and support functions have been fully organized to ensure that these markets are served efficiently and effectively.

New machinery installations have been the subject of several articles appearing in trade publications. In 1968 the registered trademarked process, Nitro-Pak®, was introduced, which enabled Victor to deliver the freshest and most consistent product possible, in addition to guaranteeing an extended shelf life. The new technology provided a virtually oxygen-free flexible package, thus eliminating the bulky, heavy cans used in the retail trade.

This scene, a familiar part of Victor packaging, represents one of the earliest and most unusual sales promotions in America. Until World War I a charioteer and four white horses traveled from town to town by railroad advertising for the local Martin L. Hall merchant.

With the exception of one company in Connecticut, Victor is the only importer, blender, and manufacturer of tea in New England. The tea is imported from the great estates of Sri Lanka, northern India, and Kenya, and packed on specialized, high-speed equipment.

While processing technology has improved dramatically over the years, one crucial aspect of the business has not changed since 1796. The high-quality coffees and teas can only be selected by the process of "cupping." Determining the essential ingredients of flavor and aroma remains the province of the taster's nose and palate. This remains the only viable means of approving the raw tea and coffee before they are committed to maintaining the consistent blends.

While many changes have occurred over the years, Victor Coffee Company continues to concentrate on its two main strengths—coffee and tea. By not diversifying, Victor is able to direct all its resources to the coffee and tea industry. Although the chariot horses have long been retired, the century-old motto—Victor wins the race strictly on quality—is alive and well.

FRANKI FOUNDATION COMPANY

In most countries of the free world today, the name FRANKI can be seen on construction projects. It all began with the Franki pile, conceived in 1908 by a visionary young Belgian contractor named Edgard Frankignoul. In that small country he thought big, and in 1911 formed La Compagnie Internationale des Pieux Armes Frankignoul, also registered as S.A. Franki N.V. Today Franki is the largest organization of foundation specialists in the world.

Some people think Franki is only a pile-driving enterprise. Nothing could be further from the truth. While the installation of piles is still its primary product (and *millions* have been installed in more than 90 countries), Franki does much more than that. In the early days the courage and skill of Frankignoul involved him in tunneling and other major construction. Since then Franki has developed and perfected techniques in deep foundations, retaining structures, soil improvement, underpinning, drilling, grouting, and heavy construction—as well as tunneling, shaft sinking, and freezing in conjuction with Foraky, a part of the Franki group. Franki also builds a great deal of the equipment it uses for

The Franki Pile has been used in the foundations of numerous construction projects throughout the world.

these special types of work.

To maintain its leadership role Franki is committed to an ongoing research and development program as a matter of course. From sophisticated studies of soil and subsurface structure behavior, to the design and construction of specialized heavy equipment, Franki's approach to subsurface construction is leading-edge.

Franki made its first appearance in the United States in Pittsburgh in 1951 as the Franki Foundation Company with the majority of stock held by Koppers Company. Three years later Koppers was bought out by S.A. Franki N.V. and the company's offices moved to New York City. In 1956 the firm established its home in Massachusetts at the Statler Office Building in Boston. In March 1987 the office was moved to a new building at the company's depot and workshops in Woburn, Massachusetts.

In the 1950s driving Franki piles— or pressure-injected footings (PIFs), as they are called in the United States—

Here, in a joint venture with Civetta and Falco, the Franki Foundation Company incorporated diaphragm walls, tie-back anchors, caissons, tie-down anchors, mass excavation, and foundations in the total basement construction of Battery Park in New York.

was the scope of the company. The PIF is still the backbone of the firm; but other systems, methods, and techniques in deep foundations, soil improvement, slurry walls, cut-off walls, underpinning, and general construction are utilized in solving highly specialized problems. Such problems include isolation of ground water, soil liquification, dam rehabilitation, suppression of noise and vibration, total foundation packaging, and more. The list is endless, and always challenging.

Franki welcomes the challenge to find the best answer—technically, logistically, and financially—to each particular construction need. At the Franki Foundation Company, it is not exclusively building foundations, rather, building solutions to subsurface problems.

BOSTON EDISON

The Edison Electric Illuminating Company of Boston was incorporated on January 8, 1886, just four years after Thomas Edison opened his first central electric plant in New York City. But it was at Boston Edison—the name changed in 1937—that many significant advances in electric utility engineering, marketing, and employee relations were first developed. By the early 1900s, when Boston was the best-lighted city per resident in the world and the first large American city served by a single electric utility, innovation and pride in performance were already deeply ingrained traditions in this company.

The firm's original generating plant was located in the basement of Cashman and Keating's printing office at Haymarket Place near Washington Street in downtown Boston. For the first six months of operation Boston Edison offered free wiring "in order to secure a full complement of customers." During the first year connected lamps increased from 647 in February

Inventor Thomas Alva Edison (left) handpicked Charles Leavitt Edgar to manage the company in 1887. Edgar, who was Edison Electric Illuminating Company of Boston president from 1900 to 1932, established himself as the most progressive leader of the electric utility industry.

President Charles Leavitt Edgar (left) and Boston Mayor James Michael Curley on April 29, 1930, just before Curley made the first electric weld on the new Edison headquarters building at 180 Tremont Street, Boston.

to 4,847 in December.

Between 1886 and the turn of the century competition among electric companies in the city was keen. The success of Boston Edison was built on marketing strength and engineering innovation. At a time when the skies over many cities were blackened by electric and telephone wires—sometimes hundreds on a single pole—Boston Edison followed Thomas Edison's lead and put its distribution network underground.

In 1895 Boston Edison began to sell steam, a product that was an important market segment through 1986. By 1901, when the firm had acquired or merged with all other power companies in Boston, a new era of suburban expansion was launched. By 1922 the company's service area had grown from 40 square miles in Boston to cities and towns within 640 square miles. During that time Boston Edison became a national leader in the promotion of electric automobiles, opening a 25-car garage on Atlantic Avenue to recharge and service the vehicles. At one point there were more than 350 public and private electric vehicle charging stations in Greater Boston.

Demand for electricity declined moderately during the Depression, but Boston Edison's marketing efforts continued. In 1931, for example, more than 33,000 customers visited the "Friendly Kitchen" at 39 Boylston Street to learn about cooking with electricity. Consumer demand spurred vigorous comsumption after World War II, and Boston Edison responded with increased capacity and improved transmission and distribution. In 1959 the company became the first electric utility in New England to use a large-scale computer, a step that led to interconnection of the vast New England electrical grid.

Since the early 1970s Boston Edison has faced an unprecedented number of challenges, from the oil embargo to developing new energy sources. The company entered the nuclear age in 1972 with Pilgrim Station and the solar era in 1984 with the construction, on national television, of the IMPACT 2000 House. The firm enters its second century as new economic, social, technical, and political forces reshape the dynamics of the electric utility industry. Boston Edison will meet these challenges by maintaining its century-old tradition of concern for customers and pursuing new programs for their benefit.

FOOT-JOY, INC.

Foot-Joy, Inc., was founded as the Stone-Tarlow Company in 1918 by Daniel S. Tarlow and Benjamin Stone to manufacture men's Goodyear Welt shoes. Richard N. Tarlow joined the firm in 1946 after teaching accounting and statistics and serving as assistant to the president of Dartmouth College. Seven years later William E. Tarlow joined the company after earning his law degree from Harvard University. Both Tarlow brothers graduated from Dartmouth College.

In 1957 Stone-Tarlow Company purchased Field and Flint Company of Brockton, Massachusetts, a century-old manufacturer of quality shoes for men. At that time Field and Flint was best known for Foot-Joy golf and street shoes, which were sold through golf pro shops and retail stores. In addition, they made orthopedic footwear for the Veterans Administration.

The Tarlow brothers quickly realized that the future potential of the business was in the Foot-Joy label, and that their best market was the golf pro shop. Therefore they immediately began to phase out the orthopedic footwear business, and when this was done they integrated both Field and Flint and Stone-Tarlow operations into one Stone-Tarlow plant, at the present site on Field Street in Brockton. Since 1973 the company has been known as Foot-Joy, Inc.

"When I was a child," remembers company chairman Dick Tarlow, "there were more than 50 shoe factories in town. Today Foot-Joy is the last remaining shoe manufacturer in Brockton, but we're part of a rich tradition. As other firms closed we inherited a cadre of skilled workers who had spent years in the shoe business. This pool of experienced employees helps us keep our product quality high. We're not a production line. Working with leather, our machinery amounts to little more than glorified power tools, and the skill of the individual craftsman directly determines the quality of the final product."

Foot-Joy was already an industry leader when golf "came of age" in this country. "As late as 1957 there were

Joe Fedele (above) and Bronis Barakauskas (below) of Foot-Joy, Inc.

only 5,000 golf courses in the United States," recalls Dick Tarlow. "By 1977 the total had jumped to over 13,000. The popularity of municipal, university, and resort golf courses, which are open to all, has expanded our customer base during the past 30 years."

Foot-Joy, Inc., currently makes one of every three pairs of golf shoes sold in the United States. More than 80 percent of pro tour golfers wear Foot-Joy shoes. The company is also a leading manufacturer of golf gloves, and is expanding its sports line to include racquetball, aerobic-fitness, and walking shoes. Since the firm carries both Foot-Joy and Ben Hogan products, the professional needs no other supplier.

245

HAEMONETICS CORPORATION

Haemonetics Corporation is committed to providing the medical community with high-quality products for the benefit of patients everywhere. Blood bankers and clinicians throughout the world use Haemonetics systems in many ways, including the collection of components from donors for transfusion to patients and source plasma for fractionation, performance of depletion or exchange transfusions, and salvage of blood shed in surgery for autologous transfusion.

Development of the scientific concepts that led to the formation of Haemonetics Corporation was initiated by Dr. Edwin J. Cohn, who headed an outstanding research group at Harvard on the physical chemistry of proteins and had developed vitally needed processes for fractionation of blood plasma just prior to World War II. Dr. Cohn recognized the need for equipment to process the cellular elements of blood and established a program for development of "biomechanical equipment" under the auspices of Protein Foundation, a research organization that became the present Center for Blood Research.

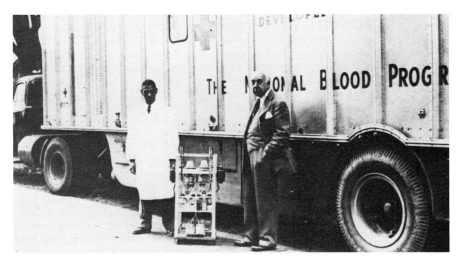

This historic photo shows Dr. Edwin J. Cohn (right) with his longtime assistant Robert J. Tinch (left) and between them, the earliest blood-processing centrifuge.

A novel centrifuge bowl that permitted aseptic flow into and out of the bowl during rotation was developed and became the centerpiece of several research programs. However, the special drive equipment for this bowl proved so unreliable that Dr. Cohn requested engineering help from Arthur D. Little, Inc. Allen Latham, Jr., who was then head of mechanical engineering at ADL, recognized such serious design faults that a complete redesign of the drive equipment was carried out at ADL. The working prototype of the new design proved so satisfactory that it was pressed into service immediately, and a total of 16 units were supplied in support of several clinical research programs. These programs established a clear need for blood cell processing equipment.

Shortly after ADL had become involved Dr. Cohn suffered an untimely death, but he left a strong group of enthusiastic, able associates who continued the program. In addition, Dr. Cohn and his associates, particularly Dr. James L. Tullis, M.D., Dr. Douglas MacN. Surgenor, Ph.D., and Robert Tinch, had so impressed Latham with the importance of their undertaking that he shifted his technical focus from cryogenics to blood processing.

Latham's prime contribution was to develop a modified bowl that was amenable to manufacture as a relatively inexpensive, disposable product. This new bowl was produced initially in a reusable form, but as soon as fa-

Gordon F. Kingsley (right), a major contributor to the early business development of Haemonetics, and Allen Latham, Jr. (left), inventor of the disposable bowl and founder of Haemonetics, at a celebration for the manufacture of the first million disposable bowls. Allen Latham, Jr., holds a sterling-silver replica in his right hand and the first successful disposable bowl in his left.

product development and the creation of manufacturing and quality-control facilities.

This brief history touches on the highlights of how Haemonetics Corporation got started. During its 14 years in operation it has grown to a $50-million business and maintains direct contact with its customers throughout the free world. The people of Haemonetics are proud to have helped carry some of Dr. Cohn's scientific concepts through to practical application in blood therapy, and are continuing to work toward further advances in this area. They are grateful for the help and encouragement of their many friends in blood research laboratories, blood banks, and hospitals.

John F. White, president of Haemonetics, led a successful leveraged management buyout of the company in 1986.

Haemonetics' blood-processing system shown performing therapeutic plasma exchanges for treatment of multiple sclerosis.

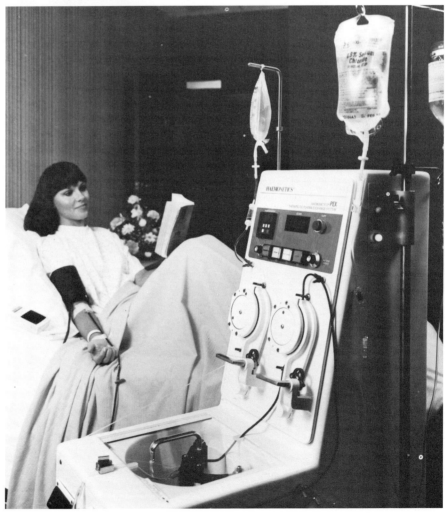

vorable clinical results began to flow in, pressure to produce the same internal geometry in disposable form mounted. Most notably in 1968 Dr. C. Robert Valeri, who was developing a blood storage program for U.S. Navy hospital ships, vigorously urged this advance. A license was arranged with the Hospital Products Division of Abbot Laboratories to manufacture and sell the disposable bowl. A few thousand bowls were produced, but Abbot withdrew from the license shortly after experiencing a complete recall of its parenteral solution product line.

In order to reestablish manufacture of the disposable bowl, Latham founded Haemonetics Corporation and searched out Breck McNeish and Nagel of Boston, which underwrote a private placement to raise the necessary start-up capital. At this time he also persuaded Gordon F. Kingsley to take on the duties of executive vice-president. Kingsley organized an effective worldwide marketing activity and led in the creation of a sound business operation. Latham continued with

NEW ENGLAND TELEPHONE

"Perhaps if Mr. Bell had realized that he was about to make a bit of history, he would have been prepared with a more interesting sounding sentence." Thomas Watson's quip refers to the first sentence transmitted by telephone, "Mr. Watson, come here, I want you!" In fact, Alexander Graham Bell couldn't have launched his new invention in a more prophetic way. Here was a call for help. Bell had just spilled acid on himself and was summoning Watson from the next room. At its birth the telephone rendered service in an emergency. From that moment on no concept better explains telephones and the people behind them than *service*.

The history of New England Telephone is linked closely to the history of the telephone, which was invented in Boston. Bell began research on the idea in 1873, and achieved success three years later by transmitting his first message.

The original New England Telephone (not a forerunner of the current company) was incorporated as a licensing agent to sell the rights for Bell telephone patents to companies throughout New England. During the next few years several telephone companies started serving different areas in the Northeast.

The year 1877 saw the first telephone put to outside use. Its line connected the Boston business and Somerville residence of Charles Williams, Jr., a benefactor of Bell. The first telephone book was issued in 1878, containing the names of 67 companies. They were listed by name only, since telephone numbers were not used until the following year.

Today's New England Telephone was officially formed October 19, 1883, by consolidating eight regional telephone companies, providing much-needed uniformity in rates and improved service. Except for southern Massachusetts and Rhode Island, all the areas in the current region were included.

Theodore Vail became the first president of the new firm, which opened for business with 400 em-

Boston was the birthplace of the telephone in 1876. Here its inventor, Alexander Graham Bell, makes one of the first long-distance calls.

ployees and 16,000 customers. Offices were originally in Lowell, but soon moved to 40 Pearl Street in Boston. Those were landmark years for the telephone industry. In 1884 the first successful long-distance call was made from Boston to New York. One year later the first multiple switchboards were installed in Boston's Tremont Street office. In 1888, when a three-day blizzard threatened to sever all communication between New York

Today's New England Telephone was officially formed in October 1883 with Theodore N. Vale as the first president. Photo circa 1885

City and Boston, lineman Angus MacDonald braved the storm in snowshoes to keep the lines open. His heroism was later depicted in Frank Merrill's famous painting, *The Spirit of Service*.

The first pay telephones were installed throughout the region in 1893 to accommodate "the public who are not subscribers to the exchanges," and many miles of underground conduit were laid, more than in any other part of the country. By 1903 the company had more than 136,000 telephones in use with exchanges and lines reaching every New England village and town of 200 or more residents. Subscribers in the town of Cambridge were able to reach the operator without even using the handcrank by simply removing the receiver from the hook.

During World War I New England Telephone was taken over by the Post Office Department as a war measure. But faltering service and increased rates proved the plan a failure, and ownership was restored to the company in 1919.

The violent Hurricane of 1938 and subsequent flooding crippled eastern Massachusetts and other parts of New England, putting one-quarter of the company's customers out of service. Operators and other personnel worked around the clock maintaining what was left of the system, while co-workers from 14 companies outside the region helped make repairs.

Over the past century telephone technology has changed dramatically. The firm has gone from manual switchboards to cord boards to the TSPS (Traffic Service Position System). Horse-drawn wagons to lay underground cable have given way to trucks with cherry pickers. Copper cable to transmit calls is being replaced by fiber-optic cables made of glass.

Electromechanical switching systems, introduced in the 1920s, made possible the remote control of coin phones and automatic toll charging. Electronic switching systems (ESS), introduced in the 1960s, brought Touch-Tone dialing, Centrex, Call-Waiting, and 911 emergency calling.

New England Telephone headquarters at 185 Franklin Street, Boston.

Future switching systems offer not only greater capacity and speed, but also more and smarter services—information networks, not just telephone lines.

In 1984 the Bell System was broken up and New England Telephone became a wholly owned subsidiary of NYNEX, one of the seven regional holding companies under which the operating companies were reorganized. (The acronym stands for New York, New England, and an "X" for the future with abundance of new opportunities.) The NYNEX family of companies also includes New York Telephone, NYNEX Business Information Systems Co., NYNEX Credit Co., NYNEX Development Co., NYNEX Information Resources (formerly the Yellow Pages Division), NYNEX Materiel Enterprises Co., NYNEX Mobile Communications, NYNEX Properties Co., and NYNEX Service Co.

Telephone wizards Theodore N. Vail and Dr. Alexander Graham Bell meet for the first time in 30 years on the steps of the National Geographic Society building. Dr. Bell was one of the founding fathers of the society and its president from 1898 to 1903. Courtesy, National Geographic Society

From 1889, when the new AT&T was founded and the concept of the Bell System crystallized, the story of New England Telephone is one of growth in customers, expansion of services, and ever-increasing reliability. It's also the story of men and women committed to providing telephone service unsurpassed anywhere in the world—people involved, often heroically, with the everyday affairs and major events of our region. Now in its second century of service, New England Telephone looks forward to continuing this rich tradition.

Linemen restore service following the blizzard of 1978.

JORDAN MARSH COMPANY

On a frosty morning in 1841 Eben Dyer Jordan sold his friend Louisa Bareiss a single yard of cherry-colored ribbon—thereby accomplishing the first transaction that was to set into motion the Jordan Marsh Company and its journey toward becoming a world-renowned mercantile establishment.

The innovative and daring 19-year-old Jordan, operating from a dry goods counter at 168 Hanover Street in Boston, had a simple principle of trading: "The better you serve your customers, the better you serve yourself." With this in mind, he envisioned and achieved steady growth.

On January 20, 1851, Jordan went into partnership with Benjamin L. Marsh, linking the two names that now stand atop Jordan Marsh enterprises throughout the Northeast. The new store, Jordan and Marsh, was located at 129 Milk Street. Its capital was only $5,000, but Jordan was already planning a bold expansion. In 1853 he traveled to Europe, where he established a substantial line of credit from the senior partner of a conservative English commission house. This credit, obtained without a dollar's worth of backing, allowed him to stock his shelves with articles strange to Boston, including linens from Ireland, silks from China, rugs from Iran, and ivory from West Africa.

The Jordan Marsh store moved to its present location at Washington and Summer streets in 1861. It is pictured here in 1880.

Jordan's trip to Europe is probably all that saved Jordan and Marsh from going out of business during the Panic of 1857, when many stores were collapsing like houses built with cards. Customers' bank accounts vanished, and Jordan faced the choice of selling

After much reconstruction the downtown Boston landmark Jordan Marsh store dominates a full city block at the intersection of Washington and Summer streets.

out or reducing prices and taking a temporary loss until the panic ended. To keep faith with creditors and customers, Jordan cut his prices in half, sustaining a loss that averaged $3,000 each day, until the economy recovered in 1858. From the gentlemen in London who had generously backed his credit four years earlier came these words of praise: "Mr. Jordan, you ought to have a monument to your pluck in preferring honor to profits."

As new properties were acquired, hoop-skirted ladies and gentlemen in top hats followed the store from Milk Street to Pearl, and on to Winthrop Square in 1859. Boston lads were volunteering for service in the War Between the States when Jordan Marsh moved to its present location at 450 Washington Street in 1861. As years passed clipper ships bringing ever-new products from foreign lands were replaced by steamships, while trucks and rail cars replaced wagon trains.

In the late 1800s the Marsh family dropped from the firm, and the Mitton family formed a partnership with Eben Jordan, who was 74 years old when he passed away in 1895. His son, Eben Jr., was just 38 years old when he took over his father's role as president. E.J. Mitton as vice-president was just 10 years older. They were as nearly perfect a team as anyone could hope for.

Young Jordan with his pince-nez and his pointed mustache was the ex-

The second-floor coat department of the Boston Jordan Marsh store in 1880.

perimeter—a man who dared to be different. Mitton, whose whiskers reminded one of King Edward VII, was a conscientious builder—a man with both feet on the ground who could mold young Jordan's dreams into practical business policies. They did things between them that are still being felt in the world of merchandising today.

Eben Jordan, Jr.'s, philanthropy became well known in Boston. Deciding one day that Bostonians should enjoy the best operatic productions, he built the Boston Opera House and ran it at his own expense for years. Recalling his father's work in helping to found the New England Conservatory of Music, he proceeded to build a new auditorium for the school, thus giving Boston its famous Jordan Hall.

Meanwhile, E.J. Mitton was the first merchant to adopt the "customer

is always right" policy. He was also the first to sell to retail customers on credit, and offer a money-back guarantee. Ideas like these jolted department store operators from Boston to Berlin, most of whom predicted ultimate ruin for "that unusual Jordan Marsh Company." But they quickly picked up the policies themselves when they discovered that the team of Jordan and Mitton knew what the public wanted.

Mitton and Jordan Jr. passed away in 1913 and 1916, respectively. Mitton's son, George W., assumed the presidency until 1930, followed by his

The second floor of the Boston Jordan Marsh store reflects a contemporary fashion image geared toward today's woman.

brother Richard, and in 1937 by his son Edward R. Under the visionary leadership of the Mitton family, Jordan Marsh became a full-line department store and a springboard in merchandising. Each descendant, by prescribing to the traditions of his forebears, initiated a move forward with the times, but retained a handclasp with the values of old New England.

When the 1950s and 1960s brought demographic changes to the area, Jordan Marsh began expanding into the suburbs. Its first shopping center store opened in 1951 at historic Shoppers World in Framingham, Massachusetts. It has since grown to a 26-store complex encompassing over five million square feet located in both urban and suburban markets, with plans for future stores throughout the Northeast. Ambitious reconstruction of the downtown Boston landmark store was completed in 1977, and today it dominates a full city block at the intersection of Washington and Summer streets. Computerized merchandising techniques and continual updating of all stores reflect a contemporary fashion image geared to the tastes and lifestyles of today's consumer.

Operations of Jordan Marsh, now the flagship division of Allied Stores, and its 9,000 employees are directed by chairman and chief executive officer Elliot J. Stone. Retail sales now approach the three-quarter-billion-dollar mark—a growth record reflecting the continued strength and dedication of the company's valued personnel.

"Building a quality image requires neighborhood involvement and sensitivity to the charitable needs of the community" says Stone. "We've combined this with our objective to make our stores exciting and have developed events that not only benefit the cultural and charitable organizations in our area but also provide entertainment at our stores." In recent years these events have run the gamut from road races to exciting and educational exhibits, and celebrity appearances to benefit the March of Dimes, United Way, the Boy Scouts of America, and other worthy organizations.

ANDERSON-NICHOLS & COMPANY, INC.

Founded in 1922, Anderson-Nichols & Company has completed thousands of architectural and engineering design assignments while building a strong reputation for client service.

The original concept of the company was to provide management consulting in quality control and efficiency for Massachusetts industry. Founder E. Ross Anderson and his colleagues succeeded in their new business by responding to the specialized needs of their clients. Their tradition of service, honesty, and pride in their work continues today in the client projects of Anderson-Nichols.

The firm's ability to provide a comprehensive range of design and follow-up services under one roof meets the needs of today's business leaders. From environmental planning and project permitting through final design and construction administration, the architects and engineers of Anderson-Nichols help clients achieve the results they need.

When the Raytheon Company's Equipment Division needed a new corporate headquarters in 1986, it turned to Anderson-Nichols. Raytheon needed a consultant firm that could deliver all site development, programming, and engineering services. The company also needed an attractive architectural design that would be compatible with the beautiful 154-acre site it owned in

Marlborough, Massachusetts. Finally, Raytheon needed to occupy its new facility quickly, in less than two years from the decision to build.

The architects and engineers of Anderson-Nichols went to work. Applying their experience in planning and designing other corporate facilities such as Wang Laboratories' headquarters in Lowell, Massachusetts, they tackled Raytheon's needs.

The result is a three-building office and research and development design that attractively blends into its lakeside location. Working on a fast-track approach, the project team completed all design and construction documents in only six months. The successful client response to the Hager Pond project has led to further work on large Raytheon assignments for the Anderson-Nichols team.

Companies such as Raytheon and Anderson-Nichols are participants in an economic rebirth in Massachusetts. One of the reasons for the new economic strength of the Commonwealth is the diversity of industries, institutions, and individuals who make Massachusetts their home. By offering such a range

The partners of Anderson-Nichols & Company are (from left) Herrick H. Spicer, Stephen P. Hassell, Joseph F. Keane, and Warren F. Daniell, Jr. Courtesy, Betsy Shapiro

of technical disciplines and services, Anderson-Nichols is well prepared to address the diversity of needs of the region's companies. The firm's recent experience includes assignments for high-technology, electronics, biotechnology, real estate development, education, and health care clients.

Joseph F. Keane, president of Anderson-Nichols, has a diversity of experience and skills himself. He began working for the company as a draftsman in 1957, an 18-year-old high school graduate working his first real job. He rose through the ranks, succeeding in several positions including designer, mechanical engineer, project manager, controller, and vice-president. Attending college at night, Keane received a B.S. degree from the Boston College School of Management.

"One of the greatest satisfactions," according to Keane, "is the fact that so many of the clients who were with Anderson-Nichols when I started here are still satisfied clients today." He attributes these long relationships to some basic themes. "Quality work, client service, and consistent performance have always been the standards of the company," he says. "We intend to keep up that tradition and build on it as we move ahead."

In January 1986 Keane and three of the firm's senior principals completed a purchase of Anderson-Nichols from the previous owners, Mark IV Industries and the LFE Corporation. The buyout was the conclusion of a year-long negotiation to create a company that would be owned and managed by employees.

The partners in the buyout, in addition to Keane, include Warren F. Daniell, Jr., executive vice-president responsible for business development and large project administration; Herrick H. Spicer, executive vice-president directing the environmental, transportation, and civil engineering divisions; and Stephen P. Hassell, executive vice-president managing the architecture/engineering divisions of the firm. The new owners bring more than 84 years of combined experience with

One of the many projects that Anderson-Nichols has recently designed is the Equipment Division headquarters of Raytheon Company, the Hager Pond facility, in Marlborough.

the company to their new roles, providing a diverse pool of ability and knowledge of their new venture.

Anderson-Nichols remains committed to its future in Massachusetts, and the firm's employees are enthusiastic about the variety of exciting projects that are developing in the Commonwealth. The company's recent projects include assignments for major Massachusetts employers such as Digital Equipment, Gillette, AVCO, Gen-Rad, Sprague Electric, and Wang Laboratories. These businesses share the distinction of having retained Anderson-Nichols for over 25 projects each. The range of client projects over the years is far reaching; Anderson-Nichols has worked for more than half of the current *Fortune* 200 companies.

Public-sector projects include interstate highway projects for the Massachusetts Department of Public Works. Other public agency clients include the M.B.T.A., the Massachusetts Water Resources Authority, the U.S. Army Corps of Engineers, and the U.S. Navy. The firm also serves as consultant to many Massachusetts cities and towns. Over 100 Massachusetts municipalities have retained Anderson-Nichols' environmental engineers for

The Wang Laboratories' Kneeland Street Manufacturing Building in Boston is yet another example of Anderson-Nichols & Company's design diversity and skill. Courtesy, Peter Lewitt

services such as water supply and distribution, wastewater collection and treatment facilities, solid waste management, environmental analysis, and flood plain studies.

For 65 years Anderson-Nichols & Company has succeeded in attracting and keeping the clients it serves. Carrying on this tradition are more than 100 dedicated and talented employees. Like E. Ross Anderson and the first group of Anderson-Nichols professionals, they know that continual response to the needs of the client is more important than any other task.

TEXON

In September 1947, 66 employees and friends invested their money, careers, and hopes in a small, unknown company called Texon. Located in the rugged and picturesque hills of western Massachusetts, Texon had its beginning in an old mill by the Westfield River. Today Texon produces a wide variety of elastomer and resin-saturated fiber materials used to manufacture such diverse products as footwear, automobile batteries, luggage and leather goods, horse saddles, and baseball caps.

The original Texon plant is still operating by the Westfield River in Russell, Massachusetts. The plant stands on the site where the river in colonial times powered a saw- and gristmill. Once owned by Cyrus Field, he sold the mill in 1858 to help finance the first transatlantic communications cable from Newfoundland to Ireland. From that period to 1936 fine writing and ledger papers were produced in the Russell mill until the Great Depression silenced the paper machines.

The mill remained idle until Du Pont, in search of man-made solutions to shortages of natural materials, leased and then purchased the property and facilities. Du Pont intended to develop synthetic replacements for leather and rubberized coating materials. Within a few years Du Pont concluded that the experiment did not hold the potential it anticipated. Again the Russell mill went up for sale.

In what has to be considered a courageous move, 66 Du Pont employees and friends raised enough funds to buy the mill. Texon was incorporated in September 1947. As it was written in literature prepared to commemorate Texon's 20th anniversary:

A small and daring band of men
Did risk their meals, their homes and dough
To chase a dream that had no end. . .
6 and 60 men of heart
A flame from tiny spark they fanned
They bent their minds and backs to find
A way to make materials
To leave what nature made behind

Texon came to life at the right time—a time when two basic facts of existence became obvious. First, World War II taught that natural resources were limited, not always available, and often expensive. Second, rapid growth in population demanded new, more ef-

---

The original Texon plant still operates by the Westfield River in Russell.

ficient, and economical ways to meet the expanding needs and expectations of man. It was a time when men and companies with foresight, luck, technology, and capacity to produce new ways of doing things could grow. Texon chose to produce man-made materials that would perform at lower cost to replace the best nature could offer.

Using Du Pont's experience, Texon personnel set out to find ways to combine neoprene elastomers with cellulose fiber structures. The goal: to create an innersole material with all the advantages of leather and none of its disadvantages. For shoe consumers, Texon wanted to create an innersoling that breathed, absorbed and desorbed perspiration, had the right balance of firmness and flexibility, and provided lasting comfort. For the shoe manufacturer, Texon needed to engineer a material that would process easily at the lowest-possible cost.

Within months after Texon was established, technical and production personnel discovered a wet-web saturating process that locked neoprene and cellulose fiber structures into a leatherlike material. It was a material that appeared to meet performance objectives, could be produced uniformly in rolls and sheets in different thick-

Today Texon headquarters is located in South Hadley Falls; its sales and distribution services cover the world.

nesses, and was low in cost. When early Texon sales representatives presented these new elastomeric fiber innersole materials, there was strong resistance. Shoe manufacturers of that era were born and raised with leather. They were not about to make shoes for their customers with "paper."

To overcome these objections, Texon contracted with a few adventuresome manufacturers in the New England area to produce wear-test shoes made with Texon elastomeric materials. These shoes were given to the presidents, sales, and key personnel of shoe manufacturers around the country to wear and test. Even the shoemen from Missouri found that the new man-made material from Massachusetts did indeed make a comfortable, durable shoe.

In the decades that followed Texon developed a line of elastomeric fiber products engineered to meet a range of shoe construction and style specifications. At the same time these materials were being modified or redesigned for use in luggage and leather goods, apparel, gaskets, and other specialized applications. Automotive battery separators were developed. Vinyl-coated and foamed products were added to the line. Texon enjoyed steady growth and expansion, establishing plants in South Hadley Falls, Holyoke, and Westfield, Massachusetts.

According to Hauke Peter, vice-president and general manager for Texon, David Schoales, a former president of Texon, recognized the opportunity for expansion on an international basis. Under the leadership of Schoales in the late 1950s, Texon took the bold step of expanding into Europe. Says Peter, "It was unique thinking at that time for a company the size of Texon to have the vision to begin exporting and diversifying into new markets around the globe."

The first export sales came from agents and representatives in the United States and abroad. As international business grew, licensed manufacturing was established in England and later in Japan. This was soon followed by a Texon plant in St. Rivalain, France, and later in Moeckmuehl, West Germany. An additional facility was built in Taiwan in the late 1970s. Texon was recognized by President Richard M. Nixon with an Export "E" Award for its export and international growth.

The worldwide Texon organization was acquired by the Connecticut-based Emhart Corporation in 1981 and, under this new leadership, the Texon overseas expansion continued, with new production facilities built in Italy and Brazil. The company's headquarters is still located in South Hadley Falls, Massachusetts. Sales and distribution services are located worldwide.

Texon manufactures more than 20 products, including elastomeric and resin-saturated fiber materials, non-wovens, and vinyl-coated and foamed materials in a variety of gauges, sizes, prints, and colors. There are innersole products such as T-437, used to produce welt constructed shoes, and Texorist for military footwear. Today almost all shoes made in the free world are produced using Texon-type elastomeric innersoling.

In reviewing Texon's history, Peter says: "As we look forward to the next chapter in our history, we know the experience and efforts of Texon people around the world will find new materials and ways to help our customers compete and grow. Dedicated Texon people made our past successful and fill our future with promise."

When Texon first began operations, the firm's goal was to create an innersole material with all the advantages of leather and none of its disadvantages. It has since developed a line of products to meet a range of shoe construction and style specifications, while also using its new material for other varied applications—as seen in the items shown here.

HOUGHTON MIFFLIN COMPANY

An abiding sense of tradition is evident at the publishing house of Houghton Mifflin Company, as befits a firm that includes among its authors Longfellow, Emerson, Whittier, Hawthorne, Dickens, Thackeray, Tennyson, Browning, Thoreau, and Twain—a company largely responsible for making Boston the nation's literary and publishing capital for many years.

Houghton Mifflin had its origins at the Old Corner Bookstore at Washington and School streets in the "Golden Age" of literary Boston. Built just after the Great Fire of 1711, the bookstore was the literary center of Boston for more than a half-century. It was headquarters for the exclusive Temple Club in 1829, the Tremont in 1851, and later the Somerset, the Union, and the Saturday clubs. In

The history of Houghton Mifflin Company began more than a century and a half ago at the Old Corner Bookstore at School and Washington streets in Boston.

1832 publishers William D. Ticknor and John Allen bought the store, but their partnership was short-lived, and Ticknor subsequently chose James T. Fields as his partner. Together they assembled one of the most distinguished groups of writers ever to share the same publishing house. They brought tact, discrimination, and generous royalties to their American and English authors while the firm took its place as a leading mid-nineteenth-century publisher. To be published by Ticknor & Fields became a mark of success among writers.

An association beginning during the Civil War with Henry O. Houghton of the Riverside Press, and later with George H. Mifflin, culminated in a merger in 1880 and the birth of the new partnership of Houghton, Mifflin and Company. By 1908 it would be a corporation.

Early on an education department was established to publish books for a growing number of students. Today the educational publishing divisions are the backbone of the company. Houghton Mifflin is a leader in developing instructional techniques and educational materials. An extensive list of elementary, high school, and college textbooks, tests, software, and other educational materials developed in Boston and by subsidiaries in Chicago and Canada now account for the largest segment of the business. Among the firm's best-selling educational publications are the *Houghton Mifflin Reading Program,* high school mathematics textbooks, college-level English and accounting programs, and standardized tests such as the *Iowa Tests of Basic Skills* and the *Stanford-Binet Intelligence Scale.*

Houghton Mifflin's general publishing activities have also remained important. Fine literature for children and adults is published under the Houghton Mifflin, Ticknor & Fields, and Clarion imprints. Through the years Houghton Mifflin authors have received numerous book awards, including a number of Pulitzer prizes and American book awards, as well as Caldecott and Newberry medals for children's literature.

Ticknor & Fields, forerunner of Houghton Mifflin Company, assembled one of the most distinguished collections of writers ever associated with one publisher. Here the founders, James T. Fields (left) and William D. Ticknor (right), are seen with one of their many authors, Nathaniel Hawthorne.

Publishing fine literary and educational works is Houghton Mifflin's heritage. For more than 150 years the firm's goal has been to shape information, instruction, and entertainment into forms that provide unique features of value to its customers. The company develops and manages ideas and intellectual properties with the help of an extensive collection of author relationships, a staff of experienced editorial talent, and a valuable storehouse of creative works.

Houghton Mifflin issues works representing a variety of viewpoints for a broad range of markets. Kate Wiggins' *Rebecca of Sunnybrook Farm,* Edward

Bellamy's *Looking Backward*, Henry James' *The Portrait of a Lady* and *The Bostonians*, Adolf Hitler's *Mein Kampf*, Winston Churchill's six-volume *The Second World War*, Esther Forbes' *Johnny Tremain*, and Rachel Carson's *Silent Spring* were all published by the firm as it built a list of distinguished, best-selling twentieth-century authors. This list also included Woodrow Wilson, Margaret Deland, and Brooks Adams, and by mid-century added Henry Cabot Lodge, Theodore Roosevelt, Amy Lowell, Archibald MacLeish, General George Patton, and Field Marshal Bernard Montgomery. Its contemporary authors include Roger Tory Peterson, who began the popular Field Guide series more than 50 years ago; Stephen Birnbaum, well-known travel guide author; as well as Louis Auchincloss, J.R.R. Tolkien, Howard Fast, John Kenneth Galbraith, Arthur Schlesinger, Pat Conroy, and Margaret Atwood.

As society has moved into the information age, the firm now publishes materials in electronic as well as print formats. In 1964 Houghton Mifflin began work on a new dictionary, the first to establish a computerized word base derived from extensive word frequency research and to be typeset by a computer. Introduced in 1969, *The American Heritage Dictionary* was ac-

Houghton Mifflin is a leading publisher of elementary school, high school, and college textbooks and other educational materials.

claimed by literary critics, academics, and the public, and remained on the *New York Times* Non-Fiction Bestseller List for 39 weeks. Other reference publications including a variety of children's dictionaries were derived

from the extensive word base, which was also used in the development of sophisticated lexical software for word-processing applications. The company continues to explore and develop new ways of distributing information electronically.

The Houghton Mifflin Company of the 1980s is still moving with the times. There is a blending of tradition and innovation even in its two separate downtown Boston offices. The firm's Trade & Reference Division occupies the handsome turn-of-the-century buildings at Two and Three Park Street, overlooking the Boston Common, where the company has been located for more than a century. Corporate headquarters and other editorial offices are at the contemporary One Beacon Street high rise. Harold T. Miller, chief executive officer since 1973 and chairman since 1979, directs the operations of Houghton Mifflin Company and its professional staff of more than 2,000.

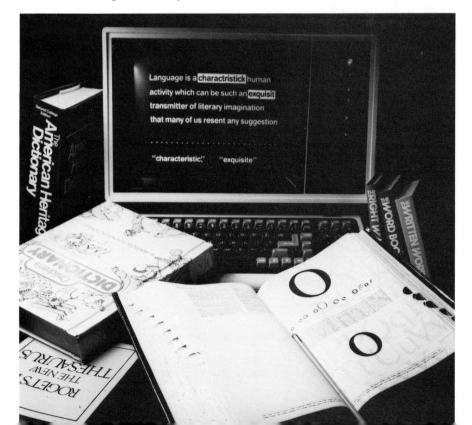

Houghton Mifflin's extensive list of reference publications and lexical software are derived principally from the company's computerized American Heritage Dictionary word base.

ESTHER QUINN REALTY

Esther L. Quinn is a vibrant and energetic woman who received her salesman's license in 1972. Quinn is the first to admit that her Pittsfield-based agency is not a business steeped in history. But, upon meeting Quinn, it becomes evident that she embodies a tradition of strong-willed, independent women in this country who have repeatedly set and achieved bigger and better goals.

One such goal, which Quinn has realized recently, is her selection as the 1986 Berkshire County and Massachusetts Realtor of the Year—a first in her county over a period of 30 years. No easy task considering there are 670 licensed realtors in Berkshire County and over 20,000 within the state's 21 counties. The criteria in selecting the honoree for this recognition involves sales, humanitarian contributions to one's community, voluntary hours to one's business community, and participation in one's realtor profession on the local, state, and national level. It also involves something rather difficult to gauge, a dedication to improving the industry overall.

Esther L. Quinn

Quinn estimates her volume of sales for 1986 to hover near the $10-million mark, placing her agency head-and-shoulders above others of comparable size in the county. The highlights of her community involvement include a weekly column on real estate in the *Berkshire Eagle,* six years as the vice-president of membership for the Central Berkshire County Chamber of Commerce, eight years as chairman of the chamber's monthly Business After Hours educational and social meetings, currently serving a three-year term on the executive board of directors for the Berkshire County Visitors' Bureau, a three-year post on the board of directors of the county's chapter of the American Red Cross, the 1985 president of the Berkshire County Board of Realtors, and currently serving a two-year term as a state director for the Massachusetts Association of Realtors.

Quinn says it took many years and much encouragement from family, friends, and members of the business community to finally establish her own agency. After receiving her salesman's license she worked for two years as the first associate in a small "mom-and-pop" realty home office. Needing a professional office, they merged with another small realty firm. Quinn stayed another three years with that firm. "I learned a lot in those years," says Quinn, "but I eventually realized I wanted to further my real estate education and own my own agency."

After obtaining a broker's license, Quinn opened Esther Quinn Realty, working out of her home with four associates for one year.

In 1978 Jack Welch, current chairman of the board of General Electric Company, considered Quinn to be one of the most honest, competent realtors he knew in the area. The last advice Welch gave Quinn before transferring to the General Electric headquarters in Fairfield, Connecticut, was to "Get out of the kitchen and get a professional office and go tell it as it is." Quinn would be the first to tell you that that advice started her career to bigger and better heights.

It was then that Quinn became a partner with the third-generation family firm of Robertson Realty, established in 1910. The Robertson and Quinn partnership lasted for seven years, at which time Quinn decided to buy out their interest and office space and become Esther Quinn Realty again. All of the previous firm's 13 associates opted to stay with Quinn. Within a year of June 1985, 15 more associates had joined the firm, and husband, Richard, a civil engineer, and sons Joseph and William took a new interest in the family business.

Quinn describes her sales technique as caring. She talks extensively with her customers in order to understand their needs and dreams when they are buying a house. She is also very committed to passing along her success to her associates.

Quinn's next goals are to establish branch offices in north and south Berkshire County and to open a commercial real estate division.

Quinn has earned the GRI (Graduate Realtor Institute) and CRS (Certified Residential Specialist) designations and currently is furthering her education in the CRB (Certified Real Estate Broker) management and commercial courses.

RED LION INN

There is a well-known Norman Rockwell painting of a huge clapboard building with an expansive porch. Giant maple trees line a snowy street upon which a red 1948 Packard with a Christmas tree atop is passing, and men, women, and children are walking and engaged in conversation. Behind the building rise green and blue hills to meet a bright blue sky. The scene was painted by Rockwell in the 1950s from his adjacent studio in the Berkshire County town of Stockbridge; pictured is the Red Lion Inn.

The original structure was built in 1773 by Silas Pepoon as a small tavern. The numbers of travelers increased when Stockbridge became a stop on the Albany-Hartford-Springfield stagecoach run, and Pepoon added a few rooms to accommodate those making the long, rigorous journey. The inn was not initially called the Red Lion,

The Red Lion Inn and the Soldiers' Monument in 1866. The building was destroyed by fire in 1896 and was completely rebuilt the following year.

though an ornate red lion has always been emblazoned on the signboard.

The small tavern and hostel had a series of owners over the next century until it was purchased in 1862 by local residents, Mr. and Mrs. Charles H. Plumb. During the 90 years of the Plumbs' ownership Mrs. Plumb, an avid collector of antique furniture and china, dramatically upgraded the quality and style of the inn, and the structure was expanded to house over 100 guests.

In 1896 the building was completely destroyed by fire. Indicative of its popularity and value, the inn as it exists today was rebuilt within one year. Over the next few decades the Red Lion Inn developed a reputation as the grande dame of country inns, and the tiny town of Stockbridge became established as a summer retreat for prominent artists, musicians, and writers.

In 1961 the hotel was purchased by Robert K. Wheeler, a resident of nearby Great Barrington. The southern portion of the inn was converted to a motor lodge and a swimming pool was dug. Business at the inn faltered during the 1960s, and by the end of the decade the inn was again put up for sale.

The Red Lion Inn was saved from pending demolition in 1968 by its current owners, former State Senator Jack Fitzpatrick and his wife, Jane. A classic tale of successful entrepreneurship, the Fitzpatricks started a mail order curtain company, Country Curtains, literally from their kitchen table in the late 1950s. They moved to Stockbridge, and their ever-expanding business required the purchase of first one and then another building. They purchased the inn with the expectation that the sprawling building would fully accommodate both guests and their retail/wholesale curtain company. While the guests and a retail shop remain, Country Curtains has outgrown the quarters and continues to expand throughout New England.

Perhaps the most meaningful contribution made by the Fitzpatricks was to return the Red Lion to a large country inn. In the past few years the inn

The 100-room Red Lion Inn today, now operated by former State Senator and Mrs. John Fitzpatrick.

has had its plumbing and heating systems revamped, and it is now open all year. There are a total of 103 rooms—90 in the main house and the rest in four adjacent homes used as suites and VIP lodging.

With stenciled wallpaper, fresh flowers, and canopied beds the rooms exceed the most imaginative expectations of a real country inn. The main dining room is elegant and dignified, offering both traditional New England and continental cuisine complemented by an extensive wine list. The Cozy Widow Bingham Tavern is filled with wooden beams, antique baskets, tools, and a collection of fascinating signboards. Downstairs, the victorian Lion's Den Pub offers lighter meals and entertainment nightly. Once again a renowned center for cultural activity, the Red Lion Inn serves as a gathering point for thousands of travelers who have come to the area to participate in the many events available for the arts enthusiast.

THE BOSTON COMPANY
Boston Safe Deposit and Trust Company

Like the city in which it was founded over a century ago, Boston Safe Deposit and Trust Company is a unique blend of past and present. Ulysses S. Grant was President of the United States when the company first opened in 1875. Its eight original staff members offered fiduciary and advisory services that were new and somewhat revolutionary—managing capital for others.

Trusteeship as we know it began in Boston early in the nineteenth century when large fortunes were amassed by successful merchants and ship owners. The new firm's name clearly identified its purpose—to offer safe deposit and trust services. As its reputation grew, many of Boston's most prominent and influential families came to rely on the company's skill, prudence, and discretion; and, within 25 years, Boston Safe Deposit and Trust Company had be-

come the largest trust company in New England.

In many respects the firm continues to carry out the objectives of its revolutionary charter by specializing in the "trust business" and its supporting services. But as times changed the demands on the investment fiduciary changed, and in 1964 Boston Safe created its own holding company, The Boston Company. This alteration was made to facilitate diversification into broader investment activities and to serve new geographic markets. In the ensuing years The Boston Company organized or acquired additional subsidiaries, thereby broadening both the type and reach of the firm's financial services.

In 1981 The Boston Company was acquired by Shearson Lehman Brothers Inc., the second-largest securities broker in the United States and itself a subsidiary of American Express. The Boston Company thereby became part of a worldwide financial services network.

Through its principal subsidiary, Boston Safe, The Boston Company has long been involved with philanthropy. In 1917, when it organized the Permanent Charities Fund of Boston (now called The Boston Foundation), Boston Safe took a pioneering step which would become a dominant force in strengthening and developing the entire range of Boston's community services. Within its first half-century the fund distributed $16 million to deserving charities, including hundreds of cultural organizations. As a leading administrator of charitable funds in New England, The Boston Company continues to place special emphasis on the needs of the homeless and the importance of community development.

As Boston has grown during the past century to become the second-largest financial center in the United States, so, too, has The Boston Company expanded. Today the firm is orga-

nized into six groups.

The Institutional Markets Group provides a wide range of financial products and services for tax-exempt pension plans of America's largest institutional clients and endowments. The primary services of this group include master trust and custody of assets, defined contribution services, active and passive investment management, and real estate investments.

The Individual Client Group provides all financial services including asset management, trust, lending, and deposit taking to individuals at the top of the economic spectrum.

The Mutual Funds Group provides advisory, administrative, custodial, and transfer agent services to registered investment companies. Through The Boston Company Advisors, Inc.,

In a unique blend of past and present, The Boston Company Building rises behind the Old City Hall (left) and the Old State House (right) in the heart of Boston's financial district.

Archival documents dating back to 1875—the year Boston Safe Deposit and Trust Company first opened its doors to the public.

Today The Boston Company and its several thousand employees are directed by George W. Phillips, chairman and chief executive officer, and James N. von Germeten, president and chief investment officer.

"Our competitive edge, the basis for our success, is commitment to quality," explains von Germeten. "Because we are dedicated to first-class service, we maintain state-of-the-art operating capabilities directed at developing competitively advantaged products and superior service delivery."

Now in its second century of service, The Boston Company has expanded far beyond its original charter privileges of receiving "on deposit for safekeeping" money, securities, jewelry, and similar items of value, and to "collect and disburse the interest or income upon such said property . . . when it comes due." But one thing has never changed: Striving for excellence is still the company's formula for success.

the group offers a family of funds under The Boston Company name. The Mutual Funds Group also provides automated investment and account processing capabilities to many banks nationwide.

The Treasury Group provides investment services and pursues funding opportunities in the global capital markets. Treasury manages Boston Safe Deposit and Trust Company's balance sheet and offers a broad range of investment-related services to institutional clients. These services include foreign exchange, economic research, and discount brokerage through Boston Institutional Services Inc.

The Corporate Administration Group manages the administrative functions of the corporation, including corporate marketing, human resources, finance, real estate, facilities management, audit, strategic planning, and legal functions.

The Corporate Operations Group provides the foundation for service delivery functions for all The Boston Company clients through data processing, custody, and banking operations. This group operates the company's computer facilities around the clock while designing and developing new and improved systems.

The Boston Company stands apart from other financial institutions in two important respects. First, its clients include both the descendants of New England's builders and people who are on their way to becoming the founders of wealth in future generations. Second, each client is considered to be unique and important and is given personal and confidential treatment by the company's officers. The hallmark of The Boston Company is personalized attention that helps clients meet their specific financial goals. The quality and style of its service foster relationships that often continue from one generation to the next.

The 10-story Boston Safe Deposit and Trust Company edifice, circa 1910. The building, still in existence, was home to The Boston Company for 60 years.

HALE AND DORR

Hale and Dorr, Boston's largest law firm with 248 attorneys, maintains a tradition of energy and innovation in its practice of law. Partners at the firm have included Reginald Heber Smith, one of the nation's founders of legal aid and an early expert in law office management; Joseph N. Welch, the distinguished litigator who opposed Senator Joseph McCarthy in the historic Army-McCarthy senate hearings of 1954; James D. St. Clair, one of the country's most respected litigators who was assistant to Welch in the McCarthy hearings and who later represented President Richard M. Nixon in the Watergate controversy; and Paul P. Brountas, nationally recognized as a pioneer in the legal representation of developing high-technology businesses.

In the heart of the downtown financial district next to Faneuil Hall, the firm occupies seven floors of modern office space at the 60 State Street office tower, built on the same site occupied by Hale and Dorr from 1919 to 1969. The firm has a branch office in Washington, D.C., which was opened in 1981 and is located at the Willard Office Building. The firm's total staff of 725 in Boston and Washington is linked by an internal computer network.

Hale and Dorr traces its legacy back to the early nineteenth century, when Josiah Parsons Cooke opened a

Reginald Heber Smith, Hale and Dorr managing partner from 1919 to 1955.

law practice in the Old State House on Boston's State Street. After a succession of partnerships, the firm commenced business under its present name on July 1, 1918, when Dudley Dorr, a respected member of the Boston Bar, became a partner of Richard Hale, Frank Grinnell, Roger Swaim,

Hale and Dorr's managing partner John D. Hamilton, Jr. (center), with Harry T. Daniels (left) and John M. Westcott, Jr. (right), assistant managing partners.

and John Maguire. Both Hale and Dorr served as partners in the firm until their deaths in 1943 and 1961, respectively.

In 1919 the partnership was reconstituted to include Reginald Heber Smith, who brought with him six legal aid lawyers. During more than 36 years as managing partner of the firm, Smith was active in furthering legal services for the poor and became the first recipient, in 1951, of the American Bar Association Gold Medal and, in 1957, of the Reginald Heber Smith Medal, now awarded annually for dedicated service to legal aid. Hale and Dorr has remained foremost among Boston firms in pro bono programs, maintaining at any one time 50 to 75 open pro bono files, involving over 7,500 hours of services per year.

The "Smith System" formula for measuring attorney productivity and determining partner compensation was developed by Reginald Heber Smith and has been a model for numerous law firms and professional service firms in this country and abroad. A series of articles written by Smith describing the system were published in the *American Bar Association Journal* in 1940 and have been republished many times in booklet form, most recently in 1984.

In 1954 Smith recommended to his partners that the firm assume the fees and expenses for a new client, the

United States Army, and the firm's leading litigator, Joseph N. Welch, was appointed special counsel to the Army in the Army-McCarthy hearings. The courtly and scholarly Welch, a deft and erudite courtroom attorney, impressed himself upon the national consciousness when, in the televised senate committee proceedings, he brought the powerful Senator Joseph McCarthy to a standstill. The senate committee hearings culminated in McCarthy's censure, and Welch, long one of the most highly regarded members of the Massachusetts Trial Bar, received national respect for his determination in the face of an aggressive and formerly intimidating adversary.

In 1956 Paul F. Hellmuth succeeded Smith as managing partner and served until his retirement in 1976. Hellmuth earned great distinction especially for his efforts in Boston on behalf of a variety of important cultural, educational, recreational, and community resources.

Today the most extensive areas of practice at Hale and Dorr are litiga-

Joseph N. Welch and James D. St. Clair, counsel and assistant counsel to the United States Army during the Army-McCarthy hearings, relax on the Capitol lawn during a break in the proceedings.

tion, corporate law, and real estate, and its practice in the fields of tax, personal law, and commercial law continues to expand. The firm's litigation practice is the largest in New England and represents one of the most active courtroom practices in the country. In recent years the firm has been involved in a variety of significant cases, including representation of John Hancock Mutual Life Insurance Company in claims arising out of the construction of Hancock's glass skyscraper in Copley Square, Boston; successful defense of the Town of Mashpee, Massachusetts, in an Indian land claim case; successful defense of Southern Pacific Company in a large antitrust case; and successful defense of Beatrice Companies, Inc., in landmark environmental litigation. The firm successfully argued in the 1984 term of the United States Supreme Court the case that confirmed that the sale of stock of a small business was governed by the Federal Securities Laws, and in the 1985 term of the United States Supreme Court successfully represented the State of South Carolina in an Indian land claim case. Jerome P. Facher, chairman of the Litigation Department, has taught a course in trial practice at Harvard Law School since 1962; James D. St. Clair taught another section of the same course for more than 25 years.

Hale and Dorr's Corporation Department, under the chairmanship of Paul P. Brountas, has grown rapidly in the past decade and today represents a number of large, public, computer-related corporations that it helped found in the late 1960s and early 1970s. The firm continues to specialize in representation of both small, start-up enterprises and the venture capital investors who often finance such businesses. More recently, the firm has developed a strong practice in the syndication area, representing public and private partnerships in real estate, re-

search and development, and oil and gas, as well as a burgeoning practice in international transactions and representation of foreign investors in the United States.

Led by Herbert W. Vaughan, Hale and Dorr was one of the first large law firms in the country to develop a significant real estate practice, playing a key role in representing both developers and lenders active in the commercial and industrial growth along Route 128 and the dramatic revitalization of Boston's downtown area. Now one of the nation's largest, the Real Estate Department currently represents syndicators, developers, lenders, and investors throughout the United States. The firm's real estate expertise has also been instrumental in the related growth of its corporate and securities practice in the real estate syndication area. As part of the multifaceted nature of this work, members of the Real Estate Department have become expert in the zoning, environmental, and permitting aspects of development that have grown so rapidly in recent years. They have also devoted much time with nonprofit community groups on low- and moderate-income housing projects.

Typical of its innovative style, Hale and Dorr has implemented a firm-wide computer network as extensive as any installed by a personal service organization. Each secretary, and also many attorneys and administrative personnel, has a desk-top computer terminal that provides word processing and other office automation functions (electronic mail, paperless files, litigation support, calendaring, mathematical spread-sheet capabilities), as well as access to central information such as billing and time records. The firm's Washington, D.C., office is linked to the system, greatly enhancing communications and the sharing of resources. The system has greatly increased productivity for clients and will position Hale and Dorr to play a leading role in the development of computer applications that permit legal services to be delivered more efficiently in the future.

BERKSHIRE MEDICAL CENTER

Berkshire Medical Center, a 369-bed, private, nonprofit hospital in Pittsfield, Massachusetts, has a rich history that mirrors the evolution of the entire health care industry. One of the state's largest hospitals, Berkshire Medical Center tended to the needs of nearly 160,000 people in 1986 with state-of-the-art medical care. It has developed as a vital and central facility for western Massachusetts following its creation from the 1967 merger between Pittsfield General Hospital and St. Luke's Hospital, which was the first merger of a secular and a nonsecular hospital.

THE HOUSE OF MERCY

In the 1870s the residents of Pittsfield, a town of 10,000, began serious discussions about the need for a hospital to care for the area's largely rural population. Although a fund was established, plans to build a centrally located hospital were scrapped on the basis that raising the half-million dollars needed was far too ambitious of an undertaking.

Despite the setback, the idea of a hospital did not dissolve, and people in the community began to consider the possibility of adopting the British concept of a cottage hospital. It is written in the "Capsule History of Pittsfield General Hospital" by Vera Fielding that a cottage hospital was an idea "expressed in a little book by an English physician who believed that the essentials of a hospital were a roof, a bed, a nurse; and that philanthropy, working in the ordinary channels, could always be relied upon to provide food and medical care." The book continues: "Considered from that point of view, the hospital problem in Pittsfield was plainly simplified." Indeed, hospitals were few and far between, and physicians worked independently of health care institutions. Those who were sick and could afford it hired doctors and nurses to care for them in their homes. The poor either nursed themselves or relied on the charity of their local parish.

In 1874, arguing the premise of the cottage hospital, Dr. J.F.A. Adams addressed a meeting of the town's wealthy

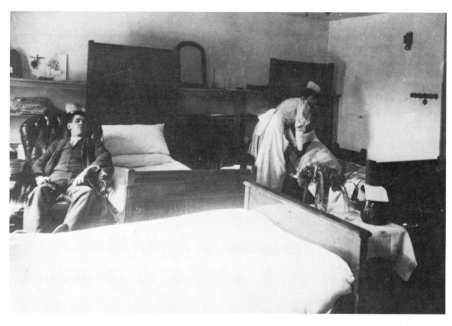

Hospital wards were the rule at the turn of the century and for many years afterward. This was the Men's Ward at the House of Mercy about 1900.

housewives, imploring them to realize that caring for the sick was an act of "housewifely ability," and assured the gathering that health care was an area in which they would discover "a field of public service in which they would be energetically at home." Inspired by his words, the group immediately

The pharmacy at Pittsfield General Hospital in 1956. Shown here is pharmacist Marc Gasbarrone at work.

formed an association with the purpose of raising money for a cottage hospital. Their efforts were a success, and in 1875 a house was rented capable of accommodating eight patients with access to five attending physicians. Christened The House of Mercy, it was the first cottage hospital in the country, and had a charter that read, "For the care of the sick and disabled, whether in indigent circumstances or not." It is clear from the first ledgers that many of its patients were indigent, or close to it; payments were often made in the form of livestock, lumber, or free labor.

Within three years, impressed by the obvious need for a larger hospital,

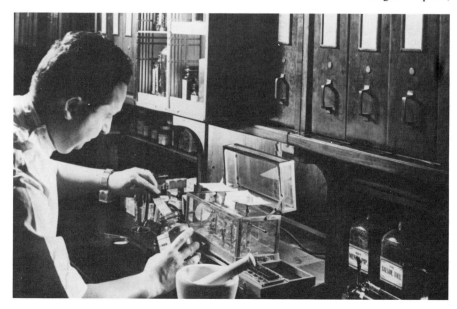

A nurse with an anesthesia machine at the House of Mercy, circa 1920.

the community donated $10,000 in cash and materials for the construction of a two-story, 13-bed facility.

Currently one of the state's valued teaching hospitals (in affiliation with the University of Massachusetts Medical School), Berkshire Medical Center began its medical education program early in its history with the admission in 1884 of four nursing students who were taught by the matron of the House of Mercy.

As the demand for the House of Mercy's services grew, so did bequests and donations, allowing it to expand in both staff and facilities. Historical documents report that it was the women of the county who contributed the most to the hospital in its early years. One source says, "Service to the hospital was almost a life work. The quality of their service animated many able women of following generations to carry on the unselfish work courageously." In 1949 the House of Mercy was renamed Pittsfield General Hospital.

ST. LUKE'S HOSPITAL

In the early 1900s the Reverend Charles Boylan left funds to the Springfield, Massachusetts, Diocese with the request that it be put to use for a charitable cause. The diocese used the modest donation to purchase two buildings in Pittsfield, which became the Boylan Memorial Hospital. The Sisters of Providence were placed in charge of its operations. The following year the Allen Estate mansion was deeded to the Sisters and remodeled into a 28-bed hospital named after the patron saint of physicians, St. Luke. Initially the plan was that Boylan Memorial and St. Luke's would function as one hospital with two wings. However, the brief existence of Boylan Memorial ended when the building in which it was housed was sold to raise funds for the construction of a five-story hospital in 1926.

St. Luke's also had a nursing school that began in 1917 with six students. The hospital successfully weathered lean times by levying Catholic parishes throughout the county. While never matching the growth and size of Pittsfield General Hospital, St. Luke's held its own and over the next decades expanded as a teaching hospital. In 1959 St. Luke's became affiliated with the Albany, New York, Medical School.

BERKSHIRE MEDICAL CENTER

Merging the operations of St. Luke's and Pittsfield General took 10 years and many long, heated debates. The reason, according to a participant in the process, was that, "There were so many years of history behind both hospitals and such deep loyalties involved that everyone felt they were somehow losing their hospital."

The first interaction between the two hospitals was in 1959, when a joint medical education program was inaugurated. The first bona fide discussions on merging the two facilities began in 1967, when Bishop Christopher J. Weldon called a meeting of hospital and community officials to discuss the city's future health care needs and to recommend unifying the two hospitals. That same year the staffs of the respective institutions voted to merge under the name Berkshire Medical Center. In 1968 the staffs of the hospitals were combined. However, it took until 1976 to fully consolidate the structure, budget, and overall operations.

At a time when the health care industry trend is the establishment of regional health care clusters, Berkshire Medical Center, under the umbrella of Berkshire Health Systems, is emerging as one of the state's foremost regional centers. Senior vice-president Keith Pryor explained that the medical center's mission is to provide complete, quality health care to the residents of Berkshire County. "We offer every major component of health care, from our special care nursery to our nursing home," he says. "In addition to our other services, we will be constructing a state-of-the-art cancer treatment facility this year."

It was many, many years ago that the nurses of the House of Mercy conceived the guiding principle that still governs Berkshire Medical Center today: to help the sick with courtesy, respect, and caring.

The emergency room of St. Luke's Hospital, 1953.

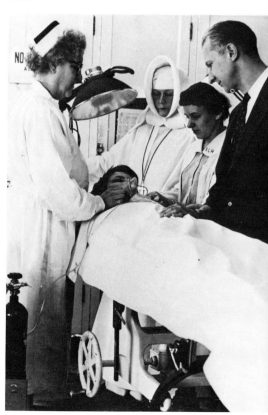

EASTCO

Eastco was incorporated in its present form in 1933, but its roots go deep into the 1860s, when Morris Steinert formed the M. Steinert Company in New Haven, Connecticut, to import and distribute Steinway pianos. In the latter part of the nineteenth century, the firm expanded vertically as well as horizontally, becoming a manufacturer (with its plant in Leominster, Massachusetts), wholesaler-importer (with headquarters in Boston), and retailer (with 44 stores at its peak as far west as Ohio). It also took on additional musical instruments, sheet music, and eventually phonographs and phonograph records manufactured by the Victor Talking Machine Company. In 1924 the M. Steinert (now "and Sons") Company wholesale division merged with The Eastern Talking Machine Company, another Victor Records distributor.

Five years later RCA bought the Victor Talking Machine Company and introduced the now-famous brand name of RCA Victor. The Eastern Talking Machine Company, still a division of M. Steinert & Sons Company then began to distribute RCA Victor products. Thus, through the late 1800s and up to the present, Eastco has enjoyed an unbroken relationship with RCA and its predecessor, the Victor Talking Machine Company.

In 1933 Alan Steinert, grandson of Morris Steinert, formed a new corporation—The Eastern Radio Company—solely to distribute RCA Victor products. It was a humble rebirth; in its abbreviated first fiscal year the firm sold a mere $30,000 worth of products to Boston area retailers. The new venture acquired its first major appliance franchise in 1936, resettling in Cambridge from its Boston location, changing its name to The Eastern Company

During World War II The Eastern Company was converted into a defense company, manufacturing electronic equipment and critically needed communications apparatus for the military and employing more than 500 people. This photo was taken in 1943.

to reflect this broader base of product lines. The firm also established a branch in Providence, Rhode Island, just before the end of the decade. The business continued to grow until World War II, when it converted into a defense company, employing, at its peak, more than 500 people, manufacturing electronic equipment and critically needed communications apparatus for the military.

After the war The Eastern Company returned to the wholesale distribution of RCA products as well as the Kelvinator and Bendix brands of major home appliances. Whirlpool laundry products were taken on in 1952, and the full Whirlpool product line followed

Today Eastco is the largest wholesale distributor of consumer durables, serving more than 2,500 retailers in the six-state New England region.

four years later. In 1970 the firm branched out into the carpeting business, and broadened further in 1974 by entering the resilient floor covering business, including, most recently, ceramic tile, in all of New England. Continuing in its expansion, Eastco recently has become the New England distributor for Canon office products, Southwestern Bell telephones, computers and monitors from Mitsubishi, and satellite television equipment from General Instrument. The name Eastco was conceived in 1969 as a result of the acquisition of distributors in Hartford, Connecticut, and Springfield, Massachusetts.

The company prides itself on its New England orientation, having as its objective the maintenance of its history of being the finest and most effective, albeit the largest, distributor of consumer durables in the six-state area, with close, personal working relationships with more than 2,500 retailers in the region. The 180 people, including 50 salespeople traveling the byways of New England each and every day who are the spirit and heart of Eastco, are dedicated to serving the very real needs of all the customers of the company. That is Eastco's creed.

PETRICCA INDUSTRIES, INC.

An integrated construction and concrete corporation, Petricca Industries of Pittsfield was started at the height of the Depression by Basilio "Patsy" Petricca with little more than a used pickup truck, an old wheelbarrow, and a loan from his godmother's cookie jar.

In 1910 Patsy Petricca left his family's farm in Monteflavio, Italy, possessing the dream of many emigrants: to find his fortune and a better life in America. Unable to speak more than a few words of English and having only a sixth-grade education, 16-year-old Patsy landed a job as waterboy at a construction site. Quickly recognized as a hard worker with an ambition, Patsy was promoted to laborer and then to foreman. Three years later he traveled to the far western regions of the state to take a job working for his future father-in-law, Peter Mancuso, on the construction of the Mount Williams Reservoir in North Adams.

After marrying Mancuso's daughter, Rosa, in 1918 Patsy accepted a higher-paying job with the Lane Construction Company. Lacking today's technologies that allow construction firms to excavate and build during the winter, Patsy and his growing family spent summers traveling to construction sites from White River Junction, Vermont, to Pennsylvania and winters working in a North Adams factory, and driving a taxi.

Anxious to establish himself in the field of construction and better provide for his family, Patsy worked nearly every day of the year from 4 a.m. to 8 p.m.

The strength of Patsy's character was revealed by his decision, during one of the hardest times for business in American history, to scrape together his life's savings and ask for his godmother's financial assistance. With less than $500 he established Petricca Construction Company.

It was the devastating flood of the Hoosic River in 1936 that allowed the Petricca Construction Company its chance to prove its capabilities for bridge and infrastructure engineering. The town of Chester, Massachusetts, had lost a total of four bridges, and access to and from the small community was literally washed out. Patsy went directly to Boston to place a bid with the state on the reconstruction of at least one of the bridges. He returned home with a contract to repair all four.

In 1947 Transit Mix Concrete and General Sand & Stone were founded. Although Patsy Petricca passed away in 1962, his daughter Virginia, and three sons, Basil, Robert, and Peter, have catapulted the company into a well-diversified, formidable construction operation busy throughout New England.

In 1968 a competitor, Berkshire

Below, right: In 1986 Petricca Construction Company celebrated its 50th anniversary in the construction industry.

Below: A mid-1960s site under construction by Petricca.

Gravel, was acquired by Petricca. The three companies—Transit Mix Concrete, General Sand & Stone, and Berkshire Gravel—were merged to form one Berkshire Concrete Corporation. Today Berkshire Concrete Corp. is a major supplier of concrete, sand, and stone products throughout Berkshire County. That same year Unistress, a fully equipped prestressed concrete manufacturing facility opened. Among its major contracts was providing prestress concrete products for the renovation of New York's Yankee Stadium. In 1982 the company diversified from the construction business and incorporated Petricca Communications Systems, a private telecommunications firm specializing in the resale of long-distance telephone service and communications equipment.

In 1986 Petricca added its newest industry with the formation of CONAC (Concrete Accessories, Inc.) to manufacture and distribute plastic accessories for the prestress concrete industry. It subcontracts with local firms to manufacture their products.

A visitor to Petricca Industries walks away from the offices filled with a sense of history. It is impressive to consider that 76 years ago a young Italian immigrant toiled long and hard to raise a family and the business that is currently responsible for the livelihoods of more than 300 employees and the existence of hundreds of highways, roads, bridges, sewer systems, buildings, and dams throughout the Northeast.

OCEAN SPRAY CRANBERRIES, INC.

American Indians were the first to harvest cranberries, one of only three native North American fruits. (Concord grapes and blueberries are the others.) Cranberries are cultivated primarily in Massachusetts, Wisconsin, New Jersey, Washington, and Oregon, as well as parts of Canada. In 1930 two cranberry operations in Massachusetts and one in New Jersey decided that "competition among them was seriously interfering with the development of a year-round market for cranberries." To remedy this, they formed a cooperative called Cranberry Canners, Inc. At first they only sold cranberry sauce—whole and jellied—under the brand name Ocean Spray. But soon cranberry juice cocktail was added to the list, advertised as "a smooth drink with delicious flavor and sure relief from faintness, exhaustion, and thirst." A concentrate called Ocean Spray Cran appeared in 1939, and the 1940s saw the introduction of dehydrated cranberries (for the armed forces) and cranberry-orange relish. New growers from Wisconsin, Washington, and Oregon joined the cooperative in the early 1940s, thus creating a cooperative stretching from coast to coast.

During World War II tin and sugar shortages limited cranberry products for the civilian sector. Only a small amount was packaged for use on the home front, but about one million pounds of cranberries each year were dehydrated to supply the armed forces. In appreciation of its dedicated growers and employees, the cooperative received the coveted Achievement "A" Award in 1944 from the War Food Administration.

After VJ-Day government demand for dehydrated cranberries fell significantly, and cranberry sauce was again widely available to American consumers. The cooperative had continued to grow during the war, boasting 15 facilities as early as 1943. Now a nationwide organization, it took the new name of National Cranberry Association (NCA) in 1946. Advertising and publicity efforts were strengthened, and membership began growing rapidly. Within five years the NCA in-

This scene, circa 1912, is the Central Packinghouse in Hanson, Massachusetts, then a new building and later the site of Ocean Spray's headquarters through the summer of 1977.

cluded 1,760 members.

The National Cranberry Association started Canadian operations when Ocean Spray Limited officially began production in 1950. Delicious new taste treats were soon introduced, such as Ocean Spray Cape Cod Cranberry Sundae Topping in 1950 and dietetic cranberry products in 1951.

Two founders of the cooperative, Marcus Urann, president and general manager, and John Makepeace, secretary/treasurer, both retired in the mid-1950s, and a series of short-term managements during the next five years detracted from the cooperative's continuity of policy. One forward step, however, was a change of name. To more closely identify the cooperative with the brand name it had used since the beginning, NCA became known as Ocean Spray Cranberries, Inc., in 1959.

Many readers remember the cranberry scare that soon followed. On November 9, 1959, Secretary of Health, Education, and Welfare Arthur Flemming announced that aminotriazole—a weed-killing chemical used by some West Coast growers—caused cancer in

laboratory animals. This front-page news led stores to remove cranberry products from their shelves. Ocean Spray immediately began testing its berries and banned the use of aminotriazole, but the damage was done. Holiday sales plummeted, and many families across America served their Thanksgiving turkey without cranberry sauce.

The fact that something as unex-

The Pilgrims gave the cranberry its name, as they believed the berry's pale pink blossom, shown here, resembled the head of a crane. Hence, they called it the crane-berry, later contracted to cranberry.

Wooden scoops (foreground) were replaced with mechanical pickers resembling large lawnmowers. These machines, still used today for cranberries to be marketed as fresh produce, gently comb the berries from the vines by means of moving metal teeth.

pected as the 1959 scare could destroy Ocean Spray's sales season forced management to seek more stable, year-round sources of income. The period from 1963 to 1968 marked Ocean Spray's full-scale entry into the consumer drinks market. In addition to the familiar cranberry juice cocktail, CRANAPPLE® cranberry-apple drink, CRANGRAPE® grape-cranberry drink, and CRANICOT® cranberry-apricot drink joined the growing product list. Today these and other popular drinks account for more than three-quarters of total sales. Im-

proved harvesting methods brought about improved yields to match America's growing use of cranberries. By 1968 North American growers were harvesting almost 1.5 million barrels of berries each year. (Each barrel contains 100 pounds of berries.) Demand also continued to grow and was about equal to supply at this time.

Larger crops and increasing demand pushed annual sales past the $100-million barrier in 1974, as processing facilities were added or improved in Washington, Wisconsin, New Jersey, and Massachusetts.

In the most common harvesting method, mechanical water reels, such as these, are guided through the cranberry bogs, which have been flooded to a depth of about two feet. The water reels stir up the water with sufficient force to dislodge the ripe berries from their vines.

Ocean Spray's headquarters outgrew its Hanson, Massachusetts, location and in 1977 was moved to a five-level building on Plymouth's historic waterfront, less than a half-mile from Plymouth Rock.

The first noncranberry growers joined the Ocean Spray cooperative in the 1970s. In 1976 a facility was opened at Vero Beach, Florida, for citrus growers in the Indian River region. Grapefruit delivered to the plant is made into concentrate and shipped in bulk to facilities across the country to be reconstituted into grapefruit juice products.

Skyrocketing consumer demand outpaced production capacity in the late 1970s, forcing Ocean Spray to seek satellite processing facilities. Several independent plants across the country now package Ocean Spray products, closely supervised by the cooperative's quality-control experts.

Continuing its entrepreneurial tradition, Ocean Spray became the first American company to offer consumers aseptically packaged juice drinks in the summer of 1981. More recently the firm has introduced products such as CRANRASPBERRY® cranberry-raspberry drink, CRANBLUEBERRY® blueberry-cranberry drink, and MAUNA LA'I® Hawaiian guava fruit drink. Sales doubled between 1981 and 1986, catapulting Ocean Spray onto the *Fortune* 500 list of the nation's largest corporations.

Professor Ray Goldberg, chairman of the Agribusiness Department at Harvard Business School and an authority on cooperatives, has been watching Ocean Spray Cranberries, Inc., for three decades. In summing up the success of this quintessentially American company, he says, "Most cooperatives were started with a production orientation, but Ocean Spray has gone further by finding out what the consumer wants and asking how it can be more creative." This consumer-driven spirit is all part of a unique marketing success story at Ocean Spray—one that has led to distribution of the cooperative's products in more than 35 countries worldwide.

THE BEAL COMPANIES

The year 1988 marks the 100th anniversary of the founding of Beal & Company, Inc., a fourth-generation closely held real estate corporation that offers professional consulting and appraisal services for selected clients while also developing and managing real estate for its own portfolio.

Boston was the hub of a complex, metropolitan area in the midst of a building boom when A.B. Beal founded his real estate firm in 1888. He was joined in the early 1900s by his sons Julius and Benjamin. The city at that time was bursting with new institutions; Fort Hill had disappeared and with it the last trace of the colonial waterfront, and the tidal salt marsh known as the Back Bay was filled, reigning supreme as a much needed residential district. Transportation by electric trolley was beyond anyone's imagination, as horse-drawn vehicles caused daily traffic tangles. It was a transitional period for the first crude applications of electricity, and a bellwether for unprecedented social and industrial progress.

The Beal family became a significant part of this progress, as it purchased and operated real estate throughout the metropolitan area and was one of the earliest firms to do appraisal and consulting work.

Beginning in 1931 Alexander S. Beal, son of Julius, became involved in Beal & Company, Inc. He specialized in real estate appraisal and tax valuation analysis of commercial, industrial, agricultural, waterfront, and residential real estate throughout the eastern and southern United States. Alexander S. Beal became one of the preeminent experts in the field of eminent domain. He served as president of the Massachusetts Association of Realtors and the Massachusetts Association of Appraisers. A lifetime member of the Greater Boston Real Estate Board, he continues as a director of Beal & Company, Inc., and consultant to The Beal Companies.

As one of Boston's oldest continuous real estate firms, The Beal Companies traditionally maintains a conservative philosophy toward its

portfolio. It purchases properties as investment builders, acquiring distinctive landmark structures. Among these are the Old Corner Bookstore, Boston's first brick building, which was owned by The Beal Companies; the historic Grain Exchange Building, constructed in 1892; and the Park Square Building, the largest office structure in the city in 1922 with a first-of-its-kind interior arcade. The Batterymarch Building, Boston's first art-deco skyscraper, was completed in 1929 and sold by The Beal Companies in early 1986.

The firm has extensive experience in the ownership, development, financing, construction, and management of real estate assets comprising commercial, retail, industrial, and office buildings; multifamily housing; and land

As one of Boston's oldest continuous real estate firms, The Beal Companies purchases properties as investment builders, acquiring distinctive landmark structures. Among those owned by The Beal Companies are (right) the historic Grain Exchange Building, constructed in 1892 and located in Boston, and (below) the Park Square Building, the largest office structure in the city of Boston in 1922 with a first-of-its-kind interior arcade.

held for development throughout New England, the Atlantic seaboard, and the midwestern United States.

The firm serves as a consultant to such clients as governmental agencies, corporations, communities, institutions, and individuals. These clients can obtain a broad range of services, including development and ownership, management, real estate counseling, evaluation and appraisal, real property taxation and assessment, financing and brokerage, and construction services.

Through its principals and related entities The Beal Companies is actively engaged in the development and ownership of varying types of real estate. In recent years it has acquired and developed extensive commercial, industrial, and residential properties. Illustrative of these are Technology Park/Southern New Hampshire, an office and industrial park containing about one million square feet of space; the American Mutual Property in Wakefield; and the Ledgemont Research Center, the largest office park in Lexington, Massachusetts. Landscaping at the Ledgemont Research Center is so artistic that it is used as an example in landscaping.

The evolution of The Beal Companies closely tracks the last century of Greater Boston history. It was one of the first firms to become involved in condominium conversion, participating in the acquisition and conversion to condominiums of the largest multifamily garden apartment complex in Boston.

Today company principals Bruce A. Beal and Robert L. Beal continue a family tradition of personal involvement in the civic, educational, medical, and charitable affairs of New England. Bruce Beal is an overseer of the Boston Symphony Orchestra and the Boston

Museum of Fine Arts, serves as chairman of the Associates of the Boston Public Library, and is a trustee of the New England Conservatory of Music and the Massachusetts Eye & Ear Infirmary. His brother Robert is chairman of the Massachusetts Industrial

Finance Agency, former president of the Greater Boston Real Estate Board, and a trustee of Beth Israel Hospital and the New England Aquarium. He is also active in causes relating to the growing need for affordable housing in the Boston area.

The Beal Companies is actively engaged in the development and ownership of varying types of real estate. In recent years it has acquired and developed extensive commercial, industrial, and residential properties. The largest office park in Lexington, the Ledgemont Research Center (top right and right) is one of The Beal Companies' most artistically landscaped commercial real estate ventures.

ST. JOHNSBURY TRUCKING COMPANY

The year 1987 will mark 66 years of St. Johnsbury Trucking Company history—from a one-truck operation in 1921 to an industry leader today with 63 terminals, 4,300 units of rolling equipment, and annual revenues of more than $260 million. Today the firm employs more than 4,000 people and maintains its executive offices in Holliston, Massachusetts, and administrative offices in St. Johnsbury, Vermont.

It all began when two enterprising brothers, Harry and Milton Zabarsky, saw a need, took a risk, and succeeded. Hauling meat up the White Mountains to summer resorts was unheard of, but the Zabarsky brothers tried it in their truck, and it worked. They had the vision to see an advantage of truck transport over railroads. In 1927, after one of Vermont's greatest floods, their truck served hard hit communities by hauling food, freight, and mail to areas where the railroad tracks had been washed away.

Originally St. Johnsbury Trucking Company hauled milk from Vermont dairy farms to local creameries. But soon the Zabarskys began to think about long-distance trucking, and convinced major outlets in Boston that they could deliver butter from Vermont creameries faster and fresher than the railroad. For the return trip frim Boston, they persuaded grocery distributors to use their truck. This "growth" in business meant additional equipment. One new truck led to two, and the rest is history.

In the early 1930s trucking became highly competitive. Prices were cut to far below the break-even point, and conditions became chaotic. But in 1935 the Motor Carrier Act was passed by Congress, and trucking as a major industry came of age.

By this time a third brother, Maurice, had joined the firm, and Milton had moved to Boston to establish new business and expand operations. With all three brothers totally committed to the business, they began opening (and building) terminal facilities. The first facility was constructed in 1941 in Burlington, Vermont, and others were soon added in Maine and Massachusetts.

In the 1950s a second generation of Zabarskys came along to carry on the great St. Johnsbury tradition begun by their fathers and uncles. For 20 more years the company continued to prove it was "one step ahead."

From a one-truck operation in 1921 to the Northeast's leading regional carrier, St. Johnsbury connects the entire Bay State with 15 northeastern states and Ontario and Quebec, Canada.

In 1975 Sun Carriers, Inc., a subsidiary of Sun Company, purchased St. Johnsbury Trucking Company. Since that time St. Johnsbury has continued on one of the trucking industry's most successful expansion and revenue growth programs. In 1986 Sun Carriers, Inc., was purchased by management and is now a private company. Today St. Johnsbury serves 16 Northeast states along with the Canadian provinces of Ontario and Quebec. The firm features daily direct service to more than 17,500 communities and is widely recognized as the service performance leader in the Northeast. Nationally St. Johnsbury ranks among the 15 largest general commodities carriers in both revenues and profitability.

Directing the corporation is William M. Clifford, president and chief operating officer, who has been in that position since 1981 and a St. Johnsbury employee since 1968. When asked what makes St. Johnsbury Trucking Company so successful in a highly competitive industry, Clifford replied, "Our people make the difference. They are trained professionals that take a high degree of pride in their performance. It is an attitude of excellence and commitment to quality. Working for St. Johnsbury is more than just a job."

MEREDITH & GREW, INCORPORATED

In 1875 James Morris Meredith began a small real estate company at 4 Exchange Place in Boston. His first properties were downtown, but the business expanded quickly. The Back Bay marshes, now solidly filled westward, provided a growing base for real estate activity. Meredith was associated with Henry Whitney in laying out Beacon Street through Brookline, and subsequent development of the district.

Meredith took his first partner, Thomas M. Nelson, in 1886. Nelson retired five years later, and was succeeded by 21-year-old Edward Wigglesworth Grew, a recent graduate of Harvard. New offices were established at 15 Congress Street under the name of Meredith & Grew.

Although Meredith's family connections had provided the initial contacts to start a new real estate business, Grew gave the firm a new dimension with the management of real estate property and real estate trusts plus extensive ties to Boston's financial community.

In 1909 the Boston Museum of Fine Arts announced plans to move from Copley Square to a new site on Huntington Avenue. Meredith organized the Copley Square Trust to purchase the old museum. On the site flanked by Trinity Church and the new public library, the Copley Square Trust erected one of Boston's most elegant hotels—the Copley Plaza.

Although Meredith & Grew continued to operate principally in Boston, the 1920s showed a rising interest in larger country estates, especially on the North Shore. The firm's first office outside of Boston was opened in Manchester, Massachusetts. Listings in newspapers of the period include the sale and rental of property in virtually every seacoast town from Lynn to Ipswich.

After more than a half-century in the Boston real estate business, Meredith retired in 1925. Twenty years later his partner, Edward Grew, died after 55 years with the firm.

Boston began to stir following World War II. No major buildings had been constructed for several years, and new projects were planned. Land for the proposed Central Artery had to be taken by eminent domain, and Meredith & Grew became active in the appraisals. Subsequent assignments included takings for the Massachusetts Turnpike, and a review of appraisals for the Federal Highway Administration of New Jersey.

Meredith & Grew's Thomas M. Horan persuaded Travelers Insurance Company to purchase land at auction in 1958 and build at 125 High Street, the first noninstitutional office building in Boston in 30 years. This was the beginning of a resurgence of the city's financial district that continues to this day.

Meredith & Grew has been a major contributor, acting as leasing agent for many of the city's new office buildings, including the John Hancock Tower and Bank of Boston. Site assemblies include those for the Bank of Boston, Shawmut Bank, Blue Cross/Blue Shield, Stone & Webster, and The

The Landmark at 160 Federal Street, Boston.

New England. During the 1980s Meredith & Grew added the Finance and Development Services departments, and in 1981 Thomas Horan retired after 42 years with the company (including 17 as president).

Today Meredith & Grew, Incorporated, led by current president George M. Lovejoy, Jr., is one of Boston's largest real estate firms concentrating on management, appraisals, counseling, brokerage, financing, and development services for commercial and industrial real estate locally and internationally through its affiliation with The Office Network. The company's full-service capability is exemplified by these contemporary projects: The Landmark, at 160 Federal Street and 150 Federal Street, Boston, where Meredith & Grew provides development, leasing, financing, and property management services for both buildings totaling 900,000 square feet; and Crown Colony Place, Quincy, where it provides development, leasing, and management services for the 176-acre site.

CODMAN & SHURTLEFF, INC.

In the spring of 1838 Thomas P. Codman, a mechanic from Roxbury, Massachusetts, designed, manufactured, and offered for sale through C. White, druggist, his Pocket Cupping Instrument. It was well received by the physicians of Boston, and he was convinced to continue the manufacture of medical and surgical items. This was the beginning of the firm that would later be known as Codman & Shurtleff, Inc., and would still exist 150 years later.

Benjamin S. Codman, the younger son of Thomas, was born in Roxbury on February 24, 1818. Graduating from Harvard Medical School in 1845, he entered the practice of medicine at an office on Tremont Street in Boston. Asahel M. Shurtleff was born in Rindge, New Hampshire, in 1832 and came to Boston at the age of 17 to enter the employ of Joseph Burnett, a druggist. It was at Burnett's establishment that he met Dr. Codman.

In 1851 Dr. Codman purchased from Burnett his entire stock of dental supplies and opened a Dental Depot on Tremont Street adjacent to his office. He took young Asahel Shurtleff as his assistant two years later, and added surgical instruments and anatomical

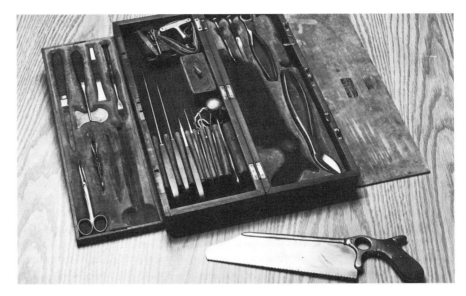

supplies to his line, thereby establishing the Benjamin S. Codman Company. The firm's business expanded rapidly due to the high quality of the instruments and supplies offered and to the inventive genius of Shurtleff, who, before his death, would be awarded 20

Codman & Shurtleff, Inc., world headquarters is located in Randolph, Massachusetts, with additional facilities in Avon, New Bedford, and Southbridge, Massachusetts, and Tuttlingen, West Germany.

Codman general surgery and amputation set, circa 1862, was used by Army surgeons during the Civil War.

patents on his inventions.

In 1857 Benjamin S. Codman, Asahel M. Shurtleff, and Franklin O. Whitney entered into partnership, and the firm was named Codman & Shurtleff Company. Moving to more spacious quarters at 13-15 Tremont Street, the company offered a full line of medical, surgical, dental, and veterinary instruments and supplies. From

his Tremont Street office, Dr. Codman continued to practice medicine while employed as head of the firm. In 1860 Codman & Shurtleff issued its first catalog of 32 pages.

During the early 1860s the atomization of liquids for the treatment of respiratory diseases became popular, and a variety of atomizers began to flood the market. In 1862 Codman & Shurtleff produced its famous Patented Steam Atomizer, which was a Shurtleff design. Heavily promoted through journal advertising, it became a worldwide best-seller for over two decades. Another major item of that period was the General Surgery and Amputation Set designed for use by Army surgeons during the Civil War. These kits were manufactured and sold for many years after the end of hostilities, and were especially popular among the frontier doctors, many of whom were former Army surgeons. These two products were the best known of the Codman & Shurtleff-manufactured items and together contributed greatly to the company's early reputation and success.

The 1870s and 1880s saw the firm continuing its prosperous growth. Manufacturing all of its instruments by this time, it occupied four stories at the Tremont Street address. The making of ear, nose, and throat instruments, many designed by surgeons of the Massachusetts Eye & Ear Infirmary, was a major part of its business. Highlights of these two decades were the conversion of the factory to steam power in 1870, the company's fortunate escape from the Boston fire of 1872, the exhibit of surgical and dental instruments at the Philadelphia Centennial Exhibition, and the establishment of stables for vaccine propagation at Stoughton, Massachusetts, in 1878. Howard L. Shurtleff, eldest son of Asahel, joined the firm in 1879.

Dr. Codman died on February 22, 1894. The partnership was dissolved, and the firm was placed into receivership and offered for sale. Plant operations continued in limbo during this period, and in late 1896 Asahel M. Shurtleff and his son Howard con-

tracted to buy the firm. Two years later an extensive catalog of surgical instruments was published.

On May 26, 1904, Asahel M. Shurtleff, Arthur A. Shurtleff, and Howard L. Shurtleff associated with the intent to form a corporation, and two days later the company was incorporated under the laws of the Commonwealth of Massachusetts as Codman & Shurtleff, Inc., and a charter was issued. Asahel M. Shurtleff became its president and Howard L. Shurtleff its treasurer. In 1905 the corporation moved its offices to 120 Boylston Street, its first move in 50 years. Asahel M. Shurtleff died on December 5, 1915, and Howard assumed his father's position as president.

Howard Shurtleff was a vigorous leader and worked hard to maintain the firm's preeminence in the surgical instrument field. He died at his Boston home February 4, 1925, at the age of 65. At the time of his death the corporation possessed more than $300,000 in cash and securities, a substantial sum for a small business in those days. He was succeeded in the presidency by his younger brother, Arthur A. Shurtleff.

With the advent of the 1930s and the Great Depression, the company faced a rapid decline in both sales and assets and was on the verge of bankruptcy. It still maintained a small key force of highly skilled, German-trained instrument makers whose ability to manufacture high-quality instruments and to train younger men in their skills was to become crucial to the firm in the years ahead. Sales manager Frank G. Ruggles purchased the company and assumed its liabilities in 1938. Although hampered by a lack of working capital he continued the manufacture of high-quality instruments, particularly neuro and orthopedic instruments developed by Boston surgeons. This and a top-notch instrument repair service helped substantially in keeping the company financially sound.

The United States went to war in 1941, and the firm was soon engaged in war work. During 1942 and 1943 it was awarded various Ordnance Department contracts, one of which was

The Codman steam atomizer was patented in 1888 for treatment of respiratory ailments.

the manufacture of parts for torpedo fuses. During this phase the surgical instrument business declined, and war's end found the company in dire need of additional capital. This was provided when Eben H. Rice, a civil engineer from Waban, Massachusetts, purchased the assets of the company on March 29, 1948. The corporation was reorganized under its existing name, and Frank G. Ruggles was retained as president, while Eben H. Rice assumed responsibilities as treasurer.

That same year the offices and plant were moved to 104 Brookline Avenue, Boston. Through the sale of shares to various local hospitals and surgeons, $100,000 of new capital was acquired. With the purchase of new machinery and equipment and the hiring of additional craftsmen, the firm

Codman manufactured original instruments for neurosurgeon Harvey Cushing, M.D., such as hypophysectomy instruments, 1914 (top), and Silver Clip instruments, 1911 (bottom).

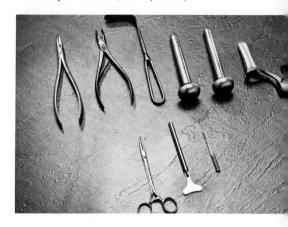

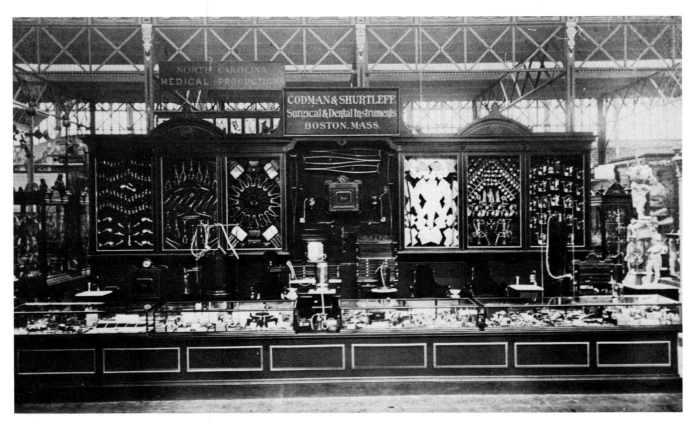

This Codman & Shurtleff exhibit, from the 1876 United States Centennial Exhibition in Philadelphia, is still on display at the Smithsonian.

began a period of slow but steady recovery and new growth. Dedicating itself fully to the manufacture and sale of surgical instruments, Codman & Shurtleff, Inc., became known as a manufacturer of fine specialty surgical instruments in the fields of neuro, orthopedic, cardiovascular, and thoracic surgery.

In 1911 and 1914 the firm manufactured the original hemostatic clip set and hypophysectomy instruments for neurosurgeon Dr. Harvey Cushing. That was the beginning of Codman's unique specialization in and dedication to the specialty of neurosurgery. In 1952 Nathaniel Simkins II, a recently discharged neurosurgical scrub technician and Korean War veteran, joined the company, and for 34 years was the major architect and driving force of Codman & Shurtleff's involvement with neurosurgery worldwide. While the firm supplies general surgical and other specialty instruments, it is primarily focused in neurosurgery and allocates the majority of its resources to this specialty.

In June 1963 all operations were moved to 130 Auckland Street, Dor-

chester. Due to illness on the part of both principals it was decided to sell the company, and in April 1964 the firm was acquired by Ethicon, Inc., a Johnson & Johnson company of Somerville, New Jersey. In September 1965 Thomas A. Jones, executive vice-president of Ethicon, Inc., was named president, replacing Frank G. Ruggles, who shortly retired. The firm moved all operations in 1967 to its present world headquarters location in Randolph, Massachusetts. Two years later the company was given affiliate status as a wholly owned subsidiary of Johnson & Johnson, Inc., reporting directly to Johnson & Johnson in New Brunswick, New Jersey.

During the next 15 years Codman & Shurtleff was expanded through construction and acquisition. Operations were added in Avon and New Bedford, Massachusetts; Irvington and Berkeley Heights, New Jersey; Sun Valley, California; and Tuttlingen, West Germany. Internally established

during this time were the CINTOR* Division of Codman & Shurtleff, Inc., specializing in orthopedic implants and devices, and the MENTOR* Division, specializing in ophthalmological instruments and equipment. The CINTOR Division has since become a part of the Johnson & Johnson Orthopedic Company, and the MENTOR Division was transferred to Johnson & Johnson intraocular lens company, IOLAB* of Covina, California, and has since been divested.

Following the transfer of Thomas A. Jones to the Johnson & Johnson

The Pratt surgical splint was produced in 1892.

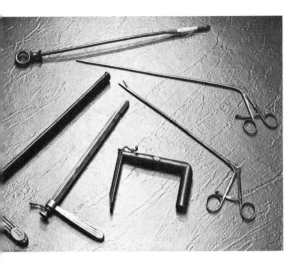

Dr. Harris P. Mosher Instruments (1905) were used for endoscopy.

Development Corporation in August 1979, John S. Assenza, formally president of the Jelco Division of Johnson & Johnson, became president of Codman & Shurtleff, Inc. In August 1983 he was appointed vice-president of Codman & Shurtleff, Inc., International, and began the development of a more sophisticated and productive international marketing system utilizing Codman & Shurtleff and other Johnson & Johnson companies throughout the world for the promotion and sale of Codman products.

At that time Roy W. Black, Codman & Shurtleff general manager, was appointed president, the ninth head of the company since its inception in 1838. More than 18 of his 25-year career with Johnson & Johnson have been with the company in a myriad of sales, marketing, and general management positions.

At this writing, Codman & Shurtleff, Inc., has accomplished a major facilities consolidation program resulting in factory locations in Avon, New Bedford, Randolph, and Southbridge, Massachusetts, and Tuttlingen, West Germany, with executive offices and world headquarters located in Ran-

Codman state-of-the-art products. A Dr. Leonard I. Malis bipolar coagulator and irrigation system for microsurgery (left), and an Aloka ultrasonic tissue aspirator and handpiece for tumor resection (right).

dolph, Massachusetts. With its focus and mission established for the long term, the company is aggressively supporting the development of its worldwide businesses through acquisition, product development, and distribution of related products. Recently Codman & Shurtleff, Inc., acquired the Kees Surgical Specialty Company of Wilder, Kentucky, and Denver Biomaterials, Inc., of Evergreen, Colorado, whose products will fortify the firm's mission and provide more growth opportunities for the future. The company markets an array of modern, sophisticated surgical products ranging from delicate microsurgical instruments, implants, and disposables to ultrasonic imaging and tissue aspiration devices for neurospinal surgery. Focused application of research and development resources and the development of worldwide trade through Codman & Shurtleff and Johnson & Johnson affiliates are but two of the more important charges of the man-

The Codman & Shurtleff magneto electric medical machine, circa 1853, was used to treat nervous diseases.

agement of Codman & Shurtleff, Inc., now and for the future.

Codman & Shurtleff, Inc., is proud of its 150 years (1838-1988) of continuous operation in the State of Massachusetts and looks forward to increasing civic, social, and professional involvement in the years to come.

*Trademark

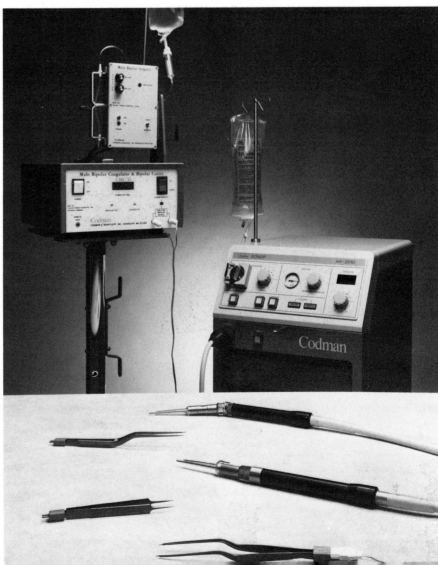

NEW ENGLAND MEDICAL CENTER

Nearly 200 years ago, during the presidency of George Washington, patriotic Bostonians signed a charter establishing the Boston Dispensary, giving birth to an institution known today as New England Medical Center. When it opened in 1796 the Boston Dispensary was the first public health facility in New England and only the third in the United States. In order to assure that "those who have seen better days may be comforted," organizers, including Samuel Adams and Samuel Parkman, urged private benefactors to sponsor the cost of care for needy persons. (One year's worth of health services in 1796 cost $2.50, while $50 guaranteed a lifetime of care.) It was, in a sense, the world's first HMO (health maintenance organization).

About 100 years later—in 1894—the Floating Hospital was established to provide health care for the children of Boston. At that time thousands of Boston children were malnourished and suffering from infections and diarrhea. Hoping that cool sea breezes might ease their suffering, the Reverend Rufus Tobey hired a barge to take children out into the harbor for a day's worth of medical supervision. By the end of the first season the "floating" hospital had provided a therapeutic outing for more than 1,000 boys and girls.

In 1906 the barge was replaced by the first vessel in the world designed and built as a hospital ship—it was the Floating Hospital's new home. On board ship, doctors and nurses examined the young passengers; they began to notice, and describe, certain patterns of illness. Over the years the Floating

Opened in 1796, the Boston Dispensary was the first public health facility in New England and only the third in the United States. Here patients wait at the entrance of the dispensary at Ash and Bennet streets. Photo circa 1910

became well known for the diagnosis and treatment of childhood diseases. It also pioneered the practice of family participation in patient care. In 1931 the Floating was rebuilt on land, adjoining the Boston Dispensary.

These two hospitals, with the Pratt Diagnostic Clinic, formed the nucleus of what would become New England Medical Center and the primary clinical affiliate of the Tufts University School of Medicine.

New England Medical Center has a long history of achievement in clinical

In 1894 the Floating Hospital was established to provide health care for the children of Boston. It became well known for the diagnosis and treatment of childhood diseases and, together with the Boston Dispensary, formed the foundation for what is today the New England Medical Center.

research, ranging from the formulation of Similac, the first synthetic milk product for infants, in 1919, to pioneering work in immunology in the 1950s, to the introduction in the 1970s of computer methods to supplement decision making by physicians and further improve the quality of patient care. Today New England Medical Center is recognized as a clinical and research leader in cardiology, hematology-oncology, cardiothoracic surgery, neurology, neurosurgery, pediatrics, endocrinology, immunology, geographic medicine, psychopharmacology, and infectious diseases.

Although it is the oldest hospital in Boston, New England Medical Center is also the newest. In the past three years every building, patient room, doctor's office, and testing lab has been carefully rebuilt, renovated, or refurbished. Samuel Adams and others who founded the Boston Dispensary would not recognize it today, but they would recognize the caring and compassion that have always been hallmarks of this institution.

FRANK B. HALL & CO. OF MASSACHUSETTS, INC.

A continuity of tradition prevails at Frank B. Hall & Co. of Massachusetts, Inc., where the primary mission for over a century has been to protect the human and business assets of its client community in an effort to assure a secure environment for growth and prosperity. Under the leadership of Colby Hewitt, Jr., and Frederic C. Church, Jr., both second-generation managers and namesakes of the firm's founders, and William F. Newell, the largest property and liability broker in New England provides full-service insurance brokerage and risk management for industry, commerce, finance, the professions, and government.

In 1933 Frederic C. Church and Charles Colby Hewitt consolidated several local agencies to establish the firm of Boit, Dalton & Church and effect competitive services and prices on the Boston insurance scene. Over subsequent decades implementation of the process of protection changed dramatically. Initially offering essentially insurance brokerage services, an expanded postwar society and global economy changed the nature of the industry. In a more vigorous marketplace new exposures in new areas increased client liabilities and government regulations complicated business management. Responding to the change, Hall created responsive new coverages and services such as exhausted value for older properties, errors and omissions for the Boston-founded mutual fund industry and for architects and engineers, as well as comprehensive self-insurance capabilities. Insulating business from a potential impact of loss became a permanent and integral function of financial management and resulted in the emergence of risk management, a new concept of insurance practice.

In creative tradition, the firm shifted from an insurance brokerage to an insurance services firm, with concentration on risk analysis, loss control, claims management, self-insurance, and other specialized efforts. With a professional staff of translators and a team approach to defining risks and developing unique coverages for unique exposures, the firm prospered.

Boit, Dalton & Church was the largest broker in New England in 1971 when it merged with, and became the northeast regional headquarters of, the worldwide Frank B. Hall & Co. Inc. Combining and building on many years of pioneering enterprise, the company later became one of the leading publicly held insurance service firms in the world. As Hall of Massachusetts, a self-contained unit autonomous in execution, the Boston operation is structured to the specific needs of its area, but, as part of the aggregate Hall team, has access to a global network of geographical and technical facilities and the resources of experts on six continents as it serves growing and multinational clients in the United States and abroad.

The firm's headquarters is at the same historic Batterymarch Building where its founders domiciled. A support branch is located in Meriden, Connecticut.

Insurance brokerage remains the central element at Hall of Massachusetts, a provider of insurance and risk management to an ever-expanding business community. Comprehensive financial guarantee programs and dealing with exposures arising from the biotechnical industries, those caused by environmental hazard, and those concerning political risks and terrorism is the focus of the future for the firm's 270 staff members.

There is active participation by Hall of Massachusetts' personnel in civic, educational, and charitable endeavors, including directorships and trusteeships in the Greater Boston Chamber of Commerce, New England Deaconess Hospital, New England Conservatory of Music, Wheelock College, Hampshire College, and Archdiocese of Boston Catholic Charities. Frederic C. Church, Jr., currently serves as president of the Boys and Girls Clubs of Boston, following in characteristic tradition the footsteps of his father. Colby Hewitt, Jr., is chairman of the Greater Boston Forum for Health Action, Inc., a group searching for creative responses for cost-effective health care.

APOLLO COMPUTER INC.

In Greek mythology, the God Apollo drew the sun across the heavens in his chariot. In the world of high technology, Apollo Computer Inc. has blazed a trail in the high-performance workstation market. The firm was founded in 1980 by a group of seven men fascinated by the emerging concept of distributed computing. Combining that interest with a belief in the importance of high-performance graphics, they introduced its first product in 1981 and established a new market for workstations. The goal then is the same as today—to help increase the individual and group productivity of engineers and professional teams.

The Apollo product concept centers on the Apollo Domain® network. Late in 1986 Apollo shipped its 30,000th Domain system, becoming the first computer manufacturer in the world to reach that workstation milestone. The shipment represented another landmark for Apollo, which by that time had recorded more than $900 million in workstation sales since pioneering the market.

Apollo delivers a complete family of compatible workstations—from the economical Personal Workstations to powerful 3-D graphics systems. Some of the key features include extensive communication capabilities; an open architecture that allows the sharing of resources within multiple-system environments that might include minis, mainframes, and PCs; and high-resolution graphics, integrated for maximum productivity.

Apollo started with a single, elegant idea—stand-alone, dedicated computing for an engineer, instead of shared time on a minicomputer or mainframe. Just five months after the presentation of a corporate plan to venture capitalists, Apollo Computer was incorporated and produced its first system. Over 100 more systems were shipped that year, and in 1982 the firm showed its first profit.

Apollo offers a complete family of technologically advanced workstations—from high-performance graphics systems to economical personal workstations.

The company's goals are precise and demanding—to offer the more powerful product at half the price every 18 months. In pursuit of this goal Apollo has grown from a handful of engineers to nearly 3,800 employees in 25 countries. The firm staffs more than 75 sales and service offices worldwide. By the end of 1986 Apollo had more than 1,700 corporate accounts, and sales for that year alone totaled nearly $400 million.

"The quality and breadth of our products continue to attract new customers while at the same time fueling the expansion of existing Apollo accounts," says chief executive officer Thomas A. Vanderslice, who came to Apollo Computer Inc. after 23 years with General Electric and GTE Corporation, where he held top management positions. "Apollo's primary aim is to remain the technological leader through innova-

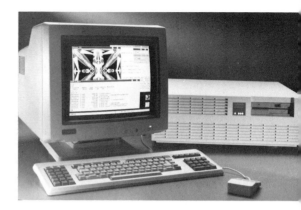

Apollo's Domain® Series 3000® Personal Workstation®, introduced in February 1986, was the first computer to bridge the gap between personal computers and high-performance technical workstations.

tion. We move forward with increased focus in our product and market development, and are confident of the future."

HEATBATH CORPORATION

It is fascinating to consider just how many steps contribute to the final production of something as complex as a piece of machinery or as simple as a hairpin. Founded in 1923 by Ernest A. Walen, Heatbath Corporation uses a variety of chemical baths and process methods to change the characteristics of metals in order to make them more resistant to wear.

A family-owned and -operated business, Heatbath Corporation's current president, Ernest A. Walen III, has just recently taken charge of the firm. As both his father and grandfather before him, he concentrates his efforts on seeking new markets and developing new methods of treating metals.

It was his grandfather who had the vision to utilize what he had learned in the field of heat treating and start his own company more than 60 years ago. That first Ernest Walen learned the basics of heat treating working for a small company in Connecticut. From there he moved north to Springfield to work on the production of firearms at the old Springfield Armory. During his tenure with the armory Ernest A. Walen, Sr., was instrumental in the development of hardening metals through the use of molten salt baths. When Walen incorporated Heatbath in the 1920s, it was with the sole purpose of cleaning, hardening, and tempering metals with salt baths. In the years to follow, as machine tooling came into the fore as a method to curtail the labor intensiveness of manufacturing, the demand for Heatbath's processes expanded from the heat treatment of metals to other surface treatments used in the fledgling automotive, aircraft, and firearms industries.

It was during the 1930s that Walen patented what his grandson describes as "our bread and butter product." The Pentrate patent, a black-oxide process, is what gives firearms their durable and lustrous indigo finish. It also dramatically increased precision tool life by reducing friction that would occur under around-the-clock production line use.

Contrary to the majority of the Northeast's industries during the Depression, Heatbath enjoyed the unique opportunity of increasing its clientele. It seems the firm's salt bath and Pentrate processes outperformed many of the metal-treating methods available, which in turn lowered manufacturers' operating costs. It was during this time that Pentrate became a generic product name like Kleenex, Coke, and Frigidaire. To fuel the war effort Heatbath kept the plant open 24 hours a day, expanding its staff from 5 to 17. Although the manufacturers of firearms continue to be one of Heatbath's largest custom-

Heatbath Corporation's state-of-the-art technical center was built in 1985 and houses a staff of technicians and graduate chemists.

ers, it was the consumer rage for the "home permanent" that created a huge market in the 1950s for the coatings on hairpins.

Ernest A. Walen, Jr., became the president of Heatbath in the early 1950s. His father assumed the role of chairman of the board. Ernest Jr. is credited with expanding the corporation with the addition of new product lines and sales territories. A perusal of his hand-written sales and travel log reveal the initial contacts with firms that continue to be customers and tremendous progress in opening up new sales territory from the East to the Midwest to the Southeast. The volume of business became such that a warehouse and later a satellite plant were started in Chicago, Illinois.

To date there are more than 80 employees working at the Springfield and Chicago plants. In 1985 a 12,000-square-foot, state-of-the-art technical center was built, housing a staff of eight graduate chemists. There are nearly 60 treatments available in the Heatbath line. Ernest Walen III says the greatest attribute of Heatbath Corporation is that it will never become an endangered industry. Its function is essentially twofold: to respond to the changing needs of industry, and, through research and development, to create new products that will aid and improve upon the ever-changing technologies of machine tooling, defense, aircraft, automotive, and aerospace.

OLD STURBRIDGE VILLAGE

It is hard to believe that Old Sturbridge Village, one of America's foremost outdoor, living history museums, is only 40 years old. To wander along the dirt paths through the village's 200 acres of gently rolling hills, pastures, homes, and shops, one is almost convinced of having been transported back to daily life in a New England farming community in the 1830s.

Attention to detail and meticulous recreation of a physical environment that represents the period from 1790 to 1840 is the reason why each year more than a half-million people come to the village to experience and learn about life in an early American village, when farming was beginning to give way to emerging industry. As voyeurs of the old days, village guests walk a peaceful route that winds through more than 40 original, restored buildings from all over New England in which historically costumed interpreters, members of the village staff, demonstrate and share the life, work, and celebrations of the early nineteenth century.

The concept of Old Sturbridge Village, located in Sturbridge, Massachusetts, was conceived in 1946 by two brothers, Albert B. and Joel Cheney Wells. Executives at the American Optical Company in nearby Southbridge, they possessed an extensive collection of antiques and artifacts. As their collection grew in size and popularity, the Wells family decided to expand their museum to include a "living" element,

information and demonstrations on how the objects were made and originally used.

One impressive aspect of Old Sturbridge Village is that it remains open all year. In the spring interpreters are hard at work plowing the fields and spring cleaning. The village's animals, which have been "back bred" to resemble as closely as possible animals at the turn of the century, are giving birth. In the summer the gardens at the homes are resplendent with flowers and the fields robust with crops. In the fall the village is a stunning sight, ablaze with the foliage of huge deciduous trees. The community literally bustles as interpreters prepare for the long winter months. Crops must be harvested and stored; hay stacked inside the barns; wheels of cheese produced; vegetables gathered for drying or pickling; and buildings and fences repaired and reinforced.

The winter is a time in which the true connoisseur of early American crafts and domesticity can revel in the activities of Old Sturbridge Village.

Inside the Freeman farmhouse, the Fitch House, and the Richardson Parsonage, hearth-cooked bread, meat, and stews are prepared. Women spend their time demonstrating knitting, weaving, and sewing. The men, if not

A team of oxen in training in the Center Village at Old Sturbridge Village, Sturbridge, Massachusetts. Photograph by Robert S. Arnold

in the woods logging, are in the dooryards cutting firewood or fence posts or operating the sawmill.

Throughout the year the interpreters are busy turning a variety of raw materials into the products necessary for day-to-day life: Wool is carded, dyed, and woven; the tinsmith makes pierced tin lanterns; the cooper makes barrels and buckets; the blacksmith hammers out tools for use throughout the village; mugs and pitchers are turned to be fired and glazed in a brick kiln; the water-powered "up-and-down" sawmill saws logs into boards; and the shoemaker sews leather shoes and boots.

Behind the scenes at Old Sturbridge Village, a nonprofit, educational organization with a staff of approximately 400 people, staff members work full time researching every aspect of the era's history and material culture and planning their interpretation.

Whether one is an antique enthusiast, a historian, an adult, a child, or just someone out for a lovely stroll into the past, the appeal of Old Sturbridge Village is extremely diverse and always fascinating.

Old Sturbridge Village is located on Route 20 in Sturbridge, approximately one hour from Boston and 45 minutes from Springfield, Massachusetts, and Hartford, Connecticut. The museum is about one-half mile from the intersection of the Massachusetts Turnpike and I-84.

DAMON CORPORATION

Damon Corporation was established in 1961 as a manufacturer of electronic frequency-control devices for use in defense and aerospace. In 1967 Damon held its initial public offering of stock. In the company's 10th year, when its revenues had reached $56 million, its common stock was listed on the New York Stock Exchange.

Early in its history Damon foresaw the need to diversify. Its first efforts were in the field of education. In 1965 the company entered this field by designing and manufacturing teaching apparatus as part of the nation's new emphasis on science curricula. From that base Damon ultimately expanded into the hobby products business with a line of model rockets and kites.

The field of health care became the primary focus of the firm's diversification efforts. In 1968 Damon acquired International Equipment Company (IEC), a leading manufacturer of laboratory centrifuges. These instruments are essential to the preparation of blood and tissue specimens for clinical laboratory analysis. IEC is the largest producer of general-purpose centrifuges in the world.

The acquisition of IEC, with its long-standing reputation in the clinical laboratory market, gave Damon a foothold in that market. In 1968 Damon began to establish a network of clinical laboratories to provide medical testing services for physicians and hospitals.

Over the next several years Damon's clinical laboratory business was the fastest-growing segment of the company. Damon was a pioneer in foreseeing the burgeoning medical services market, and in offering cost-effective diagnostic services.

Today Damon Clinical Laboratories is operating nine regional laboratories in major cities in the United States and Mexico. This network permits Damon to offer large-volume testing services to thousands of clients, including hospitals, health maintenance organizations, and the U.S. Armed Forces. Damon Clinical Laboratories now leads the clinical laboratory industry in the development of innovative partnerships with hospitals to provide timely,

Damon Corporation founder Dr. David I. Kosowsky serves as chairman and chief executive officer of the company.

accurate testing for the medical community.

In the late 1970s Damon's interest in the development of diagnostic products led to research into microencapsulation technology. Damon was the first company to apply microencapsulation technology to the production of diagnostic test kits. This, in turn, led to further research into microencapsulation

Damon Corporation and Damon Biotech headquarters in Needham Heights overlooks the Charles River and houses more than 200 of the company's 2,800 employees.

and the feasibility of encapsulating living cells.

By 1981 the firm's research and development efforts came to fruition with the patented ENCAPCEL® system, which launched Damon into the revolutionary field of modern biotechnology. Damon Biotech was founded as a subsidiary that year. In 1983 Damon Biotech conducted its first public offering of stock, and is now listed on the NASDAQ National Market.

Since then Damon Biotech has reached several key milestones. The company has applied its ENCAPCEL® system to the production of new biologicals, known as monoclonal antibodies, for human therapy. It has built a Cell Culture Facility in Needham, Massachusetts, for the manufacture of products to treat cancer and heart disease. The firm also developed the Cellular Enhancer technology, a genetic engineering technique that offers major advantages in the creation and production of new biomedical products.

In 1986 Damon established another new division to expand into a key area of medical instrumentation. The division's first product, called ScanMate®, is the first truly portable ultrasound instrument ever introduced.

Today, as Damon Corporation begins its second quarter-century, it is strongly committed to a major presence in the health care field through the introduction of innovative products and services.

CARTER RICE

At a time when the Carter and Rice names were both well known in the New England paper industry, two younger members of the families—21-year-old James Richard Carter and 20-year-old Frederick W. Rice—bought all of the "paper, envelopes, cards, and other stock" of William McAdams & Co. of Boston and went into business for themselves on January 2, 1871.

Carter and Rice had just begun to develop a reputation as paper merchants when disaster struck Boston on November 9, 1872. The great Boston fire destroyed hundreds of buildings and caused approximately $75 million worth of damage, but it missed the tiny Carter Rice establishment at 13 Spring Lane. "My little store on Spring Lane, I believe, was the only paper store not burned out," wrote Carter later, "and in the next few days we did enough extra business so that I think the profit made good our losses from customers who had been bankrupted by the fire and loss of insurance."

Within two years the burned out district had been rebuilt, and Carter Rice moved to 69 Federal Street, "a great change from our little tumble-down establishment in Spring Lane." The business recuperated slowly after the Panic of 1873, but the young entrepreneurs were always on the lookout for new business.

In 1883 Carter Rice incorporated for the purpose of "buying and selling all kinds of paper cards; cardboard; envelopes; printers', stationers', and paper mill supplies and twine; and the manufacture of envelopes, blocks, albums, and bank books."

Carter Rice moved to larger quarters at 250 Devonshire Street, a handsome building with a curved front. For the next half-century the company prospered and expanded into the manufacture of various paper products.

By the turn of the century James Carter had become an established and successful businessman who believed that "a business organization must be founded on something more than the desire of its members to promote their own selfish interests, or their narrow views will dwarf its use and make it

Boston, viewed from Back Bay by John Bachman, a New York lithographer, looked like this in the mid-1800s when James Richard Carter and Frederick W. Rice were growing up. It was a literary center—home of the North American Review *and the* Atlantic Monthly—*and publications were among the early customers of Carter Rice. Courtesy, the Bostonian Society*

worthless for the public good. Such organizations should be the centers of intelligent consideration of business affairs, and of political affairs, as they relate to business."

Carter himself was engaged in a wide range of civic interests, including prison reform; the extension of the probation system; the restriction of undue influence of corporations on legislators; the improvement of the consular service; the safeguarding of the civil service; scientific forestry; the building of the Panama Canal; commercial reciprocity with Canada; the location and construction of new public buildings, bridges, and highways; and the improvement of the railroad and telephone systems.

Carter Rice was the only paper firm in the city spared by the fire whose aftermath, on Federal Street, was photographed by J.W. Black. Within two years the burnt district, comprising the business area of the city, had been rebuilt and Carter Rice moved into it—at 69 Federal Street. Courtesy, The Boston Public Library

But paper was Carter's cardinal preoccupation. On the firm's 50th anniversary he summarized his feelings when he said that "the paper business is a clean, pleasant occupation, bringing one in contact with bright, active, and intelligent men, with whom it is a pleasure to deal. . ."

Carter died at Nashua, New Hampshire, on September 13, 1923. His partner, Frederick W. Rice, had already passed away prematurely in 1885.

In 1928 the operation merged with the Charles A. Esty Paper Company of Worcester, Massachusetts. Esty became managing director, and five years later he was named president. James Carter's son, Richard, remained as treasurer.

In 1937 Carter Rice moved again—this time to its present location at 273 Summer Street, a seven-story brick and concrete building only a short walk from South Station. This and neighboring structures, once owned by the Boston Wharf Company, were at one time the center of the wool trade. After extensive alterations and the installation of new handling equipment, the business could claim that "the building houses the largest combined stock of printing and wrapping papers in the East, representing private and mill brands from the country's foremost paper mills." Over the years Carter Rice became a leading national distributor of paper, with sales supported by offices in Seattle, Portland, San Francisco, and Denver. In the early 1940s these distant companies were sold to concentrate the firm's energies in the Northeast marketplace.

At about the same time a New York City paper merchant, J.O. Bulkley, was assuming control of his family's business. Bulkley Dunton had been established by his grandfather, Edwin Bulkley, in 1833 and had prospered despite several reverses. After merging with other merchants, it is known today throughout the New York area as Bulkley Dunton.

The younger Bulkley believed that the best paper market in the country lay along U.S. Route 1, between Boston

Dixie Cups were delivered by horse and buggy at one time. Continuity and reliability of service have always been the key to Carter Rice's growth.

Large inventories from warehouses throughout New England meet the printers' demand for next-day delivery service in the 1980s.

and Washington, D.C. His idea was to merge the paper companies on this "Main Street of America" under one management. This novel idea eventually led to the 1946 acquisition and ownership of Carter Rice, which for some time had been New England's leading paper distributor.

In the 1950s and 1960s an unprecedented series of acquisitions were made for Carter Rice. The first was Storrs and Bement Co. of Boston, Carter Rice's largest competitor. With this acquisition Carter Rice became known as Carter Rice Storrs & Bement, Inc.

Three generations of family ownership ended in December 1966, when J.O. Bulkley sold the outstanding shares of Carter Rice Storrs & Bement to the Hammermill Paper Company of Erie, Pennsylvania. This acquisition cemented the fine relationship that had existed ever since the concern began selling Hammermill's fine papers 50 years earlier. In November 1986 Hammermill was purchased by the International Paper Corporation, with which Carter Rice is now affiliated.

The history of Carter Rice is a Yankee success story; in talking with its customers, words like "reliable," "consistent," and "trustworthy" keep coming up.

"We're customer oriented, not job oriented," explains president H.S. Julier. "We'd rather lose an order than lose a customer." It's a philosophy that's made Carter Rice a New England tradition.

PEAT MARWICK MAIN & CO.

Klynveld Peat Marwick Goerdeler (KPMG) is an international accounting firm providing audit, tax, management consulting, and business advisory services to a diverse client base worldwide. In nearly every specialized industry, KPMG professionals serve start-up companies to multinational corporations, private and public entities, from more than 350 offices in 90 countries.

KPMG was formed in 1987 with the merger of two international accounting firms: Peat, Marwick, Mitchell & Co. and KMG/Main Hurdman, both rich in tradition and history. The new entity—known as Peat Marwick Main & Co. in the United States—is the largest accounting and consulting firm in the world.

More important and impressive than size, however, is the combined resources of the new firm and the subsequent scope of services offered. The strengths of the companies prior to the merger were highly complementary. Today the whole is indeed greater than the sum of its parts. The result is a unique professional services organization with geographical balance and a global delivery system, coupled with an intimate understanding of the international marketplace.

In 1910 Peat Marwick's first office in Massachusetts was established on Congress Street in Boston, employing a staff of two. Today the Boston office, located at One Boston Place, is the fourth largest in the firm's domestic

network, and there are three other offices throughout the Commonwealth of Massachusetts. The Burlington office was opened in 1983 in the heart of New England's technology region, enabling the firm to better serve the "middle market" and emerging growth companies. Main Hurdman, in addition to its Boston office, had large offices in Worcester and Springfield; both are continuing operations as part of the new firm. Together Peat Marwick Main & Co. serves the state's business community from these four strategic locations with over 700 professionals specializing in the high-tech, financial services, education, banking, health care, insurance, real estate, and commercial industries, among others.

The firm's basic philosophy is one of providing excellence in client service as well as encouraging innovation and technological advances. The strategic affiliations between Peat Marwick and Regis McKenna Inc. (Cambridge) and Pittiglio, Rabin, Todd & McGrath (Wellesley Hills) greatly enhanced the firm's capabilities in serving the high-technology and related industries both

in Massachusetts and nationwide. In addition, the recent merger between Peat Marwick and Nolan, Norton & Co., an information technology planning and management firm based in Lexington, expanded consulting services and provided a wealth of additional research materials and data base information.

Robert D. Happ, managing partner of the Boston office, believes that in addition to providing unparalleled services to clients, one of the firm's thrusts will be to continue a high level of involvement in state, city, and community affairs. According to Happ, "Peat Marwick has traditionally been a leader in the State of Massachusetts in both our business and community activities. Additionally, we encourage our personnel to pursue involvement in organizations that work to benefit others."

Peat Marwick Main & Co. professionals reside throughout Massachusetts and are actively involved in their communities through town committees, chambers of commerce, local arts and sports functions, and charitable organizations. Peat Marwick partners sit on the boards of hospitals, symphonies, libraries, museums, and other not-for-profit entities. The firm takes an active role in fund raising for groups such as the United Way of Massachusetts Bay, the Massachusetts Easter Seal Society, and local chapters of a variety of national organizations.

Peat Marwick Main & Co.'s Massachusetts leaders are (from left) William A. Larrenaga, former managing partner, Main Hurdman-Boston; Donald R. Dupre, managing partner, Springfield office; Richard J. Noonan, managing partner, Worcester office; and Robert D. Happ, managing partner, Boston office.

A.W. PERRY, INC.

In 1884 A.W. Perry established his first office at 125 Summer Street in Boston. As a pioneer in real estate, as well as other developing industries, he helped rebuild Boston's economy after its great fire.

Leasing an entire building and then subleasing it was a concept developed by Perry. He personally managed and operated the properties that he subleased. His insight in establishing enduring business relationships, combined with his personal approach to the needs of each tenant, became the foundation for A.W. Perry's philosophy. As a testimony to the strength of his vision, A.W. Perry, Inc., proudly enters its second century under the direction of the fourth generation of its founding family.

From the beginning A.W. Perry responded to the needs of the Boston business community. Sometimes this took the founder outside the realm of real estate. At the turn of the century he built an electric manufacturing plant in the basement of one of his buildings to better serve his tenants. As gas lighting gave way to electricity, Perry marketed his direct current to other properties, establishing an electric business that serviced a large segment of the Boston business community.

In addition to his real estate and electricity interests, Perry was early to recognize the potential in steam shipping, acquiring the Plant Line, a passenger service on the East Coast. It was the Plant Line that carried many immigrants to the United States from neighboring lands.

After World War I Perry and his three sons, who had joined their father in the business, began to concentrate their efforts in real estate investment. They acquired control of a large number of Boston properties, making A.W. Perry the largest individual taxpayer in the City of Boston.

Alonzo W. Perry, a pioneer in Boston real estate and founder of A.W. Perry, Inc.

The firm prospered as it contributed to the revival of Boston's economy after World War II. Its tradition of service to developing businesses—originally catering to the shoe and leather manufacturing industry and, later, to the expanding decorative arts trade—now focuses on Boston's growing service and financial sector. Presently the register of properties owned and operated by A.W. Perry, Inc., includes nearly 2,000 acres of land and more than 20 buildings in the Greater Boston area. Among these are two properties listed on the National Register of Historic Places and the landmark Berkeley Building, which is undergoing complete restoration. Several key development sites included in the portfolio represent the backbone of Perry's plans for the future.

Today A.W. Perry, Inc., has come full circle. In a joint venture it is developing a new 23-story office project at 125 Summer Street—the site of its original 1884 office. Scheduled for completion early in 1989, the 125 Summer Street structure will exemplify a new quality of Boston architecture with a responsive design, which draws character and substance from its historic neighbors. Like all of A.W. Perry's endeavors, this project continues its policy of investing in quality properties that will endure for the long term.

In a symbolic return to its roots, A.W. Perry, Inc., is developing a new 23-story office project at 125 Summer Street—the site of its original 1884 office.

BLUE CROSS AND BLUE SHIELD OF MASSACHUSETTS

The year 1987 marks the golden anniversary of Blue Cross and Blue Shield of Massachusetts. For a half-century the corporations have helped make the Massachusetts health care system one of the finest in the nation. Today Blue Cross and Blue Shield provide insurance for more than 3.2 million individuals throughout the Commonwealth. Fifty years of experience and success stand behind the corporations' creed that "quality makes the difference."

The Blue Cross/Blue Shield commitment to quality began in the fall of 1937. Fordyce Turner Blake, Jr., a Williams College soccer player, suffered a triple fracture in his leg after colliding with an opponent in a game against Army. Fortunately, Blake's father had a few days earlier enrolled the family in a new group hospitalization plan called the Associated Hospital

Service Corporation. As he recovered from his injury at Massachusetts General Hospital, young Blake knew neither he nor his family would be burdened by undue hardship because of medical bills. He was covered by what is today known as Blue Cross of Massachusetts.

Families who suffered through the Great Depression were enthusiastic about the concept of prepayment as a means of securing health care without fear of being financially burdened. For an established monthly fee they were protected from the risk of economic hardship so often created by catastrophic illness. *The Boston Herald*

In the early years after the corporations were founded, open enrollment was used to sign up new subscribers. This photo, taken circa 1942, shows female marketing personnel being employed for the first time by Blue Cross/Blue Shield because of the war.

Traveler headline of September 10, 1937, said it best: "Sickness Need No Longer Wreck Budget." Created by an act of the state legislature in 1937, the Massachusetts Blue Cross plan was the 26th created in the nation, but it was the first to offer subscribers statewide protection.

Physicians also became interested in the prepayment concept of financing health care, and in 1941 the state legislature (at the urging of the Massachusetts Medical Society) established Blue Shield of Massachusetts. The plan was unique in that it paid for covered services only with participating physicians. It produced widespread physician participation and established freedom of choice of physicians for Blue Shield subscribers.

The protection enjoyed by today's subscribers is significantly more comprehensive than the coverage provided to young Fordyce Blake, Jr., in 1937. Blue Cross and Blue Shield have grown and adapted to the changing needs of consumers, offering ever-increasing comprehensive coverage. What began as a hospital insurance plan 50 years ago has evolved into a multifaceted health care organization. In addition to traditional health insurance, Blue Cross/Blue Shield provides a full range of benefit programs, including health maintenance organizations, prepaid dental care, and health education and promotion.

The corporations initially offered coverage only to employee groups, but added nongroup direct-pay coverage in the 1940s. A new "experience-rating" system, in which a group's rates were linked to its own insurance experience rather than the community's, was introduced in the 1950s. Master Medical coverage was introduced by Blue Cross and Blue Shield in the 1950s and soon became a household name for comprehensive benefits. Members of this plan were secure in knowing they held the most complete health care coverage in Massachusetts. Not surprisingly, membership soared.

In 1961 the first computer system was installed. At the time it was the largest computer in the state.

The corporations' role was broadened in 1966 when they were appointed Medicare intermediary for Part A and carrier for Part B for the Commonwealth of Massachusetts. With this new responsibility, Blue Cross and Blue Shield evolved from underwriters of financial risk to administrators of health programs underwritten by the federal government. In 1972 Blue Shield was awarded the first fixed-price contract ever offered by the federal government for the processing of Medicare claims. This first contract was for Medicare claims in the State of Maine. In 1985 the states of New Hampshire and Vermont were added, making Blue Shield the Medicare carrier in four states.

In 1966 Blue Cross/Blue Shield developed Medex, a supplement insurance program for Medicare recipients. Medex is the most widely held Medicare supplement in Massachusetts. In 1983 Blue Cross/Blue Shield became the first health insurer in the nation to establish a health care network for senior citizens at health maintenance organizations (HMOs). By combining the benefits of Medicare and Medex, stressing preventive medicine and reg-

Today Blue Cross and Blue Shield of Massachusetts provide insurance for more than 3.2 million individuals throughout the Commonwealth. Pictured here are Blue Cross/Blue Shield representatives (from left) Christopher D. Perna, Margaret A. Moran, and Deborah J. Avant.

ularly scheduled care, Senior Plan provides comprehensive medical care at a cost much lower than traditional insurance programs for the elderly.

Utilization Review was introduced in hospital payment agreements beginning in October 1972. This gave Blue Cross the right to review and reach independent conclusions about the use of hospital services by its members, without any financial risk to members if benefits were denied by Blue Cross because of inappropriate utilization.

Blue Cross and Blue Shield helped pioneer prepaid, managed health care in Massachusetts in 1969 by collaborating in the development of the state's first health maintenance organization (HMO). After assisting in the establishment of several additional HMOs, Blue Cross opened the Springfield-based Medical West Community Health Plan, a wholly owned subsidiary, in 1978. With this event, the corporations took on still another role—that of health care providers. With the adoption of a bold, 10-year plan, Blue Cross and Blue Shield began developing a statewide network of staff, group, and independent practice association (IPA) model HMOs. Today 300,000 members, including 32,000 people with Medicare and 3,000 with Medicaid, are enrolled in the Blue Cross and Blue Shield family of HMOs.

The success of HMOs in helping to control rising health care costs led

to the development of the first Benefit Management program at the Norton Company in early 1983. Master Health, as this first Benefit Management program was called, borrowed the HMO "gatekeeper" feature and linked it to the corporations' most popular product, Master Medical. This innovative program integrated hospital preadmission approval, mandatory second surgical opinion, hospital concurrent review, and discharge planning with the traditional array of comprehensive health care benefits. Building on the early success of Master Health, the program was modified in 1985 to include coverage of well-baby care and regular pediatric checkups. Also included were enhanced prescription drugs and other benefits. Master Health Plus, as the new plan is called, grew quickly in two years to become the most widely held of Blue Cross and Blue Shield products.

In 1970 Blue Cross and Blue Shield helped develop and underwrite the first dental insurance plan in Massachusetts. In 1986 the companies introduced a new dental program called Master Dental. Quickly recognized for its benefits and delivery, Master Dental exceeded expectations with more than 40,000 members joining during the first year.

For the past 50 years Blue Cross and Blue Shield have acted as catalysts to quality health care in Massachusetts, while helping to make the state's health care system one of the most sophisticated in the nation. Continuing change, dynamic environment, highly competitive, new products, new relationships with providers, and new responses to customer needs—all are an integral part of the Massachusetts health care scene.

This record of achievements is possible because of the strong commitment of the corporations' more than 6,000 employees—men and women who never forget that customers turn to them in times of illness. Because of these dedicated individuals, more than three million people from the Berkshires to Boston feel secure with Blue Cross and Blue Shield of Massachusetts.

POLAROID CORPORATION

Polaroid Corporation, celebrating its 50th anniversary in 1987, has had a distinguished history of product development, seeded originally by scientific research begun during the 1920s, when Edwin Land was a student at Harvard College. After several years of scientific investigation Dr. Land announced in 1932 that he had developed a means of producing an extensive sheet of synthetic light polarizing material. (Polarizers reduce reflected glare by filtering multidirectional light vibrations.) Knowing that this invention would lead to a new applied science and to commercial applications, Land left Harvard that year to form Land-Wheelwright Laboratories with Harvard physics instructor George Wheelwright III.

Land-Wheelwright was incorporated in 1933 to continue Land's research and manufacture polarizers. Within one year a basic patent in sheet polarizer had been issued to Land, and Eastman Kodak had agreed to buy light polarizers for use in photographic filters. In 1935 the American Optical Company signed a similar contract for the manufacture of Polaroid Day Glasses. The trademark *Polaroid* was first used by Sheet Polarizer Company, a predecessor of Polaroid Corporation.

Land formed the Polaroid Corporation in 1937 to acquire Land-Wheelwright Laboratories and "to develop (the field of light polarization) technically and commercially." The young company rapidly developed a series of products using polarizing materials, including variable-density windows for trains, glare-free desk lamps, and glass-testing equipment. Polaroid also completed development of the Vectograph, an entirely new type of 3-D photograph that was viewed through polarizing filters. Polaroid stereoscopic motion pictures were shown at the New York World's Fair in 1939. Two years later Polaroid Corporation's annual sales climbed to one million dollars.

Prior to the outbreak of World War II Polaroid had entered into contracts to produce a number of special filters for the U.S. Navy. During the war Polaroid designed and manufactured a widely used infrared night viewing device, and devised and produced a machine gun trainer that simulated tracer bullets in flight while the operator manipulated a life-size anti-aircraft gun against a 3-D image of an

Edwin Land, Polaroid founder, reveals the first instant picture seen outside the laboratory in a demonstration before the Optical Society of America in New York in 1947.

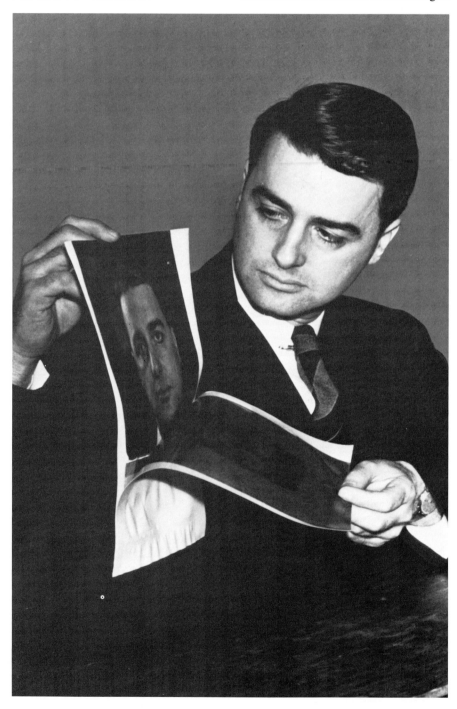

attacking plane. By VJ Day Polaroid's annual volume of business had jumped from one million dollars to $16 million, and its employee population reached a wartime high of 1,250.

Polaroid then faced the problem of reconversion to civilian production. Among the projects Edwin Land and other scientists had been working on was a revolutionary camera and film system. On February 21, 1947, Land astonished his audience at a meeting of

the Optical Society of America by announcing a one-step dry process for producing finished photographs within one minute after taking the picture. Less than two years later the Polaroid Land camera (Model 95) and Polaroid Land film (Type 40), which made sepia-toned photographs, were offered to the public in limited quantities. The product was received with great enthusiasm, and photographic sales for the first year, 1949, exceeded $5 million. By 1950, when a black-and-white film was in-

Today's Polaroid Spectra system camera represents the finest in the Polaroid line of fully automatic, instant-picture cameras.

Less than two years after Dr. Land's revolutionary 1947 demonstration, the Polaroid Land camera, Model 95, was introduced at the Jordan Marsh department store in Boston. The camera produced a sepia-toned image in 60 seconds.

troduced, more than 4,000 dealers throughout the United States sold Polaroid cameras, film, and accessories.

New adaptations of Polaroid Land photography were developed almost immediately. By 1951 Polaroid had announced Type 1001 Land film for radiography, the first of a continuing series of Polaroid instant X-ray products.

The impact of Polaroid instant photography was immediate. It changed the way people would come to think about making photographs. In the presence of the picture and its subjects, the photographer could establish what Dr. Land called "a visual conversation with the environment."

The 1950s were a decade of rapid growth. Polaroid recognized that the immediacy of instant photography was especially well suited to demonstration on live broadcast, and the firm became one of the earliest major advertisers on the new medium of television.

In 1963, following more than 15 years of experimentation, Polaroid introduced Polacolor Land film, the first instant color film. Later that year the firm introduced a new film format that used a flat film pack to produce eight 3.25- by 4.25-inch prints. Unlike previous Polaroid films, these prints were developed outside the camera.

In 1967 Polaroid announced an ambitious expansion program and the construction of a series of new factories. A secret research program was under way to design and produce cameras and film for the SX-70 system. The 1972 introduction of this product realized Dr. Land's concept of absolute one-step photography. The SX-70 camera was a fully automatic, motorized, folding, single lens reflex camera that ejected self-developing, self-timing color prints. Two subsequent models of the folding SX-70 camera were introduced in 1974 and 1975, and in 1976 the Pronto! cameras for SX-70

film were announced. These nonfolding viewfinder cameras led to the 1977 introduction of the inexpensive fixed-focus OneStep Land camera, which became for over four years the best-selling camera in the United States. That was the same year that Polaroid sales exceeded one billion dollars for the first time.

In 1982 Edwin H. Land retired as director and chairman of the board to devote his full time to the Rowland Institute for Science, a private, non-profit institution organized to engage in basic scientific research. William J. McCune, Jr., chief executive officer of Polaroid since 1980, was elected chairman. McCune had joined Polaroid in 1939 after graduating from the Massachusetts Institute of Technology. He established the quality-control operation of the company and during the war worked with Dr. Land as assistant director of the firm's Guided Missile Project.

In 1986 I. MacAllister Booth was elected chief executive officer in addition to his position as president; McCune continued as chairman of the board. Booth, who joined Polaroid in 1958, has held a variety of positions in the company's film and engineering divisions, and was responsible for the design, construction, and management of Polaroid's multimillion-dollar color negative manufacturing facility in New Bedford, Massachusetts.

Under McCune and Booth Polaroid Corporation continued its heavy investment of energy and resources toward creation of a new system for amateur instant photography. In 1986 the firm introduced the Spectra system, which embodies a host of innovations in instant film chemistry, electronics, optics, engineering, and manufacturing. The new Spectra film presents colors so brilliant that they can rival the results of conventional 35-millimeter amateur photography. Meanwhile, research in such fields as magnetic media, graphic arts, fiber optics, medical diagnostics, photovoltaics, and holography evidence Polaroid's concerted effort to continually expand the technical and business base of the company.

C&K COMPONENTS, INC.

C&K Components, Inc., with corporate headquarters in Newton, Massachusetts, is a leading international producer of electromechanical switches for the computer and electronics industries. The company was originally called Component Corporation of America, producing magnetic computer memory units for the Polaris missile and other military and space programs. Started in early 1957 by Marshall Kincaid, C&K was joined a few months later by Charles Coolidge as both employee and investor.

The two men had worked together previously as early as 1946 under Howard Aiken of the Harvard Computation Laboratory. Their work on the original Mark I computer, as well as the Mark II, III, and IV, places them among the pioneers of the computer industry. In 1952 they left Harvard and joined the newly formed firm of EPSCO, Inc., a producer of analog/digital converters. Late in 1956 Kincaid left EPSCO to form the present company, with Coolidge soon to follow.

In 1966 a line of miniature computer switches was introduced, and within five years the transition was complete. C&K made only switches. The founders foresaw a market that would respond to quality products marketed with emphasis on customer service and on-time delivery, and have created a textbook example of how to succeed against foreign competition. C&K's sales have increased rapidly

Dr. Charles A. Coolidge, Jr., chairman of the board of C&K Components, Inc.

James E. Walsh, president of C&K Components, Inc.

since 1970. Management attributes this to three basic business policies: good customer-oriented service, competitive pricing, and sophisticated manufacturing processes designed to keep costs down and margins profitable.

Foreign sales have always been actively pursued, and in 1984 accounted for one-fourth of the firm's total revenue. This achievement was due in part to the establishment in England in

C&K manufactures a broad line of electromechanical switches that is recognized around the world for quality and performance.

1978 of a wholly owned subsidiary, C&K Switches, Ltd. Two years later another subsidiary was created in Hong Kong, C&K Components (HK) Ltd., to serve clients in the Far East.

Given the dynamic nature of the industries that it serves, C&K sees an ongoing opportunity to accelerate its growth by continually expanding its line of technologically advanced products. Existing products are constantly improved while significant resources are directed at creating new designs. The product line presently includes a wide variety of miniature and subminiature switch types, including toggle, rocker, push button, rotary, slide, thumbwheel, and keylock. Special features such as illumination, sealing, and antistatic treatment are available, and C&K's ability to create special designs to suit customer needs is well known. Computers are the principal end use of C&K switches, but several other products provide substantial markets: telephone equipment, medical instruments, laboratory and production test equipment, and household appliances. The business today is so broadly based that more than 200 customer companies each purchase in excess of $10,000 worth per year, hence the firm's slogan: "C&K—The Primary Source Worldwide."

C&K has also acquired a few select companies with related product lines. The principal requirements of any acquisition are that the products produced be superior; that the manufacturing processes complement C&K's high-volume, low-cost, high-quality production standards; and that they can be sold through C&K's global distribution network.

The company diversified beyond its traditional switch business in 1982 by establishing C&K Systems, Inc., located in San Jose, California. This subsidiary produces intrusion detection devices, entry controls, and alarm systems incorporating the most advanced microwave and infrared technologies. Such dual-technology alarms are rapidly gaining favor in both commercial and residential security markets because of their self-checking capability, which limits the cost and nuisance of false alarms. The company's detector products are finding many new applications, such as door openers, heating and lighting control systems, as well as the present protection and alarm installations. C&K Systems' motion detection devices are now sold worldwide. Sales have grown rapidly from $.5 million in 1983 to $14 million just three years later.

In 1986 C&K further diversified its switch product lines by acquiring the Unimax Switch Corporation of Wallingford, Connecticut, along with its subsidiary, Unimax Switch, Ltd., of Wokingham, England. The firm is known today as C&K/Unimax, Inc., and manufactures a complete line of high-quality snap-acting, metal-cased, and illuminated switches. Applications include limit and position sensing in industrial machinery and appliances, and front-of-panel control switches.

Company founder Marshall Kincaid passed away in 1983. Since the firm's inception, cofounder Charles Coolidge has been president and chief executive officer, responsible for all of C&K's domestic and overseas operations. In March 1987 the board of directors named Coolidge chairman of the board, and James Walsh was elected president. As president, Walsh will be responsible for all of C&K's divisions and subsidiaries, both domestic and foreign. James Walsh had served as C&K's chief financial officer for 15 years.

"Today," explains Coolidge, "switches and switch components constitute approximately 85 percent of the business." In an annual survey conducted by *Electronic Buyers News,* C&K Components consistently achieves high recognition among buyers for the various types of switches it supplies, and has been named the number one switch supplier for the past several years.

Today the company operates six modern, highly automated plants devoted primarily to switch manufacturing. The main plant (and corporate headquarters) is housed in Newton, Massachusetts. Other plants are located in Wallingford, Connecticut; Clayton, North Carolina; and Kettering and Wokingham, England. In Kettering, 250 employees manufacture and supply switches for approximately 90 percent of the European market. The sixth plant, located in Hong Kong, manufactures 80 percent of the switches for markets in Asia and Australia, and also does all assembly and manufacturing for C&K Systems, Inc.

Continuous product testing and evaluation is required to ensure the consistent product quality that customers have grown to count on.

C&K's 2,000 employees at all locations share in the company's financial success through its profit-sharing plan. Other popular employee benefits include opportunities to enjoy the C&K yacht *Doric* and use of strategically located, company-owned condominiums in New Hampshire, Connecticut, South Carolina, and Hong Kong.

C&K Components, Inc., has consistently demonstrated the ability to perceive market needs and design and manufacture excellent products at fair prices. Its generous treatment of its employees has created a loyal staff of experienced personnel second to none in the industry.

Modern manufacturing methods and a high degree of automation have kept C&K more than competitive in today's switch market.

EQUITABLE REAL ESTATE INVESTMENT MANAGEMENT, INC.

Equitable Real Estate Investment Management, Inc., is one of the largest real estate investors in the United States. It is a wholly owned subsidiary of The Equitable Financial Companies, the third-largest insurance company in the world, established in 1859.

Equitable Real Estate combines the financial clout of its parent company with the entrepreneurial direction so important in the conception and development of high-quality real estate investments. The firm commands the full range of asset management disciplines with a nationwide organization that acquires, finances, develops, manages, enhances, and sells prime commercial properties of every type and size for its clients' portfolios.

Company headquarters is located

Combined in a single neocolonial building across Boylston Street from the Public Garden, Boston's centerpiece, are the new Four Seasons Hotel and Four Seasons Place, which houses 100 of the city's finest condominiums.

Contrasts are familiar sights in downtown Boston. Here One Boston Place, purchased by Equitable Real Estate in 1981, towers above the Old State House—which dates back to 1713.

in Atlanta, Georgia, and 12 regional offices are strategically located throughout the United States. Equitable Real Estate has had investments in Massachusetts since before the Depression, and a regional office was opened in Boston in 1973. "We view Boston as one of the best real estate markets in the United States," explains senior vice-president C.J. Harwood. "As the number one real estate investor in Boston, we have committed more than $2 billion to our New England/New York regional portfolio. At least half of that amount is invested in downtown Boston." Major investments in the metropolitan area include such familiar names as Rowes Wharf, One Boston Place, the Bank of Boston building, One Post Office Square, and the ultramodern Four Seasons Hotel and condominium complex.

The enterprise is also the nation's largest investor in shopping centers, and is skilled at both construction and renovation of these suburban malls. Shoppers World in Framingham, Massachusetts, the nation's first shopping center east of the Mississippi River, is an Equitable Real Estate property. "Shoppers World was a thoroughly modern shopping center when it opened in 1951," says Harwood, "and

we look forward to replacing it in the near future with a new, enclosed mall that will be state of the art for years to come."

Equitable Real Estate Investment Management, Inc., is recognized as an industry leader because it prides itself on performance excellence, thoroughness, speed, and savvy. Of Equitable's 450 real estate professionals, over 300 serve on the front lines of the company's 15 regional and divisional offices. This local presence permits constant monitoring of activity in all the country's real estate markets. Due to this unmatched market penetration and long-standing business relationships with builders and owners, the firm is uniquely positioned to review most promising acquisition opportunities and development projects. Explains Harwood, "Spotting trends, moving quickly, and taking advantage of acquisition opportunities have brought Equitable Real Estate success over many years, making us one of the nation's leading developers today."

BERKSHIRE INDUSTRIES, INC.

In 1970 and again in 1981 Berkshire Industries, Inc., in Westfield, Massachusetts, was recognized by the Small Business Administration as the Outstanding Subcontractor of the Year for the New England area. As there are many relatively small machine tool shops concentrated in the region, being selected for the award is not an easy accomplishment. The acknowledgment is for "integrity, reliability, initiative, and capability in meeting important government requirements." It comes from the nation's largest and most well established contractors, such as General Electric, Pratt & Whitney, and IBM.

Berkshire Industries, originally called The Berkshire Tool Company, was started in 1956 by Otto Essig. Essig received his early training in the machining field in southern Germany and had experience with several U.S. companies prior to founding Berkshire Industries.

His policies of maintaining an excellent work place with the most modern machinery, paying the highest wages, and providing the best fringe-benefit package have resulted in the development of a stable group of highly skilled machinists and manufacturing support personnel.

Berkshire's plant is fully air conditioned, immaculately clean, and the machinery and equipment is efficiently placed in 55,000 square feet on one floor. It is located on 12 beautifully landscaped acres, and contains playing fields and picnic areas for employee use.

The majority of the company's staff of 140 employees are intent upon the operation of sophisticated, computerized machining equipment. Around the clock, the facility produces components for almost every jet engine built by Berkshire Industries' largest customer, General Electric, and for 30 other firms specializing in areas of aircraft, armament, missiles, flight controls, and electronic devices.

Berkshire Industries, Inc., is cen-

trally located among the defense and aircraft industries in New England. The common bond between these industries is that they all manufacture products that require precision and complex parts—components that must function smoothly under conditions of high speed and, often, extreme temperatures. It is the craftsmanship and quality that goes into production at Berkshire Industries that has given the company national recognition as one of the finest machine shops in New England.

Two views of Berkshire Industries, Inc., headquarters, located on 12 acres in Westfield.

GENERAL ELECTRIC

With the advent of the industrial revolution in Massachusetts in the latter part of the nineteenth century, the area north of Boston became a focus for manufacturing activity, first in textiles, later in leather goods, then in machinery. Then, in the decade of the 1880s, a burgeoning electric power-generating industry took root in the City of Lynn, when the American Electric Company, located in New Britain, Connecticut, was brought to Lynn by its owner, Professor Elihu Thomson. A merger subsequently created the Thomson-Houston Electric Company.

Ten years later, in 1892, Thomson-Houston merged with Thomas Alva Edison's enterprises in Schenectady, New York, to form the General Electric Company. Edison had wanted to centralize the operation in Schenectady, but Thomson admired the beauty of the North Shore and valued its proximity, as he put it, "to Boston and Cambridge, and to Harvard and Technology." The genius-inventor and scholar prevailed in his objection to the combining and transfer of the business to New York State, thus strengthening and preserving the economic and industrial base of Lynn for the coming century.

The first president of the new General Electric Company was Charles A. Coffin, a Lynn businessman. Under his leadership, the plant embarked on a series of programs that would bring about the development and manufacture of steam turbine-generators for commercial use. Lynn-built units such as these helped make Edison's predictions of "cities that would glow in the dark" a reality. They also established GE as the leader in the design and manufacture of steam-driven power-generation equipment, a role it continues today.

In 1930 GE pioneered a propulsion design that linked a geared steam turbine directly to a ship's propeller shaft for the first time. This development boosted fuel efficiency and led to the building of an entire new fleet of

The Thomson-Houston Electric Company's factory in Lynn as it looked in 1884. Eight years later Thomson-Houston merged with Thomas Alva Edison's enterprises in Schenectady to form the General Electric Company.

naval battleships, destroyers, and fast cruisers.

The GE plants in the Lynn area include the River Works, located on the banks of the Saugus River, about 10 miles northeast of downtown Boston; the Factory-of-the-Future at West Lynn; and a satellite plant in nearby Everett. Two other high-technology businesses located north of Boston include aircraft instruments in Wilmington and GE/RCA electronic defense systems at Burlington.

State-of-the-art technology has characterized the activities and products of GE in Lynn over the years. Street lighting, meters, electric motors, and other products were developed and produced at Lynn, establishing and maintaining worldwide leadership. Many of these markets subsequently became important enough to merit their own separate headquarters and new factories in new locations. Today the principal activities at Lynn are associated with aircraft engines.

As early as 1917 experience gained from pioneering turbine work led to the development and production of turbo-superchargers for aircraft. In 1937 a

America's first jet aircraft, the Bell XP-59, flies over the California desert in 1942, powered by the GE 1-A engine.

supercharger business was formed, with headquarters at Lynn; GE turbosuperchargers made it possible for piston-engine military aircraft to fly at high altitudes during World War II.

On April 18, 1942, the United States was launched into the jet age when America's first jet engine successfully completed its initial test run at the Lynn plant. Calling on GE Lynn turbosupercharger experience, the U.S. government had instituted a crash program to develop this new kind of aircraft propulsion system based on a British design. A GE team of scientists, engineers, and skilled craftsmen created a 1,250-pound thrust jet engine in record time. That same year America's first jet aircraft, a Bell XP-59, took off from the desert runway at Muroc Dry Lake, California, powered by the GE 1-A engine. The site was later to become Edwards Air Force Base.

The GE aircraft engine business designs, develops, and manufactures modern, high-performance jet engines, whose technology represents the leading edge of multiple scientific disci-

plines.

Scientists, engineers, technicians, and skilled production workers interact in such fields as aerothermodynamics, acoustics, combustion, high-speed rotating machinery, electronic instruments and controls, and computer-aided engineering and manufacturing processes.

At GE aircraft engine's Factory-of-the-Future (FOF), new, advanced manufacturing technology, automated manufacturing, scheduling, dispatching, systems monitoring, and quality control combine to produce high-technology, high-quality parts for modern aircraft engines. There GE is developing the techniques for using new systems to build higher quality jet engines at lower cost for America's defense and to serve a broader range of air travelers. The aircraft engine business is a truly international one that brings the benefits of progress in avia-

tion to people and nations throughout the world.

The GE aircraft engine business, which led America into the jet age in 1941, had continued world leadership in jet engines in the 1980s. The two major engine facilities for research and development, production, assembly, and test are located at Lynn and in Evendale, Ohio. Satellite manufacturing plants are located in Everett, Massachusetts; Hooksett, New Hampshire; Rutland, Vermont; Wilmington, North Carolina; Albuquerque, New Mexico; Madisonville, Kentucky; and Bromont, Canada. There are test facilities at Peebles, Ohio, and major service shops in Cincinnati, Ohio; Seattle, Washington; Ontario, California; Struthers, Kansas; and in Singapore and Greece.

The GE plant in Fitchburg, Massachusetts, began as a defense facility in 1942 to produce turbine-generator sets to power critical services aboard combatant and Liberty-class ships. GE purchased the plant after World War II and added the manufacture of turbochargers for diesel locomotives

and welding equipment. At the same time commercial industries were attracted to the company's highly reliable single-stage turbines. Many of these durable units are still in service around the world.

Eventually these product lines were superseded by larger steam turbines as the demand for electric power grew steadily in the 1950s. During this boom in domestic power plant construction, the Fitchburg GE plant produced an average of two 6,000- to 9,000-horsepower turbine systems a week. These boiler-feed-pump systems supply water to the huge boilers at electric power-generation plants.

As the size of power systems grew in the 1960s, so did the size of Fitchburg turbines, which reached 35,000 horsepower. Likewise, the rapidly growing postwar economy and the stable price of oil fueled a building boom of large super-tanker vessels and LNG ships for transporting liquid natural gas. Many of these vessels rely on GE propulsion and turbine-generator systems to meet the dual requirements of speed and reliable onboard electrical power for vital ships services.

A 2,500-kilowatt marine turbine-generator system, manufactured by the GE plant in Fitchburg, provides onboard electrical power for vital ship services.

By the late 1960s and throughout the 1970s, the emerging petrochemical industry was calling for larger machines to drive compressor systems. Fitchburg GE mechanical-drive turbines were installed worldwide at refineries, at ammonia plants that produce fertilizer, at ethylene plants that feed the growing plastics industry, and at LNG plants that permit pipeline gas to be confined in less space for easier shipment. At the same time Fitchburg turbines reached an impressive 60,000 horsepower. In the late 1970s tens of millions of dollars were invested in the Fitchburg GE plant to make it a world-class leader in computer-aided design, manufacture, and test of integrated turbine systems. With more than 90 percent of all work being performed on numerically controlled machine tools, customers are assured of high-quality original equipment as well as precisely matched parts.

As demand for turbines leveled off

in the early 1980s, the Fitchburg GE plant once again adapted to changing times, committing itself to becoming a single-source supplier of turbocompressor systems. These systems use steam turbines to drive compressors that create thousands of pounds of pressure to move gas down a pipeline, through a refinery process, or to transport it to some other application. Presently GE turbocompressor systems are in operation around the world at installations that include ammonia syn-gas, carbon dioxide/urea, ammonia, natural gas injection, gas processing/handling/recompression, propylene, and fuel gas.

Subsequently Fitchburg became headquarters for Naval & Drive Turbine Systems, with more than one million square feet of space at its plants in Fitchburg and Lynn, Massachusetts, and Bangor, Maine. N&DTS provides fully integrated turbocompressor systems, commercial steam turbine-generator systems up to 40 megawatts, and is the leading supplier of marine and Navy steam turbine propulsion and ships service turbine generator systems.

GE's roots were already firmly established in Massachusetts when the opportunity to expand in the Commonwealth brought it to Pittsfield, the westernmost city in Massachusetts, just six miles from the New York State border and some 60 miles from Schenectady, New York, a cornerstone of the company.

GE acquired the Stanley Manufacturing Works in Pittsfield in January 1903, entering yet another core business for the growing young corporation. This facility provided a focus on large AC transformers, an essential ingredient in the transmission of electricity over long distances. The transformer business evolved into a broad line of products but, more important, it spawned two other diverse activities that have grown to become major high-tech GE businesses in Pittsfield.

The first spin-off was GE Plastics, which evolved from the need to use effective insulating materials in the building of transformers. Now among the largest enterprises in General Electric, its international headquarters and research center remains in Pittsfield Plastics Center, with production facilities and technical centers in the United States, Japan, Australia, and Europe. The second business to spring from transformer production is GE Defense Systems, a strategic supplier created in 1941 to help with our nation's defense needs during World War II, chosen because of Pittsfield GE's expertise in electronics and metal fabrication. Defense Systems' first product was a line of gun mounts and electronic directors for the Navy.

During the war years GE Defense Systems also manufactured marine motors for use on high-speed escort vessels. Following the war the company began producing the Mk 35 torpedo and later manufactured radar antennae at Pittsfield. Its missile guidance systems first became prominent in the mid-1950s, when work began on the Polaris program. This historic program

The GE Plastic Business Group's Research Center is located at GE's headquarters in Pittsfield.

was followed by the Poseidon missile guidance system, then the Trident I and the Trident II missile guidance systems.

GE Defense Systems has been a key supplier to the U.S. Army, providing an innovative high-horsepower, hydromechanical transmission for tracked vehicles. It also provides a turret stabilization system for such vehicles, permitting them to operate at high speeds over rough terrain. The division has pioneered development of both liquid propellant and electromagnetic guns, providing an array of shipboard defense systems now in use to protect ships in the United States and allied navies. These include the Aegis and Phalanx systems. As part of the GE Aerospace Group, the division in Pittsfield works closely with other aerospace components of the company.

With a century of history behind it, General Electric has become one of Massachusetts' major employers, contributing to the state's share of high-technology research and manufacturing activities.

MASSACHUSETTS INDUSTRIAL FINANCE AGENCY

Since 1978 the Massachusetts Industrial Finance Agency (MIFA) has been an important partner to the state's business community. Across the Commonwealth, companies have expanded, renovated, modernized, and, most importantly, created employment by utilizing a variety of financing vehicles offered by the agency.

MIFA was created in 1978 by Governor Michael Dukakis—then in his first term—and the state legislature. It was a time of economic decline in the state, and MIFA was seen as one of the solutions to the state's "capital formation crisis." By helping businesses get low-cost financing, MIFA enabled companies to undertake or accelerate their growth plans and thus add employment to the state's economic base.

Robert L. Beal, chairman of the board.

The track record since 1978 is testament to the success of the program. MIFA has issued over $4 billion in total financings for more than 2,200 growing companies in the Commonwealth. To put that record in perspective, $1.2 million of private capital has been invested every day since 1978 in Massachusetts businesses. One firm every day and a half has financed a new expansion project. And the bottom line—one new job has been created as a result of MIFA financing virtually every hour of every day since 1978.

MIFA issues taxable and tax-exempt bonds, insures loans, guarantees loans, and makes direct loans. In 1987 legislation was passed that enabled MIFA to raise capital internationally for public authorities and private enterprises. The legislation also greatly broadened the definition of the types of projects the agency finances In essence, MIFA has evolved into a unique quasi-governmental investment bank, structuring new financial incentives and providing access to new sources of capital.

Historically, the primary incentive offered by the agency was the Tax-exempt Industrial Development Bond (IDB). Tax-exempt financings were extremely successful in spurring additional investment in industrial expansions and commercial revitalizations across the state. When the tax bill of 1986 imposed a dramatic reduction in the program, MIFA continued to target this scarce resource to projects of greatest need.

To continue to meet the great demand for low cost-capital, MIFA introduced one of the country's first taxable IDB programs in early 1987. With the Taxable IDB, MIFA finances a wider array of industrial and commercial expansion projects. The agency issued the nation's first pool of taxable bonds, the largest single taxable IDB in the country, and the first taxable bond to be used for a commercial development project. The Taxable IDB Program greatly enhanced the agency's reputation as a national leader in public finance innovation.

MIFA has also pioneered in creating access to new capital markets on behalf of smaller businesses. Larger corporations have long raised capital in the public markets, where longer terms and attractive rates are attainable, but it is a market virtually unavailable to smaller, unrated companies. MIFA, however, developed the structure that enables the agency to raise capital for relatively small companies in the major capital markets—in the United States as well as internationally.

MIFA has further developed programs that are targeted to specific industries or areas of need in the Commonwealth. For example, MIFA has developed a Seafood Loan Fund specifically intended to spur innovation and modernization in the seafood-processing industry. Another highly targeted fund helps companies build on-site child care centers for their employees.

Creative techniques for gaining access to capital have always been a hallmark of MIFA. As a catalyst for private investment and job creation, MIFA's financings have played a significant role in the often-told story of Massachusetts' economic resurgence. Today, with new programs and initiatives, the agency continues to bring new opportunities for economic development to the Commonwealth.

MIFA's financing spurs private investment in such areas as traditional industry and commercial revitalization.

ASSOCIATED INDUSTRIES OF MASSACHUSETTS

The year was 1915. The Boston Red Sox, with a team including "Smoky Joe" Wood and a young Babe Ruth, won the American League pennant and the World Series. With less fanfare, an organization was founded that would have a profound impact on the state's manufacturing industries—the Associated Industries of Massachusetts (AIM). It was established by a small group of industrialists to provide a voice for them on Beacon Hill. By the end of its first year AIM was representing the interests of 48 companies.

Some of those early firms are still members of AIM. These include Ampad Corporation, General Electric, the Pro Corporation, and Strathmore Paper Company. Today nearly 3,000 companies are members.

AIM has been active since the beginning. During World War I it sponsored a bill creating the War Emergency Industries Commission, which enabled manufacturers to work overtime on urgent defense contracts. AIM continued to flourish during the Roaring '20s, but the Depression years were the most difficult in its history. In its darkest hour the members of AIM had the vision to elect Roy F. Williams executive director—a post he held for 23 years. Nicknamed "Mr. AIM," Williams provided the leadership that kept the organization moving until better times arrived. During his tenure *Industry* magazine, which had been established as a four-page newsletter in 1918, was expanded to a monthly magazine, a format it retains today.

During the 1930s AIM authored the Experience Rating Amendment of the Unemployment Compensation Law which resulted in major savings to qualifying employers. And in Washington the association made itself felt by supporting fair taxation of corporations, equitable railroad freight rates, and the lifting of restrictions on oil imports that especially affected Massachusetts.

When World War II began Massachusetts mobilized quickly. Within two years manufacturing employment rose from 500,000 to more than 625,000. AIM members worked

Former Secretary of Health, Education, and Welfare, Joseph A. Califano (right) accepts a Paul Revere lantern from AIM chairman Charles B. Housen, chairman, president, and chief executive officer of Erving Paper Mills. Califano was the keynote speaker at AIM's 72nd annual meeting in 1987.

closely with the armed forces, and were awarded 186 "E" flags for excellence in production.

Following the war AIM participated in a series of international industrial tours of England, France, Italy, and Switzerland to learn more about overseas markets. Argentina, Brazil, Uruguay, and the Scandinavian countries were also visited, and in 1958 AIM organized a visit to the Brussels World's Fair.

Throughout the 1960s and 1970s AIM's emphasis on legislative issues and public affairs grew. From significant and long-lasting reforms to the state's unemployment compensation system, to health, safety, and environmental issues affecting employers across the state, AIM's influence was felt.

Today more than ever, AIM is a vigorous, effective voice of Massachusetts business. Membership benefits include management consulting services in many fields, an energy and environment program, an insurance plan, an economic research department, a legislative reporting service, and much more. In the spirit of its founders the Associated Industries of Massachusetts has shown amazing foresight in meeting the challenges of changing times.

SPAULDING & SLYE

Unlike most real estate firms, which specialize in a single aspect of the development process, Spaulding & Slye occupies a unique niche in the industry by offering all of the key aspects of development in-house. The company's current base of 350 employees includes development, property management, brokerage, and construction divisions.

With a starting investment of just $8,000, Hank Spaulding and George Slye formed Spaulding and Slye Corporation in 1966. By 1968 the two had marked their first success with the completion of a 14-story office tower in Central Square in Cambridge. Soon after Spaulding and Slye began implementing its now-signature project management concept. The technique employs a project manager as the focal point/coordinator of the various services required to develop a project. Such phases include land acquisition, building design, regulatory appeals, finance, construction, leasing, and property management. Today this administrative style continues to provide the company with a tight organizational method for directing the diverse functions each project demands.

By 1972 Spaulding & Slye's two-man operation had grown into an enterprise with 56 employees. The year 1973 brought the opening of the company's first regional office in Charlotte, North Carolina. The Charlotte area now hosts three major Spaulding & Slye office parks.

Two years later Spaulding & Slye extended its geographic reach by opening an office in Oklahoma City, Oklahoma. A joint venture in the business district—the City Center Building—paved the way for a series of successful development, brokerage, construction, and property management projects. Spaulding & Slye is credited with pioneering the suburban office park concept in the Oklahoma City area.

The company's next major development and corporate headquarters

Offering all aspects of real estate development within one firm, Spaulding & Slye provides many vital yet diverse buildings to New England and other areas as far away as Oklahoma. One of its projects, pictured here, is Rockledge Centre in Bethesda, Maryland.

from 1977 to 1986 was a joint venture with New England Mutual Life Insurance Company. A 55-acre former gravel pit on Route 128 in Burlington, Massachusetts, was developed into a complex of first-class office buildings known collectively as the New England Executive Park (NEEP). NEEP served as a precedent for structuring future large joint ventures. The company's reputation continues to be built on successful partnerships of this kind.

Spaulding & Slye's Washington, D.C., office was opened in 1979. A second partnership with New England Life resulted in the development of Rockledge Executive Plaza, now one of

A future Spaulding & Slye project, at 125 High Street in Boston, is scheduled to begin construction in the fall of 1987.

Spaulding & Slye recognizes and acts upon the needs of new development and, as a result, is building within suburban locations—which have risen in popularity among large office users. An example of the firm's suburban work is 150 Cambridge Park in Cambridge, Massachusetts.

the finest suburban office locations on the East Coast. Other joint ventures with New England Life and IBM Corporation have resulted in such major developments as Shady Grove Executive Center and Rockledge Centre. Since opening this full-service regional office, Spaulding & Slye has grown rapidly into the Washington market.

Hank Spaulding and George Slye became directors of the firm in 1977 when Peter Small was selected to be president. Under Small's leadership, Spaulding & Slye has continued its commitment to excellence. As a privately held company, Spaulding & Slye is widely recognized as an innovative industry leader with an unusually high level of sensitivity to the needs of its tenants.

The 1980s find office space in the midst of an evolution. Tenants are becoming more sophisticated, viewing office space as more than a cubicle equipped with a desk and file cabinet. The demand for "livable" office space is on the rise. As a result, suburban locations are increasing in popularity among large office users who want to avoid the traditional pitfalls of urban office areas, higher rents, difficult parking, and congestion. Recognizing these trends, two of Spaulding & Slye's most recent Massachusetts developments, Cambridge Park in Cambridge and 25 Burlington Mall Road in Burlington, both feature outstanding architectural design; elegant glass, marble, and exotic wood finishes; amenities such as exercise facilities; and ample on-site parking. Simply put, these are buildings designed to make life easier, more pleasant, and more productive for the occupants.

After a 15-year hiatus from downtown Boston development, Spaulding & Slye is making its reentry into that market with New England Telephone and the Prospect Company, the development subsidiary of The Travelers, as limited partners. New England Telephone will be a major tenant in the first phase of development. The project, located at 125 High Street, is a 1.45-million-square-foot office and retail development. Situated in Boston's financial district, it is designed to provide numerous area improvements and public benefits, including the rehabilitation of three historic nineteenth-century buildings and construction of a new ambulance facility and a new City of Boston fire station. Landscaped malls will connect the central eight-story atrium courtyard to Oliver, Purchase, Pearl, and High streets. Three of the walkways and the central courtyard will be bounded by specialty retail shops, restaurants, and a museum focusing on the history and future of communications.

Spaulding & Slye continues to investigate options outside office development. Longwood Retirement Associates is the result of such research and foresight. Says Small of the project, "Spaulding & Slye has been looking for the right opportunity to add more balance to our portfolio by entering into a business that will capitalize on our many existing capabilities as well as respond to market need." At the beginning of 1987 a joint venture was formed between Spaulding & Slye and Longwood Management, Inc., a developer, owner, and operator of housing facilities for the elderly. The partnership intends to build and manage retirement care facilities for the elderly across the country.

"At Spaulding & Slye, we are working hard to combine the creative entrepreneurial aspects of real estate with solid management," explains Small. "For us, it's a winning combination."

An interior view of a Spaulding & Slye development, the lobby of 1030 Massachusetts Avenue in Cambridge.

CHOATE, HALL & STEWART

Choate, Hall & Stewart is one of the most contemporary "old line" law practices in downtown Boston. The firm's 120 lawyers and numerous support personnel are committed to providing the highest quality legal service involving the most sophisticated and challenging legal matters through attentive, creative, and aggressive representation of its clients. The first major law firm in Boston to elect women to partnership, Choate, Hall & Stewart takes pride in seeking imaginative solutions to the unique and ever-changing situations that clients encounter in the contemporary business environment.

Almost all the lawyers participate, either on their own or through the firm, in some form of pro bono work. This has included accepting civil and criminal court appointments from the Lawyers Committee for Civil Rights under Law, from various state and federal courts, from the Civil Liberties Union of Massachusetts, and from the Volunteer Lawyers Project sponsored by the Boston Bar Association. In addition, lawyers with the firm have represented small businesses organized by minority group members, have done work for state and local government agencies

and conservation groups, and have participated actively in national and local bar associations.

Choate, Hall & Stewart was founded in 1899 by Charles F. Choate and John L. Hall, who were, respectively, the sons of the presidents of the Old Colony Railroad and the New York, New Haven & Hartford Railroad.

Not surprisingly, Choate and Hall began their careers defending railroads against personal injury suits brought by victims of grade crossing accidents. In 1904 they were joined by Ralph A. Stewart, a former assistant attorney general, and the firm took its present name.

Choate, Hall, and Stewart advanced from early work for railroads to become preeminent trial lawyers of their day. By the mid-1920s the practice included 10 lawyers and had become one of the "large" firms in Bos-

---

The founders of the law firm Choate, Hall & Stewart were (left) Charles F. Choate, Jr., who practiced law from the inception of the firm in 1899 until 1927, and John L. Hall (right), who practiced from 1899 until 1960.

ton. During this era one young lawyer, Archibald MacLeish, practiced with the firm and later left so that he could pursue "interests outside of the law."

During the early years Choate, Hall & Stewart was almost exclusively a litigation firm. But in the 1930s a security law practice developed, and in 1934 it prepared the first registration statement ever to be filed with the Securities & Exchange Commission. During this period the organization also added a trust department, which remains active today. Through the 1940s and 1950s specialties in banking law, tax law, estate planning, family law, and corporate law were developed. In the early 1960s Choate, Hall & Stewart became the first large firm to establish a wide-ranging health care practice. Specialties in real estate and bankruptcy and creditors rights were also added. As client needs and governmental regulatory patterns changed in the 1970s and 1980s, the firm developed specialties in environmental law and labor and employment law. Except for patent and admiralty law, Choate, Hall & Stewart now has the capacity to provide expert advice in every area of the legal spectrum.

SAMUEL CABOT, INC.

Cabot Stains, founded in 1877 by Massachusetts native Samuel Cabot, has developed into a leading manufacturer of stain products. Today its broad line of stains for a variety of interior and exterior, residential, and commercial applications leads the industry.

It all began over a century ago, when Samuel Cabot, a young chemist who studied at the University of Zurich, Switzerland, came home to Boston inspired with the idea of starting an American coal-tar dye industry. At that time the Germans held a monopoly in the field.

In 1877 he bought a small coal-tar distilling plant on the Chelsea mudflats. This plant had previously been boiling tar to obtain pitch for caulking the seams of clipper ships and other vessels. Young Cabot was not so much interested in the pitch as in the distillate, creosote oil. His unsuccessful efforts to make dyes from the creosote left him with a large surplus of the oil, for which he needed a market. To remedy this situation, he began manufacturing wood preservatives and soon developed the original creosote shingle stain by dispersing paint pigments in the creosote oil.

Encouraged by his father who was a doctor at Massachusetts General Hospital in Boston, the young pioneer chemist also developed a disinfectant using coal tar. This disinfectant has been famous ever since under the name of Cabot's Sylpho-Nathol.

Samuel Cabot, founder of Samuel Cabot, Inc., and inventor of the world's first shingle stain.

In succeeding years Cabot developed many other outstanding products including Cabot's Insulating and Sound-Deadening Quilt, an effective house insulation made from eel grass.

Samuel Cabot passed away in 1906 at the age of 55, and was succeeded by his son, also named Samuel. The Cabot plant burned to the ground two years later in the Great Chelsea Fire. Samuel Cabot rebuilt the busi-

The new Cabot Stains plant in Newburyport, the most efficient and productive stain manufacturing plant in the world today.

ness from scratch, and remained active in the firm until his death in 1967. Under his direction, the Cabot laboratory developed the famous patented Collopaking Process by which the pigments are ground finer than in ordinary paints and are more uniformly dispersed in the oil. As a result of this process, Cabot's stains are extremely durable and nonfading.

The company has been managed by four generations of the Cabot family and continues today under the guidance of the current president, Samuel Cabot III. Continuing the tradition of being an innovative leader in the stain industry, Samuel Cabot III opened a new $9-million, state-of-the-art manufacturing facility in Newburyport in 1985. "This new facility represents a milestone for Cabot Stains as we move into our second century," says the president. "It ensures our ability to remain at the forefront of our industry by continuing to provide the broadest range of premium products to meet our customers' needs."

The name "Cabot Stains" has become synonymous with quality, long-lasting beauty, and wood preservation. Cabot's products are distributed throughout the United States, Canada, and Australia. Among the many famous places where Cabot Stains have been used in Massachusetts are Boston's Old State House, Faneuil Hall, Paul Revere's House, and the USS *Constitution,* "Old Ironsides."

BRIGHAM AND WOMEN'S HOSPITAL

As an internationally known medical institution, the 720-bed Brigham and Women's Hospital (BWH) is committed to clinical care, medical research, and academic excellence. Its long and colorful history reflects these three purposes.

BWH is the result of a 1980 union of three entities: the Peter Bent Brigham Hospital, a general adult medical facility; the Robert Breck Brigham Hospital, which was devoted to the care of arthritis and related diseases; and the Boston Hospital for Women, which provided obstetrical-gynecological care. (This institution, in turn, was the product of an earlier merger between the Boston Lying-in Hospital and the Free Hospital for Women.) The combination of these illustrious institutions marked the outcome of an idea: the desire to improve and streamline health care delivery. Today BWH's international prestige, as well as its satisfied patients and high occupancy rate, attest to its success.

The history of the hospital reflects a series of many successful ideas. Perhaps the first was in 1832, when, with the help of the Massachusetts Humane Society and the Massachusetts Charitable Fire Society (of which Paul Revere was a charter member), the Boston Lying-in Hospital was born.

A commitment to holistic care—evidenced by a schoolteacher's full-time employment—was consistently a part of the Robert Breck Brigham Hospital's tradition.

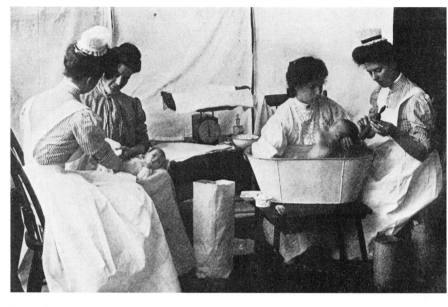

Pre- and post-natal care are still top priorities at Brigham and Women's Hospital, whose labor and delivery department expects to surpass 10,000 births in 1987.

Located at 718 Washington Street, "it embraced a house well-adapted to its present purposes, and a spacious lot of land which will admit to an extension of its buildings whenever it shall become necessary." It did not, for the hospital moved twice after this, expanding and modernizing with each relocation. Beyond the care of "poor, but respectable" maternity patients like the first, Mary Connor, the hospital became respected for its care of all women, as well as for research and clinical innovation. The first American administration of obstetrical anesthesia and use of

bichloride of mercury as an antiseptic during childbirth are among its many accomplishments.

Sharing in the charitable mission of the Lying-in—and foretelling BWH's community commitment—was the Free Hospital for Women, founded in 1875. For many years housed in an elegant Brookline building, the hospital was originally presided over by Dr. William Baker, who, like the Lying-in's Dr. William Richardson, was a professor at Harvard Medical School and a seminal figure in American medical history. The Free Hospital for Women was among the first in the world to apply radium to the treatment and study of cancer. Researchers affiliated with it also were responsible for the first clinic in vitro fertilization and the first reports on the effectiveness of oral contraceptives.

At about the same time that the Free Hospital was created, a Boston restaurateur was enjoying the prime of his life and career. The son of a Vermont farmer, he made his fortune selling oysters. His life was marked by charitable endeavors, so it is no surprise that his will specified that his estate be used for "the care of the indigent sick of Suffolk County" in the form of a hospital. Thus the Peter Bent Brigham hospital—named after its benefactor—opened in 1913, housed in an elegant, airy structure (now comprising the administrative offices of BWH)

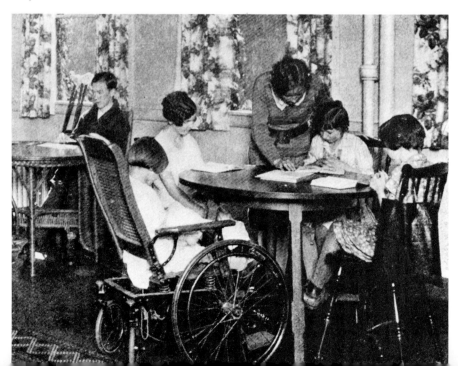

near the Fenway area of Boston.

Through the Brigham's halls walked many of the giants of American medicine and nursing. Perhaps the most venerable of these was Dr. Harvey Cushing, the founder of modern neurosurgery, but there were many others. These were men and women who contributed medical "firsts" such as the creation of the Drinker Respirator (iron lung), the Kolff-Brigham artificial kidney machine, the first successful kidney transplant, the use of electric current to restore heart rhythm, the development of fetal monitoring, and the cure of pernicious anemia. In 1934 this cure won the hospital one of its two Nobel prizes; the second was won in 1986 by Dr. Bernard Lown for his work with the International Physicians for the Prevention of Nuclear War.

Luckily for individuals suffering from arthritis and other rheumatologic diseases, charity ran in the Brigham family, and in 1914 the Robert Breck Brigham Hospital was born. (Like his uncle, Robert Breck Brigham was a restaurateur, but he made his fortune selling lemon pies.) This small facility, situated high on Mission Hill not far from the other two hospitals, broke new ground in the areas of physical and occupational therapy. It also showed a deep concern and compassion for its patients, particularly children, who were provided—through the Boston public schools—a full-time elementary schoolteacher.

In the late 1970s the parent hospitals joined forces to create Brigham and Women's Hospital. By combining talents to advance patient care, sharing staff and faculty to improve teaching, and sharing equipment to control costs, the new medical center provides a first-rate environment for clinical work, teaching, and research. The BWH patient tower, a block away from the former Peter Bent Brigham Hospital, features a cloverleaf design that places nursing units equidistant from each patient's room. Other new buildings include two ambulatory facilities and a 16-floor research building.

Today BWH is a vibrant place that attracts not only patients from all over the world, but also an impressive amount of research funding. In 1986 BWH was listed by the National Institutes of Health as first in the nation among independent hospitals in total NIH research grants, contracts, and fellowships. The hospital is deeply involved in a range of research, including respiratory distress in newborn babies, reproductive endocrinology, blood vessel diseases, cancer, rheumatoid arthritis, kidney failure and transplantation, diagnostic imaging, sleep, Alzheimer's disease, and multiple sclerosis.

As always, Harvard Medical School students serve rotations at BWH, and internship, fellowship, and residency training programs provide practical skills that prepare physicians for future careers in teaching, research, and practice. In addition, training is provided for nurses, nurse practitioners, dietitians, physical and occupational therapists, medical record technicians, and other administrative and support personnel.

Thousands of pioneering operations on the brain were performed by Dr. Harvey Cushing, first Chief of Surgery at the Peter Bent Brigham Hospital.

The award-winning Brigham and Women's Hospital patient tower stands in close proximity to Harvard Medical School and other noted health care institutions.

A great deal has changed at Brigham and Women's Hospital since the day the first patient walked into the house on Washington Street. As was true then, however, BWH today is committed to excellence and to its mission to continually provide improved care and services for its patients and the community.

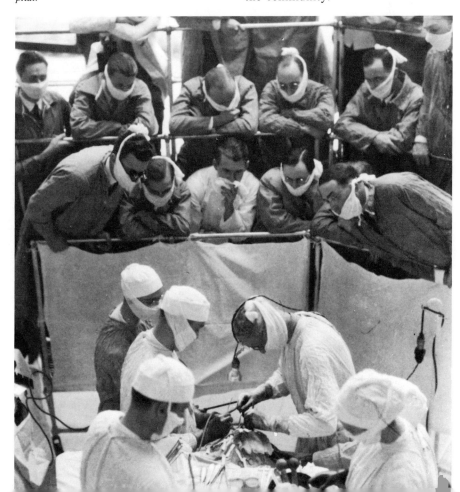

XTRA CORPORATION

Intermodal transportation—the movement of goods by the most efficient combination of rail, water, and highway—has rapidly become the standard by which freight moves. XTRA Corporation is a leader in providing intermodal equipment to the transportation industry. The use of XTRA's trailers, containers, and chassis in all of the world's transportation modes has grown significantly as the popularity of intermodal transport has increased. The advantages of this system are obvious: shortened transit time, fewer handling requirements, reduced cargo damage, and less pilferage.

The concept of intermodalism began with the introduction of piggyback (trailer on flatcar) trailers in the 1950s. XTRA Corporation was born in the autumn of 1957, when Carl P. Tomm (formerly with the Boston and Maine Railroad), Francis C. Ventre, and Selwyn A. Kudisch bankrolled $1,000 for the purchase of four used trailers. With offices in Cambridge, Massachusetts, XTRA became the nation's first piggyback leasing company. Since then XTRA has grown to become the largest intermodal equipment transportation and service company in the world.

XTRA's piggyback trailers move on railroad flatcars as well as over the nation's highways, and even on specialized oceangoing vessels. In addition,

Charles F. Kaye, chairman of the board of XTRA Corporation.

the firm's over-the-road fleet provides highway trailer service throughout the continental United States.

Containers, introduced on a large scale in the early 1970s, expanded the concept of intermodalism to water carriers, and today this equipment travels on wheeled chassis both over-the-road and on railroad flatcars. More recently containers without chassis have moved on the rail lines on specialized "double-stack" flatcars. All of

XTRA Corporation is the largest intermodal equipment transportation and service company in the world. Here an XTRA piggyback is being transported in Chicago.

these modes have been added to traditional transport in maritime container ships.

A significant milestone was reached on September 26, 1974, when XTRA took delivery of its 25,000th piggyback trailer. The following day this trailer was presented as a gift to the National Railroad Piggyback Association at its meeting in Washington, D.C., to run free for its lifetime, for the benefit of the nation's railroads. The enthusiasm with which it was received by the members evidenced a mutual recognition that XTRA, by its continuing commitment to superior service and equipment, had become a supplier-partner with the railroads in the development and strengthening of the industry, and has provided more than 75,000 piggyback and over-the-road trailers since its inception.

Today XTRA's container leasing operations span the globe from Europe to the Far East and from Africa to Australia. Almost 1,000 employees are on the worldwide payroll.

Explains board chairman Charles F. Kaye, "Intermodalism has significantly increased the productivity and efficiency of the world's transportation system. XTRA's ongoing commitment to it, as a leading lessor of the finest equipment available for intermodal transport, will continue increasingly as this market expands in the future."

GREATER BOSTON CHAMBER OF COMMERCE

Boston has never been an uninterested spectator of public movement in any portion of the continent, and its chamber of commerce reflects a historic participation in the development of the capital city from where many of the earliest American ideas sprung. The organization exists today under the same mandate of its original charter: "To Forward in a Business Way the Public Good." Consistent with the communal consciousness of that mandate, the organization has moved forward effectively to preserve and promote the business and public interests of its community. Indeed, to paraphrase James L. Sullivan, its president since 1981, "The reason for the Chamber's being is to interface between the private and public sectors, to be a convener in the collaborative efforts of a public/private partnership."

The Greater Boston Chamber of Commerce is the fourth in line of descent from one that was organized as a Grain Exchange—its 1,000 members represented the grain and produce trade especially—sometime in the years between 1793 and 1804, before Boston became a city. In 1885, for the general advantage of Boston, now both a city and a port, a 500-member Boston Produce Exchange and a 300-member Boston Commercial Exchange consolidated to be the principal trading body of a city three times its original size, and making its living from the sea. The progressive and influential group held their formal meetings at the new Quincy Market Rotunda until January 21, 1892, when, replete with incandescent lighting, the pink granite, Romanesque-style, seven-story Grain Exchange Building, which still stands at India and Milk streets, was dedicated for its interests.

In 1909 the preeminent concerns of the 670,000 people living in Mayor George A. Hibbard's metropolis were property taxation, the handling of coal fuels, education for its youth, extension of its streets, and rail and steamship transport problems. On June 15, by charter of the Massachusetts Legislature, a new organization called the Boston Chamber of Commerce was formed

by the merging of the old Chamber and a reorganized Boston Merchants Association. Its objective was to have a unified, effective voice in the public interest of just and equitable principals of trade. In common tributary concern 100 "sustaining members" adopted bylaws and contributed dues of $200.

The complexities of modern society enlarged the scope of issues affecting business and the local economy, thus broadening the Chamber's role as catalyst and coordinator in such concerns as environmental protection; governmental regulation of business, state, and municipal fiscal policy; development of new energy resources; expanded transportation services; educational needs; development and renewal issues; inner-city needs; health care; and aid to the nonprofit sector.

Boston's thriving business community conducts business in an urban environment that is renown for its unique combination of old and new, historic charm, and leading-edge technology and initiatives. The Old State House presides over State Street, one of the busiest in Boston's downtown district. Courtesy, Fay Photo

In 1952 members and directors of the city's largest business organization changed its name to the Greater Boston Chamber of Commerce, thereby extending its area of corporate representation.

The dawning of the 1980s saw a new, confident Boston, its modern skyscrapers rising over the harbor as a beacon to commerce guarding the public legacy of more than 350 years of Boston enterprise. The members, officers, directors, professional staff, and committees of the Chamber, from offices at The Federal Reserve Bank Building on Atlantic Avenue, continue to mediate and implement, in a cooperative spirit, those goals of communitywide interest that affect the economic, political, and social well-being of all that Greater Boston is and will be. Today approximately 3,000 members are participants in programs initiated and administered by the Greater Boston Chamber of Commerce, united in their efforts to enhance the quality of life for all who live and work in the Greater Boston area.

OMNI PARKER HOUSE

Boston's Omni Parker House has roots running deep in the soil of Massachusetts history. Even before Harvey D. Parker opened the doors of his five-story white marble hotel in 1855, the name was synonymous with fine dining and elegant tradition.

Parker was born in the village of Temple, Maine, in 1805 (before that state was separated from the Commonwealth of Massachusetts) and grew up in the nearby village of Paris. At the age of 20 he came to Boston with less than one dollar in his pocket, working in suburban Watertown as a stable boy and coachman.

Whenever he came to town, Parker liked to eat at John E. Hunt's small restaurant on Court Square. Saving his wages, Parker eventually purchased the restaurant in 1832 for $432, and renamed it Parker's Restaurant.

The restaurant prospered for more than two decades, and in 1854 Parker decided to expand. Hotel dining had become fashionable in Boston, both with travelers and residents, and Parker decided to build a hotel to house his new restaurant. A lot on the south side of School Street attracted his attention—a historic plot that had been occupied for more than two centuries. First a mansion, then a boardinghouse, the structure had fallen into disrepair, and Parker demolished it to make way for a new, white marble building. Five stories tall, it was built in the Italianate style. The windows on the ground and second floors were arched while those above were surmounted with cornices. Above the door was a sign engraved with the single word, "Parker's."

The new hotel flourished from day one. The Boston *Transcript* on opening day remarked upon "the gorgeous furniture of the parlors, the extent and beauty of the dining hall, the number and different styles of the lodging rooms—and, in fact, the richness, lavish expenditure, and excellent taste which abounded in every department."

The hotel's cuisine was as responsible for its success as any of its other attractions. The novel "European plan" allowed guests to eat elsewhere, but few did. Unlike other hotels, where

The Omni Parker House rooftop ballroom follows the original tradition of elegance established by Harvey Parker when he opened his hotel and restaurant in 1855.

meals were served three times each day, the Parker House restaurant served continuously, offering a menu unsurpassed in the city. Parker's French chef, Sanzian, was rumored to earn

$5,000 a year for his services, 10 times more than his colleagues in other establishments. But satisfied diners agreed that he was worth every penny of it.

The Parker House soon became more than a handsome hotel with comfortable rooms, a convivial bar, or even a fine restaurant. It was quintessentially Bostonian—reflecting the city's solemnity, dignity, and punctilious regard for style and manners, grace and good taste. Proper Bostonians, Brahmins from Beacon Hill, felt at home there. Harvard students, merchants from nearby State Street, bankers from Philadelphia and New York City, and "outlanders" from rural Vermont, Maine, and New Hampshire mixed easily in the dining rooms and bar.

Early guest lists record famous actors and opera singers, including Sarah Bernhardt, Charlotte Cushman, Edwin Booth, and Richard Mansfield. Edwin Booth's younger brother, John Wilkes, was a guest in April 1865, although Harvey Parker seldom mentioned it—

Today's Omni Parker House blends the skilled craftsmanship and opulence of the past with the most modern innovations and conveniences of the present.

". . . Such guests! What famous names its record boasts, Whose owners wander in the mob of ghosts! . . ."

With 541 restored guest rooms and 14 function rooms, the Omni Parker House can accommodate the requests of any guest or group.

only eight days following his visit Booth made the unexpected appearance on the stage of Ford's Theater in Washington, D.C., seconds after firing the shot that took the life of President Abraham Lincoln.

Two famous clubs met regularly at Parker's, although they had many members in common. The Literary Club, later called the Saturday Club, was devoted to friendship and conviviality. The Magazine (or Atlantic) Club, on the other hand, was formed to organize a magazine superior to any other in the United States at that time. After the first issue of the *Atlantic Monthly* appeared in 1857, the Magazine Club merged into the Saturday Club.

Saturday Club rosters include scientist Louis Agassiz, essayist/lawyer Richard Henry Dana, Jr., philosopher Ralph Waldo Emerson, poet James Russell Lowell, physician/poet Dr. Oliver Wendell Holmes, novelist Nathaniel Hawthorne, and poets Henry Wadsworth Longfellow and John Greenleaf Whittier. These and other luminaries met each month in a private second-floor dining room at the Parker House. For six hours, from three in the afternoon until nine at night, poems were read, stories recounted, gossip exchanged, and books criticized while members were served a seven-course meal. Oliver Wendell Holmes, in his poem, "At the Saturday Club," wrote:

The success of the Parker House led Harvey Parker to begin a program of improvement and enlargement. In 1860 he acquired the adjoining Horticultural Hall, replacing it with a six-story addition to the hotel. He continued to purchase, expand, and annex his property until, at his death in 1884, it had become a sprawling mixture of buildings, elaborate and immense for its time.

In the 1890s the Joseph R. Whipple Corp. took over the vast complex, and in 1925 all but a small annex of the now outdated marble palace of Harvey Parker was demolished to make way for a sleek and modern 1927 structure. A Parker House of steel and granite was constructed 14 stories above the corner of School and Tremont streets, and the 800-room hotel, with a grand rooftop ballroom, enjoyed a new burst of popularity. But the hard times that followed the 1929 Stock Market crash brought a mortgage foreclosure and transfer of ownership to Glenwood Sherrard, who operated the property until his death in 1958.

Eleven years later the hotel was acquired by the Dunfey family, owners of hotels and restaurants throughout New England. The Dunfeys initiated a $12-million, long-range restoration program for the historic Boston property. Elegant workmanship of a bygone era now blends with modern innovations and amenities to welcome visitors from around the world in 541 restored guest rooms and 14 function rooms.

The oldest continuously operating hotel in the country and now a premier classic hotel of Omni Hotels, the Omni Parker House is once again a grand hotel. The "white facade" is darker now than it was in the days of Harvey Parker; the remembered voices of Holmes, Longfellow, and Whittier are nearly inaudible. But the "mob of ghosts" still stalks the plush halls and corridors of the Omni Parker House, and will, if fate is kind, for many years to come.

Patrons

The following individuals, companies, and organizations have made a valuable commitment to the quality of this publication. Windsor Publications and the Bay State Historical League gratefully acknowledge their participation in *Massachusetts: Colony to Commonwealth.*

Accounting Microsystems
Anderson-Nichols & Company, Inc.*
Apollo Computer Inc.*
Associated Industries of Massachusetts*
Atlas Founders, Inc.
The Beal Companies*
Berkshire Industries, Inc.*
Berkshire Medical Center*
Blue Cross and Blue Shield of Massachusetts*
The Boston Company*
Boston Edison*
Boston's Beth Israel Hospital*
Brigham and Women's Hospital*
Samuel Cabot, Inc.*
C&K Components, Inc.*
Carter Rice*
Choate, Hall & Stewart*
Codman & Shurtleff, Inc.*
Mr. and Mrs. Thomas P. Costin, Jr.
Tony G. Couto Real Estate
Cushman & Wakefield of Massachusetts, Inc.
Damon Corporation*
Diamond Fiber Products Inc.
Disabled American Veterans
Eastco*
Equitable Real Estate Investment Management, Inc.*
Foot-Joy, Inc.*
Franki Foundation Company*
G&H Poultry & Provisions, Inc.*
General Electric*
Greater Boston Chamber of Commerce*
Haemonetics Corporation*
Hale and Dorr*
Frank B. Hall & Co. of Massachusetts, Inc.*
Henry L. Hanson Inc.
Heatbath Corporation*
Hinds & Coon Co.
Houghton Mifflin Company*
Jordan Marsh Company*
B.L. Makepeace Inc.
Massachusetts Industrial Finance Agency*
Meredith & Grew, Incorporated*
Nantucket Historical Association
New England Medical Center*

New England Telephone*
Ocean Spray Cranberries, Inc.*
Old Sturbridge Village*
Omni Parker House*
Parker Brothers*
Peat Marwick Main & Co.*
A.W. Perry, Inc.*
Petricca Industries, Inc.*
Polaroid Corporation*
Prime Computer, Inc.*
Esther Quinn Realty*
Red Lion Inn*
RTE AEROVOX
St. Johnsbury Trucking Company*
Sayed M. Saleh
Smith & Wesson
Spaulding & Slye*
Symmons Industries, Inc.*
Temple Stuart Company
Texon*
Victor Coffee Co.*
Francis W. Warren, Jr.
XTRA Corporation*
Zayre Corp.*

*Partners in Progress of *Massachusetts: Colony to Commonwealth.* The histories of these companies and organizations appear in Chapter IX, beginning on page 231.

PICTURE RESEARCHER'S ACKNOWLEDGMENTS

The pictures in this book represent the cooperative efforts of dozens of people from museums, local historical societies, libraries, colleges, federal, state, and municipal agencies, private publishers, business archives, and various generous individuals who opened their normally private collections for this history. Several artists contributed new work to illustrate this volume, and photograhic copy work from very old books and prints, as well as photography of objects, was done skillfully by many others. Finally, over 300 pictures were gathered from over 60 different sources. While the source for each picture is noted at the end of the caption, I would like to take this opportunity to thank all of the people who contributed to the work of this book, and I especially want to thank the following people who made an effort far beyond the obligation of their positions to be helpful with pictures, background information, and support for the project over the past year and a half.

Special thanks go to artists John H. Martin, Richard Wilkie, Paul Sherry, Louise T. Currin, Wilbert Smith, Evan Jones, and Marie Litterer for work published for the first time in this book. At the University Photographic Services at UM, Amherst, Brenda Lilly, Kathryn Stadler, Randy Chase, Paul Carew, and Fred Moore executed excellent work, while Donna Meisse dependably coordinated it all. Eugene Worman, Hill Boss, Walter and Sarah Jones, and Barbara K. Jones generously lent antique books, prints, postcards, and other objects from their private collections.

Thanks also go to Daniel Lombardo and Marty Noblick at the Boltwood Room of the Jones Library, Inc., in Amherst. Gerald Brophy at the Pratt Museum, and Judith Barter of the Mead Art Museum at Amherst College, also gave valuable help. At Andover Historical Society, Clark Pierce and Peg Hughes deserve thanks. In addition, thanks to Ann Souza in the public relations office, Wendy Watson at the art museum, and Elaine Trehub from the archives at Mount Holyoke College; also, Ruth Wilbur and Ingrid Miller at the Northampton Historical Society; Elise Bernier Feeley and Angela Vincent of Forbes Library, Northampton; Michael Goodison at Smith College Art Museum; and Karen Kurt at the Smith College News Office.

At the library of the University of Massachusetts at Amherst, Betty Brace gave special help, and in Special Collections and Archives there, Ute Bargman, John Kendall, Michael Milewski, and Linda Seidman were always enthusiastic and willing to help with the research. At the Berkshire Atheneum in Pittsfield, Ruth Datenhardt was especially supportive with material for the western counties. At Hancock Shaker Village, Joan Clemons trudged through mud and slush to show off the village on a wintry day, and capably advised on picture choice and where to research captions. From the Connecticut Valley Historical Museum in Springfield, Gail Nessell gave generously of her time and expertise; at the John F. Kennedy Library, Allan Goodrich; Massachusetts Archives, Richard Kaplan; Massachusetts Historical Society, Ross Urquhart. At the Museum of Fine Arts, Boston, Jane Hankins knew the collection well and made useful suggestions. At many of the repositories follow-up letters were necessary to clarify information, and these were handled swiftly and well by the above.

Gratitude is also well-deserved by Judith Lund at the Old Dartmouth Historical Society's Whaling Museum in New Bedford, by Donna DeFabio at Plimoth Plantation, by Hugh Gourley III and Margaret Wilkes at the Colby College Art Museum in Waterville, Maine, and Joan Cawood at the Christian Science Center in Boston. Mary Doering of the American Red Cross in Washington, D.C., was extremely accommodating. Bernice O'Brien at the Massachusetts Department of Environmental Management, Division of Forests and Parks, knew exactly how to help with the photographs and information on the CCC Camps, and she deserves special recognition for the consolidation and preservation of that collection. Pip Stromgren at the *Daily Hampshire Gazette* made an extra effort to help, as did Anne Speakman of the New England Medical Center, and Priscilla Korell at Boston Edison Co. Porter Dickinson, Jon McGowan, and Aubrey Weaver helped with factual information not found in books. And my special thanks go to Henry Waltermere, who helped me at Forest Park.

Finally, loving appreciation to Paul, Evan, and Cinda Jones, who supported my work at every step, gave helpful opinions about what should be included in a popular history, and without whom the deadlines could not have been met.

Gratitude is extended to all who helped, but, of course, the responsibility for the historical accuracy of the book lies only with the author and the picture researcher. In a book of this scope, people and events are often treated all too briefly, and depth of coverage is simply not possible. Certain subjects and people are featured, others omitted, but it is hoped that readers will be inspired to dig further into Massachusetts history because of something found here.

Ruth Owen Jones
Amherst, Massachusetts

SELECTED BIBLIOGRAPHY

Ahlstrom, Sydney E. *A Religious History of the American People.* New Haven: Yale University Press, 1972.

Allen, Oliver E. "The State of Medical Care, 1984." *American Heritage* 35:6 (Oct.-Nov. 1984) 33-40.

Bearse, Ray, ed. *Massachusetts, A Guide to the Pilgrim State.* 2nd ed. Boston: Houghton Mifflin Co., 1971.

Boorstin, Daniel J. *The Americans: the Colonial Experience.* New York: Random House, 1958.

————. *The Americans: The National Experience.* New York: Random House, 1965.

————. *The Americans: the Democratic Experience.* New York: Random House, 1973.

Booth, Robert. *Boston's Freedom Trail.* Globe Pequot Press, 1981.

Brown, Richard D. *Massachusetts: A Bicentennial History.* New York: Norton, 1978.

Commonwealth of Massachusetts, Annual Reports of the Metropolitan District Commission, for the years 1937, 1938, 1939. Public Document #48.

Commonwealth of Massachusetts, Report of the Post-War Rehabilitation Commission. Boston: Wright and Potter Printing Co., 1945.

Davis, John H. *The Kennedys: Dynasty to Disaster.* New York: McGraw-Hill, 1984.

Demos, John. *A Little Commonwealth.* New York: Oxford University Press, 1970.

DiCarlo, Ella Merkel. *Holyoke - Chicopee: A Perspective.* Holyoke, Mass.: Transcript-Telegram, 1982.

Fuller, Linda K. *Trips and Trivia. A Guide to Western Massachusetts.* Springfield, Mass.: Springfield Magazine, Inc., 1978.

Garraty, John A. *The American Nation, A History of the United States to 1877.* 2nd ed. New York: Harper & Row Publishers, 1971.

Greene, J.R. *The Day Four Quabbin Towns Died.* Athol, Mass.: The Transcript Press, 1985.

————. *The Creation of Quabbin Reservoir.* Athol, Mass.: The Transcript Press, 1981.

Handlin, Oscar, and Arthur Schlesinger, et al. *Harvard Guide to American History.* New York: Atheneum, 1967.

Handlin, Oscar. *The Americans: A New History of the People of the United States.* Boston: Little, Brown and Co., 1963.

————. *The Uprooted.* 2nd ed. Boston: Little, Brown, 1973.

Higginson, Thomas Wentworth. *Massachusetts in the Army and Navy during the War of 1861-1865.* Boston: Wright & Potter Printing Co., 1895-96.

Historical Data Relating to Counties, Cities, and Towns in Massachusetts. Boston, 1966.

Hodgson, Godfrey. *America in Our Time: From World War II to Nixon, What Happened and Why.* New York: Random House, 1976.

Hofstadter, Richard. *America at 1750.* New York: Random House, 1971.

Holbrook, Stewart H. *The Old Post Road.* New York: McGraw-Hill, 1962.

Hugins, Walter. *The Reform Impulse, 1825-1850.* New York: Harper and Row, 1972.

Jones, Landon Y. *Great Expectations: America and the Baby Boom Generation.* New York: Random House, 1980.

Kaufman, Martin. "Step Right Up, Ladies and Gentlemen . . . " *American History Illustrated.* 16:5 (August 1981) 38-45.

Kelley, Robert. *The Shaping of the American Past.* 2nd ed. New Jersey: Prentice-Hall, 1978.

Lakis, Stephen J., ed. *The Political Almanac, 1987-88.* 2 vols. 4th ed. Centerville, Mass.: Almanac Research Services, 1987.

Massachusetts Needs in Urban and Industrial Renewal, August 1960. House #3373.

Massachusetts Population Growth and Redistribution, 1950-1960. Publication #397. (Cooperative Extension Service and Experiment Station).

The Massachusetts Primer. Massachusetts Taxpayers Foundation, Inc., 1986.

Massachusetts Proposals for Better Industrial Relations. The Report to the Governor's Labor-Management Committee. House #1875.

Morgan, Edmund S. *The Puritan Family.* Revised ed. New York: Harper and Row, 1966.

A Quality of Life: An Assessment of Massachusetts. Prepared by Arthur D. Little, Inc., for the Commonwealth of Massachusetts. 1972.

Reid, William James. *The Building of the Cape Cod Canal.* New York: Oxford University Press, 1977.

Robbins, Peggy. "The Country Cheered Wildly When Jenny Lind Came to America." *American History Illustrated* 16:3 (June 1981) 29-35.

Tree, Christina. *Massachusetts, An Explorer's Guide.* Vermont: Countryman Press, 1979.

Trout, Charles H. *Boston, The Great Depression and the New Deal.* New York: Oxford University Press, 1977.

Vexler, Robert I. *Massachusetts: A Chronology & Documentary History.* Dobb's Ferry, N.Y.: Oceana Publ., 1978.

Weinstein, Allen, and R. Jackson Wilson. *Freedom and Crisis, An American History.* Vol. 2, *Since 1860.* 2nd ed. New York: Random House, 1978.

Wheller, Leslie. "Lucy Stone: Wife of Henry Blackwell." *American History Illustrated* 16:8 (Dec. 1981) 39-45.

Whitehall, Walter Muir, and Norman Kotker. *Massachusetts, A Pictorial History.* New York: Charles Scribner's Sons, 1976.

Young, Allen. *North of Quabbin.* Miller's River Publishing Co., 1983.

INDEX